ORIGINS OF FUTURISTIC FICTION

Origins of
FUTURISTIC FICTION

PAUL K. ALKON

THE UNIVERSITY OF GEORGIA PRESS
Athens and London

Paperback edition, 2010
© 1987 by the University of Georgia Press
Athens, Georgia 30602
www.ugapress.org
All rights reserved
Designed by Sandra Strother Hudson
Set in Bodoni Book by The Composing Room of Michigan
Printed digitally in the United States of America

The Library of Congress has cataloged the hardcover edition of
this book as follows:
Library of Congress Cataloging-in-Publication Data
LCCN Permalink: http://lccn.loc.gov/86025026

Alkon, Paul K. (Paul Kent)
Origins of futuristic fiction / Paul K. Alkon.
xii, 341 p. : ill. ; 25 cm.
ISBN 0-8203-0932-X (alk. paper)
Includes index.
Bibliography: p. 291–325.
1. Science fiction—History and criticism. I. Title.
PN3433.8 .A44 1987
809.3'876 1986-25026
Paperback ISBN-13: 978-0-8203-3772-2
ISBN-10: 0-8203-3772-2

British Library Cataloging-in-Publication Data available

All illustrations are from *Le Monde tel qu'il sera*, by
Emily Souvestre (Paris: W. Coquebert, 1846).

To Gwin J. Kolb

Creatures of an inferiour nature are possest with the *present;*
Man is a *future creature*.
John Donne, *Sermons*

Quand je serai grand, j'écrirai un roman de l'avenir,
et j'y ferai parcourir les airs par des machines en forme d'oiseaux;
il n'y a point de poésie dans l'avenir sans cela.
Félix Bodin, *Le Roman de l'avenir*

Contents

Acknowledgments   xi

Part One
PREHISTORY, 1659–1703

1. Temporal versus Spatial Imagination: *Epigone, histoire du siècle futur*   3
2. Towards an Aesthetics of Extrapolation: *Iter Lunare* and *The Sacred Theory of the Earth*   45

Part Two
STARTING POINTS, 1733–1827

3. Formal Variations: *Memoirs of the Twentieth Century*   89
4. From Utopia to Uchronia: *L'An 2440* and *Napoléon apocryphe*   115

CONTENTS

5. The Secularization of Apocalypse: *Le dernier homme*   158
6. Fantasy and Metafiction: From *Les Posthumes* to *The Mummy*   192

Part Three
THE END OF THE BEGINNING, 1834

7. A Poetics for Futuristic Fiction: *Le Roman de l'avenir*   245

Notes   291
Index   327

Acknowledgments

A John Simon Guggenheim Memorial Foundation Fellowship facilitated research for this book, as did concurrent award of a sabbatical year by the University of Southern California. The William Andrews Clark Memorial Library provided office space, hospitality, and bibliographical guidance at every stage. I am very grateful to its director Norman J. W. Thrower, to its librarian Thomas F. Wright, and to all the members of its staff, especially John Bidwell, Carol R. Briggs, Susan Green, Patrick McCloskey, Monika Savic, Nancy M. Shea, Carol Sommer, and Leonard White. Victoria Steele aided my work at the History and Special Collections Division of the UCLA Biomedical Library. Capable assistance was always available at the Houghton Library of Harvard University, the Huntington Library, and the British Library. Extraordinary courtesy and patience were extended to me at the Bibliothèque

ACKNOWLEDGMENTS

Nationale. In Yverdon, Switzerland, time and bibliographical expertise were generously provided by Pascal Ducommun, curator of the Maison d'Ailleurs.

Pierre Versins, whom I shall perhaps meet somewhere in the future, graciously approved necessary photocopying and has also provided indispensable inspiration in the great French tradition of encyclopedists. George E. Slusser, curator of the Eaton Collection at the University of California in Riverside, has been an unfailing source of practical assistance and intellectual stimulation. Valuable aid has come too from Paul-Gabriel Boucé, Terry Castle, Ronald Gottesman, George Guffey, John Huntington, Paul Ilie, Moshe Lazar, Marjorie Perloff, Richard Popkin, Kathleen L. Spencer, Halina Stephan, Pascal J. Thomas, Howard D. Weinbrot, and the late David S. Wiesen. I thank *Science Fiction Studies* and Southern Illinois University Press for permission to reprint parts of this work that have appeared in different form in *Science Fiction Studies* 12, pt. 2 (July 1985); in George E. Slusser and Eric S. Rabkin, eds., *Hard Science Fiction* (Southern Illinois University Press, 1986); and in George E. Slusser, Colin Greenland, and Eric S. Rabkin, eds., *Storm Warnings: Science Fiction Confronts the Future* (Southern Illinois University Press, 1987). Nancy Holmes provided expert copyediting. Karen Orchard of the University of Georgia Press gave steady encouragement and editorial help for which I am most grateful. If I ever write a utopia, its press will be called Georgia and its editors will all be replicas of Karen Orchard.

PART ONE
Prehistory, 1659–1703

CHAPTER ONE

Temporal versus Spatial Imagination: *Epigone, histoire du siècle futur*

By "futuristic fiction" I mean prose narratives explicitly set in future time. The impossibility of writing stories about the future was so widely taken for granted until the eighteenth century that only two earlier works of this kind are known: Francis Cheynell's six-page pamphlet of political propaganda published in 1644, *Aulicus his dream of the Kings sudden comming to London*; and Jacques Guttin's incomplete romance of 1659, *Epigone, histoire du siècle futur*.[1] Before Guttin's remarkable book the future was reserved as a topic for prophets, astrologers, and practitioners of deliberative rhetoric. Even the latter, who might have included cautionary fables of the future in their orations, lived under the shadow of Aristotle's dictum that "in political oratory there is very little opening for narration; nobody can 'narrate' what has not yet happened. If there is narration at all, it will be of past events, the recollection of which is to help the hearers to make better plans for the future."[2] As a trope for madness John Donne could use the proverbial castigation *Chronica de futuro scribet:* "He undertakes to write a chronicle of things before they are done, which is an irregular, and a perverse way."[3]

Works that break the taboo against tales of the future are a significant development marking the emergence of a form unknown to

ORIGINS OF FUTURISTIC FICTION

classical, medieval, and renaissance literature. They mark too the beginning of what is arguably the modern world's most revealing mode of literary statement. Our fantasies of utopian or dystopian futures, even more clearly than other dreams that we share, tell what we are by showing our collective desires and fears. In the hands of such masters as Yevgeny Zamyatin, Aldous Huxley, and George Orwell, futuristic fiction also offers our most powerful literary defense against unthinking collusion with the impulses behind our worst nightmares.

In the evolution of forms that prepared the way for achievements like *Nineteen Eighty-Four* the French maintained their early lead, although the next futuristic fiction after Guttin's—and the first to be located with specific future dates—was Samuel Madden's *Memoirs of the Twentieth Century*, a satire published anonymously in 1733. It was followed in 1763 by *The Reign of George VI, 1900–1925:* a fantasy of relentless conquest enthusiastically endorsed by its unknown author, who may claim the ambiguous distinction of initiating the genre of future warfare.[4] In 1771 Louis-Sébastien Mercier's *L'An 2440* decisively moved utopia from the ineffectual realms of no place to the influential arena of future possibilities. This is the first utopia set in future time. In 1802 Restif de la Bretonne's *Les Posthumes* portrayed a very far future marked by planetary and biological evolution. Jean-Baptiste Cousin de Grainville's *Le dernier homme* in 1805 initiated the secularization of apocalypse. In 1834 Félix Bodin's *Le Roman de l'avenir* provided the first literary criticism of works set in future time as well as the first poetics of that genre, for which Bodin invented the term *littérature futuriste*. Bodin also remarked, quite correctly, that no fully realized novelistic example of the new form yet existed. I believe his discussion is the first instance of generic criticism written predictively before emergence of the genre in question for the purpose of encouraging its creation: an altogether fitting sequence for futuristic fiction.

The situation that Bodin so perceptively identified, in which the possibility for a new form clearly existed without yet being altogether achieved, is sufficiently distinctive if not unique in literary history to warrant closer scrutiny than it has received. In this book I describe the most important eighteenth- and early nineteenth-century forms of futuristic fiction taking shape in contexts that deflected—and still deflect—attention from the significance or even the fact of its emergence as a distinct genre. Those very few previous investigations which do not entirely overlook this new literary development have dealt with fictional resort to future time either as a notable, though puzzling, episode in the long history of utopian thought and science fiction or as an opportunity for tracing the ways in which technology has shaped visions of the future.[5] I shall concentrate instead on the structure of some key works chosen not for what they betray of past expectations but for what they reveal about the formal problems that had to be resolved before tales of the future could achieve their full power.

If none of the pioneering efforts I discuss warrant that sustained applause earned by the masterpieces of H. G. Wells and the most skillful of his followers, neither do the originators of futuristic fiction deserve anything like the almost total oblivion into which they have fallen. Their attempts were often highly original. Even when far from completely successful, they remain of great relevance to the history of literary forms. That relevance is not diminished by our inability to trace direct lines of causation from early experiments to later triumphs. Whether *Nineteen Eighty-Four* and its peers could have existed without *L'An 2440* is an unanswerable question. I suspect but cannot prove that, without such pioneers as Mercier, there would not have been towards the end of the nineteenth century a literary climate favoring *The Time Machine* and its acknowledged progeny. What I do argue in the following pages is that issues of causation and cultural context, though relevant, should yield priority to matters of form until the forms we seek to explain have been more adequately identified. It is to such identification of futuristic fiction's formal attributes that I primarily address this study of representative works. I claim too, presenting in this book the evidence for my case but mostly leaving contemporary applications to my readers, that we can better appreciate the achievements of such modern masters of the future as Orwell by looking back to the origins of futuristic fiction. Later accomplishments can only be fully understood as solutions to problems that earlier writers had struggled with in different ways. We do not disparage Cayley, Pénaud, and Lilienthal because the Wright brothers achieved more decisive results. The first voyagers in time deserve similar courtesy. If mentioned at all, however, they have too often been dismissed with a few sentences or paragraphs. Another purpose of this book is to encourage better appreciation of the most significant early futuristic writers by inviting closer attention than has yet been given to the forms of their key works.

Let us start by glancing ahead to Félix Bodin's tour of the horizon in 1834, approaching him by glancing even further ahead to a representative text dealing with parallel problems in our own period: Robert Scholes's *Structural Fabulation: An Essay on Fiction of the Future*. I single out Scholes's excellent discussion both for its comfort to students of futuristic fiction and for the purpose of underscoring by comparison the astonishing prescience of Bodin's criticism in a book almost totally neglected, to their loss, by twentieth-century critics, who could find its insights of more than merely historical interest. Scholes argues "that the most appropriate kind of fiction that can be written in the present and the immediate future is fiction that takes place in future time." He rightly notes that such fiction can achieve a power unequalled by other kinds and supports his case on several grounds, of which two are especially relevant to the origins of futuristic fiction. There is first an ethical argument: "If we accept Jean-Paul Sartre's imperative for literature, that it be a force for improvement of the human situation, and if we nevertheless would not see fiction reduced to the level of propaganda, then the idea of fiction freely speculating on

TEMPORAL VERSUS SPATIAL IMAGINATION

possible futures must appeal to us." Secondly, Scholes addresses what he calls a metaphysical issue: given widespread rejection of the ideas that language can or should refer to anything outside its own system, a solipsistic notion that undercuts all relationship of literature to life, futuristic fiction offers a way out because "all future projection is obviously model-making, poesis not mimesis." It follows, according to Scholes, that because such extrapolation is bounded only by "current notions of what is probable"—notions that science renders increasingly latitudinarian—the resulting literature is morally useful in the sense Sartre urges as an imperative for improving the human condition. It is also a literature in which "realism and fantasy must have a more intricate and elaborate relationship with one another."[6] There is thus an aesthetic advantage along with the utilitarian possibilities of encouraging efforts to improve our lot. This is our best defense of futuristic fiction: as a form uniquely appealing because it is potentially more able than any other kind to further progress by serving a variety of cognitive purposes without sacrificing either the appeal of fantasy or the claim to probability that is a hallmark of realism.

Bodin too regards futuristic fiction as an instructive mode that, better than any other, can enlist writing in the service of progress by combining the pleasures of fantasy with the reassurance of verisimilitude. He identifies the main philosophical dispute of his day as an opposition between those who locate mankind's golden age in the past, regarding the world as going downhill to an iron age that would mark its deathbed, and those who believe in the possibility of progress and locate the golden age in a future which presents itself to the imagination "resplendent with light." In ages dominated by conviction that things are getting worse, Bodin notes, our dreams are of endings for the world and of the last man.[7] When belief in progress prevails, other dreams are possible. But as yet futuristic literature, Bodin laments, has offered nothing but utopias or apocalypses: he does not know of any *novelistic* action transported to the setting of a future social or political condition.[8]

ORIGINS OF FUTURISTIC FICTION

The trouble with utopian literature, according to Bodin, is that its authors only try to find a basis for unfolding some religious, political, or moral system without attaching it to an action, without giving either depth or movement to things or persons, and without finally achieving the living creation of any kind of world to come.[9] Apocalypses, in Bodin's view, may at best provide poetic visions of the sort exemplified in "the mysterious and gigantic scenes" found in the Book of Revelation and its derivatives focusing on the Last Judgment. But such images, although respectable, are not consoling. Nor do they encourage either hope or efforts to work for progress. They lead to despair and apathy. Bodin's critique of previous futuristic literature thus firmly links the aesthetic issue of imaginative appeal with the moral issue of how readers may best be roused from indifference to their own futures.

When Bodin considers what futuristic fiction ideally ought to be, he specifies with even greater precision the most desirable relationships between verisimilitude, imaginative appeal, and the moral consequences of the new genre:

> If ever anyone succeeds in creating the novel, the epic of the future, he will have tapped a vast source of the marvelous, and of a marvelous entirely in accord with verisimilitude . . . which will dignify reason instead of shocking or deprecating it as all the marvelous epic machinery conventionally employed up to now has done. In suggesting perfectibility through a picturesque, narrative, and dramatic form, he will have found a method of seizing, of moving the imagination and of hastening the progress of humanity in a manner very much more effective than the best expositions of systems presented with even the highest eloquence.[10]

What Bodin envisions is a literature of rational wonders that can play a useful role in the real world *without surrendering the lure of the fantastic*. He also recognizes a problem peculiar to the issue of verisimilitude in novels attempting to enact plausible dreams of possible futures: it will be harder for such works to attain universal

TEMPORAL VERSUS SPATIAL IMAGINATION

appeal, he says, because everyone shapes an ideal future according to his own fantasies, and such fantasies are more likely to differ than are those perceptions of the existing world which become our yardstick for measuring verisimilitude in realistic fiction.[11]

At the end of his discussion, Bodin turns from the relationship between literature and society to the "purely literary considerations" involved in the question of how people view the future—in terms of progress or decay. He quotes from one of his other works an aphorism which, he affirms, contains the entire poetics of the novel of the future: "Civilization tends to separate us from all that is poetic in the past; but civilization also has its poetry and its marvelous."[12] Applying this thought to novels set in future time, Bodin winds up his essay with a remarkably accurate prediction of future novelistic possibilities as well as a perceptive location of such possibilities with respect to previous literary history. The two most striking statements from this section especially deserve wider familiarity not only for their historical interest but also for the help they can still provide to students of futuristic fiction.

To find subject matter, Bodin suggests leaving what he calls "the sad past," which has been sufficiently exploited, and making a leap into the more seductive unknown future: "There [in the future] can be found the revelations of those under hypnotic trance, races in the air, voyages to the bottom of the sea—just as one sees in the poetry of the past sibyls, hippogriffs, and nymphs' grottoes; but the marvelous of the future . . . is entirely different from these other poetic marvels in that it is entirely believable, entirely possible, and on that account it can strike the imagination more vividly and seize it by means of realism. Thus we will have discovered a new world, an environment utterly fantastic and yet not lacking in verisimilitude."[13] Here the imaginative role of plausibly extrapolated scientific wonders such as voyages under the sea and aerial races—very workable themes indeed, as we now know thanks to Verne and his imitators—is clearly affiliated with those purposes formerly served by the fantastic marvels of classical literature. Bodin affirms the need for such marvels as emotional and imaginative. Bodin also suggests a way of enlisting such marvels, changed to modern form, in the service of rational speculation. This insight is still a valid answer to those who question our need for fictions of the future. Such fictions, perhaps uniquely among literary kinds, may serve cognitive purposes both necessary and acceptable to reason in a scientific age while *also* feeding our hunger for the marvelous.

The final paragraph of Bodin's essay is even more specific in spelling out the tradition to which novels of the future should be affiliated:

> For the moment the question is to know whether, after the grotesque and audacious fantasies of Rabelais, the amusing and satiric inventions of Cyrano and Swift, and the sparkling philosophical novels of Voltaire, it would be possible to find something new and at the same time analogous; something which would be neither of a too licentious fantasy, nor of a purely critical intent, nor of that philosophical spirit which is an obstacle to interest and illusion by always substituting ideas for people, and by subordinating both action and characters to the thesis which it argues; something at once fantastic, novelistic, philosophic, and a little critical; a book where an imagination brilliant, rich, and wandering can range at ease; and, finally, a book amusing without being futile. I believe such a book would be possible; but I am still perfectly convinced that it is not yet written.[14]

Bodin's own novel of the future, to which his discussion serves as preface and to which I shall return in my last chapter, was published in incomplete form. Although even this lengthy fragment is of considerable interest both as a revealing historical document and as an intriguing story, Bodin was not up to following his own counsel of perfection. That remained for the successors of Verne and Wells, whose best writing provides just the kind of analogues to Rabelais, Cyrano, Swift, and Voltaire which Bodin here urges.

Bodin's statement of the tradition for which novels of the future could be the logical next development marks a noteworthy step

TEMPORAL VERSUS SPATIAL IMAGINATION

toward that self-consciousness which has become one hallmark of futuristic fiction. But despite Bodin's foresight, his essay was neither widely known nor instrumental in bringing about the development he recommended. There was no rush to adopt his useful term *littérature futuriste* by way of encouraging the realization of a new form designed to achieve what had previously been accomplished only separately by the fantastic voyage, the marvelous machinery of epics, the utopian projection, and the *conte philosophique*. Isolation from one another is one of the most striking features of early futuristic fiction writers and of that genre's origins. I have found little evidence that futuristic writers before 1850 knew of their predecessors' efforts apart from Mercier's famous book. Nor are there textual signs that their readers were expected to recall many earlier works *of the same kind* for comparison with the book in hand. It is not until much later that one commonly finds mutual awareness manifested by writers of futuristic fiction, along with inclusion of obviously conventional elements such as time machines or future warfare in the didactic mode popularized in 1871 by G. T. Chesney's *The Battle of Dorking*.

Early futuristic fiction is indeed as Pierre Versins, I. F. Clarke, Darko Suvin and others have suggested, a series of largely independent efforts that cut across various national, cultural, and formal boundaries.[15] The degree to which previous forms were transcended by the evolution of futuristic fiction has been obscured by its scattered origins. Despite the popularity of Mercier's *L'An 2440*, there was nothing in the rise of futuristic fiction exactly comparable to what Raymond Trousson describes as the monogenesis of forms like the utopia or the Robinsonade—forms for which a single text is clearly so distinctive that it sets the parameters for recognition of all subsequent examples while also retroactively casting some earlier works in the role of forerunners, as More's *Utopia* did for Plato's *Republic*.[16] Nor on most theories of genre has resort to future time as the setting for narrative action seemed a variation sufficiently distinctive to count as a form in its own right. Usually that resort, if noticed at all, has simply been taken for granted as nothing more than one attribute of science fiction. But tales of the future are not necessarily science fiction. Although it is closely related and undeniably liberated by the possibilities of displacing action to the future, science fiction does not require such displacement, as Mary Shelley's *Frankenstein* may remind us along with other early science fiction set in the present or close past—most notably, of course, all the major works of Jules Verne.[17]

To understand the history of futuristic fiction it is useful to take what Trousson calls in his lucid account of utopias a heuristic model of genres endowed with a relative permeability that allows them, in the course of their evolution, to borrow themes and procedures from neighboring genres. On this model individual works may fall under several categories at once. Thus it is possible to identify utopias that also display to a significant degree the traits of other kinds: the mirror for princes in Harrington's *Oceana*, for example, or science fiction in Souvestre's *Le Monde tel qu'il sera*.[18] Works that, by virtue of a future locus for their action, achieve effects otherwise unattainable may often be described accurately if incompletely as satires, utopias, fables, science fiction, allegory or fantasy—to name only some of the most closely related forms. By assuming for heuristic purposes that futuristic fiction is a distinct genre which may, however, coexist to varying degrees with other genres within a given text, it is possible to address more precisely the question of how forward displacement of temporal setting alters the impact of narratives. We can then see more clearly how masterpieces like *Nineteen Eighty-Four* rely on such displacement to achieve their distinctive power. A pluralistic model of genre also accords most accurately with that interweaving of kinds to create new forms which especially characterizes the eighteenth century, when futuristic fiction took its first sure steps.

Additional precision in describing the mixture of forms operative in particular texts is afforded by Mikhail Bakhtin's concept of the

TEMPORAL VERSUS SPATIAL IMAGINATION

chronotope, by which he means "the intrinsic connectedness of temporal and spatial relationships that are artistically expressed in literature." The word signifies "time-space." It is borrowed from the mathematical terminology of relativity theory, although its origins (and the term itself) are of less moment than Bakhtin's application of the idea that what matters in literature is the *relationship* between portrayal of time and portrayal of space—the ratio or balance between attention to spatial and to temporal aspects of narration. Other critics have tended to focus on either time or space while neglecting the issue of how their relationship may alter the import of narrative prominence given to each of these dimensions. The consequences for questions relating to genre have also been neglected. Bakhtin, however, argues that the chronotope is above all "a formally constitutive category of literature" which "has an intrinsic *generic* significance"; "it is precisely the chronotope that defines genre and generic distinctions, for in literature the primary category in the chronotope is time."[19]

I believe Bakhtin is the only critic who posits portrayal of time, in its relationship to space, as the most fundamental determinant of genre. The various historically identifiable chronotopes, he insists, "provide the basis for distinguishing generic types; they lie at the heart of specific varieties of the novel genre, formed and developed over the course of many centuries."[20] His theoretical justification for this conclusion is persuasive by virtue of its emphasis, in the tradition of Lessing, on the essentially temporal character of all literature as an art form whose medium inescapably valorizes time over space throughout the duration of reading. But this is not the place to rehearse arguments for and against accepting Bakhtin's view of genre to the exclusion of more traditional definitions. In critical practice his perspective does not preclude others. It offers a complementary angle of vision allowing better appreciation of relationships between time and literature that have too often escaped notice.

In surveying "Forms of Time and of the Chronotope in the

ORIGINS OF FUTURISTIC FICTION

Novel" from Greek romances to the nineteenth century, for example, Bakhtin stresses the pervasive downgrading of the future's ontological status that is apparent in Western literature up to the eighteenth century, thanks to a kind of historical inversion expressed artistically as "myths about paradise, a Golden Age, a heroic age . . . as well as the later concepts of a 'state of nature'." In such notions, Bakhtin explains, "a thing that could and in fact must only be realized exclusively in the *future* is . . . portrayed as something out of the *past*, a thing that is in no sense part of the past's reality, but a thing that is in its essence a purpose, an obligation." Future goals, in other words, were most often articulated in fiction as myths of past happiness, thus deflecting attention from speculation about the possible shape of things to come. Goals were also located outside time altogether in religious literature focusing upon eternity as the origin and destination of life, again to the detriment of concern with future time. Eschatology in particular, Bakhtin notes, "always sees the segment of a future separating the present from the end as lacking value. . . . It is merely an unnecessary continuation of an indefinitely prolonged present."[21] These reasons for turning away from concern with the future—and by implication away also from attempts to write futuristic fiction—are, to be sure, matters that no survey of Western attitudes toward time could very well ignore.

What distinguishes Bakhtin's commentary, although he says nothing about futuristic fiction, is the attention he gives to the consequences for previous narrative genres of such persistent devalorization of the future:

> The present and even more the past are enriched at the expense of the future. The force and persuasiveness of reality, of real life, belong to the present and the past alone—to the "is" and the "was"—and to the future belongs a reality of a different sort, one that is more ephemeral, a reality that when placed in the future is deprived of the materiality and density, that real-life weightiness that is essential to

TEMPORAL VERSUS SPATIAL IMAGINATION

> the "is" and "was." The future is not homogeneous with the present and the past, and no matter how much time it occupies it is denied a basic concreteness, it is somehow empty and fragmented—since everything affirmative, ideal, obligatory, desired has been shifted . . . into the past.[22]

Other critics writing on the basis of very different conceptions of genre have not been so sensitive as Bakhtin to the balance between concern with past and with future. It is rare indeed to find so clear a statement of the fact that obsession with the past as a source of authenticity for ideas and fictions has been *at the expense* of endowing visions of the future with a kind of realistic concreteness to which they might otherwise aspire.

For centuries, the distinction most often made to the detriment of concern with the future was *not* between the future and records of a real past, with its obviously greater claim to higher ontological status—and correspondingly more detailed narrative portrayal—than possible futures that have never existed, do not exist, may never exist, and cannot easily be known in advance even if they are going to exist. The distinction most influential in the history of narrative genres has rather been one that deflected attention from the future to stories—mere fictions—about *mythical* pasts that cannot logically claim any greater reality than imaginary futures. That many of what we should term myths were taken as facts about the past does not alter the implications for narrative which Bakhtin describes: widespread inclination to believe in imaginary pasts is precisely the point. For complex reasons that would require volumes to explain even if I could do so (or needed to for purposes of describing the literary consequences), writers of all kinds until quite recently were inclined to attach to the *imaginary,* no less than to the actual past, a kind of "real-life weightiness" of detailed narrative elaboration denied to the future.

It might have been otherwise: conceivably at least, myths about the close future, whether in the form of religiously endorsed prophecies or officially authorized five-year plans, could have been endowed by the institutions of society with a legitimacy that encourages narratives embroidered with many details. Our histories of the rise of progressively more realistic modes of narration might then have included tales of the future before 1659. But in fact visions of the near future authenticated by the secular mythology of physical or social sciences do not appear until the nineteenth century. Nor in Western civilization have prophecies concerning the future this side of Judgment day, despite their proliferation in so many eras, ever achieved anything like the authority of those eschatological visions that, as Bakhtin notes, only discourage concern with envisioning time between now and the end.

Bakhtin's insight goes far to explain the situation Bodin faced in noting that proto-futuristic fiction of his day seemed always to lack depth and movement with respect to both things and persons. That deficiency may appear even more paradoxical than it did to Bodin if we reflect that most of the works he had in mind were written during or just after the eighteenth-century flowering of realistic novels.[23] As Bodin realized, it was a question not only of locating action in the future but also of endowing such narratives with a persuasive weight of details. The techniques for such verisimilitude were at hand but had not yet been applied to futuristic fiction. This issue, apparent to Bodin and now more amenable to explanation thanks to Bakhtin, has from other perspectives received insufficient emphasis. Bakhtin, perhaps for ideological reasons germane to his own difficult situation, does not apply his discussion of chronotopes to the interesting case of futuristic fiction.[24] He confines himself to outlining various ways in which deflection of artistic concern from the future impeded development of narratives that could portray the whole arc of temporal relationships within actions set in past or present time. Bakhtin's approach in terms of ratios between time and space and between past, present, and future is also useful to students of futuristic fiction, however, as we can see

TEMPORAL VERSUS SPATIAL IMAGINATION

in more detail by turning now to the first book of fiction set in future time, Jacques Guttin's *Epigone, histoire du siècle futur*.

Alexandre Cioranescu salutes *Epigone* as the first novel of the future, but nevertheless concludes that while it purports to be a history of the future century it is only "a false novel of the future." It is false, according to Cioranescu, because it fails to make any sustained use of a future setting as a basis for speculation about significant new ideas or progress in technology. The translation machine which figures in one of *Epigone*'s episodes, Cioranescu remarks, "is insufficient to sustain an illusion [of future time] or justify a choice [of the future century as a setting] that quickly becomes arbitrary." Cioranescu qualifies these charges against Guttin by adding that "in reality all histories of the future are false" because the future inevitably paralyzes the imagination instead of exciting it. No wonder then that Guttin failed, and small blame. In this view Guttin is ambiguously honored as the initiator of a genre that cannot ever succeed. Only the past and present, Cioranescu asserts, can supply any writer of fiction with the necessary images upon which to build a narrative. "It is therefore not astonishing," Cioranescu says, "to see that the first attempt [at future history] failed."[25] For Cioranescu and those of like mind—who after all, as Bakhtin reminds us, represent the mainstream of Western thought about the future as a topic for fiction—such attempts as Guttin initiated must always fail.

Tempted as I am to discuss the works by H. G. Wells, Aldous Huxley, George Orwell, Anthony Burgess, Stanislaw Lem, René Barjavel, Ursula K. LeGuin, and many others that I believe refute Cioranescu's premise, I must confine myself here to arguing that *Epigone* deserves much more credit. Though it is certainly no masterpiece, neither is it a failure simply because it does not project a plausible or ideologically challenging future. Rather, Guttin succeeded very well in what he set out to do by creating a future setting that enhances the effects of his primary genre, the heroic romance. Anyone who does not like sprawling seventeenth-century romances has my entire sympathy. But we should nevertheless applaud Guttin for inventing a highly original way of making such romances do more effectively some of the things they were intended to do and for which they were once valued by those who did like them. He was the first writer who explored the advantages of using an imaginary future to enhance effects expected from an existing genre. He also invented a type of future history that is still perfectly viable, though not to everyone's taste (and not to mine): futuristic fantasy. To appreciate Guttin's achievement, and that of his successors, it is necessary to free ourselves from the persistent but inhibiting idea that only one kind of future history—the realistic extrapolation written predictively—is possible or desirable.

Space, for Guttin, is still the dominant dimension. He displaces action forward to "the future century" primarily as a means of enhancing effects hitherto obtained by geographical distance. His book contains utopian elements together with lively satiric thrusts at French customs, French temperament, and European follies more generally. There is also a love story filled with extravagant adventures in the mode of more conventional prose romances crammed, like Guttin's, with battles on land and sea along with last-minute escapes from death or, for the heroine, from a fate worse than death. Several of the incidents, such as the heroine's lucky acquisition of a magical potion that renders her invisible to three disagreeable suitors, have about them a pleasant air of outright fantasy. For all the adventures, whether they involve magic or merely larger-than-life feats on and off the battlefield, a distant setting undercuts possible objections that such carryings-on are unusual or impossible in seventeenth-century France and that the story is therefore implausible to an unacceptable degree.

Nothing can altogether remove Guttin's plot from the liabilities—and advantages—of fantastic romance. But while his future setting does not provide any significant gain in verisimilitude, it

TEMPORAL VERSUS SPATIAL IMAGINATION

does render the fantastic more acceptable. This is one of the major uses of resort to future time. It can augment verisimilitude in narratives that, unlike Guttin's, center on scientifically or sociologically plausible speculation. It can also (and more often does) serve to disarm objections to fantasy by providing a locale where the familiar present constraints on action need not apply. As Guttin perhaps realized, it may be easier for readers of futuristic fiction to enjoy unabashedly impossible adventures by suspending their disbelief sufficiently to accept various conventions of the fantastic.

For satire the device of travels to several remote nations of the world, as Swift later demonstrated to perfection, can provide a valuable perspective. Such distancing may be rendered even more remote by adding a leap forward in time. Guttin has it both ways: his adventures are set in exotic non-European lands of the future whose customs afford by comparison and contrast many implied criticisms of life closer to the reader's home, and whose citizens even speak out occasionally on Guttin's behalf with scathing denunciations of what they know about Europe. Guttin was the first to provide for readers such a double voyage through space and time by locating action in geographically faraway future countries, although no characters in *Epigone* travel *through* time. They all remain where Guttin put them, in a future century. Mercier's eighteenth-century Parisian waking up in the Paris of 2440 was the first time-traveler in futuristic fiction, unless one counts the guardian angel who brings to the narrator of *Memoirs of the Twentieth Century* those documents purportedly *from* the future which make up the main part of Madden's book.

Guttin offers no explanation whatever to account for the narrator's knowledge of a future century. Later writers dealt with this potentially troublesome issue by a variety of opening gambits that eventually shook down to a familiar repertoire of acceptable conventions. Before Wells invented the time machine in 1895 there were, in addition to Madden's unusual device of material supernaturally transported backward through time, stories purporting to recount future events witnessed by a narrator remaining *in* the present during more or less ordinary sleep; during visions induced by mesmeric trances; and during visions caused by drugs such as opium or hashish. There were stories based upon scenes of the future made available to the narrator for viewing by divine permission in otherwise unexplained "magic mirrors." There were also books unequivocally purporting to narrate cases of physical travel from the present *to* the future by means of mesmeric trances allowing movement forwards and backwards through time; by means of drugs that could bring on such trances; by means of help from a friendly supernatural tour guide who suspends the usual laws of nature that prevent time-travel; and by means of lengthy slumber sometimes induced by mesmerism, as later in Bellamy's 1888 bestseller *Looking Backward* in which the sleeper wakes in what to him is the future. But starting with *Epigone* and continuing throughout the first two hundred years of futuristic fiction (just as in the twentieth century, when the genre is more familiar, more widely accepted, and therefore less in need of such conceits providing a narrative raison d'être), there were also books like Guttin's that simply took for granted the storyteller's license to tell a tale without pausing to explain how the information came to hand.

That Guttin, the first to tell a story explicitly set in the future, should do so without in any way justifying that leap may seem remarkable. He of all writers, one might think, would have taken pains to provide for his readers some reassuring pretense to account for his six hundred thirty-six pages supposedly reporting events of "the future century." The well-known device of a prophetic dream-vision was available for adaptation to futuristic fiction in the seventeenth century, just as it was during the eighteenth and nineteenth centuries. Certainly Guttin was imaginative enough to think of it, although I do not know if he ever toyed with the idea. Perhaps in the mid-seventeenth century it still smacked too much of serious religious topics for use in a secular entertainment that avoids all opportunities even to mention Christianity as a part of European history and that comes very close on occasion to employing *superstition* as a synonym for *religion*. We can only speculate whether Guttin explicitly rejected the possibility of some such pretense as the narration of a prophetic dream upon which to build his tale or, perhaps more likely, simply proceeded without pausing to consider the advantages and disadvantages of just plunging into the future. Either way, especially in light of the little he does say about his methods, Guttin's decision may be taken as evidence that he did not regard a future of the kind portrayed in *Epigone* as sufficiently different from other possible settings for romantic adventure to warrant much comment.

In four pages headed "To the Reader" at the outset of his book, just after its dedication to "Madame la Marquise de Gouvernet," Guttin both adopts and invites a casual attitude to his story.[26] He disclaims any ambitions for the eternal fame of his book but rather insists that his concern for it is confined to the time when he diverted himself by working on it and to the period during which it still pleases him. By this disclaimer he says that he means to invite rather than deflect criticism. He cannot hope to please in every particular and especially cannot hope to satisfy the taste of those gentlemen, the *précieuses*, who set themselves up as general censors of everything not written by members of their cabal. Thus without alluding at length to the warring literary schools of his day or mentioning particular authors of any camp, Guttin quietly aligns himself on the side of Molière in 1659, the very year when *Les Précieuses ridicules* was first performed.

Guttin next elaborates on his stance as a sturdy independent outsider who, whatever his faults, cannot be accused of slavishly following the affected modes then so much in fashion. If he is not proper, Guttin asserts, the work is at least his own. Whatever is wanting in propriety, he implies, is compensated by originality: a suggestion that may be applied to justify the future setting and is perhaps sufficient to do so, although Guttin does not explicitly make the application. Instead he elaborates upon his refusal to be a mere conformist bound by prevailing ideas of how writers should proceed. He takes greatest pride, he says, in pleasing himself and *in writing quickly:* "one can never accuse me of having lost six or seven lustra for a work." Those who take such pains, Guttin adds with scorn, merely drive up the price of their books. He ends these remarks by assuring readers that they have only the fruits of his good humor and a gathering of the useless clouds ("vaines vapeurs") which leisure has raised in his imagination.

Such explanations, despite their own somewhat mannered air of amateurish and not altogether convincing indifference to approval from the literary establishment, do prepare readers to accept on its own terms a relatively plain style of narration designed to be read quickly, as Guttin claims it was written, without pausing to worry over literary niceties. The object is pleasure; the book an amusement for idle hours. If Guttin is hardly the first to make such familiar professions of disengagement from the lofty demands that high art makes upon both writers and readers, his statement sets the tone for what follows and goes far to excuse the omission of any explicit justification for locating the story in a future century. Since the book is to be taken lightly as a bagatelle, there is no need for serious defense of its vagaries. Indeed Guttin's only overt allusion to the future setting, apart from the title of his book, takes the casual form of a compliment to the Marquise de Gouvernet. He starts his dedication of *Epigone* to her by saying that she must not be at all troubled by the unknown hero who presents himself to her view: although he is neither of this world nor of this century ("ny de ce Monde ny de ce Siècle"), he is neither so wild nor so barbaric that he would be incapable of making a noble choice or judging as justly of her merit as all those who know her better. This rather strained praise of the Marquise de Gouvernet, though clearly of a piece with conventional dedicatory flourishes not designed for close scrutiny, does hint at the extent to which Guttin sees a kind of equivalence between space and time.

To put the action of his book in a future century is in effect to remove it also from *this world*. Although the Marquise de Gouvernet and her circle may have interpreted *Monde* more as French high society than as the earth itself, Guttin's phrase also invites

TEMPORAL VERSUS SPATIAL IMAGINATION

fleeting awareness of the possible literal meaning with its suggestion of adventures in future time as tantamount to adventures elsewhere in the universe. I stress this shade of meaning, in itself a slender enough clue to authorial intentions, because nowhere else does Guttin step outside his role as narrator to provide any other statement whatsoever by way of explicit reference to the existence or effects of his most original stroke. But there is in *Epigone* no literal departure for another world, as in the flourishing seventeenth-century literature of space travel that by the time Guttin published in 1659 included such works as Francis Godwin's *The Man in the Moone* (1638), Athanasius Kircher's *Itinerarium Exstaticum* (1656), and Cyrano de Bergerac's *Histoire comique contenant les etats et empires de la lune* (1657). These and similar planetary voyages were not Guttin's models. His story deals with human societies clearly of this earth but nevertheless so very curiously removed from France that Guttin achieves through spatio-temporal displacement effects of strangeness as well as satiric distance akin to the distancing that many of his contemporaries pursued by keeping their heroes in the present while taking them off this world.

Extraordinary voyages to the moon, sun, and planets mitigate their strangeness by at least offering destinations whose location is apparent. Armchair travel with Cyrano, for example, entails a series of new sights that are sometimes beautiful and often disturbing, along with many philosophically shattering surprises. But every reader can find some comfort in knowing where the main action occurs. More important, that knowledge serves a thematic purpose. Even though Cyrano provocatively calls in question many of his readers' basic assumptions about life, he does not obscure the location of his story. Prodigious distances traveled to the moon and sun, thanks to the reader's awareness that such vast spaces do separate us from those visible but inaccessible objects, provide a kind of emblem for departure from conventional ideas. For Cyrano and his fellow seventeenth-century astronauts, however, the temporal locus of action, usually an unspecified present, is of little significance except insofar as it amounts to removal of the story from our world of real time and space to the fantasy realms of "once-upon-a-time" where anything can happen. Space so prevails over time as the dimension endowing events with a large part of their meaning that time per se hardly exists as an artistically remarkable feature.

Guttin, by contrast, endows each dimension with significant aesthetic consequences. He does so by plunging his readers into an experience that is oddly disorienting with respect to both space and time. As in most romances, utopias, and accounts of imaginary voyages over the surface of this world, Guttin precludes one class of obvious but irrelevant objections by not specifying (and possibly confusing with some real place) the exact geographical location of the countries visited by his protagonists. Nor does he provide anywhere in *Epigone* even a single date. Time spans are usually indicated, if at all, by vague statements that a notable event such as the death of an emperor happened a little while ("peu de temps") after another landmark event such as a rebellion, or that at some such conspicuous historical turning point within the story a particular character was "young" (p. 99). Guttin occasionally remarks the passage of days and nights by including references to intervals of sleep within an episode and then noting what takes place the next day. He specifies that a storm at sea lasted three weeks, during which time everyone on shipboard thought only of perishing and after which the party found themselves at a distance of three days' sailing time from their destination (pp. 331–32). Readers can figure out the sequence of episodes and sometimes their approximate duration in days or weeks. A dagger-wound suffered by one character heals in a few days ("peu de jours"; p. 311). But Guttin does not relate episodes to any fixed date in "the future century" *or* to any year of the previous centuries, as he might easily have done in recounting the early history of his imaginary countries.

This omission of all calendric reference points should not be taken for granted. The question of whether specific dates are present or absent in futuristic fiction requires closer consideration

TEMPORAL VERSUS SPATIAL IMAGINATION

than it has received, because the various ways and degrees of locating narratives in the future are far from self-evident or identical in their results. Try, for example, to imagine the effect if Orwell had entitled his masterpiece *The History of a Future Century* or even, as he first thought of doing, *The Last Man in Europe* instead of *Nineteen Eighty-Four*.[27] I shall consider this matter more closely in chapter 4 when I take up Mercier's brilliant innovation in adopting for the title of his book a specific future date.

For Guttin, there was no need to worry that even the most obtusely literal-minded contemporary readers could object that a fictitious event supposedly taking place in an imaginary country on a given date in the next century *cannot* be found there while some other event *can*. There was no risk identical to that of locating imaginary countries in places where readers may know that something else exists. Moreover, since *Epigone* has no serious predictive intention (for reasons that I shall explain), Guttin need not have worried that anything construed or misconstrued as a prediction might seem implausible if attached to a particular date or that time would prove him wrong. Besides, even if his renunciation of any ambition for the eternal fame of his work seems a little hollow in its posture of humility, there is nevertheless no reason to suppose that *Epigone* was also intended for readers of the next century in the way that Orwell surely aimed *Nineteen Eighty-Four* to stand as a warning for succeeding generations as well as his own. Guttin's audience seems intentionally limited to his contemporaries. Although his book apparently attracted attention for awhile, it did in fact sink out of sight after 1700.[28]

A more likely reason for avoiding dates is that seventeenth-century narrative conventions did not, for any genre of prose fiction, attach so much importance as later writers have given to explicit chronology among techniques for achieving verisimilitude.[29] Nor was verisimilitude a prominent concern in romances of the kind that form Guttin's most immediate model. Such indifference to bolstering realism by adding particularizing details of any sort (including dates) goes far to account for Guttin's avoidance of them. But it does not dispose of the issue. Conformity to prevailing narrative conventions was an equally strong, if not more powerful, reason for avoiding the future altogether. I believe it is noteworthy, because it was *not* inevitable, that in taking the first narrative leap to future time Guttin refrained from also taking the corollary step of providing future dates for spelling out every reader's exact temporal relationship to the story. Guttin had a choice in this matter as he did in going to a future time in the first place, and a closer look at his tale will disclose the consequences of that choice.

Epigone's narrative sequence, the order in which Guttin tells his story, is not problematic despite its vagueness in spelling out where and when its action takes place. Following a convention of heroic romance, Guttin opens *in medias res*. He describes a storm of unparalleled ferocity which from the book's title we may suppose occurs in "the future century." But from the initial sentences readers learn only that the sky has *never* in its anger thrown so many thunderbolts, the waves have *never* been so agitated, and the winds have *never* fought such impetuous battles in the air. This rhetoric displaces events from the real world of specifiable chronological relationships to a kind of ideal order outside ordinary time—an order where events are defined only by sweeping contrast with *everything* that has ever occurred previously. After further description in an equally hyperbolic mode of that awesome tumult which drowns out all other sounds and obscures the daylight, readers are told that the tempest "threw a completely ruined ship onto one of the coasts of Agnotie, seeming by the discharge of this burden to return calm to the sea and daylight to the earth" (pp. 1–2). This description hints at mysterious supernatural forces without compelling readers to accept anything more than a marvelous coincidence between the ship's arrival at Agnotie, wherever that might be, and the return of calm weather.

Survivors of the wreck include Epigone, our hero; his beloved,

TEMPORAL VERSUS SPATIAL IMAGINATION

the princess Arescie; her confidante, Idise; and Aricas, Epigone's elderly retainer and mentor. There is also a retinue of servants, who construct a cabin for their master and mistress. None of the group know where they have landed, although from the length of nights and inequality of days Epigone guesses they are somewhere on the border between the torrid and temperate zones. We learn that they are in exile from their native land, but Guttin does not at this point disclose its name or location. Strangely garbed natives appear. They abduct Idise. The rest are conducted through the jungle to a magnificent city by an enigmatic old man named Synime who turns out to be the high priest of the temple. At its altar under a great crystal dome, a strange and astonishing ("inouye") translating device also made of crystal permits communication so that Epigone, to his amazement, can understand Synime "as though he spoke the language of the Clodovists" (p. 58). Here readers have their first clue to Epigone's origin, a clue that only deepens the mystery. The initial passages of Guttin's book thus skillfully serve to arouse curiosity. Where are we? Who are the Clodovists? With whom—and with what—are we confronted?

Only starting on page 75 are events leading to the shipwreck recounted in the form of a series of conversations between Aricas and Synime that provide what the heading on that page describes as the "History of Epigone." After three "books" of this history within the one (and only) volume of *Epigone*—which as a whole is subtitled "Part One"—the account of Epigone's adventures has been brought up to the moment of the conversations between Aricas and Synime. The latter warns that for the prince and princess Agnotie will present even more dangers than the lovers have already encountered and barely survived in the perilous travels that have been recounted at such length. With this promise of more adventures to come, Guttin ends his book. There is no sequel.

Placed between Guttin's prefatory remarks to the reader and his opening account of the tempest are two pages headed "Key to obscure words." The vocabulary there unfolded may arouse expectation of a story that is more consistently allegorical than Guttin's actual narrative. *Agnotie*, we are informed, means "unknown country" ("terre inconnue"). *Epigone* means "posterity" or "successor." *Arescie* means "perfection." *Frontide, Penone, Chronise, Euphoise,* and *Technide*, the names of Arescie's servants ("who serve perfectly"), mean respectively "care," "work," "time," "spirit," and "art." *Idise* means "of a beautiful and agreeable disposition." *Aricas* means "old." *Synime* means "intelligent." The names of three rival suitors in love with Arescie—*Isique*, the *Prince of the Itlimates*, and *Philtrason*—mean respectively "idler," "Prince of nonsense" ("niaiseries"), and "he who amuses himself with foolishness." Although the names of Arescie's servants are identified as such, the list does not otherwise spell out roles in the manner of a "cast of characters." Terms such as *Proctes* ("those who were awhile ago") and *Istate* ("the latest, or the most recent arrivals") must be either kept in mind for application when they occur in the narrative or looked at again later if necessary for elucidation of puzzling episodes.

Guttin says nothing about the languages real or imaginary, past, present, or future, from which the "obscure words" are supposed to be taken. Most often knowledge of a name's meaning as explained in the key adds little or nothing to understanding of episodes in which the term occurs or to appreciation of various characters. Their dominant traits are in any case unmistakable. Thus Philtrason's absurdity is as clear from his conduct as Synime's intelligence is from his actions and Arescie's perfection from her exemplary behavior. When coquettes make trouble for Aricas because of his age, it is plain enough that in Guttin's view the elderly would always encounter similar problems with such people for the same reason. Little seems to be gained by regarding the main characters primarily as allegorical types of age, intelligence, good nature, or whatever.

Epigone chooses his name, as we eventually discover, to emphasize his independence as the maker of his own fortune when going

TEMPORAL VERSUS SPATIAL IMAGINATION

into exile to avoid entanglement in a civil war that divides members of his ancient royal family. He leaves in search of glory ("aller chercher la gloire") rather than choose sides between the rival armies led by his mother and by one of his brothers (p. 106). He is not to be taken in an emblematic sense as simply standing in general for all the posterity of Guttin's generation or of any previous generation. The key to obscure words, because of its redundancy as an aid to interpretation, is most notable to readers today and in the seventeenth century as the first sign of *Epigone*'s persistent weaving in and out of an allegorical mode. The book fluctuates between emblematic time with a universal application that minimizes relationship to particular moments or places and adventure time with its more individualized hours connected to the locus of distinct events.

One of the longest episodes, for example, takes place after Epigone's storm-driven ship shelters and then runs aground off a "dangerous headland" on which reside the *Mignones*—a word not in the key but duly specified in the narration as meaning "coquettes." Their realm shades into an amazonian kingdom of misrule named Istasie where, "because the second sex there has the first rank and exercises the principle authority, that which passes elsewhere for weakness is in these regions a high virtue; and the pleasures which are everywhere condemned by philosophy and reason are among them the most plausible and most approved motives" (pp. 555–56). Much of what follows from this deplorable premise in Guttin's topsy-turvy land where women rule has a kind of dreamlike detachment from the world of ordinary fixed relationships between men and women, farce and high seriousness, time and space.

Epigone's grounded ship is welcomed by a countless number ("nombre infiny") of little boats filled with "the most handsome men and most beautiful women in the world." These people sing love songs—we are given some of their lyrics—and appear occupied only with enjoying themselves. This scene has a nonpareil quality that gives it more affinities to the landscape of dreams and allegory than to that of the real world, where most new encounters can be readily associated with similar moments and with places previously experienced. Guttin next heightens the sense of detachment from normal waking time and space in our quotidian world: there was *never* anything more jolly or more gallant ("Il n'y eut jamais rien de plus gay n'y rien de plus galant," p. 340). Here, as in the book's opening paragraph and elsewhere, Guttin substitutes a temporal discrimination for a physical description. He does not specify what the beautiful people wore or tell us anything in particular about their physiognomy and attributes. Instead, falling back as he often does upon the romance writer's repertoire of hackneyed phrases, Guttin resorts to the one available descriptive trope that most radically dissociates what is described from the ordinary flow of time during which, according to the logic of Guttin's conventional phrase, one has *never* seen and by implication *can never see* the like of what is described. Events then accelerate as in a nightmare, taking Epigone and Arescie with disconcerting speed from comedy to the brink of tragedy.

The comic turn, which seems to proffer a happy outcome to Epigone's exile, comes just after he goes ashore and finds himself named by the queen to be Istasie's next king. Her title is *Istatesse*. Epigone will be the *Istate*—literally, "the latest arrival." In a country run by coquettes obsessed with novelty, it is the custom to enthrone each newcomer. In connection with this decision the queen summons her council of *Mastropes* ("seducers, enchanters," according to the vocabulary key, which notes also that the French word is "too free"). Then she convenes her inner council of a few women called *proctes* to fill a vacancy in their ranks. Guttin describes at length the ceremony for initiation to that office. There are solemn dances and a long oath which includes among its other clauses a vow that all thoughts and cares will be devoted to the god of love and never turned to any serious object. Lest we miss the point of this rather heavy satire, the narrator remarks that by his rehearsal of "this ridiculous custom you can well judge the spirit of the country." It is a place, he continues, where nothing is arranged in conformity with reason, where everything follows sensual caprice, and where nature seems exhausted in producing what pleases the inhabitants and in banishing reason (pp. 373–74). But Epigone's first impressions are more positive. He is easily taken in by it all.

A throne, Epigone reasons, will make him more worthy of marriage to Arescie—she is the daughter of an emperor—and will also make up for the throne he lost by going into exile. Even Arescie is at first pleased by their reception at the hands of people who seem to care only for pleasure and who treat both of them without the chilling formality that usually prevents friendship with those of high rank. Neither the prince nor the princess is alarmed at what should be for readers the telling way Aricas is shunned by the natives because of his age and is compelled to stay aboard ship when the rest go ashore. Of Epigone and Arescie's delight at finding themselves for the first time in a place where all the inhibiting ceremonies of rank are discarded, the narrator ominously remarks: "that joy did not last long; and if the beginning diverted them, the end was for them not so agreeable" (p. 343). By alerting readers to the impending shift in fortunes, this prolepsis also heightens awareness of the accelerating tempo of incidents.

The turn toward tragedy arrives with the queen's sudden decree, in a fit of jealousy, that Arescie will be executed unless Epigone renounces her. From this point forward in Guttin's account of events in Istasie, his narrative flickers in an especially revealing way between the adventure-time dictated by romance conventions and the intrusion of a less determinate temporal nexus suitable to the requirements of allegory. The contrast, I should stress, is a matter of subtle shifts in Guttin's manner of evoking spatio-temporal relationships rather than an absolute distinction between two mutually exclusive modes of narrative time. It could hardly be otherwise. Nor is the slightness of the variation at all unusual within a seventeenth-century context of narrative forms that do not rely upon the kind of temporal verisimilitude that was only to become the norm for some eighteenth- and nineteenth-century fiction. Among heroic romances Guttin's style of temporal allusion is notable, however, because an examination of it helps define the parameters limiting any attempt in his day to overcome the literary time-barrier that kept writers away from the future.

From the moment when the queen forces upon Epigone the dilemma of choosing between fidelity to Arescie and sovereignty over Istasie, the narrative largely devolves into a sequence of intrigues and adventures arousing suspense that points the reader's attention forward to a resolution of the main question: will Epigone succeed in rescuing his beloved and, if so, how? Much of what follows in this connection is the familiar stuff of heroic romance. Epigone and Arescie first resolve to die for their love. They exchange touching letters. Allegorical implications of the situation are only briefly recalled when the queen sneeringly advises Epigone to get rid of "that ridiculous virtue which the Europeans term constancy" (p. 389). Epigone spells out his quandary in a manner that echoes the familiar agonizing of all those previous noble heroes of romance caught in love quandaries once so highly interesting to readers: "It is necessary to displease she whom I love, or love she whom I hate. It is necessary to be ungrateful, inconstant, unfaithful; or be the cause, the author, and the instrument of the death of Arescie" (p. 406). The sentimental pathos of Epigone's plight, however much it may recall previous books that will seem delightful or tedious according to the reader's taste, mainly serves to focus attention upon the particular interval and spaces within which the protagonist must act to bring about a happy ending.

The generalized time of allegory recedes to the background without altogether dwindling to insignificance. As the episode unfolds, Guttin concentrates primarily upon detailing Epigone's attempts first to visit Arescie in the labyrinthine prison where she has been secluded and then to rescue her at the place of execution. Time acquires meaning in relationship to the geography of three places:

TEMPORAL VERSUS SPATIAL IMAGINATION

the claustrophobic palace where the queen detains Epigone in a room lit with perfumed torches and hung with mirrors; the prison whose secrets he must unravel to find his beloved or even send a letter to her; and the public square in which the headsman's block is being installed upon a scaffold while a crowd assembles to witness Arescie's execution. At this point in the narrative, for Epigone and for readers caught up in the adventure, there is an overpowering sense of time as a force to be reckoned with—real time, not time emblematic of some other quality. Days, hours, and minutes are running out for the lovers: first slowly for Arescie in the prison and even more slowly for Epigone trying to communicate with her; then very rapidly as the cart bearing Arescie and six armed guards moves through the crowd drawing closer and closer to the scaffold upon which she is to die.

Guttin also heightens connections between time and the geography of this adventure by narrating Aricas's attempt, amid frustrating delays, to leave the ship and go to the aid of his master, who is eventually located in the perfumed chamber surrounded by the queen's courtiers. Difficulties encountered at every step by Aricas, who must resort to a complicated stratagem in order to have a few moments of private conversation with Epigone, enhance the sense of time as an almost palpable obstacle to a happy ending. Fortune then changes again for Aricas and Epigone, and with this turn for the better Guttin minimizes all sense of time as flowing rapidly or slowly in the manner of duration experienced in real life. It is almost as though the narrative were here replicating in miniature that large historical shift that Bakhtin associates with medieval chivalric romances and their later novelistic sucessors—a shift in which the pure adventure-time of antiquity, evoking an orderly sequence of objective time within stories where "a day was equal to a day, an hour to an hour," is displaced by "a hyperbolization of time typical of the fairy tale: hours are dragged out, days are compressed into moments, it becomes possible to bewitch time itself. . . . We begin to see the peculiar distortion of temporal perspectives characteristic of dreams."[30] The dénouement of Epigone's adventure in Istasie certainly has more affinities to the magical time of dreams and fairy tales than to either the emblematic time of allegory or the classic adventure-time that was to be revived with improvements in realistic fiction of the eighteenth century and afterwards.

There is a bewildering speed and illogic in the events leading to Epigone's rescue of Arescie and their escape on the ship whose subsequent wreck brings them to the shores of Agnotie, where readers first encounter them at the beginning of Guttin's narrative. A mysterious captain of the queen's own guard corps—who inexplicably turns out to be "the adorable Idise disguised as soldier"—arranges for Epigone and Aricas to disarm and replace two of the guardsmen, thus acquiring weapons along with a means of going unchallenged to the foot of the scaffold where there might be a chance to help Arescie (p. 510). The two guardsmen turn out to be Arescie's waiting-maids Frontide and Penone ("care" and "work," according to the vocabulary key, if that helps). When the cart bearing the prisoner approaches, everyone in the crowd is moved by her calm, courageous bearing. Epigone and Aricas successfully attack the six armed guards, only to discover that the prisoner is in fact one of the rival suitors, the Prince of the Itlimates ("prince of nonsense"). He has disguised himself as Arescie and taken her place. How he managed this, or indeed how he suddenly pops up again at this juncture, is not explained. Nor, with the perfect illogic of dreams, does Guttin explain how Epigone or a crowd pressing around the cart for a close look could mistake that strapping figure—a formidable swordsman in other episodes—for a beautiful princess, despite the disguise.

Without puzzling over these matters, Epigone rushes back to the prison for another shot at saving Arescie. Further swordfights ensue. When Epigone is taken prisoner and things again look bleak, Idise somehow captures the queen and spreads word that she is dead. The whole city, rather surprisingly (as Aricas remarks), accepts this rumor for fact and turns to the customary celebrations,

TEMPORAL VERSUS SPATIAL IMAGINATION

dances, and masquerades that attend the election of another Istatesse. Arescie is chosen. For her this creates a quandary analogous to Epigone's previous dilemma, because it turns out that she would have to share the throne with Philtrason, yet another of the rival suitors who has inexplicably appeared at a most awkward moment. He now spends "four or five days" (p. 596) pressing his courtship and threatening vengeance if Arescie refuses. Guttin's specification of this rather lengthy interval in the midst of an otherwise accelerating crescendo of frenetic action adds to the episode's dreamlike atmosphere of distorted temporal and causal relationships. So does a sudden resolution of Arescie's difficulties when Idise takes her back to Epigone's ship unnoticed amid the confusion after the natives, tiring at last of squabbles over Epigone and Arescie, proclaim as their new Istate the lone survivor of another ship that has been conveniently wrecked on their coast.

Far from denying that much of what I describe as a sequence of distorted temporal perspectives throughout some parts of *Epigone* can be attributed to the conventions of heroic romance, and would not have been remarked as unusual in Guttin's day, I want to insist upon that influence. A chain of implausible coincidences magically creating complications or doing away with them was as commonplace in such fiction as agonizing love dilemmas detailed in tedious soliloquies, astonishing feats of swordsmanship, and disguises (like those in Shakespeare) that have only to be specified as disguises to be accepted as convincing. So too for the fluctuations between patches governed by adventure-time and patches of temporal distortion caused by magical or supernatural rather than natural causal relationships between events and times. Given the conventions of heroic romance, there is nothing especially distinctive in Guttin's alternations of this kind in modes of temporal representation. Nor is there anything that readers of his day would necessarily have regarded as unusual in Guttin's scattered intrusions of allegorical time. The gestures toward allegorical meaning in such matters as the Istasians' final rush to enthrone the latest shipwreck survivor are obvious; for seventeenth-century readers of romances, they were easily enough accommodated to the nonallegorical level of action.

Only slightly more problematic are satirical touches like the one Guttin includes in his detailed narration of the method for Arescie's impending execution: following the custom of the country, its priests are to open her cranium and remove her brain as a sacrifice to the evil spirits, for it is that part which is there held in most horror; her hair, however, as the part held in most esteem, must not be disturbed when the brain is removed; and finally, she is to be killed by having her head chopped off. When Aricas pauses amid the bustle of rescue attempts to ask a native why it is necessary to behead the prisoner, since removing the brain is surely fatal, he is told that experience in the land of the coquettes has amply demonstrated that brains are not necessary to live and live happily. Even such divagation to farce could have been accommodated by the conventions of a genre not bound to later notions of verisimilitude or consistency of tone.

What makes the conventional features of romance bearing on temporal representation worthy of especially close remark in *Epigone* is that Guttin's way of envisioning a future is largely determined by his application of just these conventions. They license almost any mode of spatio-temporal representation except precise affiliation of a story to the reader's present or future location in space or time.

Events throughout *Epigone* are displaced from ordinary time and familiar locations in all the ways I have illustrated and in many others less immediately relevant. Even the patches of adventure-time, which most closely focus attention on particularized sequences of action tied to relatively determinate places, do not specify with any exactitude when or where the action occurs with respect to other episodes or to the reader's world. Instead Guttin provides separate stories about the same hero—stories that, taken

TEMPORAL VERSUS SPATIAL IMAGINATION

together, are more like a picaresque series of encounters than a plot involving causal connections linking incidents in a necessary sequence from beginning to end. Each episode with its freight of excitement, allegory, and satire seems to float in a time and space only nominally connected to the rest. Interwoven too with the adventures even at their most determinate are those dreamlike intrusions of illogical coincidence and inexplicable events that disrupt all sense of time flowing in orderly relationship to space. Allegorical and satirical strokes with very general application—we are not dealing here with sustained historical allegory—further deflect attention from the real flow of time in the reader's world. Even when Guttin's satire is aimed at what he identifies as specifically French manners, the targets (such as obsessive pursuit of the latest fads in dress and entertainment) are not confined to one clearly identifiable era, much less to a particular date. In this context it is almost inevitable that Guttin's "future century" is not unequivocally a future at all, nor for that matter exactly a present or a past century.

Instead of falling indisputably into one of the ordinary categories by which events are usually located, however roughly, in the past, present, or future, Epigone's adventures are ambiguously related to the flow of calendar time in the reader's world. The book's title alludes to "the future century" with an apparent clarity which the narrative itself does not sustain. From what is told about the past of Epigone's country, it is impossible to determine precisely where its history meshes with real events. The extent and grandeur of "the empire of the Clodovists"—called *Clodovie*—is better known than its origins, Aricas tells Synime in starting to explain about Epigone's background. We then learn of Eric the Great who was succeeded by Clodovée the Just, father of the next king, Clodovée the Conqueror. At the time of Epigone's shipwreck on the coast of Agnotie, his native land is ruled by Clodovée the Eighteenth. *Clodovie* can be taken along with the name of the ruling dynasty as an allusion honoring Clovis, although Guttin's book does not explicitly mention him or any other actual historical personage. Neither the first King Clodovée nor any of his seventeen namesakes can be identified with Clovis on the basis of what we are told. There are no significant parallels. Nowhere in *Epigone*, for example, to mention only one striking omission, is there *any* mention of Christianity as a religion that has ever existed, much less been accepted by Epigone or fostered by a Clodovist king in the manner of its adoption by Clovis. Nor is any other notable event of French or European history mentioned.

It is nevertheless possible, as Pierre Versins remarks, to equate Clodovée the Just with Louis XIII (1601–1643), simply because he too was known as "Le Juste." In this case Eric the Great must be equated with Henry IV (1553–1610), and Clodovée the Conqueror must be taken as an equivalent of Louis XIV, who reigned from 1643 to 1715 but was only twenty-one years old at the time of *Epigone*'s publication.[31] On this view Epigone's wanderings during the reign of Clodovée XVIII would, from the standpoint of readers in 1659, be pushed very far ahead without being attached to any specific dates, because the narrative gives no hint as to how long the first seventeen Clodovées are supposed to have lived or reigned.

A complication of that vague chronology, which hinges upon a plausible but not inevitable equation of Clodovée the Just with Henry IV, is that Guttin's account of Clodovée the Conqueror's empire-building hardly squares with the achievements of Louis XIV by 1659. It was Clodovée the Conqueror, Aricas relates in the book's most explicit equation of Clodovie with France, who extended the limits of the French empire ("étendit les bornes de l'Empire de France") to the Caspian Sea, the African deserts, the polar regions, and finally to the very edge of the Western American continent (pp. 86–87). If applied to Louis XIV in 1659, this statement must be taken (as Versins also notes) for either a prediction or a suggestion about the future. It is quite possible that *Epigone* here flatters the young King Louis XIV by obliquely—very obliquely—prophesying for him a glorious career of territorial aggrandizement.

TEMPORAL VERSUS SPATIAL IMAGINATION

Perhaps too Guttin thus urges his king to adopt an expansionist policy. If so, it is Guttin's only invitation to speculate about what the real future might hold for those reading in 1659.

Significantly, even that prediction—if indeed it is a kind of prediction—has more to do with space than with the flow of political or other events in specifiable calendar time. *Epigone*'s hyperbolic account of how "the empire of France" expands to the Caspian Sea, the African deserts, the extremities of the polar regions, and the borders of the American continent is, to be sure, somewhat hazy around the edges except for mention of the Caspian Sea. But these are at least places that can be approximately located on a map. Guttin is far less specific about the time involved.

After remarking that Clodovée the Conqueror had in less than twenty years almost as many children ("en moins de vingt années eut presque autant d'enfans"), Guttin adds even more vaguely that Clodovée's expansion of the borders took place in the incredible and unprecedented span of time occupied by his inimitable life ("dans l'espace d'un temps incroyable & sans exemple que dura son inimitable vie," p. 86). Time is here measured by events rather than vice versa. Rather than locating actions with respect to particular dates or some known or knowable era, Guttin specifies the years in terms of incredible actions that fill them. Again it is the nonpareil quality of intervals ("sans exemple") not their relationship to calendric time, which matters for descriptive purposes. As I have remarked, such description has the effect of *removing* what is so described from the world of ordinary (and quantifiable) temporal relationships. The geographical equation of Clodovie with France is more exact than any connection readers can make, on the basis of information supplied in Guttin's narrative, between particular intervals within its story and periods of time—past, present, *or future*—in the real world occupied by readers. Guttin's portrait of a "future century" in *Epigone* is therefore more like an alternate history than like anything we might now describe as a tale of the future.

ORIGINS OF FUTURISTIC FICTION

The impression of reading about an alternate history is heightened because, even though Epigone's native land is in some sense the place we know as France, for the most part its history is not the same. Only the geographical correspondence is unequivocal. Other parallels are less striking. Thus, in addition to the sentence in which Guttin inadvertently or by design refers to Clodovie as "the Empire of France," we are told elsewhere that the Gauls and Francs are now known as Clodovists (p. 89). There is also an allusion to Marseilles as the one city among those inhabited by the Gauls which obtained from early Clodovian emperors the liberty of preserving its name and privileges. A few more sentences about the history of Marseilles mention its pride and state that difficulties it caused (they are not specified) were at last dealt with and forgiven by a patient emperor (pp. 113–14).

While the struggles of Marseilles to retain its independence are notable as far back as the time of its problems with Julius Caesar after the Punic Wars, Guttin's allusion to its history probably evoked from his readers more immediate memories: perhaps recollection of administrative arrangements made separately for the city when Province joined the kingdom of France in 1481; more likely recollection of resistance to Henry IV or even more recent antagonism to Louis XIV during the Fronde. Resurgence of this antagonism was to be dealt with in the year after *Epigone*'s publication not by royal forbearance but by siege warfare directed at Marseilles and by construction there of Fort Saint Nicholas. Guttin's account of the Clodovian emperor's patience might have been read in 1659 as a discreet suggestion about the way Louis XIV *should* handle Marseilles in the immediate future. Or it might have been taken as a polite reference to any one of several periods when perforce nothing much was done by French kings to curb that city's aspirations. In either case, Guttin's reference to Marseilles mainly serves to underscore geographical indentity between Clodovie and France.

Parallels between the real history of Marseilles and the role of that city in Epigone's world are neither sufficiently determinate in

TEMPORAL VERSUS SPATIAL IMAGINATION

time nor sufficiently specified otherwise to enforce an unequivocal correspondence between the histories of France and Clodovie. Nor does Marseilles play a role in the story except as the place from which Epigone sets out on his travels. The only thing he does there is board a ship and sail away. For Guttin's readers the paragraph about Marseilles in a book of 636 pages does not command enough attention to invite more than a fleeting and necessarily indecisive effort to correlate the city's actual part in French history with vague parallels in *Epigone*'s fictive history. By invoking such hazy parallels while alluding to a real place as the point of departure for all the adventures that are actually narrated at length in *Epigone*, Guttin mainly heightens the sense of distance between every reader's location somewhere in the same world of time and space occupied by the real Marseilles and those strange unreachable lands and times where all the book's action takes place.

If in *Epigone* there is some other scrap of historical allegory that seventeenth-century eyes could unveil better than mine, it too seems insufficiently obtruded or sustained to enforce a coherent relationship between the history of France and that of the Clodovists. There are too many striking differences. Because Epigone seems to come from a Europe that has never known Christianity, never heard of the Roman Empire, never experienced any of the landmark events of medieval and renaissance history apart from unification of Franks and Gauls into one country, the history of *Epigone*'s "empire of France"—starting with its new name of Clodovie—seems like an alternative, dream-world scenario of how France might have developed, not an allegory of what actually happened in the reader's universe. Consequently the "future" in which Epigone lives is in effect a future that might follow from some *other* history than the one we have known in our world.

Epigone thus projects a future that is not an extrapolation from any reader's past and present. It is a "future" situated altogether apart from real time but affiliated with actual space. Even that affiliation, however, is very tenuous because of the way Marseilles in particular, and all of Clodovie in its role as "the Empire of France," merely serve as jumping-off points for adventures that occur entirely in places and times doubly removed from our reality: removed not just to imaginary lands to which no ship can sail but also to a future that does not, even in imagination, clearly flow from the reader's past and present. The future portrayed by Guttin's narrative is very much of a piece with, *and shaped to accord with*, the make-believe landscapes of romance.

Seeking to augment the effects of those landscapes in a genre which depends heavily upon them, Guttin turned to the idea of the future. I cannot explain why he was the first to do so, nor why others in the seventeenth century did not follow suit. Whatever the reasons prompting his experiment, I submit that Guttin knew very well what he wanted to do and that he did it very well. But Guttin was unlucky in publishing *Epigone* just when heroic romances of the kind that he attempted to invigorate by a future setting very suddenly went out of fashion. That shift is itself puzzling. A historian of the French novel remarks that "the reasons for the abrupt end to the vogue of long *romans* remain obscure."[32] Paradoxically, however, given the prior vogue of romance conventions that valorized all sorts of inaccessible dreamscapes as the locus of adventure, Guttin could depict a time almost entirely disconnected from the real past, present, and future while nevertheless calling it "the future century," precisely because to most people the future *was* still an unreal concept. Since the past and present then had more ontological legitimacy for many reasons including the ones Bakhtin notes, an unreal, empty future severed from relationships to both the present and the actual future was most easily adapted to the needs of romance.

Whatever the exact genesis of Guttin's innovation, he spatialized time by making "the future" do even more efficiently what less original authors had been content to achieve by resorting (as Guttin also did) to banal varieties of physical distance. Guttin is important

TEMPORAL VERSUS SPATIAL IMAGINATION

not merely as the first to resort to a future setting, because his kind of alternate future is not characteristic of most later futuristic fiction apart from outright fantasy only set in a putative future. His achievement is better appreciated as a remarkably successful effort to augment by manipulation of *temporal* setting that impression of departure from real to unreal space upon which romances set such a high premium.

It is not just romance. Landscapes like those of *Epigone* are as thoroughly removed to nowhere as those in any utopia published before 1771, when Sébastien Mercier's *L'An 2440* first moved an ideal state from no place to some real place in future time. In Chapter Four, I discuss the implications of this and related shifts. Here I want merely to note a basic difference between the literary uses of future time by Guttin, along with his successors in futuristic romance, and the exploitation of future settings by writers more in the tradition of Mercier. The locus of Mercier's utopian projection is Paris; the time, although very far ahead, is unequivocally linked by a specific date to every reader's past, present, and future. Mercier thus invites sustained consideration of what may someday happen (however unlikely it might seem) and what should happen to a real, not imaginary, place throughout a future that is connected to the reader's actual present moments. But Guttin's allusions to time, no less than his allusions to space, disrupt such continuities. They deflect attention from the real future.

Though *Epigone*'s country is geographically equated with France, its history is for the most part totally different from that of Clodovie, and the notable parallels are at best temporally indeterminate. Apart from the two possibilities I have mentioned, readers therefore cannot take *Epigone* as either a prediction whose plausibility can be assessed or a prescription for future conduct that might be accepted or rejected. Nor are they encouraged to do so. It is not just that Guttin does not portray any ideal state in the manner of utopias whereas Mercier does—an obvious but trivial difference. There is a more fundamental distinction between a future like Mercier's that is fictive but ontologically related to the real flow of time by virtue of being situated ahead of the reader's present and a future like Guttin's that is disconnected from the real flow of time by virtue of being grafted onto an equally fictive past and present.

In Mercier's future, events and institutions are measured by the reader's notions of what is possible, what will be possible, and what is desirable in the real world. In Guttin's kind of alternate past, present, and future shaped to meet the requirements of heroic romance, everything is judged by accepted conventions of the marvelous. Invisibility potions, translation devices, and the like—including also in *Epigone* an astonishing suspended apartment where Arescie lives for months on shipboard insulated from all motion caused by the sea—are not referred to the real future in terms of possibility or even desirability. They are simply rendered more acceptable as marvels by virtue of the alternate timestream as well as the inaccessible space in which we encounter them, a space rendered all the more remote because of its displacement to a time cut off from connection with our own. What is important for the history of futuristic fiction is that, from its very beginning in *Epigone*, there was the possibility that future time could play the same role as imaginary space.

CHAPTER TWO

Towards an Aesthetics of Extrapolation: *Iter Lunare* and *The Sacred Theory of the Earth*

Guttin's achievement as the first to endow any kind of fictional future with a significant aesthetic role is all the more striking for its isolation. No one followed his lead. The next book set in future time, Samuel Madden's *Memoirs of the Twentieth Century*, was published seventy-three years later in another country for entirely different purposes by a writer who does not betray the slightest awareness of his predecessor. It partly explains Guttin's accomplishment to note that *Epigone*'s alternate future was invented to satisfy in a new way the conventional requirements of heroic romance by making future time augment the effects of spatial distance. Nonetheless, that explanation does not account for the lapse of almost two centuries before one can start tracing the subsequent history of romances set in futures that serve mainly to enhance the effects of spatial distance in giving free rein to improbable adventures. That lapse was not inevitable. Guttin after all proved that a writer of sufficient daring *could* break the taboo against chronicles of the future well before acceleration of technological change, along with increasing belief in the idea of progress, had created a more favorable climate of opinion. But until far into the eighteenth century there were still powerful constraints upon tales of the future, some caused by the very transformations that ultimately made it easier for writers to experiment with the new genre. Before turning in my next chapter to the conditions that helped bring into being *Memoirs of the Twentieth Century* and its immediate successors, I want to pause for some account of the inhibiting forces. They are best brought to light by attempting to recapture what I shall call "the seventeenth-century aesthetics of extrapolation."

That aesthetics was for the most part implicit rather than explicit. It was never fully worked out. It was not universally accepted or even debated, much less debated in anything like the terms that now seem relevant to a historian of futuristic fiction looking backward. *Extrapolation*, although only applied widely in and outside mathematics in the twentieth century, is nevertheless an appealing rubric because it is neutral with respect to time. One may extrapolate in any temporal direction, or no temporal direction. The idea of extrapolating from a known mathematical series to previous or succeeding figures in the same series does not necessarily involve any notions of moving from a present to an earlier or later state. Nor does the idea of extrapolating from known or hypothesized facts to their corollaries or consequences necessarily involve moving from present to future, although in current practice the notion is usually applied to scientific or fictional projections forward to a future condition that will probably follow from the present one. But extrapolation may also go backwards in time from observed facts to their causes or to likely anterior states.

It was extrapolation to a geological and evolutionary past envisioned as ever more remote from the present that by the nineteenth century had widened temporal perspectives in a way favoring tales of the future no less than historical novels. In the seventeenth century the most daring literary extrapolations were planetary voyages that required no movement in time, only movement through space.[1] Instead of being

TOWARDS AN AESTHETICS OF EXTRAPOLATION

neutral on the issue of temporal settings, however, the implicit aesthetics of such imaginary voyages most often worked to discourage fictive projection to the future. There were seventeenth-century scientific extrapolations to the remote past and distant future that could have established an aesthetics encouraging similar projections in imaginative literature. The necessary assumptions were clearly stated. But nobody applied them to futuristic fiction. For my topic this is one of the more tantalizing glimpses of an alternate past that did not materialize.

The reasons for that failure may illuminate the puzzling chronology of futuristic fiction's rather late development as a form that gathered momentum only toward the end of the eighteenth century. Its emergence has been correlated with several trends: proliferating technology culminating in the imaginatively appealing balloon flights of the 1780s; the series of shattering political upheavals surrounding the French Revolution; and the less dramatic but more pervasive rise of capitalism and its future-oriented habits of working to schedules with an eye on the clock while projecting financial outcomes. All these contexts doubtless play some role, though one surprisingly hard to trace in the earliest examples of futuristic fiction. I want to suggest in this chapter, and increasingly throughout my subsequent discussion, that ideas about literary form and the actual interplay of forms are also of the utmost importance. It begs the question to assume that invention of futuristic fiction is primarily a response to political, financial, or industrial revolutions. Even from a Marxist viewpoint, as Fredric Jameson reminds us when discussing the tales of Verne and Wells "as the symptom of a mutation in our relationship to historical time itself," it must be remembered that all types of literature "find themselves inserted in a complex and semi-autonomous dynamic of their own—the history of forms—which has its own logic and whose relationship to content per se is necessarily mediated, complex, and indirect (and takes very different structural paths at different moments of formal as well as social development)."[2] Before further theorizing about the role of social change in altering the modes of futuristic literature, we need a more detailed account of the genres for which we seek an explanation and of aesthetic attitudes underlying those genres. To illustrate here a cluster of ideas that were in effect an aesthetics of extrapolation working both against and potentially—but alas only potentially—*for* narratives set in the future, let me take up now two representative texts: first David Russen's *Iter Lunare: Or, A Voyage To The Moon;* and then Thomas Burnet's more influential *Sacred Theory of the Earth*.

Amid the rich history of early speculation about voyages to the moon, *Iter Lunare* has attracted scant attention. It was published in 1703 as a commentary on Thomas St. Serf's 1659 translation of Cyrano de Bergerac's *Histoire comique contenant les etats et empires de la lune*. Russen's tardy response to Cyrano is a revealing mélange of ideas most characteristic of the seventeenth century, although still sufficiently appealing in the early eighteenth century to warrant publication of yet another edition of Russen's book in 1707. Today *Iter Lunare* is remembered chiefly for its bizarre suggestion of traveling across space on a giant spring:

> Since Springiness is a Cause of forcible motion; and a Spring will, when bended and let loose, extend it self to its length; could a Spring of well-tempered Steel be framed, whose Basis being fastned to the Earth, and on the other end placed a Frame or Seat, wherein a Man, with other necessaries, could abide with safety, this Spring being with Cords, Pullies, or other Engins bent, and then let loose by degrees by those who manage the Pullies, the other end would reach the Moon, where the Person who ascended landing, might continue there, and according to a time appointed, might again enter into his Seat, and with Pullies the Engine may again be bent, till the end touching the Earth, should discharge the Passenger again in safety.[3]

Taken as a serious proposal, this deserves only its usual relegation to a footnote providing comic relief for historians of science.

TOWARDS AN AESTHETICS OF EXTRAPOLATION

But Russen never intended his idea as a plan for implementation in any forseeable future. While surveying previous schemes for going to the moon, Russen accurately catalogues various obstacles including those that would stand in the way of his own suggestion, such as the well-known difficulties that mountain climbers experience in breathing at great heights. Instead of trying to explain how all such problems might be overcome, thus paving the way for an actual moon voyage, Russen explains why in reality it would be futile, *though possible*, to find technical solutions:

> Now I think it possible in Nature to Effect such a Spring, as I propose, though 'tis a Query if Art will not be defective. There is Mettal enough in the World of Iron or Steel to compose it, Men enough may be had to frame it, Firing enough to work it, and Money enough to defray the Charges; but Covetousness, Vice, Intemperance, Slothfulness and Ignorance hinder those who have abilities; and such is the Poverty of those (whose Parts and Ingenuity, joyned with Industry, would prompt them to accomplish it) that they cannot perform what their Wills would undertake, if able. So that I shall despair ever of hoping for any good event thereof, till *Vulcan* and his *Cyclops* come among us to undertake it. (pp. 49–50)

The insuperable obstacle is human nature. Physical laws do not rule out Russen's idea. Adequate materials and money are at hand, even though development of metal-working techniques for applying them remains an open question ("'tis a Query if Art will not be defective"). But determination to carry out such a difficult project is—and, Russen implies, always will be—undercut by vices that paralyze the majority and doom to enervating poverty those few whose intelligence and industry would otherwise motivate them to try. Russen assumes there cannot be significant improvement in the human condition.

He is no believer in the idea of progress. For Russen, history is cyclical. To be sure, he accepts in principle the Christian doctrine of a linear progression from creation of the world to final judgment, with Christ's Incarnation standing out as another singular moment. In between these unique events and a few related ones narrated in the Bible, however, Russen sees nothing but the rise and fall of civilizations that may equal but never surpass one another: "Consider what *Egypt* is now, which formerly was eminent for all Sciences; where is *Greece*, the Mother of Learning, *Athens* the Seat of the Muses? The same Casualties will in time reduce us to that Ignorance they now labour under" (p. 76). In the quarrel between ancients and moderns that so exercised French and English literary circles around the end of the seventeenth century, Russen sides with the ancients: "To say Arts are since improved is an insufferable Arrogancy; for what do we Know that they were Ignorant of? . . . What we are now learning they had in perfection, and by those Arts improved their discoveries to a farther extent than we yet have done. We boast of Guns and Gun-powder but what else were the *Fulmina Jovis* of the Poets? We boast of Printing, but what else were *Cadmus* his Letters? Yet both these Sciences have been in use among the (by us so estemed) Ignorant *Chineses* some thousand of Years past" (pp. 73–74). To deal with a potentially embarrassing counterargument that the ancients were ignorant of the New World and have thus been surpassed by moderns in at least the realm of geographical exploration, Russen adopts a bold hypothesis of extremely rapid geological change: "Our Fore-Fathers have rounded the Ocean a thousand times, yet could never find that vast tract of *America*, which we have now discovered: Surely their Eyes were as good as ours; but then *America* was no Object for them, because it was not, or not above Water" (pp. 72–73). Although Russen's cyclical view of history would have struck a responsive chord in a majority of his readers, of whom many surely sympathized also with his defense of the ancients, few could have found this final corollary very convincing.

Nor, perhaps, would most of those likely to peruse *Iter Lunare* in 1703 have taken kindly to what is apparently a slap at methodical

TOWARDS AN AESTHETICS OF EXTRAPOLATION

programs of experimentation like those which the Royal Society had encouraged in England for some forty years: "The discovery of many useful Sciences and Arts, such as the direction of the Magnet to the North-Star [and] that useful Discovery of the Telescope . . . have not been the effect of Industry, Reason or Forecast, but meerly casual, and from uncommon Observation, yet the Persons who discovered them were prompted thereto by some Invisible Agent, who out of kindness to us, did, as it were, or as we apprehend it, by chance, discover the knowledge of those things we knew not; which discoveries being once made, Arts, Learning, and Philosophy, have polished, refined, and perfected" (p. 95). To ascribe all basic scientific discoveries to chance or supernatural intervention rather than to human reason is idiosyncratic even for a writer so steeped as Russen in the more conservative currents of seventeenth-century thought. Equally unusual are his desperate speculations on the recent emergence of America from the sea. For the most part, however, Russen's rejection of deliberate projection to the future—what he calls here "Fore-cast"—is a consequence of those cyclical views of secular history that he shares with a majority of his contemporaries. In this he is distinctive mainly for being so explicit. Russen's blindness to the possibilities of social or technological progress is sufficiently representative of his era to explain why neither he nor most of his readers would have found anything strange in the fact that his extrapolation from known principles of metallurgy to their potential application in a trip to the moon is referred not to a real future but instead to an impossible recurrence of mythic time when "*Vulcan* and his *Cyclops* come among us to undertake it."

That is a playful way of saying "never." Russen's idea of a moon-voyage via giant spring is only a jeu d'esprit. It is a kind of atemporal extrapolation in which possibilities are toyed with more for amusement than for any of the purposes to which physicists now apply their "thought-experiments." The subtitle of *Iter Lunare: Or,*

ORIGINS OF FUTURISTIC FICTION

A Voyage To The Moon explains that we are to expect a book *Containing Some Considerations on the Nature of that Planet. The Possibility of getting thither. With other Pleasant Conceits about the Inhabitants, their Manners and Customs*. *Conceit* is used here in its contemporary sense of "imagination, fancy." *Pleasant* meant "agreeable, diverting."[4] The more unusual the conceit, the more likely it is to be taken as "Pleasant." Russen invites participation in a diverting game of extrapolation abstracted from historical time but nevertheless rooted in scientific reality.

That attention to science distinguishes his outlook from what might be called "an aesthetics of fantasy." Russen represents a transitional period during which some categories of the marvelous in literature—space voyages most notably—could be measured against scientific canons of plausibility in extrapolation without, however, eliciting any reference to the time required for realization of such possibilities or to the future period when they would or might become realities.

Russen speculates about some intriguing potential consequences of known properties of our universe but deflects attention from any questions about what might accordingly happen in the near or even far future. To all questions about the time when space travel may really get started, Russen's answer is "when Vulcan and Cyclops return." The supernatural of classical mythology is only alluded to by way of discriminating between real time, with its possible futures, and a region of scientific hypothesis apart from time. Russen discards fantasy in favor of concern with theories that amount to non-narrative, speculative fictions based upon science but oriented to space rather than time. His grotesque yet unforgettable image of a giant spring simultaneously touching a planet and its satellite is an apt symbol for an imagination that is spatial, not temporal. Starting with Russen amid the realities of metallurgy, astronomy, and physics, we find ourselves winding up with Vulcan and Cyclops in the fabulous past realm of "once upon a time"—that is to say, outside of historical time—but never in any kind of

TOWARDS AN AESTHETICS OF EXTRAPOLATION

future, not even the most unlikely hypothetical future of what barely might be, someday.

To appreciate the significance for literature of Russen's atemporal outlook, it is necessary to recall that he is writing neither science nor fiction. As a response to Cyrano's moon voyage, *Iter Lunare* is literary criticism. As such it provides one of the rare early discussions of the way in which relationships between science and fiction may shape imaginative writing. Russen explains that he borrowed Cyrano's book, read it twice, and "could not part . . . without making some Notes and Observations thereon; which is the Subject of these following Lines" (p. 2). Russen adds that, like Cyrano's narrative, *Iter Lunare* itself is unavoidably "composed of serious Philosophical Reflections, intermixed with variety of diverting Thought, and as such I doubt not but the Knowing will accept it" (Preface, signature A3). His readers must be prepared for a mixture of tones that may be disconcerting but in Russen's view is inescapable when writing about a book like Cyrano's that so thoroughly mingles rational speculation with fantastic invention.

The resulting genre, for which Russen could find no accepted name, seemed to him in some ways akin to utopian fantasies and also to satiric romances in the vein of *Don Quixote;* nevertheless, he believed that it belonged to a higher order of seriousness:

> The title that the Translator gives it (when he calls it a *Comical History*) seems to be too full of Levity, and unbecoming that Gravity which a Treatise of so serious Matter doth require. For though it be interlaced with much Matter of Mirth, Wit and Invention, of things either doubtful, or meerly feigned, and so in some sence may be ranked with Sir *Thomas Moor's Utopia*, Don *Quixot's Romantick Whymseys*, or *Poor Robin's Description of Lubbardland;* yet is it throughout carried on with that strength of Argument, force of Reason, and solidity of Judgment in the Demonstration of things probable, that it may not be unbecoming the Gravity of *Cato*, the Seriousness of *Seneca*, or the Strictness of the most rigid Peripatetick

or Cartesian; and instead of *Comical*, may deserve the Epithete of the *most Rational History of the Government of the Moon*. (pp. 3–4)

The key to Cyrano's new kind of writing is thus its persuasiveness "in the Demonstration of things probable." Such works are not, however, to be measured by the mimetic standard of their accuracy in holding a mirror up to nature to show the world as it is or will be in the future. Nor are they to be measured like utopias by their moral appeal in showing a better way of life than any known in our world.

Russen goes on to praise Cyrano's moon voyage for its air of probability in recounting the narrator's "Journey to the Moon, the manner of his Ascent thither, the Observations he there made of their Shape, Figure, Manner of Living, Arts, Sciences, Government, Products" (p. 4). For Russen what counts in the new literature of planetary space is not use of distance in the manner that Swift later perfected to achieve thinly disguised satiric portrayal of known places, personality types, and customs. Instead it is verisimilitude achieved by "force of Reason" (we could say by extrapolation) that distinguishes successful tales of space travel from previous adventures, satires, and journeys to no place.

Russen also remarks early in his preface that some people—but only those who are not fit readers for his volume—"look upon the Notion of [the moon's] being Peopled as a Romance." The opposition here is not simply between fact and "romance" in the conventional late seventeenth- and early eighteenth-century general sense of romance as "a meer fiction or feigned story." The same lexicographer who provides that definition explains that "a romancer" is "a teller of lies or false stories" and that "to romance" is "to tell a magnificent lie."[5] Even though for Russen the idea of the moon's being populated is not romance, it is at best plausible conjecture rather than truth.

Cyrano's book and others like it accordingly fall somewhere in between "mere fiction" and true statements. Although he rejects

TOWARDS AN AESTHETICS OF EXTRAPOLATION

"romance" in its pejorative sense, Russen has no positive term other than "Rational history" for what we would call speculative fiction or science fiction. He leaves no doubt, however, that if such works are not to be dismissed as romance, neither are they to be accepted—even at their most plausible—as demonstrations of fact. Their plausibility arises from the likelihood that natural laws *elsewhere* may be different from those encountered on our earth:

> Indeed there are in it [Cyrano's moon-voyage] many things which among us are altogether unusual, improbable, or perhaps, above the Power of Nature, as far as Nature is understood by us, or above what our Capacities can explicate from those principles we have generally received; such as are his story of *Cardan's* Moon-men; his Spirit, which attended him in the Moon; putting Persons in the Posture of others to know their Thoughts . . . and others of this kind; which because the Principles we have in this Earth will not account for, (and yet they seem to be deducible from Natural Principles) our Author hath placed them in the Moon, as the Customs of that Country, where they may pass for Probable, on as good Grounds, as many wise Men conjecture that the Moon is an Earth, and like ours Inhabited. On this conjecture it is, that the whole Treatise is grounded. (pp. 4–5)

This notable passage provides carte blanche for a speculative literature of space travel that can "pass for probable" even though it recounts events which could only be dismissed as "altogether . . . improbable" if included in a novel set on *our* world. This critical paradox of admitting as acceptable in fiction a whole new category of improbable probabilities is based upon Russen's endorsement of the idea of a plurality of inhabited worlds.

Publishing *Iter Lunare* seventeen years after the first edition in 1686 of Fontenelle's *Entretiens sur la pluralité des mondes*, Russen welcomes as an act of religious faith speculation about a well-populated universe: "I confess it favours more to Religion to admit a plurality of Worlds, than of Pride to deny it" (p. 67). Scientific evidence bearing on the issue counts for less than adopting a stance of Christian humility by discarding the view, amounting to the sin of pride, that man is unique. Rejection of the old geocentric astronomy, with its implication that creation centers on the laws governing human existence here on this earth, has for Russen the liberating consequence that even natural laws may be variable. He remarks that God may govern other habitable globes "by a diversity of Laws suitable to their Nature: And 'tis highly probable that he displays to them some of those Attributes of which we are wholly Ignorant" (p. 67). In the same year that Fontenelle's dialogues appeared, Newton had exhibited at the Royal Society the first book of his *Philosophiae Naturalis Principia Mathematica*. But Russen avoided the imaginatively constraining though more scientifically useful assumption of Newtonian physics that nature is constant, governed everywhere by laws that are to be induced from observation of what happens in our part of the universe.

Impelled most strongly by faith in God's power, but also reasoning by analogy from observation of the widely differing environments that support life on earth, Russen insists that narratives like Cyrano's story of the sun's inhabitants must be counted among works of acceptable conjecture:

> That the Sun, as well as other Stars, is habitable, is no Novel Opinion, nor hath in it any absurdity. I know Ignorance laughs at it: and indeed to suppose Men and Beasts, composed of so gross Matter as we are, can make our abode there, would be a ridiculous Thought: But that God, who hath formed the Sun so different from all the other Works of his Creation, can also create Beings of a Temper fit to inhabit it. We may as well infer, that nothing can live in the Sea, because Man is drowned in it, as to say the Sun cannot be inhabited, because Man is burnt up in it: And we may as equally deny a possibility of Angels inhabiting the highest Heaven, because it is too Glorious for Man to behold. (pp. 99–100)

Russen's theology encourages bold speculation about strange forms of life or even different natural laws that may coexist with us in

TOWARDS AN AESTHETICS OF EXTRAPOLATION

some other part of the universe. For literature, this amounts to licensing free indulgence in science fiction about other worlds. What that theology forbids is speculation about the future.

Toward the end of his account Russen insists again that all tales of travel to the moon, including Cyrano's, are only "feigned Relations, under which they have endeavoured to teach us probable, yet doubtful Principles" (p. 61). Although not all readers of such stories would have agreed with every one of Russen's theological premises, his view of these tales is representative of the prevailing outlook in his age insofar as he considers the tales a class of fictions whose probability can be discussed, and rated by application of logic, but never brought to the test of experience. The space voyages are a literature of conjecture that is based often enough upon scientific extrapolation rather than mere fantasy to be aptly described either by his term "rational History" or by our term "science fiction." But it is a literature of lateral rather than forward extrapolation. Space dominates its chronotope. On premises like those Russen articulates so clearly, there is no possibility of writing science fiction, or any kind of fiction, in the form of speculation about the future.

After summarizing his own and other proposals for going to the moon, Russen not only insists that "all [are] . . . vain and ineffectual" but also rejects for religious reasons even the possibility of discovering in the far future what is really there (p. 61). Thus, while extrapolation by a mixture of faith and analogical reasoning inclines him to think the moon is indeed inhabited, "what kind of Creatures they are, what Dispensations of Providence they are under, what Laws governed by, what attributes the Divine Being doth manifest to them, of which we are Ignorant, is known only to the God who hath made them" (p. 62). So far as concerns the situation in 1703 when *Iter Lunare* was published, as well as the immediate future, this merely states the obvious, given those obstacles to space flight that Russen has canvassed in such detail. But to his reminder that nothing can *now* be definitely known about the moon's inhabitants except by God, Russen adds a statement implying that nothing will *ever* be learned directly about them by human observers during the entire span of future time in this life: "That we should ascend to them, or they to us, I hold not possible, Divine Providence having fixed betwixt us and them so great a Gulph, that while we dwell in these Tabernacles of Clay, we must content ourselves with this Earth he hath allotted us, reserving the farther Enquiry hereof till a future Estate, when more of the Infinity of God's Works shall be discovered to our Understanding" (p. 62). Heaven is for Russen the only imaginable "future Estate" during which conjecture about other worlds may be replaced by knowledge. Although for him religion does not forbid a new literature of "rational histories" abounding in such conjectures, a literature which Russen in fact encourages as a way of enhancing appreciation of God's glory by free speculation on the marvels He may have created elsewhere, it is only after death that anyone can hope to find out with certainty what the moon and planets are like. Despite the vast array of technical difficulties that Russen has catalogued, the overwhelming problem is not inadequate technology for travel off the earth. To him the distances and difficulties involved are only a sign that God does not will us to undertake such journeys except on wings of imagination. The insurmountable barrier is "Divine Providence."

Of course interpretations of divine providence have always varied hugely according to the lights and motives of each interpreter. For some of the religiously minded like Burnet, as we shall shortly see, neither scientific nor literary speculation about the future was entirely unthinkable. Moreover, there ebbed and flowed throughout the seventeenth and eighteenth centuries, as throughout most periods, a flood of would-be prophets bent on showing how God's providential plan for human history could be deciphered to provide glimpses of the future. The resulting literature, however, does not significantly shape in any way that I can trace either the form or content of futuristic fiction before the publication in 1805 of Grain-

TOWARDS AN AESTHETICS OF EXTRAPOLATION

ville's *Le dernier homme*—a special case that I discuss in chapter 5. Although prophetic visions modeled on those in religious writing, but not necessarily concerned with the future, do play an important and well-documented role in English poetry from the renaissance through the romantic movement, prose narratives take another path.

The divergence of religious prophecy and futuristic fiction is partly a matter of form and partly a matter of doctrine. There are prophetic works with such promising titles as the anonymous 1650 publication *A Brief Description of the future History of Europe, from Anno 1650, to An. 1710*. But such works are for the most part simply interpretive essays attempting to apply predictively a hodgepodge of biblical passages. These efforts are not coherent accounts of any future interval modeled in their telling on the methods of narrative historical writing that have a close affinity with novelistic techniques, including those in the extrapolative fictions Russen calls rational histories. Prophetic works do not encourage fictive elaboration. *A Brief Description of the future History of Europe*, for example, announces in its subtitle that it will treat events which seemingly would provide enough high drama to inspire any novelist: *The ruine of the Popish Hierarchy, the final annihilation of the Turkish Empire, the Conversion of the Eastern and Western Jews, and their Restauration to their ancient Inheritances in the holy Land, and the FIFTH MONARCHY of the Universal Reign of the Gospel of Christ upon Earth*. Here, potentially, is material for whole shelves of futuristic fiction. In practice, however, writers of religious prophecy deflect attention from attempts to imagine the detailed shape of things they predict, in favor of emphasis upon typological or other modes of exegesis providing the basis for their predictions.

Consequently attempts at persuasive argument, most often extensive and labored, take precedence over accounts of predicted future events. Narration, if presented at all, is thus minimized and subordinated to a rhetoric of abstract exegetical argument. Moreover, statements about the future are frequently put in a figurative mode, as in this characteristic passage from *A Brief Description of the future History of Europe:* "The whole Government of *Moses* (who was a second *Noah* to the Church) is a shadow of the Kingdom of Christ. The Law continued in force 1529 years to the Passion of Christ: But 1598 years to the Destruction of the Temple by *Titus:* the Destruction of the Temple by *Titus* was according to the account of *Dionysius Eziguus* A.C. 69. From thence reckon the Number of 1598 years, and you come to A. 1667; which is the year which shall smoke with the ascending up of the Flames which consume the Kingdom of the Beast."[6] As this sample may sufficiently suggest, such prophecy is more often than not designedly vague or even ambiguous in its statements about the future. It is hardly the stuff of which gripping fiction is made.

To be told that flames will consume the Kingdom of the Beast in 1667 was doubtless reassuring to many readers in 1660. But that statement is not much of a scenario upon which to flesh out a tale of the future. Apart from the specific future date, details of what lies ahead remain veiled in figurative language. As in the Book of Revelation and other biblical prophecy to which later efforts more or less closely conform in style to gain prestige, the prevailing mode of prophetic statement is more akin to allegory than to naturalistic fiction of any sort. Even where it presents the future as a metaphor of the present, however, futuristic fiction depends heavily upon novelistic piling up of details that convey a sense of the future rendered visible. Futuristic fiction in realistic modes also creates a sense of the future rendered plausible by conventions of verisimilitude that do not derive from the authority of divine utterance.

There is thus a radical incompatibility between early forms of futuristic fiction and religious prophecy as it was usually practiced in the seventeenth and eighteenth centuries. Despite passages where prophecy might veer toward less figurative, more specific statements about the course of future events, and despite later fu-

TOWARDS AN AESTHETICS OF EXTRAPOLATION

turistic fictions that encourage some degree of emblematic interpretation, the two forms tend toward opposite ends of the spectrum along which literature can be ranged from allegorical to nonallegorical. Nor do most prophecies of the period take the form of narratives except very incidentally.

Typological extrapolation, moreover, as the passage from *A Brief Description of the future History of Europe* illustrates, pointed attention backwards to the past even more insistently than it directed thoughts to the future. Because their stories are known, Moses, Noah, Christ, and Titus furnish more concrete material for meditation to any reader of that passage than its veiled language concerning the future. The past, as the only source of types whose antitypes are to be sought later in time, claims a kind of priority that turns typological exegetes away from the more single-minded attention to coming events that characterizes writers and readers of futuristic fiction.[7]

However paradoxical it may seem, forms of religious prophecy were so overwhelmingly oriented toward the past as to be an impediment to writing tales of the future. To engage in prophecy was to look backward to the bible for authority in forecasting and to biblical history as a source of types; thus, the very act of prophesying confirmed the habit of thinking more about the past than about the future. The rhetorical need to back up predictions by resort to exegesis of a small number of relevant passages with a limited range of applications, to say nothing of the narrow political motives that so often animated would-be prophets, also provided severe constraints upon wide-ranging extrapolation to various possible futures. Prophecy, which claims truth and not simply verisimilitude, is radically at variance with the impulse to invent outright fictions of the future or even to speculate about details that are not in some way suggested by a biblical text invoked as the authority behind prophetic forecast. Focus, moreover, was usually upon one wished-for outcome or a small series of desired events whose specific dates were of more concern than surrounding chains of circumstance that might otherwise have provided material for fictive elaboration. Often too, as Bakhtin notes in remarking how eschatology deflects attention from short-range possibilities, the main event of interest among students or practitioners of prophecy was the end of the world—another discouragement to invention of secular futures.[8]

Outside the perennial ranks of those obsessed with apocalypse, and consequently not much concerned with intermediate possibilities that might deserve consideration, there were many influential thinkers who vehemently insisted that it was dangerous to attempt any kind of prophecy about the future of human history, especially prophecy achieved by applying biblical passages as a guide to coming events. These warnings were variously motivated but were perhaps most frequently instigated by opposition to radical politicians who donned the prophet's mantle to agitate for drastic social change.

Among the more conservative students of prophecy, for example, was Isaac Newton, many of whose views on the subject were made widely known in his posthumously published *Observations Upon the Prophecies of Daniel, and the Apocalypse of St. John* (London, 1733). Though he was more than willing to discover laws allowing prediction in the realms of physics, mechanics, and optics, he emphatically cautioned against exegetical speculation about time to come: "The folly of Interpreters has been to foretel times and things by this Prophecy, as if God designed to make them Prophets. . . . The design of God was much otherwise. He gave this and the Prophecies of the Old Testament, not to gratify men's curiosities by enabling them to foreknow things, but that after they were fulfilled they might be interpreted by the event, and his own Providence, not the Interpreters, be then manifested thereby to the world. For the event of things predicted many ages before, will then be a convincing argument that the world is governed by providence."[9] In this view religious prophecy can no longer be practiced because God does not now inspire genuine prophets; and the reading of biblical prophecy is to be a retrospective exercise in decid-

TOWARDS AN AESTHETICS OF EXTRAPOLATION

ing which of the recorded predictions in Holy Writ have *already* been fulfilled. For all those—and there were many—who shared Newton's approach to prophecy as a form of literature that could only be understood properly by looking back over past history to note its conformity to God's plan as announced long ago in the Bible, there were powerful religious motives for turning away from thinking or writing about the future.[10]

Thus amid the various purposes served by religious prophecy when futuristic fiction emerged as a distinctive genre, it is hard to find significant encouragement for an imaginative literature of freewheeling and overtly fictive speculation about plausible futures. Quite the contrary: seventeenth- and eighteenth-century forms of prophecy and related discussions were an obstacle to the rise of futuristic fiction. Nor did fictional conjectures of the kind Russen considers point expectation forward to an earthly future, however remote, when people might discover by firsthand observation how closely their speculations about other worlds conform to the facts.

It was geology that provided a viable but short-lived aesthetics of extrapolation to the future. Ironically, the chief motive was concern with the earth's past. The key text is Thomas Burnet's *Sacred Theory of the Earth:* a work of the 1680s whose first two parts attempt a scientific explanation of Noah's flood, as well as of differences between pre- and postdiluvian geology, and whose last two parts seek a scientific explanation of the earth's final conflagration and the ensuing millennium as foretold in the Apocalypse of St. John.[11] Burnet's enormous though unintentional influence on the aesthetics of eighteenth-century English poetry is well recognized.[12] I want to remark the relevance of his ideas—and of their rejection by later geologists—to futuristic fiction.

Although historians of science grudgingly acknowledge *The Sacred Theory of the Earth* as too influential in its own day to ignore in accounting for the rise of scientific geology, they usually dismiss it rather curtly for reasons that should arouse the interest of anyone concerned with futuristic fiction. Thus Frank Manuel notes its primacy among the works known as *physica sacra*, books aimed at scientific explanation of biblical allusions to natural events and written mostly by scholars under Newton's influence whose "enthusiasm for harmonizing Scripture and science led to the proliferation of bizarre literary fantasies bearing the trappings of science."[13] This could be a detractor's definition of science fiction. In their classic study *The Discovery of Time*, Toulmin and Goodfield concede that Burnet's book "attracted as much attention as Newton's *Principia* itself." But they complain that the "*Sacred Theory* reads more like science fiction than serious geology"—as indeed it does, in ways that also caused uneasiness in the eighteenth century.[14] Buffon not only dismissed Burnet's ideas but responded to his eloquence by calling for a limitation of poetic flights of imagination in scientific writing, for a plain unadorned prose, and especially for rejection of attempts to describe the future in the manner of Burnet's "prophetic style." Buffon demotes the *Sacred Theory* to the status of "a well written novel & a book that one may read to amuse oneself, but which one should not consult for instruction."[15]

Burnet had to deal with similar charges of fictionality brought against his book in his own lifetime, even though Isaac Newton took it seriously enough to correspond about *The Sacred Theory of the Earth*, exchanging speculations with Burnet about geological realities apparently alluded to in Genesis. Newton argued that the biblical account of Creation and Deluge is neither fiction nor an objective scientific description but rather a kind of phenomenological extrapolation backwards to narrate events during planetary formation as they would have appeared to an observer on earth without any knowledge of science:

> As to Moses I do not think his description of ye creation either Philosophical or feigned, but that he described realities in a language artificially adapted to ye sense of ye vulgar. Thus where he speaks of two great lights I suppose he means their apparent, not

TOWARDS AN AESTHETICS OF EXTRAPOLATION

real greatness. . . . To describe them distinctly as they were in them selves would have . . . become a Philosopher more than a Prophet. He mentions them therefore only so far . . . as they were phaenomena in our firmament, & describes their making only so far & at such a time as they were made such phaenomena. . . . For Moses accommodating his words to ye gross conceptions of ye vulgar, describes things much after ye manner as one of ye vulgar would have been inclined to do had he lived & seen ye whole series of wt [sic] Moses describes.[16]

Genesis is here taken by Newton as using scientifically correct extrapolations to present a version of the distant past that is not fantasy (not "feigned"). It is, Newton insists in the same letter to Burnet, "not an Ideal or poetical but a true description."[17] On this view, however, Genesis is factual in an incomplete way because it resorts to a nonscientific (not "Philosophical") vocabulary that allows but does not compel informed readers to recover the real basis of its account.

Anyone trying like Newton and Burnet to reconstruct the facts of planetary formation alluded to in Genesis would face a problem strikingly like that confronting the reader of a scientifically accurate fictional narrative which presents events as they might have been perceived by an *imaginary* protagonist ("had he lived & seen ye whole series"), one who saw things that really happened though from a limited perspective in space and without the scientific knowledge to understand them. Of course Newton did not envision (and probably would not have welcomed) the prospect of a deliberate fiction extrapolating backwards—or forwards—in this fashion.

To Newton *The Sacred Theory of the Earth* was more science than fiction; doubtless it was appealing too on account of its attempt to grapple scientifically with the Book of Revelation. For most of Burnet's contemporaries, including Newton, science and theology were not only compatible in the sense of coexisting peacefully in ways less possible after Darwin but also mutually reinforcing. The stimulus provided by religious speculation to Newton's scientific thought is a complex but inescapable issue that has increasingly challenged his biographers to set aside nineteenth-century assumptions that science must always advance by a different path. Ordinary thinkers of Newton's day most often took for granted, as Russen did despite aversion to the idea of progress and consequent blindness to the future, that scientific speculation per se could only enhance appreciation of God's greatness by explaining the wonders of His universe. Burnet insists "we are not to suppose that any Truth concerning the Natural World can be an Enemy to Religion; for Truth cannot be an Enemy to Truth, God is not divided against himself."[18] Far from only constraining science by setting doctrinal boundaries that inhibited inquiry or speculation, theology was often taken as an inducement to scientific speculation, though it did not provide any direct encouragement to futuristic fiction for the reasons that I have suggested. For Burnet as for Newton and many others, the Bible offered premises inviting construction of explanatory hypotheses by a process of extrapolation.

Thus Burnet's theory of how and when mountains first arose, and indeed all his speculations about planetary geology, stemmed initially from his attempt to account for the amount of water that would have been necessary for the Deluge. Given the size of the earth and the height of those flood waters, Burnet reasoned, there must have been "a quantity of Water eight times as great as the Ocean" (1:17). But this contradicts the other inevitable consideration that, if heavy rainfall accumulates at a maximum rate of four feet every twenty-four hours, then forty days and nights of rain could only result in one hundred sixty feet of water at best—hardly enough to cover mountains or even respectable hills. Assuming no miraculous contravention of the laws of nature, where then did the water for Noah's flood originate? Again assuming no miracles, Burnet then turns to the distant future and confronts the equally vexing question of how the final conflagration will start, given the apparently incombustible nature of so much of our planet. How will all the oceans, rocks, and sand ever catch fire?

TOWARDS AN AESTHETICS OF EXTRAPOLATION

Burnet's answers to these and similar questions are less relevant than his response to charges that his theories are wrong and his book accordingly no more than a mere work of entertaining fiction. Joseph Keill, for example, anticipating Buffon and Burnet's subsequent antagonists who for three centuries have been moved to reclassify his book from science to fiction, wrote in 1698 that Burnet's "lofty and plausible stile may easily captivate any incautious reader, and make him swallow down for truth, what I am apt to think the Author himself . . . designed only for a Philosophical Romance, seeing that an ordinary Examination thereof, according to the laws of Mechanisme cannot but shew, that . . . in reality none of these wonderful effects, which he endeavours to explain, could have proceeded from the causes he assigns." After more than one hundred pages given to refutation of Burnet's ideas about the geological past, Keill ends on a note of unctuous commiseration for anyone whose pleasure in reading *The Sacred Theory of the Earth* may be destroyed by finding out that its theories are wrong: "Perhaps many of his Readers will be sorry to be undeceived, for as I believe, never any Book was fuller of Errors and Mistakes in Philosophy, so none ever abounded with more beautiful Scenes and surprising Images of Nature; but I write only to those who might perhaps expect to find a true Philosophy in it. They who read it as an Ingenious Romance will still be pleased with their Entertainment."[19] Keill takes for granted an absolute distinction between true and false writing, between science and fiction, and above all between the pleasures appropriate to each.

In Keill's view, neither beautifully described scenes of earth's paradisal state before the Flood nor striking descriptions of a drowned world or an earth aflame will redeem a work of speculation whose science is wrong. Nor, conversely, will erroneous theories matter in the least to readers who do not look for "a true Philosophy" in their fiction but are content to accept any "Ingenious Romance" as a clever fantasy whose scientific accuracy is irrelevant. Keill assumes in a perfectly Coleridgean way that science and literature are distinct: works of science have for their sole object truth, whereas literature—which may be indifferent to scientific accuracy—has for its primary object pleasure. While there is no harm in enjoying well-written fantasy intended and accepted as such, there *is* something wrong with allowing literary pleasures to sway or even accompany judgment of a scientific hypothesis. This idea of an absolute barrier between science and aesthetics still commands more adherents, I suspect, than an accurate statement of their resemblances like Arlen Hansen's assertion that "scientific theories . . . are functional fantasies, not absolute truths. As products of human inventiveness and creativity, they are as rich a subject for the critic and analyst as is science fiction or any other form of verbal art."[20] For Keill and others like him then and now, aesthetic properties are an attribute of literature and the arts; science, on the other hand, displays only truth or falsehood, not beauty or ugliness.

Burnet denies that proposition. Although he defends his theories at every point where they come under attack, thus claiming for his book the virtue of scientific accuracy, Burnet is not content to rest his defense on the issue of whether his extrapolations are true or false, probable or improbable, as accounts of the distant past and future. Nor is he content to accept the idea that aesthetic considerations are irrelevant to judgment of whether a scientific hypothesis is properly framed. Burnet refuses to accept an absolute dissociation of science and aesthetics. He insists that there is an aesthetic dimension to any theory and also that this artistic aspect of science should not be treated merely as a kind of irrelevant side effect.

Burnet first characterizes opponents like Keill as people too "apt to distrust every Thing for a Fancy or Fiction that is not the Dictate of Sense, or made out immediately to their senses" and who are therefore inclined to "call such theories as these philosophick Romances, and think themselves witty in the Expression; they allow them to be pretty Amusements of the Mind, but without Truth or

TOWARDS AN AESTHETICS OF EXTRAPOLATION

Reality" (1:xxi). He does not admit either the charge of falsehood or its implied confinement of all science to induction from observable cases and experiments that may be repeated in a laboratory—conditions impossible for the cosmologist and historical geologist, among others. Burnet retorts that "If an Angel should write the Theory of the Earth, they would pass the same Judgment upon it," because "where there is Variety of Parts in a due Contexture, with something of surprizing Aptness in the Harmony and Correspondency of them, this they call a Romance; but such Romances must all theories of Nature and Providence be, and must have every Part of that Character with Advantage, if they be well represented" (1:xxi–xxii). Here Burnet's response takes the extraordinary tack of admitting the charge that his theories read like and in fact *are* like a romance.

They are exactly like an entertaining fiction that offers the aesthetic pleasure of variety along with harmonious correspondence of parts that do cohere as a pleasing whole but are not at first perceived to hang together: hence the quality of *surprising* aptness in a properly written ("well represented") theory or romance. Burnet, however, does not mistake their likeness for identity. While conceding that all skillfully explained theories will indeed have the aesthetic attributes of a good romance, and have those attributes moreover to an even more perfect and pleasing degree than the best fiction can hope to attain ("Must have every Part of that Character with Advantage"), Burnet denies that his or any theories are on that account necessarily false.

Because scientific theories reflect nature, which Burnet takes to be harmonious and well contrived by its great Artificer, it follows that the more accurate a theory is (the more truthfully it describes the properties of nature) the more such a theory will necessarily have the aesthetic properties we also expect in well-designed fiction: "There is in them [all theories of nature], as I may so say, a *Plot* or *Mystery* pursued thro' the whole Work, and certain grand Issues or Events upon which the rest depend, or to which they are subordinate; but these Things we do not make or contrive our selves, but find and discover them, being made already by the great Author and Governor of the Universe" (1:xxii). Far from admitting that a theory is rendered suspect to the extent that it offers aesthetic satisfactions like those afforded by fiction, Burnet thus counters with an argument that such pleasures are more likely to be a sign of accuracy. He winds up this part of his defense with an eloquent assertion that when the laws of nature "are clearly discover'd, well digested, and well reason'd in every Part, there is, methinks, more of Beauty in such a Theory, at least a more masculine Beauty, than in any Poem or Romance; and that solid Truth that is at the Bottom gives a Satisfaction to the Mind, that it can never have from any Fiction how artificial soever it be" (1:xxii). Burnet's conviction that valid scientific theory offers better "satisfaction to the mind" than fiction can ever provide does not lead him to renounce the pleasures of poetry and romance. Instead he appropriates them for science.

Throughout *The Sacred Theory of the Earth* Burnet scatters observations spelling out further ramifications of the aesthetic affinities linking scientific theories and fiction. Thus after some two hundred pages explaining his view of planetary formation from the original chaos mentioned in Genesis through those geological changes that he thought resulted in transformation of a smoothly spherical earth to the mountainous postdiluvian world that we inhabit, Burnet pauses to anticipate the potential objection that he has indulged in a bit of fictionalizing. Again as in defending himself against Keill, Burnet admits the charge but denies its power to discredit theories which, because of the very nature of all theories, *must* be like fictions: "How fully or easily soever these things may answer nature, you will say, it may be, that all this is but an *Hypothesis;* that is, a kind of Fiction or Supposition that Things were so and so at first, and by the Coherence and Agreement of the Effects with such a Supposition, you would argue and prove that they were really so. This I confess is true, this is the Method, and if

TOWARDS AN AESTHETICS OF EXTRAPOLATION

we would know any Thing in Nature further than our Senses go, we can know it no otherwise than by an *Hypothesis*" (1:201). Burnet is willing to recognize that any hypothesis is "a kind of Fiction." He accepts on pragmatic grounds the utility of even those unsatisfactory hypotheses which inspire investigation leading to their own displacement by more accurate conjectures, as successive explanatory fictions approach the status of true statements.[21]

Burnet also faces the fact that scientists must invent such fictions in order to perform the imaginative exercise of extrapolating from the very narrow sphere of what we can observe to the circumstances governing other realms whose conditions are beyond direct observation on account of their remoteness in space or time: "When Things are either too little for our Senses, or too remote and inaccessible, we have no Way to know the inward Nature, and the Causes of their sensible Properties, but by reasoning upon an *Hypothesis*. . . . if you would know the Nature of a Comet, or of what Matter the Sun consists . . . you can do this no otherwise than by an *Hypothesis;* and if that *Hypothesis* be easy and intelligible, and answers to all the *Phaenomena* of those two Bodies, you have done as much as a *Philosopher* or as *human Reason* can do" (1:201–2). To this caveat that a satisfactory hypothesis, however akin to fiction, must fit all the relevant known facts and account for them as clearly as possible, Burnet adds further clarification of the relationship between the form and content of scientific theories: "As to the Form, the Characters of a regular Theory seem to be these three: *Few and easy Postulatums; Union of Parts; and a Fitness to answer, fully and clearly, all the Phaenomena to which it is to be apply'd*" (2:327). This is not merely a restatement of the familiar principle of Ockham's razor in its stress upon economy of explanation ("few and easy Postulatums"). It is also a definition that includes a logical principle of formal unity ("Union of Parts") that for Burnet is also an aesthetic virtue in scientific theory, no less than in any other "kind of Fiction."

Accordingly Burnet finds it necessary to warn his readers against the fallacy of mistaking such unity, which is the mark of both a well-designed theory and a well-designed story, for proof of validity: "bare coherence and Union of Parts is not a sufficient Proof; the Parts of a Fable or Romance may hang aptly together, and yet have no truth in them; This is enough indeed to give the Title of a just Composition to any Work, but not of a true one; till it appear that the Conclusions and Explications are grounded upon good natural Evidence, or upon good Divine Authority" (2:328). If truth is beautiful and if scientific theories should be no less well composed than romances in point of unity, it does not in Burnet's view follow that beauty is a proof of truthfulness. This issue would be less problematic for him if he thought there were no aesthetic response elicited by scientific theories. But since in Burnet's opinion all such theorizing will elicit pleasure to the degree that it satisfies the formal requirement of "Coherence and Union of Parts," it becomes especially important to guard against accepting merely attractive extrapolations as valid without some external basis for judging their probability.

For Burnet the Bible is one such basis, providing "good Divine Authority" for many of his premises, as he notes again in reminding his readers that "The Matter and principal Parts of this *Theory* are such things as are recorded in Scripture: We do not feign a Subject, and then discant upon it, for Diversion; but endeavour to give an intelligible and rational Account of such Matters of Fact, past or future, as are there specified and declared" (2:324). Burnet is so very careful to draw the line between fiction and science in terms of intention because of his acute awareness that no such distinction is necessarily apparent, from the standpoint of how scientific writing affects readers. There would be less need for him to insist so much upon biblical and other evidence for the veracity of "the principal Parts of this *Theory*" if any well designed and well argued theory did not provide the same kind of entertainment ("Diversion") as that produced by writers of fiction who simply make things up ("feign a Subject"). Paradoxically, Burnet so often distinguishes

TOWARDS AN AESTHETICS OF EXTRAPOLATION

between science and fiction because he realizes better than most that they differ in the claims they make upon our assent but not necessarily in the pleasures they afford.

Where the Bible does not provide statements serving as a basis for extrapolation to the past or future, there are for Burnet especially acute problems in separating the incidental pleasures afforded by science from the application of logical tests for veracity. The difficulty is that such tests may often be measures of that "coherence and Union of Parts" within a theory which testify to its proper scientific economy of explanation but also account for its resemblance to "the Parts of a Fable or Romance" that "may hang aptly together, and yet have no Truth in them." Thus when Burnet considers possible natural causes of the future conflagration that will destroy the earth as we know it and usher in those geological changes necessary in his view for establishment of the millennium as it is described in the Revelation of St. John, two theories are dismissed: Burnet rejects as unsatisfactory extrapolations both the idea that the earth will move closer to the sun, thus scorching the planet's surface, and the idea that central fires will erupt from the earth's core.

He concedes that both the sun and fires burning within the earth "are potent Causes indeed, more than enough to destroy this Earth, if it was a thousand Times bigger than it is." But he then applies a test that is at once aesthetic and probabilistic: "For that very Reason, I suspect they are not the true Causes; for God and Nature do not use to employ unnecessary Means to bring about their Designs. Disproportion and Over-sufficiency is one sort of false Measures, and 'tis a Sign we do not thoroughly understand our Work, when we put more strength to it than the Thing requires. . . . This Supposition of burning the Earth, by the Sun drawing nearer and nearer to it, seems to be made in Imitation of the Story of *Phaeton*, who driving the Chariot of the Sun with an unsteady Hand, came so near the Earth, that he set it on Fire" (2:66). This shrewd guess that the myth of Phaeton underlies one current theory explaining the future destruction of the earth is further evidence of Burnet's sensitivity to the role of fiction in the formation of scientific extrapolation.

His objection is not so much to the fictive origin of a theory in the Phaeton legend as to the resulting fallacy of postulating a stronger force than is necessary to account for the phenomenon in question. "Over-sufficiency" of causation is equated in Burnet's phrase with "Disproportion"—presumably disproportion between cause and effect (imbalance between their respective sizes). While to Burnet such disproportion implies a lack of symmetry that could be equated with ugliness of a kind absent from God's well-proportioned universe, use of "disproportion" as almost a synonym for "over-sufficiency" here evokes a standard for measuring theories that is more logical than aesthetic. It is a standard, moreover, that Burnet applies to discard a theory derived from a famous myth—a myth rejected as the basis for a scientific hypothesis not because it is a fiction but because it is a fiction that leads to an implausible extrapolation about the future.

Establishing credibility, as Burnet was keenly aware, is the fundamental difficulty for any writer who invites us to imagine things to come: "We are naturally heavy of Belief, as to Futurities, and can scarce fancy any other Scenes, or other States of Nature, than what is present, and continually before our Eyes" (2:130). One way to "cure our Unbelief" about accounts of the future, Burnet notes, is simply to "take Scripture for our Guide, and keep within the Limits of its Predictions" (2:130). This method of dealing with the future is appealing on account of its certainty, because the Bible can be relied upon for true accounts of the future: "We must not imagine," Burnet insists, "that the Prophets wrote like the Poets; feigned an Idea of a romantick State, that never was, nor ever will be, only to please their own Fancies, or the credulous People" (2:243). The catch, however, is that even if prophecy is taken as truth rather than fiction and accorded a higher degree of certainty than the best

TOWARDS AN AESTHETICS OF EXTRAPOLATION

scientific extrapolations, "the limits of its Predictions" are notoriously hard to determine because the prophetic style of writing is vague: "though the Sum and general Contents of a Prophecy be very intelligible, yet the Application of it to Time and Persons may be very lubricous. There must be Obscurity in a Prophecy, as well as Shadow in a Picture" (2:59). This vagueness creates for any writer of science (or fiction) who attempts to stay within the limits of scriptural predictions the interpretive problem of clarifying what in the Bible is obscure, a problem with which Burnet, Newton, and so many others wrestled extensively.

One result apparent throughout *The Sacred Theory of the Earth*, though most striking in its chapters on the conflagration and millennium, is what might be called "hermeneutic extrapolations": predictions about the future and speculations about the past determined more by principles of biblical interpretation than by application of natural science.[22] Scientific extrapolations to possible futures devolve to the status of arguments bolstering the credibility of biblical exegesis. Burnet follows what he calls "the receiv'd Rule of Interpreters" that "the literal Sense . . . is never to be quitted or forsaken, without Necessity" (2:218). Accordingly he rejects the view "that *darkening of the Sun, shaking of the Earth*, and such like Phrases of Scripture . . . are to be understood only in a moral Sense" (2:131). Eclipses, earthquakes, and other phenomena apparently predicted in the Bible thus always invite Burnet to attempt scientific explanations even when the phenomena would not be anticipated at all merely on the basis of known scientific laws. I have mentioned some of the general ways in which attitudes toward prophecy constrained efforts to imagine the future. Burnet's attempt to work out and make explicit an aesthetics appropriate for writing scientifically about apocalypse is the best available illustration of what those constraints meant in practice.

There are several places where Burnet momentarily abandons scientific speculation in favor of biblical exegesis. He does so in dealing with "the Time of the *Conflagration*" which "no Foresight of ours or Inspection into Nature, can discover to us" and where consequently the "Method . . . of Prediction from natural Causes" must be "laid aside as impracticable" (2:35). It is only in Book Four, however, where Burnet probes the most "dark and remote Futurities" of the postapocalyptic millennium that he almost totally renounces the role of scientist in favor of turning for guidance to prophecy. This fourth section, "Concerning the New Heavens, and New Earth, and Concerning the Consumation of all Things," opens with a "Preface to the Reader" urging those unwilling or unable to make such imaginative leaps into the distant future to stop reading: "rest here, and be content with that Part of the Theory which you have seen already" (2:177–78). I cannot think of another topic which inspired so earnest a warning toward the end of a book that it might not be best for everybody to finish it. The idea of urging readers to at least consider stopping before the end is certainly at variance with ordinary authorial psychology. Burnet, unlike most of those who dabbled in millennial speculation, here articulates a seldom-noted but nevertheless profound seventeenth-century uneasiness, even among students of prophecy, at the prospect of attempting actually to depict the future.

Burnet assumes a kind of absolute temperamental distinction between those future-oriented (or future-obsessed) readers willing to engage in the mental time-travel with which he proposes to conclude, and those who refuse to see any value at all in such exercises: "To whom . . . such Disquisitions seem needless, or overcurious, let them rest here; and leave the Remainder of this Work, which is a kind of PROPHECY concerning the STATE of things after the Conflagration, to those that are of a Disposition suited to such Studies and Enquiries" (2:178). He recognized what I believe is still the case: that speculation about the distant future is not only a matter of finding appropriate methods (scientific, religious, or literary) and choosing a suitable style of writing but also of addressing an audience for whom the very possibility of such speculation

TOWARDS AN AESTHETICS OF EXTRAPOLATION

seems worth pursuing. Many who accept other topics eagerly or at worst with indifference angrily resist visions of the future.

Burnet saw what the hostility so often aroused by futuristic fiction still demonstrates: that even the right aesthetics of extrapolation will never work for the wrong readers. All genres must find a sympathetic audience, to be sure, but that quest has perhaps been hardest for forms concerned with envisioning the future. If not the first, Burnet is among the earliest English writers to draw such a sharp distinction between those for whom extrapolation forward in time *may* succeed because they accept the legitimacy of probing the future and those for whom such extrapolation can *never* succeed, no matter how it is done, because the very activity is suspect. What aroused Burnet to the step of warning off the latter class of readers—a warning he did not find necessary for the first three books of *The Sacred Theory of the Earth*—was his belief that, when dealing with the postapocalyptic millennium and what lies even further into the future, "*natural Reason* . . . sees no Track to follow in these unbeaten Paths, nor can advance one Step farther." That leaves only the writer's imagination aided by ability to interpret the hints provided in "Holy Scriptures" which are "the Oracles of God . . . and where *Human Faculties* cannot reach, a seasonable Help and Supply to their Defects" (2:202).

Turning to Scripture for such help and making extrapolations based upon interpretation of it does not, however, resolve the aesthetic problem of how to find an appropriate style for presenting those extrapolations in the part of his work that Burnet calls "a kind of PROPHECY." It is a kind very different from the Bible itself, calling for development of another style. Burnet's effort to solve this problem throughout the fourth book of *The Sacred Theory of the Earth* offers an excellent view of the options that seemed available at the end of the seventeenth century to a writer dealing with the distant future in a transitional form—one that is neither pure religious prophecy, nor simply exegesis of biblical passages, nor primarily science (taken in Burnet's definition as application of "natural Reason" to the "method of prediction from natural causes"), nor yet outright fiction of the kind that we encounter only much later in Cousin de Grainville's *Le dernier homme* with its outright storytelling on an apocalyptic theme.

One possibility for dealing with the past as well as the future was to mimic the obscure style of prophecy itself. Thus, in commenting on the difficulties of squaring with the Bible his or similar scientific extrapolations far backward in time to the period of planetary formation, Burnet notes: "The Reflections that are made in several Parts of the divine Writings, upon the Origin of the World, and the Formation of the Earth, seem to me to be writ in a Style something approaching to the Nature of a prophetical Style. . . . the Expressions are lofty, and sometimes abrupt, and often figurative and disguis'd. . . . And it commonly happens so in an enthusiastick or prophetick Style, that by reason of the Eagerness and Trembling of the Fancy, it doth not always regularly follow the same even Thread of Discourse, but strikes many times upon some other Thing that has relation to it, or lies under or near the same view" (1:124). This prophetic way of writing about the distant past is in Burnet's view also the style of apocalyptic visions of the future. He goes on to remark that it is a style of which "we have frequent Examples in the *Apocalypse*, and in that Prophecy of our Saviour's *Math. xxiv* concerning the Destruction of *Jerusalem* and of the World" (1:125). But from the standpoint of modern readers, there would be overwhelming disadvantages to adopting an equally apocalyptic style of lofty, abrupt, figurative, disguised, and digressive writing when attempting to explain in scientific terms—as Burnet does—"the Origin of the World, and the Formation of the Earth," or its future destiny.

More desirable for such works, as the Royal Society had recognized in urging all scientists to adopt a plain style, is clarity achieved by sticking to the point at hand in straightforward prose that avoids the obscurity of figurative language. Seventeenth-century science encouraged expression of even the most visionary apocalyptic imaginings in a secular prose style.[23] Hence Burnet's attempt to reassure his readers that, "As to the Style, I always endeavour to express myself in a plain and perspicuous manner; that the Reader may not lose Time, nor wait too long, to know my meaning" (2:"Preface to the Reader"). At odds with scientific pressure to adopt such a plain style throughout any work dealing with the future, however, is Burnet's conviction that everyone is more resistant to such speculation than to accounts of the past or present. Convinced as he was that "we are naturally heavy of Belief, as to Futurities," Burnet remarks of his own style, and by way of advice to other writers, that "especially when Things future are to be represented, you cannot use too strong Colours, if you would give them Life, and make them appear present to the Mind" (2:"Preface").

Thus accounts of the future call for vivid descriptions that may clash with the requirements of a plain style. Attempts to envision the Apocalypse even in its scientific aspects, moreover, cannot be altogether separated from moral concerns or a tendency to arouse terror; accordingly, in Burnet's view they must be designed to express as well as elicit some emotion: "For to see a World perishing in Flames . . . one must be very much a Stoick, to be a cold and unconcerned Spectator of all this. And when we are mov'd ourselves, our Words will have a Tincture of those Passions which we feel. Besides, in moral Reflections which are design'd for Use, there must be some Heat, as well as dry Reason" (2:"Preface"). For Burnet, clarity in scientific writing about the future did not imply either drabness or cold detachment.

Far more problematic than intrusion of especially colorful emotion-laden prose, however, is Burnet's disturbing thought that the more successful he or anyone is in painting a vivid picture of the final conflagration, the less credible that picture will seem to its audience: "If one should now go about to represent *the World on Fire*, with all the Confusions that necessarily must be in Nature, and in Mankind upon that Occasion, it would seem to most Men a Romantick Scene: Yet we are sure there must be such a Scene" (2:155). Of the writer's problem with such apocalyptic events, Burnet also remarks ruefully: "He that comes nearest to a true Description of them, shall be look'd upon as the most extravagant" (2:144). There will be a weakening of verisimilitude caused by the difference between such remote future possibilities and everyday reality as it is experienced in the reader's present life. Burnet thus confronted the paradox that the closest possible approximation to "a true description" of an apocalyptic future will *seem* more fantastic the more fully its implications are portrayed in passages of vividly rendered detail. The more accurately that future is imagined, the more inclined readers will be to reject the account. Here then, on purely aesthetic grounds arising from the requirements of maintaining verisimilitude, is another powerful constraint upon efforts to write any kind of narrative that invites its readers to imagine the full particulars of even a theologically authorized version of the future.

Burnet admitted this difficulty more candidly than most writers who face it. He also responded by ending his book of scientific and religious extrapolation in a way justified *neither on scientific nor on theological grounds* but instead on the basis of aesthetic considerations arising from the need to provide an appropriate sense of an ending within limits that readers would accept as credible. He sets limits by the literary test of verisimilitude, not by religious doctrine or by scientific laws of probability. Instead of closing *The Sacred Theory of the Earth* with a portrait of the postconflagration millennium based on details suggested by the Bible, Burnet takes up the even more highly conjectural matter of the earth's final fate: "The last Thing that remains to be considered and accounted for, is the Upshot and Conclusion of all; namely, what will become of the Earth after the thousand Years expir'd?" (2:316). Because Revelation is silent on this topic, "all Parties are equally . . . free, to give their Opinion, *What* will be the *last State and Consummation*

TOWARDS AN AESTHETICS OF EXTRAPOLATION

of this Earth" (2:316–17). Here at last is a part of the future upon which imagination may speculate freely, bound only by known laws of science and by the constraints of literary verisimilitude.

Burnet explains why he believes "that the Earth after the last Day of Judgment, will be chang'd into the nature of a Sun, or of a fix'd Star, and shine like them in the Firmament" (2:317). He concedes, however, that his theory is more appealing on account of its pleasingly harmonious vision of a world ending as it began than on account of any hard scientific evidence in its favor: "I have no direct and demonstrative Proof of this I confess, but if Planets were once fixed Stars, as I believe they were, their Revolution to the same State again, in a great Circle of Time, seems to be according to the Methods of Providence, which loves to recover what was lost or decay'd . . . and what was originally good and happy, to make it so again, all Nature, at last, being transform'd into a like Glory with the Sons of God" (2:318). In the last paragraph of Book Four, Burnet reiterates that this idea cannot be proposed "otherwise than as a fair Conjecture" (2:319–20). But he invites readers to join him in imagining this final transformation of the earth into a sun, and with that sublime thought bids farewell both to our planet and to his survey of its past and future: "There we leave it; having conducted it for the Space of seven thousand Years thro' various Changes, from a *dark Chaos to a bright Star*" (2:320).

That eloquent final sentence with its evocative juxtaposition of planetary beginning and ending is surely intended to linger in the reader's mind. The antithetical clause is a memorable departure from Burnet's usually plainer style. The aesthetic principle underlying his entire, and almost equally memorable, concluding speculation is apparent in Burnet's earlier statement of why he refrains from beginning *The Sacred Theory of the Earth* with an even more neatly balancing account of what he takes to be the earth's original state as a bright star, not a dark chaos: "We took our Rise no higher than the Chaos, because that was a known Principle, and we were not willing to amuse the Reader, with too many strange Stories; as that, I am sure would have been thought one, TO HAVE brought this Earth from a fixed Star, and then carried it up again into the same Sphere; which yet, I believe, is the true Circle of natural Providence" (2:Preface to Book Four, signature N2r). Burnet's scientific conviction about the earth's origin as a fixed star thus gives way to an aesthetic consideration that sets limits on his book's backward reach in time.

Rather than begin its discussion of planetary formation "higher" (earlier) than creation from the chaos mentioned in Genesis, Burnet chooses to start with that "known principle" not primarily because of its biblical authority or truthfulness (which he accepts) but because of its familiarity. Burnet hopes thereby to avoid the danger of straining credibility by providing *too many* strange stories. Again the interchangeability here of terms such as *story* and *principle*, as elsewhere of *fiction* and *hypothesis*, is telling. Burnet never evades the resemblance of hypothesis and narration so far as concerns their effects on readers. Rather, he faces the consequence that scientific speculation, no less than other forms of writing, may be constrained by the literary test of verisimilitude. Truth as determined by scientific canons of probability gives way as a principle governing the temporal boundaries of discussion to the question of what will *seem* true to readers. Burnet is willing to provide extrapolations to the past and future that will read like "strange Stories," but he is not willing to provide "too many" of them because that would diminish credibility of his work as a whole. He considers it better to publish a scientifically incomplete theory of the earth than to risk rejection of a more accurate—because more completely explained—version that, paradoxically, would have seemed false because of its unremitting accuracy.

Burnet does not provide a rule for resolving conflicts between the scientific requirement that explanations be as complete as possible and the literary requirement that extrapolations must also manage to seem credible—even, where necessary, at the expense of com-

TOWARDS AN AESTHETICS OF EXTRAPOLATION

pleteness by suppression of astonishing details. But then no one else has arrived at a rule for dealing with that kind of conflict, nor perhaps would it be good to look for one. Appreciation of the problem is very much to Burnet's credit. So is his acute awareness that *all* speculations, no matter how scientific, about the far past and future will have the air of "strange Stories." This is of a piece with his many other perceptive comments on the resemblance of hypothesis-making in science to fiction, and of a piece also with his sensitivity to the constraints imposed upon both by accepted boundaries of verisimilitude as well as by standards of coherence, proportion, unity, and what he calls the necessity in scientific writing to pursue "a *plot* or *Mystery* . . . thro' the whole Work" (1:xxii).

If Burnet's carefully articulated aesthetics of extrapolation had prevailed, it might have been easier for novelists to see liberating affinities between their art and new developments in science that were expanding temporal horizons. In geology, which played a pivotal role in suggesting the immensity of both past and future time, there might have been a further narrowing of the apparent distance between narrative fiction and treatises like Burnet's that endeavored to present credible hypotheses about the distant past or future. Despite Burnet's uneasy emphasis upon all the theological and literary reasons to avoid envisioning any remote future in much detail, his very statement of the pros and cons of doing so amid a serious scientific extrapolation to the earth's ending was a step forward that offered encouragement for those who might dare go further in considering the future a legitimate, if difficult, topic. Equal encouragement, at least potentially, was provided by Burnet's famous paragraphs describing the earth's final apocalyptic convulsions. These passages moved even Buffon, in the midst of repudiating Burnet's theories, to remark that he "knows how to paint and present forcefully noble images and place before one's eyes magnificent scenes."[24] Given Burnet's ideas, there might have been an easier and earlier leap from the genre of *physica sacra* to apocalyptic works like Cousin de Grainville's 1805 futuristic fiction of the last man.

In fact, however, Grainville did not take his inspiration from Burnet or his successors in speculative geology. Nor did any of the others who first devised futuristic fictions. Burnet's impressive aesthetics of extrapolation was never stated in a separate essay and consequently fell into oblivion, along with his entire *Sacred Theory of the Earth*, when its ideas and style of scientific writing were discredited. William Whiston, Newton's eccentric successor for a brief time in the Lucasian Chair of mathematics at Cambridge, fared no better in 1696 with his *New Theory of the Earth, from its Original, to the Consummation of all Things*. Its attribution of the Deluge and final conflagration to close passes by comets earned mostly derisive laughter. But, however regrettably for the history of futuristic fiction, Whiston did at least achieve some small impact by following Newton in minimizing the role of hypotheses generally while also differing from Burnet in stressing the veracity of acceptable hypotheses rather than their resemblance to fictions of any stripe. If Whiston accomplished nothing else, he at least quickly returned to geological speculation the absolute disjunction between fact and fiction that Burnet alone had questioned. Buffon, writing later to better effect for the development of geology, did not clutter his *Théorie de la terre* with provocative invitations to note similarities between hypothesis and romance.

Nor did Buffon focus geological speculation upon the future as Burnet and even Whiston, under the sway of their theology, had done. Buffon turned attention to the more pressing step of working out an accurate time scale for the earth's past. His extrapolations, cautious but ultimately crucial, were turned backward. He even conducted experiments in cooling metals to work out by analogy a time scheme for planetary cooling. The resulting subversion of widespread belief that our planet had existed only four or five thousand years, a subversion also abetted eventually by Darwinian

TOWARDS AN AESTHETICS OF EXTRAPOLATION

views of evolution, led Buffon's successors to renewed scientific speculation, on a far different basis from Burnet's, about earth's final destiny.[25] Only in that nineteenth-century context was it finally possible in 1895 for Wells's Time Traveller, "drawn on by the mystery of the earth's fate," to recount his existential "deadly nausea" experienced in the far future during an eclipse on that vividly described dark beach in the world's last age.[26] If Burnet's ideas on the aesthetics of extrapolation might have inspired a similar tale in a somewhat more religious vein during the eighteenth century, they never had the chance. The first time-traveler in English literature is a guardian angel who returns with state documents from 1998 to the year 1728 in Samuel Madden's *Memoirs of the Twentieth Century*. Turning next to that work, and away from the constraining influences of science and theology, I want to show how futuristic fiction was stimulated by its literary context.

PART TWO
Starting Points, 1733–1827

CHAPTER THREE

Formal Variations: *Memoirs of the Twentieth Century*

Ever since the Christian Gauss seminar at Princeton was devoted to science fiction in 1958 by Kingsley Amis, critics have tackled with increasing refinement the problem of adequately defining that genre.[1] Its affinities with the tale of the future have been so close that distinction between them is necessary in any account of either genre lest their early relationship, especially during the eighteenth century, be misunderstood as simply a case of identity. I accept Darko Suvin's argument that science fiction is best considered as the literature of cognitive estrangement rather than, according to Brian Aldiss, merely as "a lively sub-genre of the gothic" in which some alarming future locale is substituted for the old castles favored by Horace Walpole, Ann Radcliffe, and their imitators for transporting readers to a disturbing past.[2] Suvin derives his idea of estrangement from the Russian Formalist concept of *ostranenie* elaborated in Bertolt Brecht's definition of what he called the *Verfremdungseffekt:* any mode of representation allowing recognition of something while at the same time making it seem unfamiliar. Cognition is involved whenever the defamiliarized subject is then understood on a more rational basis. Suvin states that science fiction is a genre "whose necessary and sufficient conditions are the presence and interaction of estrangement and cognition, and whose main formal device is an imaginative framework alternative to the author's empirical environment."³ In this view the defamiliarizing locus of action in science fiction may be achieved by either temporal or spatial displacement—and in fact the grand archetype for all science fiction becomes *Gulliver's Travels* by virtue of Gulliver's voyages to places where he has estranging encounters with alien creatures who so often make us think about ourselves.⁴ Conversely, resort to a future setting may be for purposes that have nothing to do with the aims of science fiction.

By identifying a kinship between gothic tales and science fiction during the romantic period when that genre was at last unequivocally exemplified in Mary Shelley's *Frankenstein*, Aldiss shows the relevance of eighteenth-century theories of the sublime that provided a necessary aesthetics for the new form by legitimizing the terrifying strangeness of setting and incident, eventually including future settings. Aldiss rightly suggests that, by a displacement to the future, science fiction can manage better than its precursors "to encompass those fears generated by change and the technological advances which are the chief agents of change."⁵ However science fiction is defined, no one can very well deny that its rise is closely connected with the tale of the future.

Not everyone, to be sure, would agree with Thomas Hanzo's provocative assertion that all science fiction "is a proleptic structure," a kind of writing which follows in a fictional mode that rhetorical strategy in which for persuasive purposes "the future is treated as the past" so that "what is to come is . . . put into the past tense." Still I find among academic critics a consensus for which Hanzo speaks, when in the same challenging essay he asserts of science fiction: "Space may be its scene, the extraterrestrial its locale, but time is its peculiar realm; the future gives science fiction its energy and purpose."⁶ For the genre thus energized if not defined by its attention to the future, Suvin accurately locates "its central watershed . . . around 1800, when space loses its monopoly upon the location of estrangement and the alternative horizons shift from space to time."⁷ As I remarked briefly at the

FORMAL VARIATIONS

outset of chapter 2, various explanations for this shift have been offered, usually in terms of widened temporal horizons and heightened awareness of change induced by the new geology, by theories of biological evolution, and by the political and industrial revolutions of the late eighteenth and early nineteenth centuries.

Granted that these transformations all play some part, Suvin is nevertheless right to say of the shift from space to time: "This turning, that cuts decisively across all other national, political and formal traditions in culture, has so far not been adequately explained." He maintains that setting narratives in the future became appealing partly because that was the easiest means of getting away from the constraining demands of "naturalistic plausibility"—demands looming ever larger throughout the eighteenth and nineteenth centuries in conjunction with a "strict positivist ideology" at odds with genres that aimed at eliciting by astonishing stories the effects of cognitive estrangement. Whatever the role of positivist ideology in putting a greater premium on plausible fiction, there can be little doubt that the generic or purely formal pressures toward verisimilitude exerted so vigorously by Defoe, Richardson, and their successors made it harder than ever before to locate tales like *Gulliver's Travels* in the present. More important for Suvin as an underlying cause of that difficulty, and hence of the shift to fictions of the future, is "the strong tendency toward temporal extrapolation inherent in life based on a capitalist economy, with its salaries, profits, and progressive ideals always expected in a future clock-time."[8] There is surely some truth to this suggestion. But it too strikes me as only a partial explanation of the shift to chronicles of the future.

Though one does not find such chronicles in the Middle Ages, one does find the new money-oriented attitudes toward time notably emerging if not yet triumphant well before the Renaissance.[9] Even more to the point, there were in the sixteenth, seventeenth, and eighteenth centuries transformations quite as profound in their consequences for human relationships to time as the shift to capitalist modes of production: the rise of experimental science and the new astronomy, along with related mathematical developments such as calculus and probability theory; exploration of the Americas and the Pacific; and increasing skepticism about those religious convictions that had deflected writers from concern with the secular future by focusing attention instead upon apocalyptic visions of time's end and eternity's beginning. It begs the question to lump all such transformations together as epiphenomena of changing modes of production caused by the rise of capitalism. I believe the formalist part of Suvin's argument points in a more rewarding direction than the Marxist part. We must still ask what literary as well as social pressures pushed writers toward setting stories in the future. A look at the second book of futuristic fiction, Samuel Madden's *Memoirs of the Twentieth Century*, will provide some answers.

Perhaps in deference to the unspoken taboo against tales of the future, *Memoirs of the Twentieth Century* was published anonymously in 1733 and then immediately suppressed by its author, an Irish Anglican clergyman who destroyed almost all copies of his extraordinary work as soon as they came from the press.[10] Consequently *Memoirs of the Twentieth Century* had no apparent impact on later eighteenth-century fiction. Nor has it figured even in histories of science fiction as anything more than one of those legendary works that are duly mentioned but not discussed in any detail. It has been ignored partly because it is satire rather than science fiction or any kind of serious extrapolation to a possible real future and partly because copies, even of a Garland Press reprint, are very scarce.[11] *Memoirs of the Twentieth Century*, however, provides excellent evidence about the origins of both futuristic fiction and science fiction.

Madden found a new way of distancing narrative setting from the targets of satire. Seven years earlier *Gulliver's Travels* had used distance in space. *Memoirs of the Twentieth Century* uses time. No previous English writer had done so. Even *Epigone*, though it includes satiric as well as utopian passages and resorts to a putative future by way of augmenting the remoteness favored as a locus for adventure in heroic romances, is not set in a chronologically specified future. Because it is more like an alternate history, *Epigone* could hardly have served as a pattern for *Memoirs of the Twentieth Century*. Nor is there any evidence that Madden knew of Guttin's book. Madden deserves great credit for originality. Unfortunately he was not up to sustained exploitation of his innovative future setting. Although Madden wrote anticipatory satire instead of predictive fiction and should be judged accordingly, on the basis of any criterion known to me *Memoirs of the Twentieth Century* is failed satire. There are passages reminiscent of Swift at his best. But Madden's few palpable hits lose their force in a welter of tiresome religious satire and other incoherent attacks that miss the mark or hit the target too bluntly. Moreover, the tone frequently wavers between satiric and utopian in ways that make it unclear whether some passages are satirically or prescriptively intended.

Without making any brief for *Memoirs of the Twentieth Century* as a neglected masterpiece, then, I do want to suggest that Madden created a viable form in the shape of a tale of the future that could work perfectly well as a framework for futuristic fiction in any of its modes—despite his failure to write a coherent anticipatory satire or a work that is truly science fiction. I shall suggest, too, that examination of the self-reflexive comments which Madden includes within *Memoirs of the Twentieth Century* reveals important evidence of how literary conventions and social change interacted in eighteenth-century culture to provide a climate of opinion that at last allowed writers to cast aside the ancient prejudice against tales of the future. Finally, I shall argue that, although Madden failed as a satirist, he made a respectable showing as a critic. His explanation may still go far to account for the way science fiction and related forms can present narratives of imaginary history—usually but not invariably future history—that are often most powerful when they run most strongly counter to our intuitive canons of probability.

ORIGINS OF FUTURISTIC FICTION

Memoirs of the Twentieth Century is described by its subtitle as "Original Letters of State, under George the Sixth: Relating to the most important Events in Great-Britain and Europe . . . from the Middle of the Eighteenth, to the End of the Twentieth Century, and the World. Received and Revealed in the Year 1728; and now published . . . In Six Volumes." There were no sequels to volume one, nor were any intended. Allusion to five more volumes satirizes long-winded memoirs. Classification as letters of state would have prevented eighteenth-century readers from expecting an account of the private life of some individual, even in satiric form, and would thus have excused in advance any lack of that suspense created by arousing curiosity about the fate of a protagonist. The closest approach to a fully realized character is the nameless narrator of three bizarre "prefaces" which cannot be taken as straightforward statements from the anonymous real author. Given the novelty and, according to conventional wisdom, the evident absurdity of such future records as the subtitle promises, eighteenth-century readers would have registered at first glance the book's satiric intention. They would accordingly have taken its allusion to revelations concerning the end of the world as satire aimed at millenarian prediction.[12]

Laughter at such targets is sustained, and directed also at those who cling to belief in guardian angels, when early in the book's first preface its narrator explains that he received the ensuing letters from *his* guardian angel on the evening of January 20, 1728. He claims no credit for prophecy but only for the hard work of translating each letter from "the *English* that will be spoke in the XXth *Century*" (p. 5). Although primarily a satiric entry in controversies over the existence of guardian angels, Madden's resort to the fiction of documents transported backward through time is as viable as H. G. Wells's conceit of a time machine which defies the laws of physics in carrying his narrator forward on a tour of the future. By 1895 it was easier to suspend disbelief in any sort of machine, however impossible it might be in the real world. Even today, as every critic

FORMAL VARIATIONS

of science fiction is bound to remark, the genre makes ample use of such convenient impossibilities as faster-than-light space travel. Only a small part of science fiction confines itself to situations that accord exactly with scientific canons of possibility. Though guardian angels would now relegate a narrative to the realms of fantasy, the situation was less clear-cut in 1733. Belief in guardian angels was waning and under attack. They were nevertheless still defended by some as part of a scientifically correct—because theologically accurate—picture of the universe as it really is.[13] The lines between theology, superstition, and science were being redrawn in a way that allowed the idea of a guardian angel with documents from the future to be used as a narrative framework and also as a vehicle of satire that by various means, especially a lengthy mock defense of belief in such spirits, ridicules those who take them seriously.

Prominently, at the start of that mock defense, Madden includes one of his few hints of a possible model for *Memoirs of the Twentieth Century* by referring ambiguously to the *irrelevance* for that defense of allusions to "Kircher's good Genius, who carried him through the Planets in his *Iter Extaticum*" (p. 225). Madden thus invites readers to take his book, despite its odd format, as merely an acceptable comic variation on a familiar literary device. After the hint has been dropped, it is easy enough to regard documents brought by the narrator's guardian angel as equivalent to the tour of our solar system provided in 1656 by Athanasius Kircher for his protagonist in the *Itinerarium Extaticum*. Again Madden substitutes time for space. An angel provides access to the future just as an angel had provided access to space. Madden's variation of Kircher's idea deserves credit for seizing on the possibility of a kind of time-travel instead of following the already trite convention of spatial journeys on or off the earth.[14]

It would be stretching our generosity to praise Madden for being the first to show a traveler arriving *from* the future. Still, the appearance of the narrator's guardian angel one evening in 1728 to

95

hand over twentieth-century documents calls to mind such tales as Robert Silverberg's 1968 novel *The Masks of Time* (in which one day in 1999 there arrives in Rome a visitor from the year 2999 who can reveal future history but cannot give any satisfactory explanation of how he managed to travel backwards in time). To my knowledge, however, Madden is the first to write a narrative that purports to *be* a document from the future. He deserves recognition as the first to toy with the rich idea of time-travel in the form of an artifact sent backwards from the future to be discovered in the present. This too is an original variation on a familiar literary tradition: the discovery and interpretation of some ancient document (an artifact from the remote past) containing political or other prophecy. This convention had been used both seriously and satirically. In eighteenth-century England satiric applications prevailed, as in Swift's *Windsor Prophecy* (1711) and Samuel Johnson's *Marmor Norfolciense* (1739).

Madden's artifact from the twentieth century is a series of letters to the British "Lord High Treasurer" from English ambassadors in Turkey, Rome, Paris, and Moscow, together with a few replies sent from the English foreign office. The first letter is from "Constantinople, Nov. 3, 1997"; the last is dated "May 1, 1998." Each ambassador sketches local conditions in the late 1990s and, on one pretext or another, also gives some outline of events from the 1940s onward in the country where he is stationed.

In a report from France in 1997, for example, the English ambassador tells of quarrels between Louis XIX and Rome, then sketches by way of background the earlier loss of French conquests that resulted in a situation where "the Pope is now the entire Object of the fears of *Europe*, instead of the conquering *French*" (p. 78). This letter also describes internal problems plaguing a militarily weak France whose people are poorly governed, overtaxed, and suffering from a condition in which "the Luxury of the Nobility and Gentry is increas'd beyond all Bounds, as if they were not only insensible of, but even rejoyc'd in the publick Calamities of their

FORMAL VARIATIONS

Fellow-Subjects" (p. 85). Such passages partly reflect Madden's view of France as it was in his own day, and partly display the rather tediously elaborated fantasies of a British patriot and Protestant whose most ignominious biases against the French and against all Roman Catholics are indulged in deplorable ways that need not concern us further here.

In a lighter vein, Madden often attempts to satirize perennial human dilemmas by means of obviously absurd fantasies of progress. Thus, in response to reports of medical reforms in the Russia of 1998, and English foreign office official writes to the British ambassador in Moscow reporting that English physicians have at last found a cure for violent love: "Now whenever people find their passion is unsuccessful and desperate, without hanging or drowning, shooting or poisoning, which was the usual method, they calmly send for Dr. *Howard*, who immediately puts them into the Love-course, as they call it, and so they get rid of it at once, and then very quietly go about their affairs; and as soon as they have recover'd from the cure, (which, as in most other cases, generally takes up as much time as the distemper) they chuse a more proper, or at least a less cruel person for their adorations" (p. 431). Several correspondents also allude to British history as far back as the mid-eighteenth century and thereby provide readers in 1733 with glimpses of more immediate possibilities.

References to the close future are most often in the mode of prescriptive satire, as when a correspondent remarks with approval how eighteenth-century kings "peremptorily drove the *Italian* Opera and Music twice from *Great Britain*, and forbid their acting . . . as enervating our Spirits, and emasculating the *British* Genius" (p. 138). The moral of this bit of future history is of a piece with many eighteenth-century attacks on English addiction to Italian opera. Madden puts other suggestions in a more utopian mode. There is, for example, a description of how the Royal College of Saint George at Oxford was "founded by his Majesty's Ancestors in the Eighteenth Century" in order to establish twenty-six fellowships for deserving continental refugees as well as four new professorships in such useful subjects as agriculture, gardening, mechanical arts, and meteorology. We learn that, thanks to establishment of a chair for "the Weather Professor" whose task is to keep meteorological records as an aid to weather forecasting, "Six Volumes in Folio of these Calendars have been publisht from 1840 to 1991" (p. 144). Such passages, whether satiric or utopian, are prescriptive rather than predictive. They are scenarios of what should be done, not prophecies of what will be done.

As a framework for a tale of the future, Madden's scheme is more flexible than that adopted in 1771 by Louis-Sébastien Mercier for *L'An 2440*—and indeed in some ways more flexible than that employed by Wells in *The Time Machine*. Madden's epistolary narrative allows for a portrait of life in England, France, Italy, Turkey, and Russia during the 1990s, together with attention to eighteenth- and nineteenth-century developments. Mercier's protagonist dreams that he wakes in the year 2440 to walk around Paris observing the city and discussing its social institutions with twenty-fifth-century Parisians. Developments elsewhere are glanced at in extracts from newspapers but not described in much detail. Wells's time-traveler can set the controls for any date but, once he arrives, is essentially confined to observing how things are at that target moment in history. Madden's device of letters from diplomats with a professional knowledge of history allows for presentation of a synchronic portrait of Europe at one historical period (the 1990s) and also for a diachronic account of previous events. Mercier presents an eyewitness narrative that results in a vivid but static portrait of Paris in 2440, without much attention to the stages by which eighteenth-century conditions gave way to those of the distant and better future which his narrator describes. Madden's epistolary framework more easily allows for depiction of historical change.

For Mercier's purpose of arousing discontent that could motivate political action, it is effective enough simply to plunge readers into an encounter with a utopian Paris devoid of eighteenth-century shortcomings. Indeed, by withholding any account of how such perfection had been achieved, Mercier sharpens the contrast between 1771 and 2440. This method encourages readers to supply the missing causal links in their own imaginations and thereby consider what might actually be done to move the France of 1771 toward Mercier's vision of a better future. In his preface to the 1798 edition of *L'An 2440*, Mercier claims—with some justice—that he had been the prophet of the French Revolution. By way of proof, he states that his book is being reprinted without the slightest change so that readers can judge for themselves its predictive power as "a dream that had announced and prepared the French revolution." Mercier only disclaims responsibility for encouraging the terror, which so nearly cost him his life and was impossible to foresee, he insists, because one cannot imagine a handful of scoundrels suddenly dominating an enlightened country.[15] Mercier thus notes in retrospect (though only in retrospect) that the implausibility, and hence unpredictability, of past events is occasionally a bar to accurate future history. Reality is sometimes so incredible as to hinder fictive extrapolation beforehand. But Mercier does not discuss this as a problem for his genre.

Concerned above all with public affairs, Mercier, like Madden, avoids opportunities for depicting personal relationships among the characters inhabiting his future. He could certainly have done so effectively within the framework of a first-person narrative. Yet Madden's device of letters from several correspondents is an even better matrix for suspenseful narration of developing emotional encounters in the manner of later Richardsonian fictions, had Madden cared to do so or had he been sufficiently talented. A series of dated letters also allows more easily sustained awareness of a future setting. There can be no doubt, for reasons explained in greater detail in the next chapter, that *L'An 2440* is the superior book. It is coherent in sticking to a utopian mode; moreover, it exercised influence as a widely read work that helped prepare for social change and also, through its success, encouraged other writers to invent tales of the future.[16] Madden nevertheless deserves recognition for his achievement in designing, though not fully exploiting, a better framework for such tales.

The self-reflexive quality of *Memoirs of the Twentieth Century*, its insistent invitations to consider in relationship to previous literature what *kind* of book we have in hand as we read, is achieved mainly by the device of a narrator who uses "prefaces" at the beginning, middle, and end of the work to comment on the main text of letters from the future. But this narrator is so obviously demented that we cannot simply equate his opinions with those of the anonymous real author, much less always accept them at face value as an account of how the work we are reading came to assume its unusual form. Instead, as in Swift's *Tale of a Tub* (1704) with its mad narrator commenting in lunatic ways on the strange story he tells of three brothers, or the parallel situation of Pope's *Dunciad Variorum* (1728) with its surrounding parodic apparatus of Scriblerian commentary, there is every reason to be wary of supposing that Madden's letters from the twentieth century were intended for serious acceptance as a new kind of writing. For readers in 1733 that would have been tantamount to believing every word about the dunciad as a genre provided by Pope in the amusing essays and notes supposedly written by Martinus Scriblerus. The difference is that dunciads have not become a major form of literature (however much we still need them), whereas chronicles of the future have. Although Madden's narrator foresees no such development, what he says about the book nevertheless provides significant clues to the influences that led his creator Madden to discard the idea that narratives can only be set in the present or past.

Addressing people of the future ("I do hereby declare beforehand to *Posterity*"), the narrator, a corrupt ex-politician who bribed his way into Parliament and then turned student of astrology (pp. 11–18), gives two reasons why all discrepancies between the

FORMAL VARIATIONS

prophetic elements of his book and events subsequent to its publication must be the fault only of careless future readers: "First, that either they do not understand what is or appears to be written, thro' the disguises I necessarily made use of . . . or 2dly, Men are deceiv'd, either by reports of others, or their own fallacious senses, persuading them they have seen things happen otherwise, than they really have. . . . Pretended *facts*, are never to be set in competition with unquestionable Predictions" (pp. 517–18). Through the narrator's obdurate conviction that no mere fact could possibly invalidate his predictions, Madden makes the same satiric point, although less brilliantly, that Swift made in *The Bickerstaff Papers* against vague astrological prophecy: Partridge's witless insistence that he was still alive after the predicted hour of his death became in Swift's hilarious response an irrefutable proof that in fulfillment of the prophecy Partridge was (mentally, at least) indeed dead.

In another moment of concern over ways in which inept future readers could be led to misunderstand his book, Madden's narrator takes precautions against those who might alter his text:

> That Posterity may not be impos'd on, by any spurious Additions, Forgeries or Obliterations in this Admirable Work, I have with great Labour number'd and reckon'd up the whole of what is in it, which is a sager and fairer Way than a Table of Contents, which our modern Publishers tack to their mangled Volumes. I find therefore that there is in this Collection, (Publish'd and to be Publish'd) 28,967 Sentences that have meaning in them, 1,232,356 Words, 2,125,245 Syllables, 6,293,376 Letters, and thro' the Roughness of our barbarous Tongue, but 2,992,644 Vowels, (exclusive of *y* and all Diphthongs) as any careful Reader may find, who will cast them up with equal Diligence. (p. 30)

This flight of deconstructive fantasy does not inspire confidence in the narrator as a reliable spokesman for the implied real author. Nor is it easier to accept with a straight face the narrator's explanation of why he is publishing letters from the twentieth century that include an account of the exploits in high political office of one of his descendants:

> When I saw . . . that the World and my Descendant's Ministry would end together; I was the more willing to have my fame and his laid open to the present Age, since it was impossible for future Times to do us Justice, by assigning us that shining place in History, which Printing these Volumes will so fully entitle us to. . . . [A]s my Fame has been entirely conceal'd, and his reduc'd to take up with the short-liv'd Applause of a few Years, in his old Age, the Dregs of Life, and the Last Moments of the World, I resolv'd to be before-hand with the Glory of my self and Family, and to enjoy some part of our Reputation before we had earn'd it. (p. 23)

Here the statement in the book's subtitle that the world is to end at the close of the twentieth century is reiterated, as it is in several other places, by way of satire aimed at dire millennial predictions. Madden encourages readers to laugh at this kind of prophecy coming from a credulous narrator, whose ready acceptance of a specific date for the end of the world leads him to abandon so cheerfully the laws of cause and effect along with their necessary temporal sequence as he endeavors to help himself and his family enjoy fame two centuries before they become famous.

Such passages create a context in which there is thus primarily comic force in the narrator's insistence that he alone has "the Honour and Misfortune, of being the first among Historians (if a mere Publisher of Memoirs may deserve that Name) who leaving the beaten Tracts of writing . . . the accounts of past Actions and Times, have dar'd to enter by the help of an infallible Guide, into the dark Caverns of Futurity, and discover the Secrets of Ages yet to come" (p. 3). By stressing in this and similar passages the novelty of an account of the future which is neither religious prophecy, poetic imitation of religious prophecy, nor astrological forecast but is instead a kind of *history* (even if only a memoir), Madden succeeds in playing with some originality the eighteenth-century game of inventing mock forms.

Memoirs of the Twentieth Century results in part from the same literary climate of exuberant formal experimentation that led Madden's more skillful contemporaries to produce those masterpieces of mock form *The Rape of the Lock, The Dunciad, Peri Bathous, A Tale of a Tub, The Bickerstaff Papers, Gulliver's Travels,* and *The Beggar's Opera*. Pope, Swift, and Gay parodied such familiar forms as epic, critical treatise, travel narrative, astrological prediction, and opera. Madden chose history, perhaps the only major genre not yet turned upside down for comic purposes, and created another absurdist mock genre: the future history.

If most subsequent chronicles of the future, or even such later eighteenth-century efforts as *L'An 2440*, were primarily intended to evoke laughter, or if Madden's narrator provided nothing but explanations in the vein which I have just sampled, the emergence of futuristic fiction might be adequately accounted for on purely formal grounds. One could argue that, once writers as powerful as Pope, Swift, and Gay so brilliantly set the example of turning established generic conventions around to provide parodic mock forms serving as vehicles of satire, it was inevitable that someone would fasten on history for the same purposes. By converting narration of the past into narration of the future, someone would create a new form that could then be adapted to nonsatiric purposes, just as *The Beggar's Opera* led to musical comedy. But this is only part of the genesis even of *Memoirs of the Twentieth Century*. Attitudes less exclusively literary than a taste for parodies also account for its creation, as for the ensuing proliferation of future histories.

The social as well as literary pressures encouraging establishment of the tale of the future as a respectable mode of writing are suggested when Madden's narrator takes up an issue that is fundamental to the aesthetics of futuristic fiction: the question of probability. In the *Poetics* Aristotle defined the boundaries within which this problem has mostly been debated ever since. He remarks ambiguously that "the impossible" can sometimes be justified "by reference to artistic requirements," but usually "a probable impossibility is to be preferred to a thing improbable and yet possible." Aristotle adds a reminder that, because reality is often so surprising as to seem unlikely, it is not always easy to decide whether a represented event is improbable: "there is a probability of things happening also against probability."[17] The history of criticism on this vexing point is alluded to in eighteenth-century England most significantly in Fielding's chapter on the marvelous in *Tom Jones* (book 8, chapter 1). Typically for the period, that discussion remains within the framework set by Aristotle, with whom Fielding essentially agrees in stressing the importance of probability. Even in a fiction modeled to some degree on factual narratives by, among other devices, a title announcing *The History of Tom Jones, A Foundling* and claiming by virtue of its affinity to history the liberty of showing how people actually behave rather than how we might wish them to behave, Fielding insists that unlikely events not crucial to the story should be suppressed in the interest of preserving an air of probability.[18] In *Memoirs of the Twentieth Century*, however, Madden's narrator abandons this traditional narrative strategy of caution.

To the potential charge "that these vast discoveries and improvements, these changes and revolutions of things below, which are mention'd in the subsequent letters, cannot possibly happen, nor consequently be true, many of them are so improbable," the narrator answers with a lengthy argument that for this very reason they *must* be true (p. 550ff.). By "subsequent letters" the narrator means the five unpublished volumes, about whose contents readers are in no position to argue. This aspect of Madden's comedy ensures that attention centers on the general issue of probability, not particular episodes. For the new genre of future history, *improbability* becomes a touchstone by which to measure verisimilitude.

Madden's argument is reminiscent of that passage in *Childhood's*

FORMAL VARIATIONS

End wherein a character remarks that a report of strange events struck him as true *because* it was so incredible.[19] If Madden were merely turning the Aristotelian tradition upside down for satiric purposes, his narrator's subsequent discussion would be noteworthy only as another moderately talented attempt at imitating those comic modes of mock criticism put to more brilliant uses by Swift in *A Tale of a Tub* and by Pope in *The Dunciad Variorum* and *Peri Bathous*. In elaborating on the question of probability, however, Madden veers gradually away from comedy to provide some arresting observations on the literary implications of the history of science and its impact on society.

First Madden's narrator denies that he would go so far as "to say with Tertullian, *Certum est quia impossibile est*." But if his guardian angel had given him fraudulent letters, or if he himself wished to deceive readers, then the twentieth-century documents "would have been contrived with greater approximation, (as the learned speak) and verisimilitude to truth" (p. 506). After remarking too that nothing is easier or more common than fictions "cook'd up" to provide a plausible resemblance to everyday life, the narrator insists that "the small regard . . . here, to such little tricks . . . in [narrating] many prodigious discoveries in arts and sciences, travels, revolutions, and alterations of all kinds, and especially in the 4th and 6th volumes, ought to stand as evidence of their truth; and that they are not forgeries and impostures, but real facts, which time will produce, and which are delivered to mankind with the carelessness and simplicity of an honest publisher; more solicitous to reveal actual facts and events, as he receiv'd them, than to disguise them so craftily to the world, as to seem more likely to happen, and easy to be believ'd" (p. 507). In fact, as I. F. Clarke suggests in dismissing *Memoirs of the Twentieth Century* from extensive consideration in his study of seriously predictive tales of the future, Madden offers no picture of a world radically different from that of the eighteenth century.[20] What Clarke takes as a deficiency in predictive power is on one level simply an obviously intended (and effective) part of Madden's comedy: the narrator's defense of unpublished letters showing "prodigious" future alterations is unnecessary because those particular letters remain unavailable. The future actually depicted is only superficially unlike the world of 1733. There is little need to disarm objections to the first *and only* volume by proposing implausibility as the true test of verisimilitude, because that test applies mainly to unwritten and unpublished volumes that readers can only imagine.

Carrying on this joke for a bit, the narrator remarks that "were there occasion for it"—as there obviously is not—he could "say a great deal here on that famous observation, *Aliquando insit in incredibili veritas, & in verisimili mendacium;* and convince my readers, how little weight any objection ought to have with him, that is bottom'd on this sandy foundation" (p. 507). The Latin phrase, which means "let there sometimes be truth in the incredible and in the probable a lie," may be from some well-known source that has eluded me, or it may be Madden's own mock-authoritative variation of Aristotle's statement that sometimes it is probable for things to happen against probability. Since the Latin tag is in any event not prominent among eighteenth-century commonplaces, I take the reference to its fame as comic hyperbole.

The next comment, however, brings up a consideration that cannot be taken so lightly: "Indeed whoever are knowing and learned enough, to be acquainted with the infinite incredible verities in the world of science, the vast numbers of improbable and unimaginable truths, to be met with there, and the heaps of plausible errors and delusive falsehoods, that men are so usually led away with; will never consider the improbability of some relations in this work, as an argument for any thing, but their being more unfeign'd and genuinely true" (pp. 507–8). Any reference to the "incredible verities" of science will of course ring more solemnly in our century for readers who have struggled to understand a universe filled, so we are told by our scientists, with quasars, quarks, black holes and the like, all governed by the counterintuitive laws of quantum mechanics and relativity theory. But eighteenth-century readers with knowledge of current advances in astronomy, physics, and biology must also have seen that Madden's tone veers at this point decisively away from comedy.

There is no satire when Madden's narrator piously states that nothing foretold in the book need seem improbable in view of "the infinite power of the great Source of all events below." Nor is there any levity in a catalogue of secondary causes of drastic change such as "operations of nature" and "the vast fields of art and knowledge, which the new world hath brought forth among us, by the labours of different voyagers." In 1733 neither allusions to the power of God nor invitations to consider natural forces ("deluges and earthquakes . . . vulcanoes, tempests, and innundations"), much less allusion to the impact of the New World, could be taken as sure signs of irony. Quite the contrary. Madden's narrator pursues this more serious line of thought with an invitation to those "that are buried in the present state of the earth, and think it will continue in a manner unimprov'd and unalter'd" to "look back, if they know any thing of it in former ages" (p. 507). That backward glance over history is not merely to note previous geological and social changes in order, as was then more conventional, to see the past as a mirror of possible futures. While the logic here does rely in part on a traditional premise that a look at the past can reveal the shape of things to come, this assumption is invoked for the unusual purpose of proving that the future will be different, that all one can tell from the past is that everything changes not only drastically but *unpredictably*.

It is the past as a history of unforeseeable transformations that Madden stresses next by inviting readers to alter their temporal vantage point. They are to consider how the history of the world since the rise of Rome would have seemed *if narrated as a prediction of the future* to those living at the dawn of the Roman Empire:

Let them consider how absurd and incredible it would have appear'd, if a man, . . . at the building of *Rome*, had . . . foretold the vast growth of that Monarchy, the overturning all others by that embryo state, the majesty of the pagan religion there, the birth and rise of the Christian, the breaking of the *Roman* Empire into several little scraps and pieces, which are now miscall'd Kingdoms; the spreading conquests of the Pope and his Monks . . . the reformation of Religion, and all the wars, factions and revolutions. . . . Let them reflect, I say, if such a relation (or prediction) would not be receiv'd as more ridiculous and impossible, than those that are mention'd in these six volumes. (pp. 507–8)

This argument for the implausibility of history assumes for its persuasiveness that readers will mentally transport themselves backward in time for a moment to imagine a book like the one in their hand—only real, not fictive; predictive, not satiric—in which authentic revelations from the future are presented but inevitably dismissed as improbable. Most striking here is a rhetorical strategy, adopted throughout *Memoirs of the Twentieth Century,* that is based upon devices enforcing a double temporal perspective.

Events from the establishment of the Roman Empire to the Protestant Reformation must be viewed as simultaneously in the past (from the vantage point of those reading Madden's book) and in the future (for someone in the early days of Rome looking ahead). For its audience in 1733, the letters in *Memoirs of the Twentieth Century* likewise had to be viewed as dealing at once with the past and future: with later eighteenth- and nineteenth-century events imagined as in the future for readers but *also* in the past for the imaginary twentieth-century correspondents looking backwards.

All stories narrated in the past tense invite some degree of temporal doubling, of course, especially if they are told by first-person narrators. In a work like *Robinson Crusoe,* for example, readers are invited to notice differences in outlook between the narrator's earlier and later selves, or to notice that a given episode such as Crusoe's rescue from the island must be taken as both a past event from the narrator's vantage point while writing and a future event with respect to himself as he was at prior moments in the story.

FORMAL VARIATIONS

Typological modes of narration and their derivatives, such as Dryden's *Absalom and Achitophel* and Defoe's *Journal of the Plague Year*, as well as allegories like *The Faerie Queene*, also collapse past and present or even present and future in ways that create complex temporal doubling. Such works are nevertheless very different from *Memoirs of the Twentieth Century* in their manner of conflating past and present.[21]

No matter how inept a satire, Madden's book remains noteworthy as the first prose narrative to adopt the central technique of those modes of futuristic fiction formally distinct from previous traditions by virtue of inviting readers to imagine themselves looking backwards from a far future to their own present and immediate future, which are thus also to be regarded as the past. Here for the first time in prose fiction is the proleptic structure identified by Hanzo and others as the narrative method most necessary for viable science fiction.

The social transformations encouraging experiment with that proleptic structure are suggested most explicitly when, to the argument that major episodes in Western history were not in fact probable but only seem so in retrospect, Madden's narrator adds a survey of "the amazing alterations, in the manners and customs of particular nations" from ancient Greece to the eighteenth century. He concentrates on "the state of learning in the last two ages," thereby stressing the acceleration of change. It is during this interval, he remarks, that Aristotle fell into disrepute along with "the schoolmen, who gave laws to heaven and earth" but who have been supplanted by "the great improvers of knowledge, who have made such important and successful discoveries, in this wide world of matter and life, which the others had so long kept us strangers to" (pp. 512–13). By singling out recent discoveries, Madden invites as much attention to the rapid pace as to the surprising nature of scientific advances.

This emphasis on the quickening tempo of progress bolsters

ORIGINS OF FUTURISTIC FICTION

Madden's argument for the sheer improbability of past history and thus, by implication, of what lies ahead:

> If we consider how few years are past, since we improv'd Astronomy by a true system, verified by demonstration, and founded Philosophy on actual experiments, not on imaginary notions and opinions; since the compass and the needle trac'd out the mariner's unerring road on the ocean, and war join'd fire to the sword, or muskets banish'd bows and arrows; since the invention of printing had a new birth in the world; since regular posts were first invented, and set up by *de Tassis* in Spain, and trade and correspondence got wings by land, as well as by sea; since Physicians found out either new drugs or specificks, or even the secrets of Anatomy, or the circulation of the blood; since our own nations learn'd to weave the fleece of our sheep, or that even one half of the earth had found out the other; and above all, if we reflect, that the small compass of time, which all these great events have happen'd in, seems to promise vast improvements in the growing centuries; it will not appear surprising, and much less absurd, that such discoveries and improvements are allotted to our posterity, in these volumes. (p. 513)

This passage cannot now and could not in 1733 be dismissed as nothing more than the ravings of an amusing character mouthing ludicrous arguments for satiric purposes. Whatever Madden's intentions may have been for the overall effect of *Memoirs of the Twentieth Century,* in this passage—as sometimes also in Swift's more well-controlled satire—the comic mask is set aside for a moment, and we hear an authentic voice stating an important truth.

Although Madden again quickly dons the disguise of his bizarre narrator at whom both we and he laugh, and neither Madden nor his grotesque editor of letters from the twentieth century claims to be formulating an aesthetics for some new and more serious genre that may develop from the parodic future history inaugurated in *Memoirs of the Twentieth Century,* it is here that Madden becomes the first to articulate one of the basic aesthetic postulates of futuristic fiction. By noting that *unpredictable* change is a distinctive corollary of the accelerating pace of scientific discovery, as well as

FORMAL VARIATIONS

a somewhat less conspicuous feature of all Western social and religious history from the time of the Roman Empire, Madden derives a new canon of probability and accordingly a paradoxical new test of verisimilitude that applies especially to narratives of the future: acceptance of the implausible (we might say the counterintuitive) as the most likely shape of things to come.

It follows that, for tales of the future alone among genres, there is a premium on enhancing verisimilitude by eliciting astonishment at stories that depict apparently (though only apparently) implausible new developments in society or, better yet, strange new developments in science. It follows too, although Madden does not explicitly remark this consequence, that the reader's initial response of disbelief when confronted with tales of an apparently fantastic future is analogous to the surprise experienced at contemplating in retrospect real scientific discoveries that could not easily have been predicted beforehand. In this view, aesthetic response to science corresponds to the aesthetics of narratives relating the future with most verisimilitude.

Memoirs of the Twentieth Century thus reveals that, within the mind of the writer who inaugurated English futuristic fiction, there was a close connection between awareness of accelerating scientific discovery and awareness of inevitable corresponding alterations in our very concepts of probability in life as well as in literature. Madden certainly understood that alterations in accepted standards of plausibility derive not only from the increasing tempo of social change and scientific progress but even more from recognition that science discovers *implausible* truths: what Madden calls "the infinite incredible verities in the world of science," and what more recently has led to the dictum that our universe is not only stranger than we ordinarily imagine but even stranger than we *can* imagine.

To the arguments of Aldiss, Suvin, and others about the conditions that made tales of the future possible if not inevitable by the end of the eighteenth century, I can add a new hypothesis on the basis of

Memoirs of the Twentieth Century. I do not deny that some role was played by the rise of capitalism and related future-oriented modes of thought, along with heightened awareness of change and resulting concern with the future induced by eighteenth-century industrial and political revolutions. Also relevant, certainly, were eighteenth-century theories of the sublime that created an aesthetics favoring strange narratives. Increasing pressures from realistic fiction against setting fantastic narratives in the present must also have helped persuade some writers to set stories in the future. But pressure to locate strange adventures in the future was not merely negative, not merely pressure to avoid the present. The early eighteenth-century literary scene in England was distinctive for its extraordinary encouragement of formal experimentation: a positive trend that led, most notably in the hands of Swift, Pope, and Gay, to creation for satiric purposes of unusual works that parodied recognized genres and sometimes almost accidentally created viable new forms as well—as in the genesis of musical comedy by way of the *Beggar's Opera*. *Memoirs of the Twentieth Century*, and with it the tale of the future as a new form, is in part another such outcome of a literary climate strongly favoring innovation.

Amid these experiments Swift even wrote an acclaimed poem set in the near future: "Verses on the Death of Dr Swift."[22] Moreover, England's second book of futuristic fiction, *The Reign of George VI, 1900–1925*, starts by inviting comparison of its method with that of *Gulliver's Travels*. At first glance this may seem farfetched. Clearly Swift's masterpiece, whose action takes place in its first readers' immediate past starting with a voyage to Lilliput in 1699, cannot be regarded as a precedent for the particular novelty of imagining a future setting for narrated events. The anonymous author of *The Reign of George VI* seems instead to be remarking a more general resemblance of books that, like *Gulliver's Travels*, find new ways of disguising political commentary. *The Reign of George VI* is a jingoistic fantasy of future warfare conducted by an improbably efficient ideal ruler in a twentieth century that is just like the eigh-

FORMAL VARIATIONS

teenth century except for the presence of a King George who does everything successfully and finally even conquers France.[23] The preface explicitly invites readers to see both the hero-king and other characters, along with many imaginary twentieth-century events, as unmistakable allusions to eighteenth-century public life. The preface also remarks that *Gulliver's Travels* had similar intentions as a political roman à clef. For Swift the main device of disguise had been voyages to strange places. For *The Reign of George VI* the device is a "history . . . taken up at a what's-to-come period, and begun at an aera that will not begin these hundred years." Accordingly, we are told too in the preface, it is a work about which "it may be necessary to say a few words, whether critical or explanatory, whimsical or elaborate, shall be entirely submitted to the determination of the reader." Although the tone here betrays uncertainty about identification of the book's new form as well as about its prospects for success, there is no reason to dismiss as evidence either this statement or the author's equally hesitant conviction that *The Reign of George VI* would be regarded as a literary novelty whose form, at least, should be no less acceptable than that of *Gulliver's Travels:* "The modesty which is ever the companion of true merit, would by no means admit our author to think of a parallel between this history and the travels of Captain Gulliver.—Even to say he does not, is a sort of presumption, as it is tacitly aknowledging the possibility of such a comparison."[24] As a statement hinting at the merits of *The Reign of George VI*, this annoyingly coy remark is presumption indeed. Still it reveals unmistakably where its author looked for inspiration. It reveals too one major stimulus to invention of futuristic fiction in eighteenth-century England: not primarily technological change, or political and social revolutions, but literary experimentation of the kind manifested in Swift's magnificent formal variation on the theme of *Travels into Several Remote Nations of the World*.

Also emulating most immediately Swift's willingness to ring changes on existing genres, but setting out to vary the form of history rather than of travel literature by writing a parodic chronicle of the future for purposes of satire, Madden created a genre capable of wider uses than mere parody or even satire. Moreover, he was not only the first English writer of futuristic fiction but the first anywhere to note the importance for that form of transformations induced by science in accepted standards of probability. The coincidence is another telling clue to the origins of futuristic fiction. By the late seventeenth century, if comment on the acceleration of scientific discovery was something of a commonplace, there was nevertheless little understanding of the potential consequences for literature. Although Madden was not sufficiently talented to work out the implications of his insight in a successful narrative, *Memoirs of the Twentieth Century* provides unequivocal evidence that by 1733—almost a century before proliferation of futuristic fiction as an established genre—science had suggested the possibility of a new aesthetics, with corresponding forms such as the future history, based upon reversal of hitherto-accepted connections between plausibility and verisimilitude.

CHAPTER FOUR

From Utopia to Uchronia: *L'An 2440* and *Napoléon apocryphe*

When Charles Renouvier coined the term *uchronia* in 1857 he defined it as a utopia of past time, alluding to the new fictional genre of alternate history: works in which some crucial turning point is given a different, and from the author's viewpoint better, outcome.[1] The first uchronia of this kind was Louis Geoffroy's *Napoléon et la conquête du monde—1812 à 1832—Histoire de la monarchie universelle* [Paris, 1836]: (Napoleon and the conquest of the world—1812 to 1832—History of the universal monarchy). This is an account of Napoleon's victorious Russian campaign, his successful invasion of England, and the consequent establishment of a universal French monarchy that first governs all Europe and later takes over the entire world. Geoffroy provided a Bonapartist's nostalgic dream of a utopia that cannot ever exist because it did not exist. Renouvier published the completed version of his own alternate history as *Uchronie (l'Utopie dans l'histoire), esquisse historique apocryphe du développement de la civilisation européenne tel qu'il n'a pas été, tel qu'il aurait pu être* [Paris, 1876] (Uchronia [utopia in history], An apocryphal sketch of the development of European civilization not as it was but as it might have been). This is a complex uchronic history of an early Renaissance based upon the premise that Marcus Aurelius had been succeeded as emperor by Avidius Cassius instead of by Commodus, thus averting the misrule that contributed so much to eventual collapse of the Roman Empire and the long interval of stagnation that followed. Renouvier's main object as philosopher and historian was to employ uchronia as a means of speculating on lines of historical causation. Alternate history was for him primarily a way of identifying crucial turning points with potentially very different outcomes. Twentieth-century critics have used *uchronia* in referring to works of alternate history but also and more frequently to mean utopias set in the future. This usage mirrors the fact that futuristic uchronias have been more common. Their greater appeal for writers and readers has many justifications, but it has nevertheless obscured a significant affinity to alternate histories.

Here I wish to consider the books by Geoffroy and Louis-Sébastien Mercier that initiated both forms of uchronia. Mercier's *L'An 2440* is undeniably more important because of its wider influence on subsequent fiction. It is better known and has attracted increasing attention on both sides of the Channel and the Atlantic as futuristic fiction of all kinds has become more influential. On the other hand, there is neither an English translation of Geoffroy's intriguing book nor any discussion of it, so far as I know, in our language—and very little commentary even in French. Although critics have remarked many innovative features of *L'An 2440* while giving Mercier something like due applause, neither his dream of a perfect Paris nor Geoffroy's legend of Napoleon triumphant has been sufficiently considered in relation to such later uchronic masterpieces as *Nineteen Eighty-Four*. The power of much recent futuristic fiction, especially Orwell's, is better appreciated by comparison with the first efforts at uchronia. Important features of the form stand out very sharply when seen in their earliest manifestations and, once identified, can then be more easily recognized in other avatars. Alternate history, moreover, is closer to futuristic

FROM UTOPIA TO UCHRONIA

uchronia than to ordinary historical novels; consequently, it is best understood within the context of eighteenth- and early nineteenth-century movement toward viable forms of futuristic fiction.[2]

The eighteenth century, as Raymond Trousson pleasantly remarks, was the "golden age of utopia."[3] He rightly sees the invention of new utopian forms as one hallmark of that period and correctly identifies as the culmination of its experiments with this genre the transition to uchronia accomplished in 1771 by Louis-Sébastien Mercier's *L'An deux mille quatre cent quarante: Rêve s'il en fut jamais* (The year 2440: A dream if there ever was one). Published anonymously—Mercier did not sign its preface until the edition of 1791—this first utopia set in future time was one of the eighteenth century's most successful books. It was immediately banned in France, put on the Inquisition's list of forbidden books in 1773, and condemned in Madrid in 1778 as a blasphemous work whose distributors, if discovered, would be fined five hundred ducats and sentenced to six years in prison. *The Year 2440* had eleven editions in French between 1771 and 1799, as well as two English translations and translations into Dutch, Italian, and German. Investigation of its printing history leads Everett Wilkie to conclude that "there were 18,000 copies in print in three languages by the end of 1772 and 30,000 copies by the end of 1782, at which point it had spread thoroughly over Europe. . . . 63,000 copies had been printed by Mercier's death" in 1814. The book was less successful across the Atlantic, but a 1795 Philadelphia edition was "nevertheless, the first utopian novel published in North America."[4] George Washington and Thomas Jefferson owned copies of *The Year 2440*.

Its unnamed narrator tells of going to sleep one evening after a discussion with an Englishman about the shortcomings of Paris. The narrator then dreams that he wakes to find himself transformed into an old man who walks outside and discovers that he is in Paris still, but in the year 2440. Walking around the city, he finds everything far better than it was in his day: the Bastille, for example, is gone; the streets are wide and beautiful; everybody seems polite and happy. He discusses these and other transformations with a Parisian of the twenty-fifth century. Each chapter is devoted to some aspect of the future Paris that Mercier proposes as an ideal city in an ideal society—but not just a fictitious city in no real place. His utopia is given a local habitation, a real name, and a real if distant date. By thus putting utopia in the future it can be located at home, where readers live. Mercier's book ends with its narrator's excursion to the ruins of Versailles, where he talks with the penitent ghost of Louis XIV who says, weeping with regret, that he is condemned by divine justice to haunt the place symbolizing his misuse of power. The site is swarming with adders, reminiscent perhaps of Louis's courtiers. One of these snakes bites the narrator, who then, we are told in the book's last sentence, wakes up to find himself again in the eighteenth century. Mercier's implication is plain: the dream of a perfect Paris represents a good life; return to eighteenth-century reality after suffering a poisonous snakebite represents waking to a kind of death. This framework puts the venerable device of a dream-vision to strikingly new use as a vehicle for utopian speculation set in a specific secular future.

Even Frank and Fritzie Manuel are compelled to note Mercier's achievement, despite their preference for systematic exposition of utopian political theory over attempts to embody such ideas in imaginative fiction. They single out the eighteenth century as initiating "a major departure in Western utopia and utopian thought that occurred when good place, good state of consciousness, and good constitution were all translated to a good future time." But for the Manuels this new departure is puzzling on several accounts. To them the eighteenth century seems a bewildering interval during which "the utopian fantasy of Western society had lost an inner core," with the result that "in their attempt to fill the moral emptiness men conjured up a multiplicity of wild, even grotesque forms." Instead of "a single masterpiece," there is "a babel of uto-

FROM UTOPIA TO UCHRONIA

pias" dominated by "gigantic shapeless novels" appealing to "the growing assortment of female readers of all ages." Worse yet, "a magnificent dystopia, *Gulliver's Travels*, holds the place once occupied by More and Bacon." For these intellectual historians, there is also something strangely inexplicable in the development of uchronic forms so long before the nineteenth century stamped its seal of approval upon the idea of progress: "Turgot, Condorcet, and Mercier, the initiators in different styles of the new euchronia, in which good place gives way to good time, had the bad grace to be Enlightenment stalwarts, bred in its Parisian womb. In this instance nothing avails but to call the dialectical principle to the rescue: In the bosom of a utopia of agrarian calm felicity a utopia of endless, dynamic change in science and technology was born. . . . [It was] heralded with the awakened sleeper of Sébastien Mercier's *L'An 2440* and with the utopian projections in the Tenth Epoch of Condorcet's *Esquisse*." Appeal to "the dialectical principle," because it can always be invoked as a last resort to account for the unaccountable, explains nothing so far as causes are concerned. So too for the Manuels' observation that late eighteenth- and early nineteenth-century varieties of "un-Christian euchronia represented a resurgence of a strong millenarian, paradisaical, and apocalyptic current in secular form."[5] This is accurate—but only as a description of how secular uchronias may serve for the nonbeliever *some* of the same social and psychological purposes furthered by millenarian ideas among the faithful. Uchronias also serve very different purposes, ranging from sheer entertainment to serious modeling on probabilistic principles of possible futures in order to investigate (not predict) their characteristics. There is no connection that I have been able to discover between the ebb and flow of chiliastic thought and new uchronic forms of literature.[6] The question of causation is best set aside until we have a more complete description of those new forms.

I cite the Manuels' inability to explain on ideological grounds why utopia gives way to uchronia, because their diligent investigation of everything that may be called utopian writing over the past two thousand years of Western civilization gives special weight to their impression of the eighteenth century as the one period in all that time when the most prominent features of utopian literature are, first, "a multiplicity of wild, even grotesque forms" and, second, the emergence of uchronia. Perhaps these two features are themselves related, as my investigation of other early futuristic fiction leads me to suspect. As in the case of Madden's *Memoirs of the Twentieth Century*, I suggest starting with the hypothesis that a climate of exuberant formal experimentation and variation, whatever *its* ultimate causes (which were doubtless many and complex), was a necessary and perhaps even a sufficient condition for the impulse to set narratives, including utopias, in future time. Far more important in any case than speculation about causation is appreciation of exactly what each innovative text contributed to the potential repertoire of its genre. To understand Mercier's role, the key fact is that no previous book of futuristic fiction achieved anything like *The Year 2440*'s degree of connection to the flow of historical time.

Epigone's putative future century is more like an alternate history almost totally divorced from historical events known to its readers, as I have remarked. Madden's satire is so insistently directed at eighteenth-century institutions and customs that, despite its superior novelistic potential, *Memoirs of the Twentieth Century* invites very little attention to actual possibilities for the future development of European history. Its 1763 successor *The Reign of George VI* neither describes nor encourages any significant changes in politics or technology beyond elimination of corruption and inefficiency to bring about familiar advantages symbolized by the future triumphs of George VI as he leads England to domestic harmony and victory over France. Nor is there any convincing portrait of significant historical change in the tedious pages of an anonymous English publication of 1769 entitled *Private Letters from an American in England to his Friends in America*. The decadent, depopulated future England that is here described as a warning against unchecked emigration and various religious abuses in the reader's eighteenth century is less a dystopian vision of any particular future than another attempt at Madden's kind of temporal distancing for satiric purposes.

By contrast—a contrast far too easily taken for granted—Mercier's *The Year 2440* is the first book of prose fiction, and I believe also the first book of any kind, to adopt for its entire title a specific future date.[7] The implications of that choice, or any such choice, including Orwell's, are still insufficiently understood. Use of a date, especially a future date, for the title of a book will focus both expectation before reading and memories of the text afterwards in ways that cannot otherwise be attained. It will anchor the story in time. Of course that will not always ensure engagement with the reader's sense of history. But neither is even the most striking story enough in itself to guarantee a memorable degree of such engagement without the assistance of an apt title. It is difficult to imagine, for example, that *Nineteen Eighty-Four* could have achieved anything like its actual power as enduring commentary on the totalitarian currents of modern history had Orwell called it, as he first thought of doing, *The Last Man in Europe*.[8]

The usual distinction made by students of futuristic fiction is between near future and far future settings. The former, as Orwell's choice in 1948 of 1984, locates fictive action at a time that many readers might themselves hope (or fear) to see; far future settings are displaced beyond the reach of anything but imagination, as in the successive jumps by which H. G. Wells's Time Traveller goes first to and then far beyond A.D. 802,701, the date registered by the dial of his time machine when he arrives among the Eloi and Morlocks. Brian Stableford remarks of Mercier and his contemporaries that "in early futuristic fiction there is no trace of either the near future or the far future. . . . Events take place in the disconnected, generalized imaginative space distanced by its dating . . . not futures that anyone expected himself, or his children, to live in."[9] This is only partially true of Mercier's uchronia, which is detached from the immediate flow of time by placement in the twenty-fifth century without any detailed account of intervening events, yet connected to history in ways that previous utopian forms never achieved.

The disconnection from history is most apparent at first glance. Mercier's twenty-fifth century, as Stableford suggests, is certainly not designed as a plausible vision of any real future. In a strangely arbitrary way, *The Year 2440* is set exactly seven centuries after what the narrator mentions as the date of his birth in 1740, although its first readers in 1771 had no way of knowing this was also the real author's birthdate because Mercier published anonymously. For them in any case the action was located 669 years ahead, a figure that has no particular resonance except perhaps for its divergence from the number of the Beast (666) in Revelation 13. Even with knowledge of the author's birthdate as a reference point, there is no clear answer to the question of why Mercier chose seven centuries rather than eight, six, or ten. Nor would it have been clear why the seven centuries did not date from the year of publication or the preceding year. That might have seemed at least a little more logical by virtue of alluding to a public reference point shared, however diversely, by all initial readers. Mercier's very arbitrariness in the matter of choosing a future date linked most closely to the narrator's life makes his choice of a remote (though not inconceivably distant) future setting serve in the first place simply to disconnect readers' thoughts from the present.

The seemingly random date with at best a private rather than public significance also provides a faint aura of verisimilitude, as all random facts in literature do by reminding us that life is filled with incidents and moments that are only accidentally significant. But this verisimilitude counts for little. What Mercier conspicuously avoids is some future date, such as the year 2000 or 2666, with possible millenarian or other religious significance. He focuses attention upon the secular future. When Mercier's book was first translated into English in 1772, its translator was evidently disturbed by the apparently pointless choice of 2440, and rounded the figure off by changing Mercier's title to *Memoirs of the Year Two Thousand Five Hundred*. This is also arbitrary and avoids any hint of millenarian or other religious prophecy; but it has an English tidiness that is slightly at variance with Mercier's invitation to think about a future year notable primarily for its inexplicable ordinariness and, by the same token, its availability as a kind of empty receptacle for whatever the author chooses to put there.

Mercier fills that blank interval, too far ahead for contradiction of any reader's preconception about the future, only with his utopian dream of what a better Paris should be like, as both the narrative structure and subtitle of his book insist. This dream is not described as prophetic. It is not in any way fictively presented as a mystic experience that pretends to tear away the veil concealing the future. Whether or not we suppose the narration based upon a real dream recounted with ideologically appropriate embellishment by Mercier, he gives the dream in his story an obviously naturalistic explanation as just the kind of wish-fulfilling fantasy a Frenchman *would* be likely to have after enduring an Englishman's catalogue of the problems with life in Paris. The pretense of telling about a real dream is sporadically maintained in the text, as when the narrator remarks that giving all the details of his stroll around twenty-fifth-century Paris would be impossible because one always loses something when recollecting a dream (p. 113). Such loss is surely not the hallmark of dreams supposed to have supernaturally inspired prophetic force as visions of an actual future. Mercier thus encourages readers to take *The Year 2440* as an embodiment of hopes rather than expectations for the future.

The distinction is even more emphatically made in Mercier's dedication (to the year 2440), which dwells first on how splendid it might be actually to see instead of merely dream about wonders of the twenty-fifth century. Mercier winds up this dedication, which shapes every reader's view of the ensuing narration, with a grim (and perhaps truly prophetic) thought about the probable Paris of the future: "Delivered from the seductions of a favorable sleep, I fear, alas, I fear rather that your sun will only come to shine sadly on a shapeless pile of ashes and ruins."[10] This possibility alerts readers against the dangers of mistaking a utopian dream for prediction. Destruction of civilization seems more likely to Mercier than its perfection.

The ashes and ruins serving as images of what may well be the real future serve too as apt emblems for the moral wasteland of eighteenth-century France. As Mercier also remarks in the dedication, there prevails under the oppressive tyranny of its rulers a calm resembling that of tombs, in a land of walking cadavers where the neglected voice of philosophy cries as if in the midst of an immense desert (p. 78). The affinity of these images of ashes, ruins, tombs, corpses, and desert landscape, all standing for future and present moral desolation in the real world, underscores by contrast the fictive quality of Mercier's extended dream of an ideal Paris.

Attentive readers could not mistake that ideal for an account of what they or their descendants should really expect the future to bring. Quite the contrary. While yearning perhaps for better things, Mercier clearly warns at the outset of his book, readers can expect a dreary present to produce only a ruinous future. The pessimistic tone of Mercier's dedication is notable. Despite his imaginary demolition of the Bastille and other odious institutions of the old regime, he did not anticipate or call for a French revolution although, as I noted in chapter 3, he was happy enough after the event to claim in retrospect that he had been its prophet. The dedication that introduces and thus frames his outline of a more perfect France is designed to prevent readers from surrendering to what Mercier calls the attractions ("des prestiges") of his appealing dream. There is little temptation to suspend disbelief in what is so insistently presented as *only* a dream.

Distance between every reader's expectations for the real future and Mercier's dream of an ideal Paris is also maintained by the presence throughout Mercier's text of footnotes from the narrator in his waking moments, notes that most often contrast the beautiful Paris of his dream with the horrible realities of eighteenth-century life. These notes, as Bronislaw Baczko remarks, are situated outside the twenty-fifth-century time scheme and thus create for *The Year 2440* in effect a twofold narration that proceeds simultaneously along eighteenth- and twenty-fifth-century time tracks. This double temporal perspective further reinforces awareness of Mercier's fiction as such—an awareness, as Baczko also remarks, that ensures for *The Year 2440* not primarily the pleasures of verisimilitude that might attend realistic depiction of a probable future but the very different "pleasure of a game which depends on a permanent interchange between dream and reality."[11] This satisfaction is akin to what Michael Holquist describes as the pleasure experienced by those engaging in any form of utopian speculation that allows rearrangement according to the heart's desire of symbols standing for what cannot in reality be so neatly manipulated.[12] Mercier's uchronia, however, is connected to history in ways unattainable by previous players of the utopian game.

Without sacrificing the attractions of serious play, Mercier therefore removed utopia, as Raymond Trousson observes, from the category of gratuitous speculation to that of an instrument for investigating the future.[13] Such exploration of possible futures differs radically from prediction. Even today the distinction is too often misunderstood, especially by those who read all tales of the future as exercises in prediction and accordingly write off most futuristic fiction as nothing more than bad prophecy because it seldom provides an accurate forecast of the real future. Works that actually attempt to foretell the future, whether on a religious, scientific, or pseudoscientific basis, for the most part have a different purpose from speculative fictions investigating the future as Mercier's uchronia does. Forecasts invite more narrow judgment according to degrees of success or failure as prediction. Investigations of the future, on the other hand, including utopian speculations and other fiction set in future time, are more explicitly ways of considering present alternatives by working out their consequences. Prediction implies a fixed future, if only rhetorically for purposes of persuading readers to a course of action presented as advisable because it bows to the inevitable. Investigation of the future, whether in uchronic or other modes of futuristic fiction, assumes—and tacitly argues for—an open future with many possibilities.

The categories of predictive and investigative fictions of the future occasionally overlap. But without an effort to distinguish between them and between corresponding textual elements even in mixed cases, misreading (especially of nonpredictive futuristic fiction) is likely to result. Certainly despite Mercier's expedient post facto claim to have been the French Revolution's prophet, his intention for *The Year 2440* was investigative, not predictive.[14] Only thus could Mercier have liberated utopia from the futility of gratuitous speculation without subjecting it to the constraints imposed on works that actually aspire to the status of prophecy, even secular prophecy. Like so many Enlightenment thinkers, Mercier was more concerned with planning than with prophesying. He notes this preoccupation of his day, to which he contributed a new mode, by having the narrator of *The Year 2440* say to his twenty-fifth-century guide: "Everything has its time. Ours was that of innumerable projects; yours is that of implementation" (p. 108). As Alexandre Cioranescu remarks, Mercier's resort to future time changes utopia from a demonstration to a project: "the new temporal category of utopian writing transformed it automatically into a program."[15]

Other differences between Mercier's uchronia and previous modes of utopian fiction are precisely analyzed by Bronislaw Baczko in his superb study of Enlightenment utopians. For earlier spatial utopias taking the form of imaginary voyages, according to Baczko, the topographical rupture is also a rupture in time, because the journey to a distant land stands also for a passage from real history to an imaginary experience in a private time utterly cut off from the flow of events in the reader's world. The narrator who

FROM UTOPIA TO UCHRONIA

tells of his trip to some faraway utopian country perforce tells also, but more implicitly, of sailing away from the history of the real land from which he parted—which is also of course the reader's history, *our* history. The protagonist of such voyages encounters a country whose institutions have not been shaped by the events of our past and cannot shape our future. The utopian island thus entails an insular time as well as space. This time does not run parallel to that of our world, even if the voyage is set in a putative present, but is in effect superimposed upon it for our contemplation as a model of an utterly *other* and different history implying as well a future totally unlike that to which our past and present points the way. Voyage utopias therefore neither propose models for imitation nor suggest how a reorientation of actual past history, along the lines of the utopian society's development, would have been possible in our world. Mercier's resort to uchronia, on the other hand, initiates a new paradigm for utopian literature not only by setting action in a specific future chronologically connected to our past and present but even more crucially by characterizing that future as one belonging to progress and thus linked causally if not immediately to the reader's time. Despite Mercier's arbitrary choice of 2440 as the locus of his dream, its future is not just any future, even any conceivably better future. It is a future in which not only Paris but in fact (as Mercier's chapter on newspapers makes clear) the whole world has been improved by application of eighteenth-century ideals.[16] Adoption of these ideals throughout Mercier's twenty-fifth century transforms the uchronic utopia's time to that of universal history shaped by progress, not just French history. Finally, and equally important for the paradigm of uchronia initiated by *The Year 2440*, because its narrator finds a future in which the ideals of his own century have been realized, the fantastic quality of Mercier's book comes not from strange ideas but from a reversal of usual relationships between an imaginary utopian reality and ideas widely held in the eighteenth century by enlightened readers. An engaging air of fantasy, in other words, is created not by the ideals per se of Mercier's future society but by his account of their actualization in a familiar city, a real place which is thereby made strange.[17]

Baczko's precise identification of this new eighteenth-century paradigm of uchronia created by Mercier allows better understanding of temporal features in all varieties of utopian fiction. Appreciation of these formal attributes of futuristic uchronias should in particular dispel the widespread notion that all utopias (and dystopias), whether set in the past, present, or future, are, as Michael Holquist puts it, removed to an equally indeterminate "hypothetical or heuristic time . . . marked off from clock time just as surely as the time of a chess game."[18] Utopian time may always be to a degree heuristic, and certainly of a different order from clock time, but there are nevertheless crucial differences among the nature, purposes, and effects of such heuristic time in the various forms of utopia and uchronia. Displacement of utopia to the future was not simply a matter of replacing space with time as the distancing medium in the manner of a satire like *Memoirs of the Twentieth Century* or a fantasy of marvelous heroic action like *Epigone*. Rather, it was a matter of altering the nature of *relationships* between fictive space and time so that utopia could be linked to history instead of disconnected from it as in those imaginary-voyage utopias which remove speculation to a kind of lateral timestream that cannot intersect with our own.

In literature as in life, space and time cannot really be opposed, much less detached from each other for separate treatment, as Bakhtin has reminded us in arguing that the chronotope, the time-space relationship, is a fundamental determinant of all generic distinctions. In altering that relationship so drastically by displacing utopia to the future while keeping it in the reader's own country, Mercier connected utopia to history without sacrificing the playful quality of an overtly fictive (not predictive) game in which readers are invited to imagine events of their own future, shaped to the

FROM UTOPIA TO UCHRONIA

dictates of human desire and not simply arranged by the hand of providence or the blunders of human history.

The other variety of uchronia, alternate history showing events as they might have been if key episodes in the past had worked out differently, is a nineteenth-century development. Both forms of uchronia are nevertheless closely related, even though sixty-five years including the French Revolution, Waterloo, and all their consequences stand between *The Year 2440* and Geoffroy's tale of Napoleon's world-state—and even though Mercier's uchronia points attention to future possibilities, whereas Geoffroy's invites us to rethink past history by comparing what happened with what might have happened. An alternate past entails a different present along with prospects of a future unlike the one that will seem most probable on the basis of actual events. Indirectly therefore, but more or less insistently according to the degree and kind of their deviations from actual past events, narrations of an alternate history provoke speculation about futures that, no less than Mercier's twenty-fifth-century Paris, will seem utopian or dystopian departures from present and potential realities. Uchronias of alternate history, moreover, may also be more or less explicitly intended as portraits of possible futures presented for convenience as though their distinctive features had already come into being.

Renouvier's avowed purpose in *Uchronie*, for example, is partly to show that the rise of Christianity was a contingent, not inevitable, historical phenomenon and that it is possible to envision a secular society of the kind he believed would (and should) inevitably succeed the disappearance of Christianity at some point in the future. His uchronia is presented as a book of fictional alternate history written early in the seventeenth century by a victim of the Inquisition before his execution; it was supposedly smuggled out of prison by a friend who keeps the manuscript as a kind of family treasure to be preserved and hidden by his descendants until its publication is no longer dangerous. The author's friend explains to his son how the manuscript was acquired and remarks that, in reading its account of events as they would probably have unfolded for the Roman Empire had Christianity never achieved its actual ascendance, "the future centuries, which must follow the extinction of Christian faith, will seem to you like present centuries, and your thought will soar above time."[19] Thus Renouvier invites readers to see his uchronia of a political order based on reason, not faith, as the narration of an alternate past which is *also* in significant ways the picture of a likely utopian future. This in turn gives the subtitle of *Uchronie—Utopia in history*—very specific twofold meaning as a utopia located at once in a past that never was and, though only by implication, in the kind of future that Renouvier thought inevitable. Paradoxically, Renouvier sketches an imaginary past as a picture of what he believed would ultimately be the real future of relationships between church and state.

Geoffroy never explicitly presents *Napoleon and the Conquest of the World* as anything but an alternate past. To think of a nineteenth century in which all Napoleon's enterprises succeeded, however, is inevitably to think also of how different our present *and future* would be under those circumstances. Geoffroy encourages such speculation by incorporating into his account of the empire's growth from 1812 to Napoleon's death in 1832 a vision that readers of 1836 would clearly regard as similar to their inevitable technological, if not political, destiny. Chapters on the flourishing of the sciences under Napoleon's universal monarchy survey developments that by 1836 were among the conventional ingredients of speculation with a strong predictive component.[20]

Men have in effect been given wings, Geoffroy explains, thanks to development of dirigible balloons that can be steered "by a combination of magnetic forces with electricity."[21] Diverse applications of steam "create supernatural forces and increase one hundredfold those forces already known" (p. 338). Carriages moving "with lightning rapidity on iron tracks" cross the empire (presumably its

FROM UTOPIA TO UCHRONIA

European part) in less than two days (p. 338). There were "ships of ten, sixteen and twenty paddlewheels moved by numerous steam engines, crossing the ocean in less than a week to bring the Emperor's commands to America." Other steam engines power earthmovers that level mountains or dig canals. A vaguely specified combination of steam and explosive devices allows dissipation of clouds "by prodigious detonations," thus averting storms and controlling the weather (p. 338). Electric telegraphs link cities and continents so that Napoleon, Godlike, heard simultaneously "all the human words, knew all the events, sent his orders to the extremity of the globe, and held in his hand . . . all the strands of that magical network ['ce réseau magique'] which surrounded the earth" (p. 339). Medicine has become largely preventive thanks to discovery of vaccines for the majority of diseases. There is a cure for blindness. A technique has been developed for rendering sea water potable by "an electrical discharge combined with some other physical forces" (p. 340). The accelerating tempo of invention has resulted in what amounts to greater speed of thought itself, so that shorthand becomes the common notation and typewriters ("pianos d'écriture") are the usual instruments for recording as quickly as possible the new ideas that now abound.[22]

Napoleon has especially encouraged geography, his favorite science, to good effect. Cartographers accompany his armies to Asia and Africa. Voyages of exploration complete the great task of mapping the earth. En route home from his Asiatic campaign, Napoleon himself leads an expedition to the interior of Australia where he discovers an inland sea. Major remaining geographical mysteries are dispelled in 1828 when Vice Admiral Parry discovers the Northwest Passage and then leads a group of sailors from *le Conquérant* to the North Pole. Amid shouts of "Vive l'empereur, vive le monarque universel!" Parry of course plants the tricolor "in the name of God Omnipotent and his monarch on earth, Napoleon" (p. 344). Subjection of the entire world, indeed all of nature, to Napoleon—and to science—is symbolized by publication in 1831 of the lavishly printed eighteenth and final volume of *Le Grand Atlas impérial*.

Insofar as Geoffroy presents as alternate past history the kind of beneficent technological progress that would have seemed inevitable, give or take a few details, to many readers in 1836, he enhances the rhetorical appeal of his case for Napoleon. If only Napoleon's political ideals had prevailed, so runs the implied argument of Geoffroy's chapters on scientific advances under the universal monarchy, a better future of the sort we can now imagine would already be part of our present and immediate past. Had Napoleon only won the Russian campaign in reality as he does in Geoffroy's uchronic history, the future—a good future—would already be upon us. Time, as measured by material progress, would have accelerated. History in effect would have been speeded up rather than retarded as it has been, Geoffroy implies, by Napoleon's defeat. To whatever nostalgic appeal his book has for those Bonapartists who long for a return, replay, or continuation of the good old days of Napoleonic glory, Geoffroy skillfully adds another attraction by drawing upon widespread convictions about the likeliest technological advantages of the real future and associating them with the past as it might have been shaped by a victorious Napoleon.

In part, then, Geoffroy incorporates within his uchronia an already familiar cluster of images portraying the most probable shape of things to come as seen in speculative literature of various kinds by 1836: a world of medical advances; electric telegraphs; railroads; steam power applied to many other uses including rapid transatlantic ships; and dirigible travel across a well-mapped globe. This part of Geoffroy's utopian vision required little argument in favor of either its desirability or its probability *as a forecast of the future*. Its likelihood as a consequence of Napoleon's establishment of a world state is another matter. Whether his triumph could have thus accelerated arrival of the future in its technological aspect is certainly dubious, although the question becomes some-

FROM UTOPIA TO UCHRONIA

thing of a moot point within the context of *Napoleon and the Conquest of the World* taken as a whole—for reasons that will become apparent in considering Geoffroy's decision to give verisimilitude a lower priority than the marvelous. Before proceeding to examine the consequences of that decision, I want to stress that the uchronia of alternate history, from its inception in Geoffroy's book onwards, easily accommodates implicit or explicit visions of possible futures. Ability to do so is one of its strengths as well as a point of formal affinity with the kind of futuristic uchronia initiated by Mercier.

Despite his quickness to exploit available images of future progress, Geoffroy was no more interested in prediction per se than Mercier or most writers of early (or later) futuristic fiction. Like Mercier, Geoffroy was concerned with evaluating possibilities more with respect to their desirability as projects that could be realized in whole or in part than with respect to their actual *likelihood* as events that either will or *might have* come into existence by a given date in the immediate past or future. His purpose was to investigate the future, not to predict it. When Geoffroy published his book in 1836, eventual development of railroads, telegraphs, transatlantic steamers, dirigibles, and new vaccines could be taken for granted. They were mentioned less for purposes of prediction than in order to explore the advantages or disadvantages of a world in which such things are commonplace, and also in order to suggest the political conditions that favor or hinder actualization of such a world. Instead of confining himself to the pros and cons of a technological utopia and circumstances favoring its existence, however, Geoffroy subordinates its portrayal to his argument in favor of Napoleon's political ideals and makes imagery of a beneficent technocratic future serve as one emblem of those ideals to enhance their appeal. He also subordinates exploration of historical possibilities of all kinds (whether past or future) to a variety of other purposes that cannot very well coexist in a perfectly coherent work stressing verisimilitude but that certainly combine in this highly original book in fascinating, thought-provoking ways. That, arguably, is more than sufficient justification.

There are elements of political utopia and dystopia as Geoffroy outlines the organization of his ideal world state, while showing too some of its disadvantages. There is a portrait of Napoleon's personality as it was, extrapolated to imaginary situations where Geoffroy endeavors to show how the real Napoleon *would have* behaved. There is a devastating critique of him in Geoffroy's characterization of Napoleon as he *should* have been in order to succeed during and after the burning of Moscow. There is encouragement to speculate seriously about whether the Russian campaign, and with it world history, could have worked out differently in fact as well as in a wish-fulfilling fantasy. There is attention to ways that literature and the arts, no less than science and technology, might have flourished differently had Napoleon achieved a universal monarchy or even stable dominance in Europe. Thus many notable books published in the splendid decade between 1820 and 1830 under Napoleon's triumphant regime are listed in a chapter that catalogues such works as *Richelieu*, a historical novel "written in France and in French" by Sir Walter Scott; *Jupiter*, "the last and strangest work" by Goethe; and *Théorie de l'Esprit* by Stendhal—an excessively spiritual book which irritated Napoleon, who "exiled M. Beyle to Rome, where he completed his beautiful *History of Painting in Italy*, 1829, 12 vol. in–8" (pp. 157–58). There is an episode of the uncanny that nicely exploits many novelistic possibilities of what we would now call the science fictional premise of alternate universes: while sailing past St. Helena on his return from the victorious Asian campaign, Napoleon falls into an unaccountable depression followed by an equally mysterious rage, during which he orders his engineers to destroy the island with explosives.

More problematically, as a framework Geoffroy resorts to the marvelous in a manner reminiscent at once of heroic romance and futuristic fantasy. After victory in Russia, difficulties melt away as

FROM UTOPIA TO UCHRONIA

though by divine fiat. England is invaded with incredible ease. There is something almost magical about the collapse of English resistance after the battle of Cambridge on June 4, 1814: "In effect the moral force of England no longer existed. At the moment of landing on that unapproachable land, the charm was broken; she became an ordinary nation, bound to be vanquished" (pp. 73–74). During Napoleon's African expedition tribe after tribe surrenders to his armies without a fight, accepting his advent as the accomplishment of ancient prophecies and gladly burning before "the victorious cross" their idols, "of which the divinity is exhausted, they said" (p. 288). Mohammedan tribes decide to reject Islam "and their impetus was so violent that they came spontaneously to meet the French to renounce earlier [than necessary] their religion and their independence" (p. 288). The Turks, and with them Islam as a major religion, are disposed of with hardly more credibility.

After a French army is defeated by Sultan Mahmoud's forces at Acre on June 9, 1821, Napoleon quickly rallies his troops. At the battle of Jerusalem only eleven days later, he suffers no more than 1,500 French casualties while destroying 300,000 Turkish soldiers in a confrontation that marks the end of Islam both as a temporal power and as an ideology. Geoffroy makes this clash on the plains north of Jerusalem just beyond the Valley of Kidron seem like a continuation and culmination of some medieval romance. He describes the French army marching towards the scene displaying the cross alongside the tricolor and repeating as chorus the chants of priests, while in the background toll the church bells of Jerusalem: "Everything had taken on a religious aspect on that solemn day when, for the last time, the armies of Christ and of Mohammed came together to decide finally the destiny and the religion of the world, as formerly, in the time of Charles Martel, on the fields of Tours and Poitiers" (p. 219). In the ensuing lopsided victory it is not only the French who see the hand of God: "Western Asia was struck by the same thought at the news; she saw that the reign of Mohammed was over and that the new prophet *Buonaberdi*, as he was called, had come from the West" (p. 220). Napoleon is seen by Mohammedans, Geoffroy explains, as fulfillment of an Islamic tradition about the arrival of "another messiah" who, paradoxically, will complete their religion by bringing it to a close.[23]

Napoleon himself has fleeting regrets about this role as he returns next day in a pensive mood to contemplate a battlefield still littered with 300,000 corpses of the defeated army: "Before this debris of Mohammedanism he almost groaned at the destruction of that belief to which he had just given the last blow; he had no hatred of it, it was a sacrifice made more to his politics than to his opinion. One could even believe him pleased by that religion with its fanaticism, its oriental complexion, its enthusiasm, its energy, and its entire submission to a leader" (p. 222). Geoffroy leaves readers to make what they will of his nicely imagined reflection on Napoleon's sympathy for those aspects of Islam that (as Geoffroy characterizes it) seem political counterparts of a Bonapartist creed. The affinity as Geoffroy states it is far from flattering to either side. In any event, his Napoleon wastes little time on such musings but quickly dispatches an army under Eugene's command to destroy Medina and Mecca. Both cities are razed. Of the Kaaba only the black stone is saved for display at the Imperial Museum in Paris.

After recounting these events in detail, Geoffroy explains why they warrant so much space in his narrative: "If I have devoted long pages to destruction of the religion of Mohammed, it is because that event was the most important one in the Emperor's expeditions and conquests; Mohammedanism was the only force in the world able to fight against his: that destroyed, Napoleon was soon master of the earth" (p. 226). However implausible the collapse of Islam in favor of Bonapartism may seem as alternate history at the narrative level, Geoffroy's point as political analyst in giving that twist to his plot seems well taken: the real Napoleon's success depended in large measure upon inspiring a quasi-religious devotion to his cause. From this point Geoffroy extrapolates to the valid insight that a modern world state, *even aided by the most advanced*

FROM UTOPIA TO UCHRONIA

science and technology, could not endure while competing for loyalty with conflicting faiths of equally powerful appeal. To imagine Napoleon—or a ruler like Napoleon, or a technocratic world state of the kind prefigured by his ideas—entirely successful is almost inevitably to imagine, however fantastically, not only the disappearance of warring nationalisms but the abolition of all competing religions. Of course they are impossible to abolish as easily as Geoffroy's Napoleon does away with them. Hence Geoffroy's dilemma in writing his uchronia: to dramatize an accurate political insight about the power politics of modern empires that aspire to world dominance, he was compelled to sacrifice a large measure of plausibility in order to create an alternate history that could serve as an apt symbol for the nature of any nineteenth-century *or future* world state.

Accordingly in Geoffroy's narrative the air of fantasy is further augmented as all Protestants willingly reaffiliate themselves with Roman Catholicism, the established religion of Napoleon's universal monarchy. In 1814, at Geoffroy's conveniently arranged early death of Pius VII, Napoleon, after toying with the idea of making *himself* Pope but concluding that the time is not yet ripe to go quite so far, persuades the College of Cardinals to elect his uncle, Cardinal Fesch. This further collapses distinctions between religion and state by keeping matters in the family. Under the name Pope Clement XV, Fesch "took for his coat of arms the imperial eagle of France" (p. 89). Much later, after the disappearance of Islam, after the successful African and Asiatic campaigns, and after absorption of North America into the universal monarchy when the United States has disintegrated because of a civil war, the Jews convene at Warsaw what proves to be their final Sanhedrin. Swept along by the tides of history, they too see Napoleon as the fulfillment of their prophecies and decide to become Catholics, thus ending the long history of Judaism: "such was the empire of ideas which had seized the world, that those ancient beliefs, so profoundly anchored in the hearts of the Israelites, weakened and were cast adrift amidst the general enthusiasm: the times, they said, were come, the traditions fulfilled; and fear and admiration swept away the rest of their doubts" (pp. 324–25). There is only one dissenter: Rabbi Samuel Manasses of Strasbourg, who dies while denouncing the impending conversion. Whether he is struck down by God as a divine omen or merely collapses out of exasperation the narrator leaves for readers to decide, after explicitly noting the two possibilities (p. 325). Perhaps somewhat inconsistently, the erstwhile Jews who have embraced Catholicism are banned from Jerusalem (which they request for their city) as too newly converted to the faith to be entrusted with its holy places. But Napoleon allows them to end their long dispersion by establishing on Cypress (recently depopulated by a plague) "a new *Jerusalem* . . . called *New Judea,* which continued as a part of the French Empire subject to the imperial administration" (p. 326).

Departing still further from plausibility to establish Napoleon as a symbol for the quasi-religious forces underlying—or potentially underlying—the politics of modern empires, Geoffroy includes other episodes that have about them an even more fantastic air of heroic romance. Separated from his companions during a hunt, Napoleon encounters a lion which he tames by mere force of will, looking him in the eye and "overcoming him with that regard which until now had only been used to overcome men" (p. 248). When news of "this marvelous scene" spreads, "the Asiatics, who began to believe that Napoleon was a God, asked themselves 'is this merely a man, whom lions obey?'" (p. 251). There are interludes of Napoleon as archaeologist almost magically dispelling time's mysteries and thus in effect conquering all of the past and uniting it too with his empire in the present world. He commands his engineers to divert the Tiber, from whose bed innumerable Roman treasures *in perfect condition* are recovered for shipment to museums in Paris, where the glory of Rome is thus reconstituted for consolidation into the universal monarchy.

Even more fantastically, Napoleon directs the excavation and

FROM UTOPIA TO UCHRONIA

restoration of Babylon. Hieroglyphic tablets there, when deciphered, not only confirm biblical accounts of antediluvian events but also provide information omitted in the Bible, thus in effect making Napoleon an instrument of revelation: on the tablets are "antediluvian writings and traditions which provide with certainty the history of the earliest times of the world, confounding the [geological] systems, and confirming while completing the narrations of the Sacred Books" (p. 240). Napoleon next amazes his own skeptical archaeologists by discovering foundations from the Tower of Babel, which is then excavated. During another campaign he finds two living unicorns. These, more prosaically, turn out to be merely a species of antelope with intertwined horns. But when Napoleon orders them shipped to France they are successfully bred to become useful as well as beautiful additions to the stock of domesticated animals: "Their behavior is gentle, they are easy to tame, and we have already seen applied to industry and luxury the force of this gracious animal, of which the elegant proportions approximate those of the horse, to which in some respects it is preferable" (p. 254). As with the ruins of Babylon and the Tower of Babel, in bringing unicorns to France Napoleon resembles a magician who transforms legend into reality.

In these episodes Napoleon's accomplishments have an aura of the supernatural, although his methods are natural, indeed scientific—archaeological excavation and animal husbandry. So too for the related episode in Africa when "history itself, so to speak, was rediscovered" (p. 293): at the oasis of Theot in the Libyan desert, Napoleon's army finds a colony of Egyptian priests which has been isolated for over three thousand years and has preserved, unaltered, since the Pharaohs "the Egyptian language, religion, and history . . . ; they handed over the old secrets of the hieroglyphics and other Egyptian languages, and with that discovery the mysterious veils fell away" (p. 293). In Italy, Mexico, and elsewhere, other astonishing archaeological finds proliferate under the universal monarchy: "Bizarre discoveries! Singular mummies of cities from other times, which Providence had preserved in their tombs so that all past ages could, so to speak, be witnesses to the spectacle of the universal monarchy!" (p. 346). Most incredibly of all, at the Oasis of Boulma in Africa, Napoleon's soldiers find some of Shem's descendants who have been living in isolation ever since the Flood. They provide living records that go back to the very beginning, "preserving the traditions, the customs, and the language of the first men" (p. 346). Whether demystifying legends about unicorns or confirming the truth of what skeptics regard as only biblical myths, Napoleon is by such actions himself metamorphosed from a historical figure to the hero of his own myth. Geoffroy willingly sacrifices verisimilitude in order to build a messianic myth for the modern world upon the legend of Napoleon, as it had taken shape by 1836.

Accordingly for the second edition in 1841, Geoffroy provided a new title, *Napoléon apocryphe*, that wittily suggests both the deliberately fictional status of his story and its pretensions to consideration alongside histories of Napoleon that Bonapartists might take for something akin to sacred truths. In addition to that ambiguous title with its simultaneously self-deprecating and self-aggrandizing comparison of the book to parts of Scripture that may or may not be accepted as canonical and truthful depending on one's faith, Geoffroy provides another more extensive opportunity for readers to play a game of simultaneously reversing and declining to reverse accepted relationships between truth and fiction. As the first chapter of Book Five, after some two hundred previous pages taking Napoleon from victory in Russia to the glorious end of his Asiatic campaign with the capitulation of China and Japan, Geoffroy interrupts his narrative to denounce "A Would-be History."

First the narrator remarks that, while he is almost crushed under the weight of "that glorious and truthful history" he has been recounting, he can at least pause in the midst of his enterprise to do himself the justice of saying that he has always considered the honor of his country and the glory of his emperor, omitting nothing

FROM UTOPIA TO UCHRONIA

that enhanced them. For that purpose he had only to look toward the past and describe what he saw, thus producing a monumental work so filled, as he notes earlier on the same page, with "innumerable victories, actions so brilliant and things so marvelous, that history tends to get lost" in trying to sort them all out for narration (p. 263). How then, he asks rhetorically, could he refrain from expressing his indignation at the culpable novelist ("romancier coupable") who took for his task the work of insulting a great man and debasing his country by fashioning for posterity an "ignoble and detestable invention of which the shame should fall back upon its author" (p. 264)? Readers will have guessed, Geoffroy says, that he is about to comment on "that fabulous history of France from the capture of Moscow to our days, that history, accepted by some incomprehensible caprice, that one finds everywhere in all forms, and which is so widespread and well known ["répandue"] that in the centuries to come posterity will wonder if that novel is not true history" (p. 264). To "flog" this "odious fable" Geoffroy will suspend his own "great history" between its account of Asia, which has just fallen to Napoleon, and an account of "the rest of the world, which will fall in its turn"; he will devote the interlude to showing where "the anonymous author of that lie has turned his imagination" (p. 264). There follows a recapitulation of French history as in our world it unfolded from the burning of Moscow to Napoleon's actual death in 1821.

Amid that summary of what readers will perforce accept as real events, Geoffroy interjects comments made as though he were here recapitulating the plot of a bad historical novel: a story that misrepresents the past, is tedious, is insulting to France, and, worst of all, is *improbable*. "Horrible impostures!" he exclaims, while summing up the account of Prussia's betrayal of Napoleon in 1813 by joining Russia and Austria to form a triple alliance that successfully invaded France, even reaching Paris. Before proceeding, he exclaims even more vehemently: "My God! But all this is as false as it is absurd!" (p. 265). Resuming his summary, Geoffroy describes Napoleon's banishment to Elba and the provision of caretakers for a dormant France through a so-called restoration of the "stale race of kings who had been away from France for twenty years." Once the word *restoration* had been chosen, Geoffroy notes, the author of this bad novel, "who was doubtless pleased" by the term, set about applying it to events in neighboring kingdoms such as Spain, where Ferdinand too has his "restoration" in chasing out Joseph (p. 266). Geoffroy concedes that nevertheless "the author, in the middle of this culpable novel ['ce coupable roman'], did hit upon one sufficiently great thing": Napoleon's return to France in March 1815, where after a twenty-day journey amid universal acclamations he arrives in Paris to sleep in the hastily departed king's still-warm bed and wake on the morning of March 21 to find himself once again emperor of France. "But as if that great invention had exhausted him, the author immediately falters and falls again to the greatest depths; he does not know how to create anything but horrible disasters" (p. 266). He invents the baleful name of Waterloo, in which he immolates a hundred thousand Frenchmen, "and unable to imagine anything new after that infamy," his story simply repeats itself. He refashions the same calumnies: another invasion of France by its enemies; more "restorations"; and the casting away of Napoleon, now for the last time, to another "tiny island in the ocean, two thousand miles from Europe, where the great man dies several years later of a stomach tumor." This, Geoffroy exclaims with indignation, is what "that liar has made of Napoleon and of history." Even more unaccountably, the story has been accepted everywhere so uncritically ("avec complaisance") as to give it "an appearance of reality," despite its unbelievable confusion of absurdity and shame ("cette confusion inouïe d'absurdité et de honte," pp. 266–67). Geoffroy's irony here is obvious and certainly amusing as a way of expressing distaste for a history that ardent Bonapartists like himself could only take as a dreary tale with an utterly unsatisfactory denouement.

There are, however, more subtle purposes to Geoffroy's game of

FROM UTOPIA TO UCHRONIA

treating reality as fiction and applying to it the criteria by which novels are judged. In remarking the unbelievable absurdity of Napoleon's actual end, along with its tediously repetitious as well as unimaginative banishments to little islands, Geoffroy raises the issues of probability and verisimilitude in ways that stress the *improbability* of real life and, conversely, the verisimilitude of events in fiction that may likewise seem improbable. Samuel Madden made the same point in a different context, as I noted in chapter 3. Whereas *Memoirs of the Twentieth Century* mainly notes the impact of scientific progress in altering accepted notions of verisimilitude when thinking about the future, Geoffroy is influenced by the astonishing political events following the French Revolution. It is not just change (scientific, technological, or social) that impresses both men, however, but rather the apparently unpredictable, and hence improbable, nature of change. By implication, this conspicuous improbability of so many real events gives wider latitude for literary forms—futuristic fiction and alternate history most immediately—that cast aside canons of verisimilitude enforced by realistic novels about ordinary present-day life in the tradition of Defoe, Richardson, and their successors.

When Geoffroy stresses the incredibility of Napoleon's actual career, he also invites readers to consider his fantasy of a *successful* Napoleon as perhaps only a shade more unbelievable than the amazing true account of his improbable failure. This is to imply greater verisimilitude for *Napoleon and the Conquest of the World* than it might otherwise claim. Even by implication Geoffroy does not altogether equate the degree of the probability to be accorded his two parallel tales, one of a triumphant Napoleon told at length and one of a defeated Napoleon recapitulated briefly in the book but familiar in more detail to most of its readers. There are simply too many utterly astonishing events in Geoffroy's story of history as it should have been for his tale to be considered of exactly the same likelihood as the real Napoleon's improbable career, even after readers have duly noted that accounts of his actual downfall only have an air of verisimilitude because we *do* accept them for true rather than vice versa. Geoffroy's emphasis on the improbability of reality does serve, however, to lessen the discrepancy between fictional and factual narratives in a way that legitimates both alternate history as a form and its resort to the marvelous.

Most immediately, Geoffroy's critique of reality as though it were a badly written novel riddled with improbabilities allows for severe criticism of the actual Napoleon within a work that is also designed to glorify him. The "author" of the wretched novel everywhere accepted for true history is never named. But Geoffroy implies that insofar as the absurd tale of defeat can be attributed to any one person, its author is Napoleon. He more than anyone is responsible for what happened—the plot of the bad novel. Events in that dismal story of the emperor's downfall take inexplicable and unlikely turns for the worse, Geoffroy suggests, at just those points where Napoleon for no plausible reason acts out of character in ways that astute readers of the "culpable novel" can only criticize as lacking in verisimilitude. Thus when in the miserable novel masquerading as history Moscow burns, "Napoleon—the man of activity and genius—can find nothing better to do than immobilize himself for thirty-five whole days to kick around ashes from the burnt city" (p. 264). Geoffroy clearly objects to the sheer improbability of such paralysis as well as to its disastrous consequences. The story then proceeds, Geoffroy remarks with equally withering sarcasm, "as if the emperor had done so many things en route only in order to witness this distant fire, retreating soon afterwards towards France." While a terrible catastrophe next overtakes his army amid the Russian snows "the emperor, wrapping himself in his fur coat, leaves his soldiers frozen and dying to go at top speed back to Paris" (pp. 264–65). There could hardly be a more damning critique of Napoleon's actual conduct during the Russian campaign.

By contrast with histories of what Geoffroy here condemns as improbably uncharacteristic as well as ignoble actions, his own account of the burning of Moscow begins his book with a response by Napoleon that readers can now see as having greater verisimilitude than what really happened, because it is more in keeping with the personality of Napoleon the man of action and genius: a decisive March toward St. Petersburg and defeat of the Russian army at the battle of Novgorod. Geoffroy's chapter on the false history accepted as truth ends with an emphatic assertion that "it is the duty of a true historian to repudiate all these fables ['contes'], and to say loudly to the world that such history is not history, that Napoleon not the true Napoleon" (p. 267). This statement, carefully placed in a chapter which serves as preface for the last part of *Napoleon and the Conquest of the World*, the part containing three chapters on "Unity" outlining most explicitly the advantages of a universal monarchy, offers a key to Geoffroy's intentions. His uchronia is not designed primarily as a study of what really might have resulted from other possible decisions at crucial moments in history—although his readers are invited to consider a few such possibilities, mainly at the outset of the tale before its events have so totally diverged from actual history as to render comparisons of cause and effect difficult. Instead, *Napoleon and the Conquest of the World*, even in its most extreme glorification of Geoffroy's hero, is largely a commentary on the disparity between Napoleon as he finally was and Napoleon as he should ideally have been, given his personality and goals.

The central question for Geoffroy accordingly becomes not merely how Napoleon might have achieved success toward the end of his career by acting more in consonance with his character as manifested to better effect in the heady days before his Russian campaign, or even what consequences that success might actually have had. His main question is how the world might have benefited—or might yet benefit—from pushing to their logical extremes and *then* implementing Napoleon's plans for a new political order. Geoffroy invites his readers to think about "the true Napoleon" as a kind of platonic ideal never fully embodied in the real Napoleon. Directly or indirectly throughout his narrative, Geoffroy returns to the issue of those Napoleonic plans—what they were and ideally should have been if perfectly articulated and then totally implemented by "the true Napoleon," not the disappointing man who ultimately betrayed himself as well as his followers. Consequently the first uchronia of alternate history is, like Mercier's futuristic uchronia, very much intended as a new kind of utopia.

Because *Napoleon and the Conquest of the World* shows a utopia that ought to have been created by an ideal Napoleon, not just Europe as it ideally might have been if the real Napoleon had succeeded, Geoffroy introduces episodes that sacrifice much of the verisimilitude he might otherwise have achieved by recourse to alternate history in a work that also points out so cleverly the implausibility of real history, at least where it concerned Napoleon. This difficulty, if it is a difficulty, is not inevitable in uchronias of alternate history. Even in Geoffroy's case the resulting problems are perhaps more bothersome to those applying standards derived from other forms such as the realistic novel or its counterpart the nineteenth-century historical novel than to readers content to enjoy on its own terms Geoffroy's ambitious attempt to depict at once a complex departure from the actual outcome of the Napoleonic wars, a departure from the shortcomings of Napoleon as he really was, and a departure from many limitations of the world as it really is. For those who like fantasy—and why should one not?—the gains may outweigh anything lost by Geoffroy's departures from credibility. Without taking sides on this issue, I merely wish to stress that uchronias of alternate history lend themselves as readily to realism as to fantasy. Geoffroy's resort to the fantastic was not made necessary by the form he so brilliantly invented.

As in most previous utopias, the question of how exactly the ideal society could be (or could have been) brought into existence attracts less attention than outlining details of a fully achieved utopia in its perfected state. The very form of alternate history nevertheless enforces markedly greater concern with the mechanics of creating utopia than is necessary in either conventional voyage utopias or even futuristic uchronias of the kind inaugurated by Mercier.

If everything narrated is put far enough into the future, questions about the evolution of a utopian society can easily be left unanswered or vague, as in *L'An 2440*. Fictive alterations of known history to produce a different *present* from the one in which readers live will encounter greater resistance from the sheer weight of facts that readers will know about their world—facts they will have to set aside imaginatively in order to accept the fiction as anything other than outright fantasy with *no* possible application to the real world at *any* time in its history. By comparison, the future is empty and thus more easily accepted as the author decides to present it. Except perhaps for works set only a few months or years ahead, there is never a competing future that must inevitably be taken as already endowed with an unalterable existence precluding the one envisioned. Even to the imagination, past events are more like immovable objects. For writers of alternate history, and certainly for Geoffroy, there results a potentially bothersome paradox. More than other kinds of utopian fiction, the uchronia of alternate history necessitates relatively detailed portrayal of the means by which a utopia may be created; but at the same time it is harder to use alternate histories for utopian purposes of speculation about a radically different society while *also* providing a convincing account of the ideal society's genesis.

That paradox need not always be so troublesome as it is in *Napoleon and the Conquest of the World*. To portray an alternative past or present utopian society that is sufficiently different from known reality to seem significantly better, one may start as Renouvier did in the very distant past in order to show plausibly how the gradual accretion of changes could have resulted in a markedly different present. Or one may start in the immediate past and retain plausibility by confining changes to matters that will leave the altered present far short of radically utopian (or for that matter dystopian) differences from the real present. But a uchronia of immediate past history that portrays an altogether ideal society rather than mainly attempting to show how the close past might have varied to produce changes that will nonetheless fall short of achieving utopian perfection risks sacrificing much of the verisimilitude otherwise available to the form. Geoffroy chose to minimize the credibility of his alternate history not only by creating a mythic hero of almost superhuman powers but also by accelerating changes in order to bring about his utopia in what seems an unacceptably brief interval.

Both that decision and Geoffroy's related decision to show a utopian world unified in ways arguably beyond the reach of any historical changes, no matter how protracted, have consequences that should be apparent in even this brief sketch of the ideal society for which he argued by inventing alternate history as a rhetorical device. Geoffroy's universal monarchy deserves more attention than it has received from historians of utopian thought. It also deserves to be read on its own account as a story with more intriguing details than I can do justice to here. I hope others will seek it out now that a Tallandier edition has again made it accessible. For my purposes of concern with literary forms rather than the transmission of ideas, however, it may suffice to close this discussion by showing how Geoffroy qualifies his utopia in ways that anticipate the French dystopian tradition inaugurated in 1846 by Emile Souvestre's *Le Monde tel qu'il sera* (The world as it will be).[24] Geoffroy's technocracy has features that are clearly a step down the path to Orwell's Oceania. Geoffroy's ideal Napoleon is an ambiguous messiah who prefigures Big Brother.

Utopian features predominate in Geoffroy's alternate past, to be sure. After Napoleon's Asiatic campaign the world is at last unified under one government. Consequently, international politics as previously understood is abolished. Different countries still exist for administrative purposes but are either part of the French Empire or linked to it in a feudal relationship of subservience. Because war is caused by the existence of competing independent states, there is no more war. The universal monarchy brings universal peace. There is a uniform code of laws and a uniform system of weights and measures. One language—French, of course—is adopted everywhere as the official language of public transactions in business dealings, the law courts, and the legislatures. It is also the language for all religious services: "The French Language was thenceforward the language of God, as it was of the world."[25] It is learned by everybody—with difficulty at first by adults outside France but easily enough by their children in school, who then talk French at home too, so that soon French replaces all other languages even in private relationships. Education is provided in free public schools available alike to poor and rich children. After defeat of Mediterranean pirates, over two million poor French families eagerly emigrate to North Africa where they establish a thriving colony and prosper. Because religious differences are abolished when Roman Catholicism is universally accepted in place of all other creeds, there is no more bigotry or religious conflict.

Under the universal monarchy, scientific research is stimulated to produce advances beyond the ones that comprised in Geoffroy's day a widely accepted vision of technological progress expected in the relatively close future. In June 1819, for example, Bichat, Corvisart, and Lagrange publish their great work *Discovery of Life and Death in Man and the Organized Beings*. This report of experiments demonstrating the exact galvanic and magnetic basis of the vital force has far-reaching philosophical consequences. It establishes on a scientific basis the unity of all life, ranging from "that of an insect to that of a sun and its enslaved planets" (p. 137). Scientific and mystical ideas are here reconciled in a work that Geoffroy says will be the ornament of its age by virtue of revealing "the system of man just as Newton revealed the system of the universe"—thereby teaching inhabitants of the earth more about the divine intelligence (p. 137). Geoffroy's mysticism clearly underlies the appeal that ideas of unity (political, social, or metaphysical) have for him in shaping a utopia characterized at every level by abolition of differences.

Napoleon even convenes a scientific congress to inquire whether racial differences, which cause so many controversies, can be abolished by mathematically calculated arrangement of marriages and, if so, how many generations would be required thus to unify biologically the human race. He is haunted by the idea of fighting against nature itself by doing away with "those varieties of races and colors . . . forms so diverse, colored white, yellow, and black, with intelligences and thoughts so contrary. . . . He would have made of this humanity a single man" (p. 333). At first stunned by such an unexpected question, the scientists eventually report that seven generations would be sufficient but that the project could not be implemented. There would be too much resistance. Napoleon gives up the scheme, though regretfully. It is almost the only imaginable form of unity which Geoffroy does not attempt to envision as an accomplished fact under the universal monarchy.

However impracticable or distasteful Geoffroy's vision may be, it is not contemptible. Abolition of war, abolition of religious disputes, and abolition of racial discord are noble goals. Equally noble is the idea of a planet whose inhabitants enjoy a uniform code of justice along with universal education, a uniform system of weights and measures, and scientific advances that lead to such benefits as high-speed transportation, rapid communication, and eradication of most diseases. It is the means to these utopian ideals that will of course seem odious to readers who do not share Geoffroy's Bonapartist enthusiasim for a military dictatorship. But Geoffroy, to do him justice, also points explicitly to the dystopian aspects of such a society. Moreover, he does so in ways that should gain *Napoleon and the Conquest of the World* more recognition alongside early French dystopias as a farsighted analysis of just that combination of advanced technology, quasi-religious zeal for a

FROM UTOPIA TO UCHRONIA

leader or a cause, and imperialist ambition which has too often since 1800 made the modern state so peculiarly horrifying.

Thus even amid the fantasy of Napoleonic success on a scale far beyond the most optimistic plans ever entertained by Napoleon himself, Geoffroy does not allow readers an easy decision about the merits of a universal monarchy. For example, after remarking that international politics as we know it in a world of separate nations had been abolished, rendering meaningless the very word *politics* ("le mot politique n'était plus qu'un non-sens"), Geoffroy adds this disquieting corollary: "There was indeed a politics, permitted only to the emperor: that was the *police*, an immense network enveloping the universe, which everybody sensed, and which no one dared to notice."[26] The universal monarchy is very much a police state.

Towards the end of Geoffroy's narrative, General Oudet, leader of a small group of dissident officers, contrives to meet alone with Napoleon, draws a pistol, and accuses the emperor of being a tyrant who has destroyed liberty. Napoleon is unmoved, calmly offering Oudet the chance of retirement from the army "to go live somewhere in freedom and tranquillity." Oudet responds indignantly that there is no corner of the earth left where even such private freedom is possible: "Tell me if there is a wave in the oceans which is not entirely yours? Tell me if there is a bit of air left in the atmosphere that is not poisoned by your universal despotism!" Napoleon's response to these words is "animated" but only "with inner joy; he had never appreciated better his power than in that imprecation by an enemy, and a smile forced its way to his mouth." After again denouncing Napoleon, Oudet kills himself in despair at reforming or abolishing the world state. Remarking only that Oudet was brave but lunatic, Napoleon orders the corpse taken away. On the night of his funeral, five soldiers who conspired with Oudet commit suicide at his grave. With their end, Geoffroy winds up this chapter with a chilling eloquence worthy of Orwell: "there was to be found on the earth neither man nor word to express the idea of liberty" (pp. 318–22). So much for the ideals of the French Revolution. Geoffroy makes readers balance against their loss the abolition of history's bloodbaths. Is peace a fair trade for liberty? To his credit, the nostalgic Bonapartist did not evade this question.

Along the entire spectrum ranging from wholly fantastic episodes to utterly realistic scenarios, Geoffroy provides tantalizing possibilities to contemplate: what if Napoleon *had* defeated the Russians, the British, and then eventually the Turks, the Chinese, and the Japanese—thus establishing a world empire that could take over North America as well, after the United States had torn itself apart in civil war? What if Moslems, Jews, and Protestants had all responded to Napoleon's victories by embracing Catholicism, thus abolishing religious differences? Geoffroy's narrative provides answers that even at their most fantastic—perhaps especially at their most fantastic—challenge every reader to the interesting mental exercise of thinking about how, or whether, such events could actually have taken place as well as thinking about their desirability. Some are easily enough dismissed from serious consideration; others much less so than these highlights may suggest. More than most kinds of fiction or nonfiction, the uchronia of alternate history, the form invented by Geoffroy, constantly compels readers to consider the actual boundaries of the possible and the probable.

Mere narration of a different history from the one we know enforces that consideration. So does the frequent interweaving of real and imaginary events. As even my few examples from Geoffroy may have suggested, readers must be constantly alert for small as well as large departures from, or intrusions of, familiar history. Geoffroy invites us to think also about the more utopian question of whether such a universal monarchy as he depicts *would have been* a good thing. In an alternate history this issue becomes far more complex than the usual utopian invitation to consider whether a particular imaginary government *would be* a good thing. Readers must compare the real past with the fictional past to decide which, on balance, seems best. Geoffroy's readers must also consider the ques-

FROM UTOPIA TO UCHRONIA

tion of desirability partly with reference to a hypothetical future, because if the universal monarchy had come into existence it would be continuing past the reader's present into an alternate future. For this reason too, Geoffroy's uchronia of alternate history and Mercier's uchronia of future history are significantly related. Both forms compel serious speculation about the possibilities of shaping real events. Both prevent the game of imagining past or future utopias from being played without attention to the historical realities that constrain or facilitate actual implementation of utopian ideals.

The interchange between dream and reality, to borrow Baczko's useful and beautiful phrase, acquires remarkable prominence in both forms of uchronia (although not the same prominence in every instance). Both forms depend for their existence upon artistic license to depart radically from representation of present time without merely divagating to previous kinds of fictional time. Uchronias of future and alternate past history are among the modern world's most significant new ways of imagining human temporal relationships. Their originality is striking. Neither form of uchronia resorts to the lateral time of voyage utopias disconnected from the flow of events in our world. Neither form resorts to allegorical sequences locked in one-to-one relationship with the rhythm of human history. Neither form resorts to the mythic past of fabulous history and epic or to the "once-upon-a-time" in so many varieties of romance where flight to the temporal indeterminacy of dreamscapes overwhelms any possibility of meaningful application of the dream as a model for improvement of our waking lives. Before the emergence of futuristic fiction in the eighteenth century, a phenomenon most signally marked by Mercier's achievement, there was no precedent for any form allowing radical displacement of fictional time away from the present while also allowing for insistent speculative connection of the imagined time to the possible shapes of real history.

The absence of alternate past histories from Western literature before 1836 is as striking as the total absence of futuristic fiction before 1659 when, significantly, Jacques Guttin putatively placed a work in the future while actually writing a work that is closer to a uchronia of the way France might have developed, and might continue to develop, if its early history had been different. Apart from *Epigone*, even embryonic uchronias of past history are scarce before the form was fully realized by Geoffroy. Buried in Delisle De Sales's twelve-volume *Ma République* (1791), there is a uchronic chapter suggesting how things might have gone during the French revolution had Louis XVI behaved differently in the days just before the Tennis Court Oath. Amid the dystopian fantasies of *Gulliver's Travels* Swift places (bk. 3, ch. 7) an "Island of *Sorcerers* or *Magicians*," where ancient and modern history is "corrected"—that is to say, retold with differences—by summoning up the spirits of past notables such as Alexander the Great to tell what really happened. This chapter too is only embryonically uchronic in form. But its presence is notable in an eighteenth-century dystopia from the pen of the only English poet in that era who also set a poem in the future, albeit a near future: *Verses on the Death of Dr. Swift*. Initially a kind of futuristic fiction in verse, this poem has the interesting property of having partly switched genres with Swift's actual death. It subsequently has taken on many attributes of a uchronia of alternate history to the extent that its readers must wonder how actual responses to Swift's death corresponded to the fictional responses in the poem. Apart from such scattered efforts, however, nothing like the uchronia of alternate history existed before *Napoleon and the Conquest of the World*. Nor has the form much flourished subsequently, although it includes a few superb efforts from writers as diverse as Philip K. Dick and Winston Churchill.[27]

The greatest work to combine features of futuristic and alternate past uchronias is *Nineteen Eighty-Four*. But its dystopian form is such an unmistakable source of power that other equally crucial attributes of Orwell's novel, especially its uchronic features, have been neglected. The hideous world that Orwell depicts is quite bad enough on its own terms to be memorable. By the end of the book

FROM UTOPIA TO UCHRONIA

every reader is surely tempted to accept O'Brien's advice to Winston Smith: "If you want a picture of the future, imagine a boot stamping on a human face—forever."[28] Echoes of past and present realities in Orwell's story give this image a chilling plausibility. And *Nineteen Eighty-Four* is all the more striking by virtue of its departure from the long-established utopian convention of endeavoring to invent societies that are better than those we know in the real world.

All varieties of utopia, even those with whose premises we disagree, are inherently comforting to the extent that as a genre they are affirmations of the consoling possibility that life might be better. Dystopias, conversely, are disturbing negations of that possibility not only because they show dismal worlds where life is even worse than in ours but because they displace and deny that form—the utopia—which assures us that better things are at least imaginable. Orwell makes the contrast explicit within his text when O'Brien says to Winston Smith while brainwashing him: "Do you begin to see, then, what kind of world we are creating? It is the exact opposite of the stupid hedonistic utopias that the old reformers imagined."[29] Orwell, like Zamyatin, Huxley, and the other masters of political nightmare, gains much power by inviting us to contemplate the doubly horrifying prospect of an imagined world opposed to all our dreams of perfection and a real world where we cannot even momentarily lose ourselves in utopian fantasies of perfectibility: a world whose books have created a universe of discourse where dystopias are replacing their utopian ancestors after a kind of Darwinian struggle for survival of the politically most fit genres.

For all its impact as a dystopia, however, I believe the enduring power of *Nineteen Eighty-Four* is at least equally due to Orwell's brilliant combination of the two possible kinds of uchronia. I hope my consideration of the transition from utopia to uchronia underscores and allows more precise identification of this source of Orwell's power. In his story of Winston Smith's destruction, Orwell succeeded in transforming the near-future date of his title from the marker of a specific historical year into a symbol standing for the future itself. No one should say—as so many recently have said—that the time is safely come and gone. In one sense, *Nineteen Eighty-Four* will always remain the story of an emblematic year looming ahead of us in exactly the same threatening imminence to the present as it did in 1949—not more, not less. It is a disturbing realm of mythic time measured not by calendars but by the speed of our approach to or recession from that changeless world of unideal platonic forms where a boot is smashing a human face—forever. Equally noteworthy is the fact that Orwell created a dystopian future which will not only retain its status as an emblem of all the most horrible possibilities of future political history, while echoing some of the worst features of wartime England, Soviet Russia, and Nazi Germany, but which after 1984 has also shifted to become a uchronia of alternate past history inviting comparison of what happened in postwar England with what might have happened if things had been worse, perhaps only a very little worse.

This partial shift to the form of alternate history is, moreover, only more overt with the actual arrival of 1984. From publication onwards, readers of *Nineteen Eighty-Four* had to note small or large divergences between their immediate present and that present described (differently) as Winston Smith's past. For readers in, say, 1964 no less than in 1985 or beyond, comparison of Orwell's fictive past and their real past was necessary. With the passage of years from 1949 to 1984 and afterwards, the work simply became more prominently a uchronia of alternate history as well as a uchronia of future history. Because Orwell's future is such an accurate metaphor of past and present totalitarian states and states of mind, readers looking at *Nineteen Eighty-Four* from now on may decide that it is hardly an alternate history at all, but simply real history turned into a kind of symbolism that, like all the best art, portrays particular situations by means of universal types. These ways of reading the novel are not mutually exclusive. Orwell's supreme achievement—foreshadowed and perhaps made possible, though hardly equalled, by the eighteenth- and nineteenth-century invention of uchronia—was to locate the action of his most powerful fable in a chronologically specific emblematic future that is also an alternate past.

CHAPTER FIVE

The Secularization of Apocalypse: *Le dernier homme*

Surveying tales of the future known to him in 1834, Félix Bodin complained chiefly that, instead of attempting to narrate any truly novelistic action centering on relationships between characters realistically presented in the milieu of a future society, previous writers experimenting with the form had provided nothing but utopias or apocalypses.[1]

Today's tales of the future, especially after the "new wave" of experimental science fiction in the 1960s and 1970s, can hardly be accused of insufficient attention to novelistic action. Nor of course are they confined to science fiction, although the majority of such tales are so classified, often incorrectly, by most critics. More ironically, among current students of the genre which Bodin was the first to advocate, a favorite term for characterizing the most familiar kind of futuristic fiction is *apocalyptic*.

"Insofar as science fiction is committed to the humanization of time," according to Mark Rose, "it naturally tends toward fictions of the apocalypse."[2] Robert Galbreath notes it is with respect to "attitudes of apocalyptic eschatology . . . not to generic properties" that one usually encounters "the often-heard claim that science fiction is the contemporary form of apocalyptic literature."

THE SECULARIZATION OF APOCALYPSE

From this primarily thematic rather than generic perspective, Galbreath sees in much recent futuristic fiction "a fundamental ambivalence" manifested by "fascination with traditional images of the End" alongside an equally conspicuous "tendency to disconnect these images from formal belief and, indeed, to place them in contexts of ambiguity, skepticism, or heterodoxy."[3] Galbreath views this persistence of traditional apocalyptic imagery in contexts dissociated from religious orthodoxy as a continuation of the nineteenth-century trend that M. H. Abrams calls "natural supernaturalism" and describes as "the assimilation and reinterpretation of religious ideas . . . in a world view founded on secular premises." During the Romantic period the main result, according to Abrams, was displacement of concern with relationships between man and God by concern with "the human mind or consciousness and its transactions with nature."[4] For Galbreath as in various ways for many others, "the creation of a credible natural supernaturalism is the focus of speculative fiction," including tales of the future, whose effect accordingly "is to challenge the reader's conceptions of reality; the basic function is epistemological."[5] In this view apocalyptic themes in recent fiction are usually not intended to provide a true vision of the future but to raise disturbing questions about the present.

A compelling statement of the case for continuities of apocalyptic imagery serving epistemological purposes is David Ketterer's *New Worlds for Old: The Apocalyptic Imagination, Science Fiction, and American Literature*. In affiliating futuristic apocalypse more widely to the mainstream of American literature, Ketterer too stresses apocalyptic attitudes, beliefs, and imagery more than formalist distinctions of genre. He nevertheless insists that achievement of credibility for the apocalyptic elements, or failure to do so, is the criterion for discriminating among realistic forms that merely show the world as it is without raising epistemological questions, forms of fantasy that are so far removed from reality that we suspend epistemological doubts, and forms that force such doubts upon readers by achieving a significant degree of credibility in presenting apocalyptic themes: "Apocalyptic literature is concerned with the creation of other worlds which exist, on the literal level, in a credible relationship (whether on the basis of rational extrapolation and analysis or of religious belief) with the 'real' world, thereby causing a metaphorical destruction of that 'real' world in the reader's head."[6] This is to suggest that all kinds of apocalypse serve essentially the same purposes, provided they resort to ideas (but not necessarily forms) that achieve credibility. At first glance it might seem that, if Abrams, Galbreath, Ketterer, and the others who have argued so persuasively for continuities between older and newer kinds of apocalyptic literature are right, Bodin must have been wrong to suppose that apocalypses—no less than utopias—were an obstacle blocking development of futuristic fiction.

Bodin's concern, however, was with novelistic action more than with ideology or reader response, although he too had much to say about the importance of credibility and new possibilities for achieving it in futuristic fiction without sacrificing the marvelous. A key to understanding the paradoxical role of apocalypse in the emergence of futuristic fiction, I believe, is Bodin's notably clear-sighted recognition that, unless the prevailing domination of ideas over action was adjusted in favor of action, there could be no novels of the future—only monotonous variations of utopia and apocalypse. While futuristic fiction was still taking shape as a distinct form, the main issue from Bodin's perspective was not to free the genre from domination by religious values; he was equally dissatisfied with utopias showing future societies whose virtues were largely secular. What is easier to see with the advantage of hindsight is that by the 1830s a decisive alteration of the balance between ideas and action was in fact taking place along the lines that Bodin urged, not only in his own incomplete novel and in some equally pioneering futuristic fiction that he apparently had not seen but also in the literature of apocalypse. In this chapter I want to show how far the secularization of apocalyptic forms was in fact manifested at the

THE SECULARIZATION OF APOCALYPSE

outset of the nineteenth century and why Bodin was nevertheless right to see apocalypse as more of an obstacle than an asset to futuristic fiction. The key text is Jean-Baptiste Cousin de Grainville's *Le dernier homme*.

Grainville first planned *The Last Man* as an epic poem and finally published it in 1805 as a prose narration signaling its poetic affiliations by division into cantos rather than chapters.[7] The following year it was anonymously translated into English and published with more conventional chapter headings as *The Last Man, or Omegarus and Syderia, A Romance in Futurity* (London, 1806). Identification by this subtitle as a romance deflected attention from Grainville's epic affinities in order, perhaps, to make his unusual work more attractive to English purchasers by affiliating it with an easier genre. In 1811 Herbert Croft devoted three pages of his book on Horace to extravagant praise of *The Last Man*, seeing it as a sublime sketch for the kind of epic that might one day outdo Homer and Milton: the model, in other words, for successful future epics.[8] A second French edition of *The Last Man* published in 1811 with an enthusiastic introduction by Charles Nodier gave the work its widest currency in France. He speculated that the first edition received insufficient notice because, appearing as it did without any prefatory explanation, it was mistaken for a novel and accordingly read mostly by those with low tastes who were incapable of appreciating its poetic virtues; the few who did recognize it as the outline for a beautiful epic were (except for Croft) put off by awareness of its shortcomings as a poem.[9] Another French edition appeared in 1859 with no preface or commentary. A 1976 Slatkine Reprints edition of the 1811 text with Nodier's introduction has made Grainville's work again available.

In 1831 Grainville's text was versified (with variations) by Auguste-François Creuzé de Lesser as *Le dernier homme, poëme imité de Grainville*. In 1859 Elise Gagne versified it anew as *Omégar ou le dernier homme: Proso-poesie dramatique de la fin des temps en douze chants* [Paris, 1859] (Omegarus, or the last man: Dramatic prose and poetry about the end of time in twelve cantos).[10] In 1875 Grainville's reputation reached a high-water mark when Jules Michelet devoted a chapter of his *History of the Nineteenth Century* to a moving account of Grainville's difficult life, a romantic reading of *The Last Man* as a story showing that the world will endure so long as love exists, and, most significantly, an argument that Grainville ranks alongside Malthus in exemplifying the spirit of the early nineteenth century—that time when the forces unleashed by Watt's steam engine and Napoleon's Grand Army were in their different ways inaugurating "the great destructions of men." Michelet notes that "in the same year when Grainville seems to have commenced writing his poem, another poem, not less fictitious, in a form abstract and serious, appeared in England, a book which one could call the *Economy* of despair." Even *An Essay on the Principle of Population*, however, ranks in Michelet's view below *The Last Man* as a sign of the times: "Of all the books of that era, Grainville's is the most historical, in the sense that he shows with profound truthfulness the very soul of the time, its pain, its somber thought."[11] Toward the end of the nineteenth century, Grainville's plot still retained enough vitality to serve as inspiration for the story of Omegarus and Eva in Camille Flammarion's popular *La Fin du monde* (Paris, 1894).

Tales of the future before Grainville's *Last Man* do not waver so ambiguously between poetry and prose, inviting adaptation to either form as though the right mode were not at all apparent and had yet to be determined through trial and error. Nor do they dwell seriously on apocalyptic themes. Mercier provides no apocalyptic model of transition to the better world of 2440. Nor, as I noted before, does he adopt a prophetic vision as the framework for his account of a utopian Paris, which is seen by his narrator in a naturalistic dream that cannot claim anything like the status of a revelation. Madden only refers to apocalyptic visions as a way of mocking both millenarian expectations and obsessive preoccupation with

THE SECULARIZATION OF APOCALYPSE

fame. *Memoirs of the Twentieth Century* provides nothing more than a partial comic inversion of apocalypse. Angelic revelation of future history up to the world's end is set down not in an obscurely symbolic document challenging interpretation but in a series of letters containing perfectly lucid diplomatic reports from future English ambassadors scattered around twentieth-century Europe. Nothing is revealed about the actual events ushering in final judgment; however, in a satiric hit at those millenarians who predicted the exact date of the end, readers are informed that it will coincide with the close of the twentieth century. The narrator's purpose in communicating this "revelation" to others is merely self-aggrandisement to be achieved, he hopes, by touting the glorious deeds of his descendants. Madden's apocalyptic allusions, moreover, do not shape *Memoirs of the Twentieth Century* as a whole. It is, as its title suggests, a mock memoir in epistolary form which even for comic purposes never invites sustained comparison with any kind of biblical prophecy, much less the Book of Revelation.

The Last Man, however, begins and ends in a way that makes it an unmistakable analogue to the Book of Revelation. At the outset Grainville's unnamed narrator tells of being attracted to a mysterious cave "near the ruins of Palmyra" where "the celestial spirit to whom eternal futurity is known" informs the writer that he has been summoned as "a spectator of the scenes that will terminate the destinies of the universe": "In the magic mirrors thou beholdest around, the last man will stand revealed to thy sight. There, as on a stage, where the actors represent heroes who are no more, thou shalt hear him converse with the most illustrious personages of the last ages of the world . . . and be witness and judge of his last actions" (1:6).[12] The narrator's dual role as both witness and *judge* of events at endtime may complicate for readers the question of how their situation compares to that of those who only try to interpret the difficult visions of Revelation in order to understand—not judge—them. Biblical prophecy sets uppermost the task of interpretation. The meaning and present application of obscure symbols must somehow be decided. Grainville establishes for his implied readers the stance of those faced also and more immediately with an ordinary novelistic situation calling for judgment of fictitious characters.

Nevertheless Grainville's conceit of his narrative as the record of what is seen in a kind of prophetic theater unambiguously establishes an analogy between the form of his work and that of biblical prophecy, especially the Book of Revelation. Grainville reinforces that analogy when his narrator responds to the celestial spirit in a way that is partly invocation of an epic muse but primarily acceptance of the particular task thrust also upon the prophet of Revelation: "Inspire me . . . with thy spirit, shed the illumination of prophecy into my soul, and bestow on my voice the fierce sound of the trumpet!" (1:10). At the conclusion of the last man's story, its framing situation of magic mirrors animated with scenes of the final days is again recalled as a context for the celestial spirit's parting command to the narrator: "I consign to thee the revelation of this history of the last age of the earth" (2:204). By ending his story with a reminder that its *form* is an analogue of the Book of Revelation, Grainville reiterates the importance of a literary model that is obvious enough on thematic grounds but problematic as an aid to interpretation.

A glance at Grainville's complicated plot will suggest its difficulties if read only as a gloss on the Book of Revelation. The story unfolded in the magic mirrors begins with Ithurial's visit to Adam on a barren island outside the gates of Hell where Adam is doomed to watch the entrance of all damned souls as they descend to the eternal punishment which, but for his fault, they might have escaped: "Whenever he heard the infernal gates creak on their hinges, his whole frame trembled, his white hair stood erect, and he either averted his head, or strove to fly; but an invincible power chained him to the spot" (1:13). Adam's misery is described at length. Not least of his tortures is ignorance of Eve's fate during the long time of his confinement to the island, a question to which

THE SECULARIZATION OF APOCALYPSE

Adam unhappily returns with understandable persistence but which the book never answers. Through Ithurial, God offers Adam the chance to end his torment by persuading the last fertile couple on earth, Omegarus and Syderia, not to have children. If they agree to refrain as God now wishes, human time will come to an end, the final judgment will take place, and eternity will begin. Although Adam, in seeking out Omegarus, arrives on a planet suffering from a kind of old age marked by exhaustion of natural resources along with infertility of the soil and depopulation, there is still a possibility of inaugurating another cycle of human history and even restoring the world to abundance if the endtime counterparts of Adam and Eve, Omegarus and Syderia, decide to have children. In that case the first Adam would return to his island punishment instead of going to heaven, and the final cataclysm would be deferred. Grainville thus creates a myth stressing the role of human choice in accelerating or retarding the world's end.

Sympathy for Adam may at first incline readers to hope that his mission to Omegarus and Syderia will succeed. But as the story of their meeting and marriage unfolds in a series of flashbacks included (in the epic manner) within their long conversation with Adam, whose identity remains concealed during most of the encounter, it becomes harder to see the end of human history as an emotionally satisfactory outcome—even though Grainville presents this end as doctrinally desirable because it is God's will. The issue of obedience is not so clear-cut as in Genesis. Nor is the divinely ordained shape of history's close so apparent as in Revelation. Grainville allows neither his characters nor his readers easy recourse to biblical texts that could provide unequivocal moral guidelines for deciding the right course of action at the story's most difficult moments of choice.

Omegarus and Syderia live in a world without any trace of Christianity. Remnants of an advanced technology, including the beautifully decorated airship in which Omegarus flies from Europe to South America in quest of Syderia, provide appealing glimpses of what human civilization might achieve if its reversion to barbarism could be turned around. There are priests and oracles reminiscent of those in pagan antiquity. But there is no mention of Christ, no mention of the Bible, not even any allusion to specifically Christian precepts of morality. It is seldom clear to Omegarus whether any apparent revelation, and there are many, really has prophetic force or authentic standing as a divine commandment. Most often readers must remain equally puzzled.

Grainville further confuses matters for his protagonists (and his readers) by weaving into his tale the mythological figure of a Terrestrial Genius entrusted by God at the earth's creation with the task of protecting it, doomed to die when the planet does, and busy working in his underground laboratory throughout the final days to renew earth's resources by scientific methods while also trying to persuade Omegarus and Syderia to have children so that the natural cycle of life will continue. For Michelet the protagonist is not Omegarus but the Terrestrial Genius, despite the work's title and its outcome. Michelet views him as a heroic figure whose struggle for survival embodies Grainville's most central message, an affirmation of the value of life rather than (as in Malthus's economy of despair) a gloomy statement that love must be curbed and that limits are inescapable: "The subject of his poem is *The Last Man* or, if one will, the death of the world; it is the story of the supreme combat of the Genius of the Earth who, having arrived at the end of time exhausted and condemned, despite his sentence persists in living and, forced to continue human love in order to live himself, acts to ensure the continuation of love—because, says the sublime poet, so long as there remains one couple for love here on earth, the world cannot end."[13] But the Terrestrial Genius fails.

Finally, in a climax now seen as foreshadowing later preoccupation with the mad-scientist motif that acquires prominence most notably with *Frankenstein*, time as humans know it yields to eternity when the Terrestrial Genius, cornered in his underground laboratory by Death, blows up the world: "Suddenly the Genius flung

THE SECULARIZATION OF APOCALYPSE

his torches around the cavern, the fire caught, and the tremendous explosion hurled the convulsed earth back upon her orbit. . . . The Genius of the Earth being no more, the darkness vanished. A light, softer than that of the stars, and more lucid than the sun, gilded the vault of the firmament, unassisted by any fiery orb. It was the dawn of eternity!" (2:203).[14]

All this, especially the love story of Omegarus and Syderia set against the backdrop of a dying planet that is inhabited only by a few half-savage tribes living in the ruins of once-great cities, makes it impossible to apply the Book of Revelation as a definitive guide to Grainville's tale. It has too many elements for which traditional eschatology alone cannot account. The poignant if at times mawkish love affair of Omegarus and Syderia deflects attention from doctrinal issues. If their relationship also strikes a few chords familiar in more conventional French literature from Prevost onward, the strange milieu of their affair makes it hard for readers to fall back on memories of other fiction as a guide to interpretation of Grainville's book.[15] This difficulty does not signal a defect, however. Grainville's departures from precedent are in one way or another now acknowledged as his greatest virtue. Most recently, for example, W. Warren Wagar finds that "nearly all the imaginative force of *Le dernier homme* derives from its secular events, and from its detailed history of the future of the human race."[16] This gives deserved credit to Grainville's inventiveness in breaking away from the restrictive mold of eschatological doctrine. But I believe such a view of *Le dernier homme* goes too far in discounting both the uses to which Grainville puts the events of apocalypse and his adaptation of those events to novelistic modes of representation.

By taking into the final cataclysm itself characters with whom we have been encouraged to sympathize and identify throughout a long narrative, Grainville becomes the first writer, so far as I know, to achieve anything like a credible novelistic portrait of the phenomenology of apocalypse. Some earlier works like Burnet's *Sacred Theory of the Earth* attempt, in a manner reminiscent of Last Judgment paintings, a vivid pictorial description of the end; they do not, however, take readers inside the mind of anyone caught up in the final events. Burnet's viewpoint is that of a painter who sees a sublime spectacle from afar and records the scene on canvas as it appears to a distant eyewitness looking on rather than participating. Poetic attempts to show what it would be like to experience the Last Judgment also abound in the tedious genre of last-day poems such as Edward Young's widely read *A Poem on the Last Day* (1713) and John Bulkeley's deservedly ignored *The Last Day: A Poem in XII Books* (1720). But the characters evoked are mostly stock figures from the homiletic repertoire: the sinner facing damnation with suitable pangs or, as in Bulkeley's poem, the Atheist and the Deist quite predictably dismayed after resurrection at finding that everything, including their impending eternity in Hell, is just as the preachers said it would be. What little power such portraits attain is achieved more from their reader's prior inclination to accept the Book of Revelation as true doctrine than by any imaginative involvement with the experience of particularized characters. Grainville, however, concentrates upon such experiences and succeeds to a remarkable degree in rendering them vividly as well as plausibly, given the premises of his story. He enhances verisimilitude by altering the form of Apocalypse.

Grainville's crucial step is to adjust the flow of apocalyptic time to accommodate the tempo of human experience. The resurrection becomes a multi-stage process rather than an essentially instantaneous stroke. After a more conventional prelude of storms, comets, erupting volcanoes, and other familiar signs of the end, the last day itself commences in the usual way as "angels, placed at the foot of Jehovah's aethereal throne, now blew the golden trumpets of the last day, the clangor of which pierced the most hidden recesses of the vast universe" (2:95).[17] What immediately follows also appears conventional, so much so that its reference to men arising out of gaping graves is a traditional last-day image whose

THE SECULARIZATION OF APOCALYPSE

suggestion of instantaneous action does not quite square with Grainville's subsequent strategy of putting events into slower motion: "In an instant ['Aussi-tôt'] all the parts of matter, which contained any portion of man's substance, hastened to throw it up. In the north, the ice broke to afford them a passage: under the tropics, the ocean heaved, and vomited them on the shore. Men arose out of gaping graves, splitting trees, adamantine rocks, and edifices crumbling to pieces. The earth resembled one extended volcano, whence, through an infinite number of mouths, human bones and the ashes of the dead were ejected" (2:95). This upheaval with its eerie fallout of human ashes terrifies Omegarus, who "is afraid to tread on re-animated dust" (2:96). Actually the ashes are not yet brought back to life. The dust only *seems living* to Omegarus, as Grainville makes clear with a nuance that is lost here in the usually faithful English translation of 1806: "il craint de fouler aux pieds la poussière qui lui paroît vivante" (2:81). The appearance of life underfoot is caused by earthquakes ("mouvemens onduleux de la terre") which the volcanic action induces (2:81). Grainville's emphasis is upon phenomenology as he stresses how the changing landscape appears to Omegarus and not just what is actually happening.

During the earthquake Omegarus clings to a tree, resigning himself to death only to find that he remains alive at the end of what proves later to have been merely the first phase of resurrection: "Omegarus was astonished that he still existed, and dared not believe in the return of peace" (2:97). Grainville alerts readers to the leisurely tempo of his apocalypse by noting the moment when Omegarus begins to suspect that the upheavals he has just survived are only a long prelude to resurrection of the dead.[18] Then in a work hitherto devoid of any allusion to clocks, Grainville begins carefully to specify the passage of time: "Three hours proved sufficient for the resurrection of human bone and fragments, so rapid and violent was the eruption! As soon as God, who knew the number of atoms in the universe . . . saw that the earth had vomited up the ashes of men, he bid it rest. . . . A mournful silence succeeded this convulsion of all things" (2:97).[19] Obscured perhaps by the rhetoric of Grainville's insistence on the sublime violence and relative speed of the eruption that disgorges all human remains so quickly, and equally obscured perhaps by his praise of God's precision, is the assignment of three hours as an adequate interval. Whatever symbolic overtones the figure three may have invoked for Grainville's Catholic readers, this figure here mainly naturalizes the supernatural by treating it as an event whose duration is determined by natural law: the time necessary, as the narrator explains, for a given quantity of matter to be transferred by volcanic eruption from the earth's interior to its surface. This explanation also significantly humanizes the time scale of Apocalypse by choosing a duration that is both large enough and small enough to fit the time scale of daily life. It is neither instantaneous as in other versions of resurrection nor spread out over many days as it might well have been to achieve even greater scientific plausibility, given the many remains waiting throughout all history to be disgorged.

Moreover, Grainville protracts his narration of the resurrection to accommodate accounts of it as experienced not only by Omegarus and other witnesses who understand what is happening but also by Syderia, who does not. After following Omegarus through the rest of his terrifying day and its sequel, Grainville reverts to the moment of volcanic eruptions, making readers follow events over again as seen through the eyes of another character, Syderia, who perceives them differently. By narrating the same interval of plot time more than once from different perspectives, Grainville further slows the tempo of his narration in a way that reinforces, for his readers, the sense of resurrection as a slow series of events rather than as a single instantaneous transformation. Thereby too Grainville shifts his story even further away from a more conventional focus on the situation of resurrectees about to face judgment. His narrative follows those alive before and during

THE SECULARIZATION OF APOCALYPSE

the events of Apocalypse; it even includes, incongruously, a few ordinary householders who cope as best they can through it all.

When Omegarus quits the tree to which he had been clinging in terror during the first three hours of resurrection, he sees a world in ruins covered by a strange coating of ashes through which he makes his way toward Paris. The city has vanished: "her gardens, temples, and noble edifices, had disappeared. . . . The whole presented only an extensive waste, an immense field of dust" (2:100). A statue of Napoleon is the sole object that survives, although perhaps for patriotic reasons Grainville's description of it is omitted in the 1806 English translation. Even Omegarus has heard of the emperor, to whose memory he pays due respect before turning again to the difficulties at hand: "He knew that this monarch was among his ancestors, he stretched his hands respectfully towards [the statue] and said: O my father! if it is true that the spirits of the dead are consoled by the homage accorded them on earth, receive again the tribute of the love and respect of men; it will be the last, but your name cannot live longer in memory. In saying these words he bathed with his tears the statue of this great man" (1811 ed., 2:88; my translation). This allusion to Napoleon is Grainville's only explicit connection of the nineteenth-century reader's calendric and historical moment with that of Omegarus.

Otherwise neither his story nor the time in which it takes place is linked in any specific way to events of European or, for that matter, world history. There is no date anywhere in *The Last Man*, let alone one serving to anchor the story in time as Mercier does by locating a utopian Paris in the year 2440. Grainville's dying planet is so far in our future that—except for the statue of Napoleon amid the ruins of Paris—no traces remain of the readers' present or past history. Allusion to dirigibles and other technology of the future only underscores the disconnection of plot time from that of known history. Patriotic motives aside, the English translator was following a sound instinct in suppressing Grainville's allusion to Napoleon: it is an incongruous intrusion of real history in a work otherwise set entirely in a mythic future that connects mainly to an equally mythic past of Adam's transgression and punishment.

After weeping again and talking emotionally about what he thinks may be the world's last sunset, Omegarus takes shelter for the night in one of the few houses remaining outside the ruins of Paris. Grainville provides the exact time when Omegarus enters by noting that "opposite the door, and over a couch, a secular clock still continued to advance, the hand of which pointed to the ninth hour of the evening" (2:107). He finds some food, eats, and then wanders through a room filled with books, which prompt him to meditate on the unfair impending abolition of all human creations, no matter how noble. Grainville again specifies very carefully the passage of time: "The secular clock now announcing the last hour of the day, it drew Omegarus from his reverie. These mournful sounds, twelve times repeated by that symbol of time, and reverberating thro' this abode of darkness, affected him deeply. In a doleful voice he uttered, 'The last day of the earth is now commencing!'" (2:116).[20] It is an ordinary clock which tells the last hours of the world, and tells them in the usual way even for a person who must take note of their peculiar import under the circumstances. Grainville thus calls attention to the continuing flow of normal human time for his protagonist right up to the brink of eternity.

The owner of the house, an old man named Tibes, lies dead in its bedroom alongside the corpse of his wife in an open coffin where, as the narrator also carefully informs us, they are in the process of resurrection. Overnight, while Omegarus sleeps, both bodies are restored to youthful appearance "but they were as yet bereft of their souls, which, still wandering amidst the shades, anxious to re-animate the bodies they had been separated from, waited impatiently for the happy instant of re-union" (2:115). Even for some of the resurrectees, time—and the progress of the miraculous—still flows at the customary pace of all human experience.

It is at this point that Grainville's narrative reverts to an earlier

THE SECULARIZATION OF APOCALYPSE

moment in the chronology of its plot and follows Syderia who, pregnant at last, is "abandoned by Omegarus, unconscious of the cause, and alone during the most dreadful day the world had ever experienced" (2:122). She has no idea of what that day holds in store or why its events are taking place. Nor does she understand what they mean. Adam's account of the reasons for terminating human history and his disclosure of the role to be played by Omegarus and Syderia were missed by Syderia, who at that point in the long conversation with Adam had left to fix lunch; she returns to find her husband and their guest mysteriously absent. She follows their footprints, which eventually lead to a broken column bearing an enigmatic inscription from her husband: "Omegarus is not guilty!" (2:89). However much this statement and its venue might delight Freudian critics, it understandably infuriates Syderia, who then exhausts herself with a crying fit and faints. She revives just as the last events commence: "She came to life again at the moment when the eruption of human bones and ashes was beginning to take place; when the earth, opening her bowels on every side, was throwing up the dusty matter all around her" (2:135–36). She is so confused that she cannot tell whether this cataclysm is dream or reality or whether she is alive or dead. She suffers briefly from amnesia until she looks again at the inscription and decides to keep following Omegarus. Because of the earthquakes and fallout, however, she cannot find his footprints: "Here the gaping earth had devoured them,—there the ashes of men, falling, had covered them, as the snow covers the furrows in the fields" (2:138). In thus presenting Syderia as a totally uncomprehending witness of the last scenes, who is unprepared for them by any revelation and preoccupied with her personal affairs to the extent that the beginning of the world's end only induces temporary anomie, Grainville invites imaginative participation by readers in the phenomenology of the Apocalypse detached from its doctrinal dimension.

Despite the obvious affinities of Syderia's predicament to the most stale sentimental fiction about mistreated wives, and despite equally obvious difficulties for readers trying to reconcile some of the other jarring narrative elements drawn from usually incompatible conventions of realism and allegory, Grainville's fiction of the Apocalypse here attains its greatest power. Its imaginative force derives not only or even primarily from secular events recounted as a future history of the human race as it vainly uses scientific means to contend against what people in Grainville's strange post-Christian world consider a natural, not divinely ordained, winding down of planetary resources. That history of dwindling possibilities and collapsing civilization before the birth of Omegarus is mainly glanced at in expository flashbacks, not dramatized in a way that invites much imaginative participation by readers. Rather, the distinctive power of Grainville's narrative is achieved by an extraordinary combination of realism, fantasy, and allegory allowing the intrusion of a purely secular viewpoint—Syderia's inability to understand on the basis of revelation what is happening or why—within a narrative framework that is apparently dominated by theology. *The Last Man* thereby goes a long way toward undermining conventional uses of eschatology by providing a phenomenology of the Apocalypse that calls in question the doctrines of Apocalypse. Despite Grainville's recurrence to the Book of Revelation for values by which to judge the events of his narrative, the pathos of Syderia's plight undercuts acceptance of the doctrine which accounts for the horrors of her predicament. In this as in some other respects *The Last Man* is self-contradictory, though in ways that increase rather than diminish its power.

As Syderia wanders angry and confused amid the ruins, "at times, clouds of flame and smoke surrounded and threw her down. The fragments of buildings struck her . . . blood flowed from the wounds she received, and her face, arms, and garments, were covered with the sanguinary fluid" (2:140). The sentimental tale of an abandoned beauty next takes a more gothic turn as darkness suddenly descends; after the catastrophes there is no longer any interval of twilight. Syderia struggles to reach a lighted house where she hopes to find Omegarus. Instead, she only terrifies the couple who live there, Policletes and Cephisa, who mistake her blood-stained figure for that of a reanimated corpse: "Not daring to abandon themselves to the soft refreshment of sleep, so much had the eruption of human bones terrified them, they were yet watching, kept awake by the powerful impression of fear. The knocks they had heard at their door had increased their terror. Policletes thought that some of the dead, issuing from their graves, were come to solicit hospitality. . . . The appearance of Syderia, pale, dejected, and covered with blood and dust, confirmed them in their opinion. They imagined her to be a shade, returning from the infernal regions, and hence they were afraid to speak to her" (2:146–47). In a future world whose inhabitants do not read the Bible or apparently even remember its existence, fear of shades returning from what sounds like a pagan underworld may be logical even for people who somehow understand a little (but only a little) more than Syderia about what is taking place. The reaction of Policletes and Cephisa nevertheless seems more appropriate for a Gothic novel set in the Roman past than for an apocalypse of the future. But Grainville thus invites readers to ask how ordinary people *would* respond to a knock at their door during the world's last day. Grotesque as this and related passages may seem to modern readers for quite a variety of reasons unintended by Grainville, it raises an odd question that cannot be put aside as irrelevant to his reshaping of apocalypse as a literary form: given the doctrine of eventual resurrection, what after all *should* be the attitude of the living toward the newly resurrected? The impossibility of either knowing what to do with such a question once we have it, or of relating it to previous novelistic moments by way of precedent, is another measure of Grainville's innovation in *Le dernier homme*. He secularizes the Apocalypse *without* discarding its theological framework.

Grainville actually attempts to dramatize the last day as foretold in Revelation. Of course it is not foretold there in such mundane detail as Grainville supplies, and his version has other material that can easily be regarded for better or worse as heterodox. C. M. Le Roy de Bonneville, for example, writing in 1863, found a deplorably deistic tendency in Grainville's omission of any allusion to Christ's role as redeemer.[21] Michelet ignored the framework of events adapted from Apocalypse to praise Grainville's originality in borrowing nothing at all from either pagan epic machinery or Christianity.[22] Elise Gagne, as anxious to find Christian doctrine as Michelet was to ignore it, was content to adapt Grainville's story as a part of her "crusade against the materialist tendencies of the century, persuaded that the mission of the woman of letters, in this world, is to combat vice ceaselessly and exalt virtue."[23] Grainville's debt to Revelation is partly a matter of perspective that could only be settled by a theological excursion unnecessary for my purposes. In the history of futuristic fiction Grainville's apocalypse is distinctive less for its exact degree of orthodoxy or heterodoxy than for its portrayal of normal human duration by resort to novelistic methods in several modes (particularly gothic and sentimental), along with allegory and some residual conventions of epic narration that I have only suggested. It is resort to such procedures in order to suggest the phenomenology of Apocalypse, rather than any particular departure from received eschatology, that creates Grainville's kind of natural supernaturalism with its secularization of form more than of doctrine.

The nature of Grainville's formal innovations can be seen most clearly by noting how he reverts to a more traditional mode of prophetic narration at the close of his story. After Syderia flees from the house where she has terrified a couple already frightened by events signaling the world's end, she loses all hope and in despair "entered a neighbouring temple, the doors of which were broken in pieces, and sat down on the steps of the altar, to breathe her last sigh in peace" (2:148). At this same moment, elsewhere, Omegarus finally thinks of praying that God will take pity on his wife.

THE SECULARIZATION OF APOCALYPSE

God does, "and charged the angels, who watch the sleep of mortals, to surround her with consolatory dreams. They obeyed, and instantly environed her sleeping form, presenting to her a thousand agreeable images in the mirror of visions" (2:149). Here again as in Grainville's framing fiction, although less obtrusively, is the metaphor of prophetic vision as a sight glimpsed in a magical mirror. In these visions within the larger vision which comprises the entire narrative except for its framing account of the narrator's visit to a cave near Palmyra, Syderia is presented with a succession of scenes—an experience which thus takes the conventional shape of revelation.

Le dernier homme as a whole takes this shape too in theory, but in fact there are so many complex episodes told at length that readers cannot sustain the impression of watching a succession of *pictures*. For Grainville's entire work the conceit of describing scenes viewed by the narrator in a magic mirror gives way to a more novelistic progression. Narrated moments are not presented in the order of their occurrence. The book starts after the epic manner *in medias res* and makes ample use of flashbacks. But, for readers, episodes are nevertheless organized and mentally assimilated with reference to a chronological structure of plot time rather than a scenic succession.

In Syderia's dream, which is easier to grasp as a series of animated tableaux, there is first a vision of Eve restored to youth. Without disclosing where she has been all these years since her separation from Adam when he was consigned to his punishment on the island outside Hell's gate, Eve explains that her rejuvenation is owing to Omegarus's decision to obey God. Eve also tells Syderia that her troubles are over: "tomorrow thou wilt ascend to heaven by his side!" (2:150). In another vision "the Grand Priest Ormus" appears to explain that, although Omegarus at first rebelled against the commandments of heaven by consummating his marriage and propagating a child, "he has quitted you and his crimes are forgiven!" (2:151). Thus comforted, Syderia is next granted an extended vision of the Last Judgment—a vision more conventional than the entire narrative within which it occurs.

In Syderia's private dream of apocalypse, its progress is very different from the experience she has just lived through in her waking life where apocalypse has been real for her. There events have proceeded in stages at the pace of ordinary duration, with time for human response to cataclysms that defy human understanding, especially in her case before sleeping to encounter a vision of the Truth. But in her vision everything proceeds in a flash of instantaneous response to God's signals:

> In the next vision, the scene of the last judgement was displayed before her. At the sound of the trumpets, in the twinkling of an eye ["à-la-fois"], every tomb was rent open, and thence sprang incessantly such an inconceivable multitude of renovated dead, that the affrighted imagination could not comprehend how the earth could have borne and fed them! Some were seen shaking off the dust and ashes which stained their faces and bodies; others, covered with the garments of mortality, were stripping them off hastily, and throwing them away with horror. The mariners, whom the waves of the ocean had swallowed up, now cast upon the shore, arose, struck with astonishment, while the water flowed from their nostrils, their hair, and their bodies: they shuddered at the sight of the briny fluid, and seemed yet afraid of the element which had proved their destruction. (2:151–52)

Here the dead spring to life "in the twinkling of an eye," thus providing for spectators a sublime picture that is frightening to its beholders because of what it implies about the sheer immensity of human history: "the affrighted imagination" of spectators cannot understand how the earth could have sustained so many people. But their return to life is taken as self-evidently consoling: an astonishing miracle that affords only hope to those like Syderia (and in theory Grainville's readers) who become witnesses.

THE SECULARIZATION OF APOCALYPSE

In this kind of conventional apocalyptic scene, moreover, there is no confusion about what is happening or why. Syderia easily understands its meaning, as do readers familiar with the Book of Revelation and traditions of interpreting it. Nor is there any breaking down of the resurrection into stages whose effects are bewildering and therefore raise questions that may not be resolved either emotionally or intellectually by the usual answers: no three-hour volcanic eruption of human ashes accompanied by earthquakes and followed by an interval of silence allowing for confused wandering—or vicarious participation by readers in such wandering— amid the fallout. Nor in Syderia's vision is there time or occasion for her to question God's justice as Omegarus did while meditating somewhat rebelliously in Tibes's library about the obliteration of human civilization, whose most noble books and works of art are about to be destroyed indiscriminately. Everything in Syderia's vision, as in so many post-Reformation representations of the Apocalypse, is essentially comforting and static.[24]

Grainville's inclusion of Syderia's dream-visions within his story subordinates them to a narrative structure ostensibly like that of her revelation only insofar as *Le dernier homme* as a whole purports to be a description of supernatural visions seen in a magic mirror. For Grainville's readers no less than for Syderia, however, her dream, like conventional versions of Apocalypse, is experienced as a series of related but largely independent scenes without overt narrative continuity or causal progression. There is only thematic movement from least to most important: in her case from what immediately concerns only Omegarus and Syderia to a picture of the final judgment of all mankind. Because *Le dernier homme* is otherwise organized in terms of plot, not picture, it renders Apocalypse in a narrative mode. While not totally without precedent in the quasi-dramatic structure of Revelation itself, as well as in some epics and related forms that include a plot of action subordinated to a more static framework of prophetic statement, Grainville's method runs counter to the mainstream of apocalyptic writing. From the Renaissance through the eighteenth century and on into the Romantic period, as Joseph A. Wittreich notes, prophecy as a mode of literature was usually taken as "a 'no plot, no action' genre" concerned "not with the imitation of an action but with the portrayal of a character's mind, with the projection and improvement of thought-processes." Its method was regarded as basically "repetition, amplification, and accumulation" rather than linear progression.[25] In other words, prophecy as a literary kind usually resorted to what Joseph Frank has called spatial form: structures that invite apprehension of all their elements simultaneously rather than sequentially.[26]

Grainville managed to retain—indeed enhance—portrayal of mind, of the phenomenology of encounter with Apocalypse, while also resorting to the more sequential rather than spatial forms of narrative structure that allow presentation of such phenomenology through the appeal of action and plot. Primarily scenic progression of the kind traditionally associated with apocalypse is only dominant in the episode of Syderia's dream, within which the point of view is external rather than internal: we see what she sees and draw the same doctrinal conclusions, but we cannot so easily share the emotional comfort which she finally attains. Grainville's narrative prior to its account of Syderia's dream, however, has both invited and allowed more complete identification with her mental states as she encounters an apparently inexplicable—and accordingly all the more shattering—series of apocalyptic events. So too for the stages by which Omegarus experiences the world's end: his bewilderment is more fully portrayed and is thus easier to comprehend and identify with than his final rejection of Syderia in accord with God's commandment as conveyed by Adam, although Grainville makes it clear enough that readers *should* approve of whatever decision conforms to God's will. The trouble—and from an aesthetic point of view the advantage—is that we have been given such a powerful representation of an estranging encounter

THE SECULARIZATION OF APOCALYPSE

with Apocalypse that epistemological doubts raised by the narrative cut in all directions.

From the perspective of Apocalypse, Grainville's narrative calls into question our desire to see the human race perpetuated and human history prolonged on this world. We are shown (in more detail than I have suggested here) doctrinal and otherwise valid reasons for taking the end of the world as a consummation devoutly to be desired. Grainville thus rejects the ideology of progress toward any form of utopia. But we are also shown in powerful novelistic detail the human agony involved in the renunciation by Omegarus and Syderia of what most readers can only regard as proper, even sanctified, human pleasures of marriage, parenthood, and life on this world. Creuzé de Lesser, for example, identified as the work's major fault Grainville's "false" idea that readers should agree with Adam (and God as characterized in *The Last Man*) about the desirability of ending human history: "No one shares Adam's opinion. But when one sees that the author does and wanted to focus interest on the destruction of the human race—according to him very desirable—one regrets that he could have deceived himself on this point."[27] Either because he misjudged his readers, as Lesser supposes, or because he intended to provoke them (or both), Grainville was certainly uncompromising. He does not even suggest a thousand-year millennium as a kind of halfway point easing the pain of transition from time to eternity. Moreover, he shows suffering experienced not in the manner of last-day poems by sinners who deserve what they are about to get at the final judgment but experienced by an attractive man and woman who have not themselves done anything (apart from existing as members of a fallen race) to deserve their terrible ordeal. If that is enough doctrinally it is not sufficient emotionally. Consequently the doctrines of Apocalypse are themselves called in question.

Perhaps for some readers the ending resolves all doubt. But that possibility is further undercut by Grainville's allegory of the Terrestrial Genius. In trying to save the world and prolong the cycle of human history along with his own existence, he appears only to be carrying out the sacred task entrusted to him at Creation. By so dutifully following his instructions to the very last, however, the Terrestrial Genius finally seems out of control and in dire conflict with God. This satanic aspect of the Terrestrial Genius and his scientific devices does not quite square with the fact that *he* has been given no countermand of his initial instructions to protect the earth and sustain the life of its inhabitants. Nor is he given any opportunity to earn his own salvation by obedience. His only options during the last days seem to be successful defiance of God or annihilation if the world ends. When it goes, he goes. For him there is not even any prospect of continuing to exist like Milton's Satan, reigning in Hell if not in Heaven. This too may somehow be doctrinally acceptable; but the Terrestrial Genius, though allegorical, is a sufficiently developed character that readers will both puzzle over and to a considerable degree sympathize with his strange predicament. Revelation itself offers no obvious clue to the meaning of that predicament. Accordingly Grainville's own mythology of apocalypse, along with his often effective portrayal of its phenomenology, serves the aesthetically valid epistemological purpose of raising questions *about* the Apocalypse.

If difficult, those questions are by the same token interesting. They admit a variety of answers, as in other fiction whose complexity challenges interpretation. However readers answer the questions, Grainville's book is all the more effective because it does raise such issues. For most readers its appeal is enhanced by doctrinal inconsistencies created by the clash between overt doctrine and covert implication of situations and characterizations that undercut explicitly stated doctrines. The recurring nineteenth-century efforts to recast Grainville's story are one measure of that appeal, no less than Michelet's romantic reading of *The Last Man* as a work endorsing not the end of all history but the idea that love, symbolized by the fruitful union of Omegarus and Syderia, can

THE SECULARIZATION OF APOCALYPSE

save humanity from destruction. While critics like Bonneville found ample cause for complaint, just as Nodier and Michelet did for praise, writers as different as Creuzé de Lesser, Elise Gagne, and Camille Flammarion—though aware too of Grainville's weaknesses—were inspired to adapt one or another element of his tale as most effective for their own purposes. Their variations on Grainville's theme show both the diversity of ideas embedded in his work and, above all, its uneasy but stimulating amalgamation of disparate genres in quest of the right form for a tale of the far future.

The adaptation of Grainville's somewhat indeterminate solution to that formal problem is most attenuated by 1894 in Flammarion's *End of the World,* with its odd but engaging mixture of satire, utopia, scientific forecast, philosophical dissertation, popularized astronomy, history of beliefs about the world's end, and spiritualist preachments dramatized in a final episode when the spirit of the Pharaoh Cheops arrives during the last day to take the souls of Omegarus and Eva to Jupiter, the next destination for human evolution in our solar system.[28] Where Grainville juxtaposed the beginning and end of human history in the persons of Adam and Omegarus, Flammarion moves further away from the Bible by resorting to Cheops, whose presence nevertheless serves the same function of linking distant past and far future in a way intended to suggest their coherent relationship. Mainly, however, Flammarion borrows Grainville's idea of telling a romantic story of people at the world's end as a vehicle for a new mythology that serves to illustrate an unconventional theology. In its advocacy of spiritualism, *La Fin du monde* departs more completely than Grainville from Christian doctrines of apocalypse. Flammarion also relegates his story of Omegarus and Eva to the second part of *La Fin du monde*, entitled "In Ten Million Years." As in those memorable scenes set on a dying planet at the end of *The Time Machine,* published by Wells the following year, Flammarion's far-future setting allows a glimpse of changes on an astronomical time scale.

Flammarion's more optimistic cosmology, however, permitted

him to add by way of philosophical epilogue some comforting thoughts about the cyclical nature of such changes, which he believed would lead eventually to regeneration of decaying planetary systems. He foresaw no apocalyptic ending of time itself. The first part of *La Fin du monde* is set in a closer twenty-fifth-century future whose society is a wittily drawn satiric analogue of nineteenth-century civilization. Here Flammarion deals with the problem of a comet headed for collision with Earth. Part One may be considered a secularization of apocalypse so complete as to abandon almost completely the structural affinities manifested in the second part to Grainville's version and through it more distantly, to the Book of Revelation.

A. Creuzé de Lesser in 1831 and Elise Gagne in 1859 were more under the sway of Grainville's form. Both chose poetry, thus reverting closer to Grainville's original intention, although Gagne relegated poetic passages to service as preludes for "cantos" that are largely a combination of dialogue and narrative. Doctrinally Gagne claimed scrupulous conformity to Revelation but stressed too that her work aimed at originality by a deliberate "mixture of several literary genres so different from one another." She emphasized that in the resulting work with its attributes of poem, drama, and novel "the marvelous plays a very active role." She thus signals an epic affinity. Her end of the world is placed far enough in the future, she says, that no reader need be frightened by her account because its events are not imminent. To encourage imaginative connection with that future, however, her Omegarus lives more than one thousand years, from the eighteenth to the twenty-eighth century: "From 1774 to 2800, he witnessed all the upheavals, all the revolutions which have stained the world with blood." Her readers follow the adventures of Omegarus before their century, through it, and on to the very last day. Gagne thus attempts by a rather problematic method to create a sense of historical continuity between the reader's present and a far future. Anticipating the possible charge that such a long-lived hero is a mere fantasy unparalleled in reality and is therefore unserviceable as a moral example, Gagne blandly responds that piety, devotion, courage, and all the noble qualities which render us fit for heaven are not measured by the length of life but by its quality.[29]

If this response evades the issue of properly defining boundaries between the marvelous and the credible, its very evasiveness is another index of what Gagne clearly saw as a license *for* the marvelous created by Grainville's kind of apocalypse. Her apocalyptic future is intended to be doctrinally unimpeachable in its biblically derived account of the last day itself, and thus credible for those who accept Revelation, while it also allowably serves as an arena for the very free play of fantasy.

Creuzé de Lesser puts his entire narration into verse but tries in its preface to minimize differences between epic poetry and novels. Since epics are fundamentally narrative poems, he reasons, they should be as attractive as novels and as accessible ("facile à lire"), although most are not. Grainville, however, achieved originality, Lesser says, by an entirely new story owing nothing to the themes of previous epics and also avoiding the most frequently imitated—and hence banal—epic conventions. Grainville thus came very close to solving the problem of endowing an epic with novelistic qualities of readability, according to Lesser, who adds that he has tried to come even closer. But there must still be differences: "Of course one cannot exactly achieve the relaxation of a novel." *The Last Man*'s subject matter, for one thing, precludes familiar novelistic pleasures: "This poem is written on the tripod, and one will easily see that it is in effect *an oracle*."[30] As with Gagne's laborious attempt to rationalize inclusion of outright fantasy, Creuzé de Lesser entangles himself in an attempt to explain a mixture of genres that is hard to defend without falling into some contradiction. More important, he no less than Gagne winds up stoutly defending stronger doses of the marvelous: in changing Grainville's story, Lesser says, "I have above all tried to put the marvelous on a firmer course, at once bolder and more regular."[31]

ORIGINS OF FUTURISTIC FICTION

The question of how to achieve acceptable venues for the marvelous haunted Grainville's imitators as it had haunted him and was to concern perceptive critics from Bodin onward who have found it necessary to cope in one way or another with the persistence of fantasy in futuristic fiction. In 1772, long before harsh experiences during the French Revolution turned Grainville away from reality to thoughts of suicide while intensifying too his craving for solace in fantasies about the world's end, his prize essay for the Academy of Besançon had argued the need for fantasy in a drastically changing world whose future could no longer be seen as a continuation of its present.[32] Grainville stressed historical discontinuities caused by the new philosophies, although he acknowledged that a few useful discoveries also resulted. As Newtonian science based on demonstration, experiment, and belief in material progress gained supremacy over religious faith and its attendant acceptance of poetic imagination, not only was the stability of society threatened, Grainville then wrote, but literature was also becoming impoverished and destabilized. The new rationalism, he maintained, had destroyed generic distinctions ("les traits caractéristiques des genres"). It had also banished from literature the pagan gods. "Men remain to be portrayed. But what men! Cold and reasoners like the philosophy which has shaped them, do they offer any large trait to seize? They follow one another with the same care as a herd going over a mountain, and the number of probable actions ['actions vraisemblables'] decreases with the progress of the imitation."[33] Thus as men become more uniform—and uniformly rational—there is less scope for the marvelous or fantastic, because differences of *any* kind from the commonplace will have less and less verisimilitude.

Instead of painting the heart, Grainville also laments, writers substitute "silences, monosyllable, and dots." Worst of all, "the need for actions with verisimilitude multiplies didactic poems, the uniformity of characters produces metaphysical dramas; mythology being destroyed yields to scientific and scholarly descriptions—in

THE SECULARIZATION OF APOCALYPSE

other words philosophy seizes the crown of literature."[34] Thus for Grainville as for many others writing in the wake of Rousseau, an age of science is more the enemy than the inspiration for literature except in the sense of inspiring a deliberate turn to fantasy by way of antidote. Grainville's essay of 1772 is our best clue to the origins of his turn to the far future. It provided an excellent setting for the restoration of fantasy and the marvelous as allies of religion.

Lesser for his part sought to enhance the marvelous elements in *The Last Man* by putting them on a more plausible footing as dramatic action. He replaces Grainville's conventional personification of death with a Genius of Death who is sometimes manifested as a Celestial Spirit playing a role analogous but only analogous to that which Grainville gives to Ithurial as God's messenger. In Lesser's poem God is only a distant spectator of a more equal contest between the Genius of Death, striving to close human history, and the Terrestrial Genius who fights bravely for continuation of life on earth. Lesser's Celestial Spirit is not actually an angel sent by God on the cruel mission of enlisting Adam in an attempt to put an end to his own descendants. For Lesser there is an obvious difficulty with Grainville's cast of characters: "Against the All-Powerful what can be done by a Genius who is himself mortal? Evidently there is no equilibrium, no chance possible in such a rivalry, and with this system the destruction of man is not a difficulty, it is merely a sentence."[35] Lesser redresses the balance to make a more suspenseful contest between agents of equal power and also makes the conflict between his Terrestrial Genius and the Genius of Death more explicitly a conflict between good and evil.

In Grainville's work it is hard to see the Terrestrial Genius as an evil figure opposed to God or, emotionally at least, to accept Death as an agent of God's will (and therefore good). What is worse, despite Syderia's dream with its affirmation of the doctrines in Revelation that mark the last day as a desirable conclusion, there is some danger of taking Grainville's God as a villain destroying the lovers' chances for happiness. Lesser attempts to eliminate that awkward possibility by making the Genius of Death easily identified as the sole agent of an evil destructiveness, while God remains sufficiently in the background not to be implicated. These changes remove fantastic elements from the realm of Christian theology and allow readers greater freedom of response to fantasy unencumbered by doctrinal constraints. Lesser's *Last Man* thus retains the framework of Grainville's book while becoming more of a naturalistic fantasy that develops its own mythology and sets its own standards of acceptability for the marvelous. What results is an extension of Grainville's form to the logical end of its possible development as a secularization of the Apocalypse itself, not a metaphorical analogue of apocalypse like those which twentieth-century critics see all around us, nor even the kind of slightly closer analogue that Mary Shelley provided in 1826 in her *Last Man* with its plague destroying the human race in a narrative that draws on biblical Apocalypse mainly for imagery to reinforce a secular tale of the future.

Shelley's introductory fiction of a visit to Sibyl's cave where fragments of the ensuing story are found scattered on sibylline leaves hardly suggests a revelation of the importance claimed by Grainville's narrator. We are told in Shelley's introduction, moreover, that writing up the tale pieced together from documents in the cave, and by implication reading it too, serves mainly for escapist private consolation in the realms of imagination, not public instruction on any especially important doctrine: "My labours have cheered long hours of solitude, and taken me out of a world, which has averted its once benignant face from me, to one glowing with imagination and power."[36] Nor is Shelley's initial fiction of a story derived from prophetic fragments of sibylline writing sustained as a framing device in the way that Grainville sustains his by reverting at the conclusion of *Le dernier homme* to the narrator's experience in the cave at Palmyra. Here, at parting, the celestial spirit commands the narrator to publish what has been revealed in the magic

THE SECULARIZATION OF APOCALYPSE

mirrors so that the tale can serve as a lesson in the necessity of obedience to God.[37]

Whereas Grainville resorts almost exclusively to mythic time in an undated future, Shelley's story is set unequivocally in the twenty-first century. It begins with abdication of England's last king in 2073 and ends with arrival of the Last Man—Lionel Verney, only survivor of the plague—in now-deserted Rome, where he "ascended St. Peter's, and carved on its topmost stone the aera 2100, last year of the world!" (p. 340). In fact, it is only the last year in the sense that no one remains to make calendars. Unlike Grainville's earth, which has even lost its moon through volcanic action some years before finally being destroyed altogether at the moment when time itself ends and eternity begins, the world at the conclusion of Shelley's story continues to exist as usual with its natural stock of plants and animals, although without humans. The year 2100 is their last, not the end as foretold in Apocalypse.

A Methodist preacher who sees the plague in apocalyptic terms as a final judgment visited upon a race of sinners is depicted as a superstitious religious fanatic doing great psychological harm to the dwindling band of survivors who struggle across Europe in a futile effort to escape infection. Meteors and other strange apparitions in the sky evoke conventional imagery of Apocalypse to enhance a gothic atmosphere of doom without excluding naturalistic explanations: "Many cried aloud, that these were no meteors, but globes of burning matter, which had set fire to the earth, and caused the vast cauldron at our feet to bubble up with its measureless waves; the day of judgment was come they averred, and a few moments would transport us before the awful countenance of the omnipotent judge; while those less given to visionary terrors, declared that two conflicting gales had occasioned the last phaenomenon" (p. 270). W. Warren Wagar is right to call such allusions to Judgment Day and its portents "decorations" that are "tacked on, in casual obeisance to the traditional vision of the world's end." He is right too in noting that for Shelley "the end is not a gateway to a new world, nor a judgment, but simply an end, produced by the cold necessity of natural causes."[38]

Mary Shelley's story is a complete secularization of Apocalypse that reduces Revelation to a source of imagery decorating a work whose structure is more like that of a futuristic *Journal of the Plague Year*, told with romantic embellishments and given a bleak ending that foreshadows existentialist eschatologies of the sort now so much in vogue. Indeed the most significant formal affiliations of her work are suggested very clearly by allusions to Defoe's account of the 1665 plague and to *Robinson Crusoe* as a saga of isolation paralleling Verney's tale. Verney's irremediable final predicament without hope of rescue and return to human society, however, outdoes Robinson Crusoe's, just as Shelley's plague goes Defoe's one better by destroying everybody except the narrator.[39] Unlike Grainville's attempt to combine epic, biblical, and novelistic structures, Shelley's *Last Man* is firmly rooted in the realistic tradition of Defoe, although there are strong affinities with the gothic as in *Frankenstein*. If her *Last Man* may be read as a kind of dialectic questioning of Revelation by the method of total secularization of apocalyptic form as well as doctrine—and certainly it may thus be interpreted—then so of course in varying degrees may the majority of subsequent futuristic fictions that tell of mankind's last days.[40] In this as in other respects, Shelley's *Last Man* inaugurates a more viable structure for futuristic fiction than *Le dernier homme* provides.[41] But Shelley could only do so by turning away from the conventional form as well as the doctrines of apocalypse.

While its elements do not finally cohere altogether successfully or provide so workable a model as Mary Shelley does for subsequent tales of the future, *Le dernier homme* deserves wider recognition for what it achieves as a transitional form of futuristic fiction. It avoids the doctrinal straitjacket of much apocalyptic literature. It takes the Apocalypse as a source of ideological credibility while adapting techniques of realistic fiction to create a phenomenology of apocalypse that is credible enough psychologically to create a

THE SECULARIZATION OF APOCALYPSE

significant degree of verisimilitude amid episodes of the marvelous. It also introduces through Grainville's myth of the terrestrial spirit a surprising element of the fantastic—surprising because it is not part of the accepted mythology of Revelation. Ground rules for interpretation are thereby complicated in a way that looks forward to later fictions of apocalypse that more fully serve the epistemological purpose of challenging our conceptions of reality. Fictions by Creuzé de Lesser, Elise Gagne, and Camille Flammarion modeled directly on *Le dernier homme* show both the force of his innovations and the inadequacy of existing genres to develop much further the structure created by Grainville's mixture of elements taken from epic, novel, and the Book of Revelation. Although Félix Bodin was thus clearly right to suggest that novels of the future could only develop by first putting aside obsession with the very end of time, Grainville had come remarkably close to adapting the Apocalypse itself to the form of a futuristic novel.

CHAPTER SIX

Fantasy and Metafiction: From *Les Posthumes* to *The Mummy*

The transformation of utopia into uchronia is not the dominant pattern for early futuristic fiction. Neither is the secularization of apocalypse or the satiric future history as pioneered by Madden's *Memoirs of the Twentieth Century*. In the first half of the nineteenth century, there is a proliferation of tales that seem to have little in common beyond their resort to future time. It is tempting to find order in this diversity by noting that, as the idea of progress became an acceptable myth for modern civilization, its devotees more frequently wrote tales of the future to argue for their faith and thereby also prompted skeptics to adopt the same method for expressing doubts. But this paradigm, though relevant, applies most widely towards the end of the nineteenth century.[1] It describes only one line of development. It ignores the effect of comic modes even in many works that were indeed shaped in part—but only in part—by debates about progress. More to the point of my concerns, that paradigm does not fully account for the emerging aesthetics of futuristic fiction, especially its increasing self-consciousness and its frequent predilection for the fantastic.

From its earliest days, futuristic fiction has often manifested the "more intricate and elaborate relationship" between realism and fantasy that Robert Scholes rightly posits as an appealing attribute of the genre in our century and one of its greatest claims to attention.[2] Equally evident is what Eric Rabkin has described as a catalytic role of the fantastic in facilitating generic change. I agree with him that "our literary history is much more complex than a mere ordered series of reflexes to cultural needs."[3] However much ideas of progress and the facts of accelerating cultural change are reflected, as they surely are, in the emergence of tales of the future, it is also the continuing appeal of fantasy within the system of literature itself that shapes new forms of futuristic fiction. In tales of the future, moreover, fantasy very often signals a movement toward metafiction—that is, toward the various techniques by which a text may invite rather than discourage awareness of its own fictionality and its relationship to other books. Where fantasy is avoided, various metafictional devices often play an equivalent role in moving futuristic fiction away from unselfconscious realism. To illustrate these developments, I shall turn to Restif de la Bretonne and Jane Webb after first glancing more briefly, by way of context, at how some other writers of futuristic fiction during the first half of the nineteenth century adjusted the balance between plausibility, fantasy, and metafiction.

If the first wave of writers who extended the boundaries of futuristic fiction had mainly been concerned with predictive speculation about the future or with debating various programs of reform, their highest premium might have been on verisimilitude, not on fantasy or metafiction. Devices calling attention to fictionality could have been minimized. It would have sufficed to provide uchronic versions of utopia or dystopia showing ever-more-plausible social improvements or visions of imminent disaster. As in Mercier's prototype, works based on this model of uchronia could have maintained their distance from the novel of plotted action and from any intrusion of fantasy beyond the dream which transports a narrator into some utopian or deplorable future. As in *L'An 2440*, moreover, such dreams could have been given a naturalistic explanation that minimizes their air of fantasy. But this pattern did not prevail. Even Emile Souvestre's *Le Monde tel qu'il sera* (The world as it will be), which so brilliantly inaugurated the French dystopian tradition in 1846, maintains a self-reflexive tone of comic detachment from actual future possibilities.[4]

Souvestre's opening scene starts on a note of outright fantasy that very explicitly calls attention to its role *as* fantasy and thus to the book's status as fiction. When Souvestre's newlywed protagonists Martha and Maurice wonder what the future will be like, Martha first wishes she had a fairy godmother to show them, then laments that in the modern world there are no spirits to invoke: "The angels have ceased to visit as they did in the time of Jacob and Tobias; neither Jesus, Mary, nor the saints leave paradise, as in the Middle Ages, to test souls or help the afflicted; have all the superior powers thus abandoned the earth? Is there not here below either god or sprite who could serve as intermediary between the real world and the invisible world? All countries, all ages had their guardian spirit; where is that of our times, and who is he?"[5] This last question is answered by the arrival outside Martha and Maurice's garret window of a "little God" named John Progress, who looks like a combination of banker and solicitor and flies through the air amid "fantastic clouds" of smoke on his "English locomotive" to grant their wish: "Voila! . . . you called me, I arrive" (pp. 8–11). After giving them his business card, he proposes to satisfy their curiosity by arranging a one-way trip to the future: "say the word, and you will fall asleep instantly, not to wake until the year three thousand." They agree, and John Progress, gesturing towards them "like a mesmerizer," soon puts them into a deathlike trance from which they awake in a dystopian future Tahiti: Captain Cook's New-Cythera, as they are reminded, but now named the Isle of the Black-Animal on account of its role as a center for greedy industrialists like M. Omnivore, to whose warehouse crammed with goods from around the world the coffin with their sleeping bodies had been eventually taken (pp. 11, 17).

FANTASY AND METAFICTION

The rest of *Le Monde tel qu'il sera* recounts Martha and Maurice's tour of a world that includes steam-machines for nourishing infants in "colleges" from birth until age eighteen; physicians who diagnose *everyone* as mentally ill; writing machines for producing different genres at top speed; a "perpetual newspaper" printed on an endless sheet of paper that flows through each house on a conveyor belt; theatrical performance of "Kleber in Egypt," a fantastic historical drama (whose script is reproduced) featuring a talking crocodile named Moses; a feminist named Mademoiselle Sparticus who sells subscriptions for printing in ninety-two octavo volumes her "novels, poems, philosophical treatises, voyages, and vaudevilles" aimed at converting all women to her liberated opinions—"the world's revolution in manuscript"; a republic ruled by an empty armchair (known as "l'impeccable"); and purchase of Switzerland by an enterprising capitalist who converts it into a giant park with tollbooths selling tickets for all the major sights. Souvestre's satiric purpose is serious enough: to warn against a "world where man had become enslaved by machines and where interest had replaced love" (p. 321). But his method is not realistic extrapolation to a future whose details are all intended to ring true—except as comic exaggerations of the worst features of his own time. Souvestre stresses the entertaining *improbability* of that extended mesmeric trance by means of which an obliging supernatural spirit with an unlikely name transports the protagonists to a bizarre future—one whose amusingly horrific *implausibilities* are employed to satirize recognizable nineteenth-century attitudes by reducing them to absurdities.

It is not until 1851 that one finds a work of futuristic fiction with a fully developed plot of realistic action *and* an explicit injunction to regard its narrative as the portrait of an altogether possible but avoidable series of potential disasters. This advice comes at the conclusion of *The Last Peer*, whose anonymous author has devoted three fat volumes to the adventures of Lord Ashby—the last peer—in a dismal, impoverished, crime-ridden twentieth-century

England. His country has fallen into evil days because of industrialization, the rise to power of merchant classes at the expense of all others, abandonment of England's established religion in favor of toleration for every sect, and, worst of all, abolition of hereditary aristocracy: "My tale is ended. It is but a sorry one. Why should it be true? The past is beyond recall; but the future has hope for its rainbow. Its doom is not sealed. Its dangers may be averted. Its woes dispelled. Its vices avoided."[6] Some such moral is implicit, to be sure, in one strand of futuristic fiction starting with the anonymous cautionary tale of 1769 called *Private Letters from an American in England to his Friends in America*. This tale also portrays a depressed future England in ways that suggest possible actions which could be taken in the present to avoid the problems it depicts. Uchronias modeled on *L'An 2440* also call attention to an open future that remains to be shaped toward the depicted ideal by present action. But evolution from such works to the didactic mode of *The Last Peer* is not marked simply by appropriation of techniques from realistic novels to enhance verisimilitude while painting increasingly persuasive pictures of what the future may actually hold. Fantasy remained attractive.

Cousin de Grainville had obliquely rejected utopian programs by portraying a fantastic apocalypse that cannot be taken as a convincing prediction of any future close enough to matter, or perhaps any real future. But, for all its originality, his narrative echoes the Book of Revelation while providing too a familiar epic pattern of marvelous interactions between human and divine realms. Within these biblical and epic structures there is no problem in recognizing, whether with approval or distaste, the essentially conventional role of fantastic elements (such as the Terrestrial Genius and his angelic antagonists) or Adam's reappearance on earth as God's messenger. Far from requiring a new poetics of futuristic fiction in order to justify its resort to the fantastic, *Le dernier homme* was praised by its admirers as the sketch for a highly original epic—that is, nothing more (or less) than the latest example of nearly the

FANTASY AND METAFICTION

oldest form of Western literature. Even at its most fantastic, Grainville's story could thus be assimilated more readily to widely shared literary and religious traditions than could Mary Shelley's new myth of the last plague and its sole survivor.

Her *Last Man* was not so easily referred to available critical categories, despite its evident affinities with Gothic fiction, with quasi-historical accounts like Defoe's *Journal of the Plague Year* (itself a generic anomaly), and with narrative conventions of formal realism in the eighteenth-century novel. Indeed because of those very affinities with so many non-epic forms, Shelley's introductory account of transcribing "Sibylline leaves" found in a cave outside Naples, unlike Grainville's frame-tale of encountering a celestial spirit in the Palmyrian cave, cannot be taken as an altogether acceptable equivalent of epic conventions that suggest dictation of the story by some appropriate muse. There are too many discrepancies between those conventions and Shelley's mode of realistic prose fiction. But if her *Last Man* thus poses more of a challenge, its difficulties are also minimized by avoidance of the fantastic. Shelley's final plague, though unlikely, is at least possible and has about it no air of the supernatural. Nor does her future contain any striking departures from nineteenth-century technology or manners. Once readers have accepted the disturbing idea that a plague *might* conceivably spread to the point of destroying all human life, her book can be taken on its own terms without much thought of related works, of its own fictionality, or of the need for a new aesthetics. Not all writers of futuristic fiction, however, attempted equal verisimilitude. Many shared Grainville's predilection for the fantastic but nevertheless avoided his entanglement with such dead forms as epic and biblical prophecy.

Accordingly the question of origins for a story about the future had to be dealt with by creation of new conventions. Long before proliferation of technology allowed Wells to invent the time machine in 1895, it was no longer satisfactory to explain matters by perfunctory recourse to celestial spirits, sibylline leaves, or a dream-vision. Such conceits could still be used—at worst in banal imitation of already trite conventions; at best in witty metafictional variations like Souvestre's creation of John Progress as a new-model celestial spirit casting spells by mesmerism instead of by the older magic. Attempts to provide fresh rationales for resort to future time are among the first hesitant steps towards a new aesthetics for futuristic fiction.

The least fantastic but most overtly metafictional way of justifying a future setting is that adopted in 1810 by Pierre-Marc Gaston, Duc de Levis, in *Les Voyages de Kang-Hi, ou nouvelles lettres chinoises*. This is a very self-conscious literary exercise inviting readers to think almost as much about other books as about the future. Immediately after an italicized announcement that "it is indispensable to read" the preface for an understanding of this work, the author explains that it is based on a double fiction: "A Chinese man travels to Europe with his wife. The epoch of his arrival in Paris is fixed at the year 1910."[7] Literary precedents are cited by way of reminder that "these two kinds of fiction are not new" and to warrant their use: Montesquieu's *Lettres persanes*, of course, for creating a visitor from another culture; and Mercier's *L'An 2440* for the resort to future time.[8] Levis explains that a future setting permits him to show "as if they existed" advances in science and arts which the pace of present improvement renders so probable ("vraisemblables") that only the dates of their adoption remain uncertain. But he rejects the idea of attempting to speculate, as Mercier had, about utopian political and religious institutions that may alter human conduct for the better. Believing instead that human nature can never change and most certainly will not improve by alteration in forms of government, Levis states that he "will paint present manners without worrying about the date which I will write under my pictures" (p. ix). *Les Voyages de Kang-Hi* is thus presented as a deliberate amalgamation of the *Persian Letters* and *The Year 2440*, but with more complex goals than either of these forms. *Les Voyages de Kang-Hi* is designed partly to describe *present* French manners from a distancing perspective as Montesquieu had done, partly to show plausible developments in technology, and partly to establish an explicitly dialogic relationship with Mercier's book by recourse to an opposite method. Whereas *L'An 2440* shows altered customs as well as physical changes in a future Paris, Levis projects *present* customs of 1810 into a future France of 1910 whose surprising *resemblances* to the reader's world thus become a refutation of Mercier's utopian dreams.

Replacement of Montesquieu's Persian travelers with a Chinese couple writing letters about their experiences in France also permits more complex temporal juxtaposition than Mercier had attempted, as Levis suggests in explaining the basis for his choice. In the first place China allows a more estranging perspective: "Its customs, its language, and its laws separate it from the rest of the world, as if it belonged to another planet" (p. xiv). Therefore, Levis implies, Chinese commentators allow for spatio-cultural distancing of the kind exploited by planetary voyages, utopias before Mercier, and such fantasies as *Gulliver's Travels*. More important, China represents another time: not the future, but the remote past. Unlike the pyramids, about "whose most minute details we read with so much pleasure," China, because of its resistance to change, "is the only living and animated monument which high antiquity has transmitted to us. . . . an empire whose inhabitants have remained the same as in the time of the Chaldeans, the Etruscans, the Pelasgians, and whose mores do not have any of the resemblances to ours which one finds among the Romans" (pp. xvii–xviii). Moreover, and equally important, travelers have provided detailed information about China since Marco Polo's account. More recent reporters are the most reliable and Du Halde's *Description de la Chine et de la Tartarie chinoise* (1735) "the most authentic and the most complete" (p. xxi). Highest marks go for authenticity.

Levis surveys such material briefly in his preface while referring readers to an extensive annotated bibliography at the end of his book (2:269–83), in hopes that showing the sources he has conscientiously employed "would give some authority to my writings" (p. xxv). His work thus claims the advantages of authenticity, not fantasy: an exact realism in the cultural attitudes expressed by Kang-hi. Achievement of this verisimilitude, in turn, depends upon the reader's awareness not of China but of those myriad factual books about China to which *Les Voyages de Kang-Hi* is put in explicit metafictional relationship.

If Chinese attitudes have for Europeans the exotic air of reflecting a culture that might as well be from another (and perforce imaginary) planet—because from another time *but one that really existed*—so much the better. Levis manages to have it both ways without any implicit or explicit recourse to fantasy: he gains some of the quasi-fantastic effects of allusion to a seemingly imaginary culture while nevertheless claiming verisimilitude as the distinguishing attribute of his narrative by virtue of its reliance on books about China. He also refuses to envision any future changes that are not rendered plausible by existing trends in politics or technology: "If it is absurd to propose recipes for radically curing the ambition of princes, the depravity of courtesans, the coquetry of women, egotism and cupidity, it is not ridiculous to work at diminishing physical evil: one can reasonably search for ways to make diseases less common, to prevent contagions, to correct the deficiencies of climate, to improve public health, to improve nourishment and make it less dependent upon the seasons, to make transportation easier . . . in short, *to enhance the pleasures of the rich, and above all to diminish the suffering of the poor*" (pp. x–xi). As for political speculation, Levis remarks that "this sort of prophecy, even when it does not lack probability ['vraisemblance'], lends itself to ridicule when it pretends to fix the date of events . . . but in giving myself the latitude of a century, I am placed in a more favorable position, and I have been able to anticipate the consequences of widely expected events" (pp. xxvii–xxviii). Accordingly an appendix provides a future history narrating the revolution by which India achieves its independence from Britain.

FANTASY AND METAFICTION

Again the criterion is plausibility. This future history is grounded in the India of 1810 and is thus justified as a source of accurate information: "The details of customs and geography relating to that country, always interesting, which one will find in this account, make me hope that it will not appear too long" (p. xxviii). India's war of independence must be referred to the future, but the narration of it in *Les Voyages de Kang-Hi* claims attention not only as prediction but as an accurate picture of present realities in that country. Only a future political event widely regarded as inevitable is portrayed, and the warrant for that portrayal is the conviction of its inevitability: this too is an implicit rebuke to futuristic utopian speculation as (among its other deficiencies) lacking in verisimilitude.

Levis makes one grudging concession to fiction: "In a time where the taste for novels is almost universal, I did not believe I could excuse myself from placing an intrigue in a book whose form, at least, is frivolous ['légere']" (p. xxvii). Accordingly Kang-hi experiences difficulties because of an infatuation for a French woman whose husband eventually challenges him to a duel. But this is only one episode (predictably dull) in a work whose organizing principle is not that of a novel about human relationships. Even this episode focuses mainly upon present rather than future cultural differences in attitudes towards women, marriage, and dueling. Levis also justifies including Kang-hi's love affair on grounds that it will enhance verisimilitude by showing that his Chinese traveler is not unbelievably perfect: "I have not tried to depict models of a perfection which is too ideal, I have simply represented what one often finds in the world, a man endowed with a true heart and a just spirit but who, giving in to example and seduction, does not recognize his aberration until he sees himself . . . a victim of the consequences of his weakness" (p. xxvii). Psychological realism of a novelistic sort is what Levis prepares his readers to expect in a love story that is included in *Les Voyages de Kang-Hi* because it is published in an age whose taste runs to novels. And psychological realism as defined by novelistic conventions is exactly what readers get, along with a plausibly depicted clash between ancient Chinese attitudes and *current* French manners in a future that is explicity confined to expectations considered realistic in 1810. *Les Voyages de Kang-Hi* is thus intended to define the present of 1810 with respect to probable future history and actual past history as represented by living exemplifications of an age long vanished from European experience. The method is metafictional: in a preface and bibliography readers discover the books about China and India that are Levis's time machines.

In 1837 R. F. Williams provided a very different but equally metafictional defense of resort to future time in his anonymously published romance *Eureka: a Prophecy of the Future*. This story has neither outright fantasy nor much realism in its account of how the Lady Eureka disguises herself as a page boy named Zabra to follow her true love Oriel Porphyry during adventures at sea—adventures that include capture by a pirate who calls himself "Captain Death" and that terminate happily for all when Oriel becomes emperor of the Columbians. Other characters have such names as Professor Fortyfolios and Doctor Tourniquet. This tale is identified by the narrator of *Eureka*'s introduction as a manuscript written by one "Wilhelm," a dying fellow student at Göttingen, to illustrate his theories about the desirability of writing tales set in the future as a means of getting literature "out of the beaten track."[9] Objections raised by the unnamed narrator as he talks to Wilhelm are dealt with (in between coughing fits) by a lengthy romantic defense of the imagination as a power which "can conquer any difficulty."[10] It follows for Wilhelm—and at a somewhat more playfully metafictional level for the author and readers of *Eureka*—that, "instead of being satisfied with attempting illustrations of historical periods, or of an existing state of society," writers of fiction may "attempt to describe an imaginary time as well as imaginary characters. If a man possess a powerful imagination, let him conceive the state of the world a thousand years hence, or at any other time remote from the present" (p. x). Here futuristic fiction is given the same status due to all imaginative writing, albeit somewhat trivialized by the introduction's comic tone and the blatantly unrealistic romance that follows. In this view tales of the future need no more warrant than any other kind of fiction: the more powerful the writer's imagination the better the tale, and all such tales are to be judged simply as exercises of the imagination.[11]

The impulse toward a more Wellsian quasi-scientific realism and high seriousness in justifying an account of future time can be seen in the introduction to John Banim's anonymously published 1824 satire *Revelations of the Dead-Alive*. It starts with a chapter explaining in great detail how its narrator reached an apparently real future through experimentation with prolonged trance states whose effects are very different from mere dreams: "In what manner or fashion I was in the future, whether actually or spiritually, I am not permitted or competent to declare; but I was in it, not as a dreamer . . . but seeing, and hearing, and understanding, as previously I had seen, heard, and understood, in my past world."[12] But the elaborately explained distinction between trance and dream is rendered irrelevant as a naturalistic explanation for what follows by a tone of comic exaggeration that prevails throughout the ensuing satiric narrative. *Revelations of the Dead-Alive* winds up in a far less realistic mode than its introduction allows. It is as though the introduction were designed as rationale for a tale of Wellsian realism which could not yet be sustained.

The issue of rationalizing a future setting might be avoided by simply plunging into narration, as in the first sentence of *Mrs. Maberly; or, The World as It Will Be:* "In the year 2036 two ladies were occupying a small double-bedded room in Wilson's Hotel, a second-rate inn, or rather boarding-house, in that pleasant and fashionable watering-place, Civita Bella, which, as everybody knows, is situated on the north-western coast of Australia."[13] But eventually even this beginning is assimilated to a metafictional statement. After almost two hundred pages setting in motion a tedious love story that revolves around a group traveling to the glass-domed city of Vitria on the site of a hot springs near the North Pole, Mrs. *Maberly*'s twenty-first-century narrator decides "to throw a somerset backwards into the nineteenth century" for a thematically related adventure (1:186). There ensues a Shandean dialogue between the narrator and some imaginary readers who question the propriety of this digression. A "young lady" from the nineteenth century asks: "Is it because *I* belong to that period, and you feel anxious to return once more into *my* neighborhood?" (1:186–87). A twenty-first-century "hypercritic" objects that such leaps backward and forward in time violate the rules of criticism: "Consider the Unities!—You commenced your tale in the year 2036; there let it remain, if you please, till the end of the third volume. When you are safely arrived at the word 'Finis,' we will allow you afterwards to wander wherever you please." The narrator's retort diverts attention from his story to the book as creation and artifact:

> A fiddlestick for the Unities! say I in return, with a magnanimous flourish of my goose-quill pen. . . . Let the printer and the bookbinder take care of the Unities: if *they* stamp and stich my rambling narrative into three neat, soul-stirring, and gentlemanlike volumes, it will be all that I or any good-natured reader will care about the business. . . . Your over-nice people should write their own novels, and then they would be certain to have something that suited them. Those who delight in "'orrid murders" might kill a man or strangle a child in every other page: those who love to melt in softness and in sentiment, might pour out their tender souls upon the tear-stained paper. . . . This would be the commencement of a new era in literature. . . . But I grow prosy, and must perform my projected somerset without delay. Now for a good long run upon the spring-board of imagination!—and whisk!—presto!—heels over head!—here I am, standing before you, in the midst of the year one thousand eight hundred and thirty-six! (1:187–90)

The digression ends with equal ease: "We will now return to the twenty-first century, and proceed smoothly and straight-forwardly with our novel. . . . so, *allons!*—let me throw another somerset forwards, and 'tumble up' without further ceremony into the year two thousand and thirty-six" (1:206). A potentially bothersome shift in temporal setting is perhaps rendered acceptable by this reminder that anything an author can imagine is possible, because in works that are *only* fiction *all* things are possible. Epigraphs from Chaucer, Shakespeare, Milton, Dryden, Pope, Sterne, Byron, and others scattered throughout *Mrs. Maberly* serve as further metafictional reminders that it is to be judged as a work of literary imagination, not an exercise in prediction.

But such metafictional gestures in *Mrs. Maberly* serve no coherent purpose with respect to its complex plot, which is otherwise narrated in the manner of a realistic novel that concentrates on psychological portraits of such familiar types as a domineering mother and young lovers bothered by her meddling. Nor does their future world especially enhance appreciation of such character studies. If anything, it is a distraction. Their story gains little from being played out in a century when England is part of the Russian Empire and the chief scientific wonder is the city of Vitria. A chapter describing this polar resort has for its epigraph a statement on hothouses from "Loudon's Encyclopedia of Gardening, p. 816, Third Ed." The technology of a city under glass with steam engines powered by hot springs is thus presented in part as an extrapolation from nineteenth-century ideas. But the possibility of a hothouse large enough to shelter a city in the Arctic depends upon an arbitrary supposition that in 1880 a warm area is discovered close to the North Pole. This supposition veers away from plausible extrapolation toward fantasy.

Allusions to creatures from the realms of fantasy are then employed to augment the sense of strangeness created by locating the action of a rather humdrum love story in a remarkable future city. Its gardens, we learn, shelter mythical as well as real animals: "There was the unicorn from Africa, so long deemed fabulous; there was the phoenix, whose real nature approaches much nearer to the mythological fable, than our sceptical forefathers were willing to believe; there were clouds of Williams'-dell butterflies wheeling about as if in joyous exaltation; there were birds of paradise, so strange and so lovely, that their extreme beauty seemed almost unnatural" (3:57). Here in the account of Vitria, fabulous creatures are naturalized and real ones affiliated to fable. For anyone standing at the center of Vitria's glass enclosure and looking around, "the effect was certainly more like magic than reality" (3:58). This is not primarily an invitation to speculate about the possibilities of technology. In *Mrs. Maberly* at its most evocative the future becomes an arena where reality and fantasy coincide, their distinctions crumbling. But the effect is not sustained. It was Restif de la Bretonne and Jane Webb who most clearly saw futuristic fiction as a form encouraging new ways of relating fantasy to reality.

Even Restif de la Bretonne's most devoted admirers have found *Les Posthumes* something of an embarrassment, although not for the usual reasons. It does not quite fit into any available category. Charles A. Porter in his excellent study of Restif's novels relegates it, along with *La Découverte australe*, to a chapter headed "Science Fiction" and winds up a brief discussion by stating that "as a novel, it is one of Restif's most signal failures."[14] I do not disagree with this harsh judgment; however, I do want to argue that *Les Posthumes* is also a work of signal interest for my topic because of what it shows of the interaction of realism and fantasy within early futuristic fiction. Precisely because Restif here fails, as he so often does, to integrate coherently into a unified or easily readable work those disparate modes which he tries to combine, his narrative offers clear evidence of how fantasy and realism could enter new relationships by resort to future time. Restif's unusual blend of naïvete with sophisticated avant-garde experimentation that verges on genius makes it possible to identify in his writing the interaction of features often more artfully concealed by others. As a novel *Les Posthumes* is certainly a failure. It is too diffuse. Its philosophy is hard to take seriously. Its critique of mob violence during the French Revolution gains little from being situated within a futuristic fantasy. Nevertheless, for the history I am tracing, *Les Posthumes* is crucial. In it we see for the first time in futuristic fiction a sustained attempt to interweave fantasy and fact within a narrative that is insistently metafictional.

Resort to the future is for Restif an indispensable technique, though far from the only one, for liberating his tale from the usual constraints that prevent actual historical events from intruding on a universe imagined as the setting for fantasy. Instead of locating *Les Posthumes* unequivocally with respect to the reader's time, Restif blurs many conventional distinctions between past, present, and future. Authorship is the first temporal issue on which Restif deliberately equivocates. Published in four volumes in 1802 with no mention of his name as the real author, *Les Posthumes* is described by its subtitle as "Letters received after the death of a husband by his wife, who believes him to be in Florence. By the late Cazotte." The book's abridged title is "Letters from the Tomb."[15] This tale of posthumous correspondence thus seems itself to come posthumously from the hand of Jacques Cazotte, who had been sent to the guillotine by a revolutionary tribunal on September 25, 1792, a full decade before publication of *Les Posthumes*.

Apart from the circumstances of his death, which he met with great dignity, Cazotte was most famous for bizarre Illuminist beliefs and for a widely read fantasy *Le Diable amoureux*, published in 1776. This is the story of a Spaniard called Alvare, who dabbles in necromancy in order to summon the devil. The latter duly appears: first in the form of a camel's head uttering frightful words, then as a white spaniel, then as a man, and finally as a beautiful woman wooing Alvare throughout a complicated series of adventures which put his soul in peril.[16] Restif thus arouses expectations that *Les Posthumes* will be in the same fantastic vein as *Le Diable amoureux*. But fantasy as a kind of writing is also related to the reality of Cazotte's life and death by the false attribution of *Les Posthumes*.

ORIGINS OF FUTURISTIC FICTION

Restif tries to capitalize on whatever piquancy there might be in reading what is presented as a truly posthumous work in the form of a story about a lady receiving posthumous letters without realizing that they come from a dead man. This frame-story is grotesque enough to defy credibility, but it is not in itself fantastic in the manner of *Le Diable amoureux*.

In Restif's frame-tale a man named Fontlhete falls in love with a married woman, Hortense de Chazu. Despairing of success he takes a slow-acting poison, only to learn that she is now free and willing to marry him, which she does. Knowing that he will die in about a year, Fontlhete prepares 366 letters and says he is leaving for a trip to London, Rome, and Florence. He arranges for the letters to be mailed to her at intervals over the year following his death, with postscripts added by a friend in response to her replies, so that Hortense will believe him still alive. In the letters, the first dated February 1, 1779, are a series of fantastic narratives more in the style of *Le Diable amoureux* than is the frame-story. Throughout volume one these letters deal with the afterlife as experienced by two lovers, Yfflasie and Clarendon, who die on their wedding night while consummating their marriage; they are killed by an earthquake (reminiscent perhaps of the famous Lisbon disaster of November 1, 1755, that so differently inspired Voltaire). Starting in volume two, the letters also recount adventures experienced over several thousand future years by an immortal, Duke Multipliandre, who has the power to place his consciousness in the bodies of other people by displacing their souls. Fontlhete hopes these tales will prepare Hortense for the shock of learning that he is actually dead. He intends to provide consolation by suggesting ideas of immortality while also getting Hortense accustomed to thinking about death instead of simply having that disagreeable topic thrust upon her suddenly by an announcement of his own demise. For those readers who believe *Les Posthumes*'s false ascription to Cazotte, Hortense's situation becomes an emblem of their own relationship to the supposed author of *Les Posthumes*.

FANTASY AND METAFICTION

From the retrospective viewpoint of readers in 1802, its framework of imaginary posthumous correspondence also becomes an ironic foreshadowing of that relationship—a kind of unwitting prophecy on the part of Cazotte, who had some reputation as a prophet foretelling the French Revolution. The "Letters from the Tomb" duplicate fictionally the circumstances under which *Les Posthumes* would be read: as a legacy from Cazotte rather than as the actual work of a living writer Restif. The situations of the fictional lady and Restif's real readers are apparently reversed. They know that Cazotte is dead (the false ascription reminds or informs them of this fact), whereas the lady in the story is deceived by letters designed to conceal her husband's death. She believes him still alive. Of course anyone who took *Les Posthumes* at face value as Cazotte's was deceived in an equal but opposite way; at publication in 1802 its real author was still very much alive, although he must have known that he was nearing the end of his days. Restif died four years later.

This game of deception is not quite so pointless as it may seem. Surely while writing the book around 1796 or perhaps as early as 1788, and while publishing it in 1802, Restif was somehow coming to terms with his own impending death. This awareness may partly account for his themes and for his narration of Multipliandre's adventures in the far future.[17] More significantly from any reader's viewpoint, Restif's lifelong compulsion to record his own ideas and experiences was accompanied by an equally powerful impulse to conceal himself under a remarkable variety of assumed identities. These were mostly fictional characters, although for *Les Posthumes* Restif took on the persona of a real man, Cazotte, who was not only the author of a notable fantasy and an Illuminist would-be prophet but also one of the more poignant Royalist victims of the Revolutionary tribunals. The sources of Restif's drive to concealment, along with its consequences elsewhere in his enormous oeuvre of over two hundred volumes, are of less immediate concern than the sheer persistence of his quest for new ways to interweave fact and fiction. Toward the end of Restif's life, this quest resulted in an imaginative identification with Cazotte that was expressed as a tale about the adventures of Duke Multipliandre both in the far future and also, as we shall see, during the immediate past of the French Revolution. Elsewhere in Restif's writing, as in *Les Posthumes* but with less complexity of temporal setting, fictions very often refer in surprising ways to actuality. Even his most fantastic flights of imagination may present themselves less as mere escapism than as the vehicle of more or less overt historical record and also of philosophies which, however hard for readers to accept, at least invite serious consideration rather than mere surrender to the pleasures of dreaming.[18]

Thus, in an "editor's note" at the beginning of *Les Posthumes*, Restif insists that the stories embody Illuminist doctrines advanced by Cazotte and actually believed by him: "There has been much talk of the Illuminists, and people speak of them all the time without much knowing just what Illuminism is: the author of this work wrote guided by their principles. Everything that Fontlhete says to his wife, Cazotte really believed. These are his opinions on the situation of souls after death. . . . What Duke Multipliandre says also conforms to Cazotte's ideas. . . . If he himself could not put his spirit in another body, he believed that others could do so and that [only] the technique of doing this was unknown to him. . . . This little elucidation was necessary." (1:22). This claim introduces another uncertainty that is partly generic and partly temporal. Readers are invited to take the stories not simply as fantastic amusement but also as fictional exposition of beliefs held by Cazotte and other Illuminists. To accept this invitation is to see *Les Posthumes* as more of a *roman philosophique* purveying important ideas than as a merely amusing fantasy. This is also to regard it as a work of deliberately historical interest, because its Illuminist ideas are not only presented for acceptance by readers around 1802 but also and even more conspicuously referred to the life and times of Cazotte during the eighteenth-century heyday of Illuminism.[19]

FANTASY AND METAFICTION

Under the conventional guise of an unnamed "editor" who tells of getting the manuscript from Cazotte and says something too about his death and beliefs, Restif further stresses the connection of *Les Posthumes* to ideas flourishing in the 1780s and 1790s. There follows a short preface which, we are told, Cazotte *would have thought necessary to include*. In it readers are informed that the purpose of this unusual work ("de cet Ouvrage extraordinaire") is to cure people of vain fears of death, fears which Christianity has doubled or trebled (1:*2). Whatever one finally makes of the book, its attack on Christianity here and in subsequent passages cannot be dismissed as aimed at a trivial target. The method adopted might have been abstract reasoning, we are next told, but Cazotte preferred to establish truths "in an active and dramatic manner based on a real incident related to me by Mme de Beauharnais, aunt-in-law ['belle-tante'] of General Bonaparte, that savior of the French nation. It is by means of these extraordinary stories ['Récits extraordinaires'], which are in the class of possibilities because the human imagination cannot depart from nature, that I accomplish two purposes equally moral." (1:*). By crediting the basic idea of *Les Posthumes*'s frame-story to Fanny de Beauharnais's account of something that really happened, and by advancing a theory that everything imaginable is possible because nature constrains within her laws the limits of what we *can* think, Restif here argues not only the inseparability of fiction and fact but also the claims of even the wildest fantasy to some degree of verisimilitude.

That he will hardly persuade many on the latter point is of less moment than the fact that he tries. He tries, moreover, without any reference to the new science and technology that for Samuel Madden in 1733, as for Félix Bodin in 1834, offered a more telling argument for altering the literary relationship of plausibility and verisimilitude. From another perspective altogether, that of Illuminist belief in chains of analogical relationships linking all of nature (even everything thinkable), *Les Posthumes* is explicitly intended to dissolve *in a new way* the usual boundaries between fiction and reality, fable and philosophy, the plausible and the marvelous. Along with Restif's attempts to refer the Illuminist ideas of his book to the real world of Jacques Cazotte, Fanny de Beauharnais, and Napoleon Bonaparte, there are reiterated attempts to dissociate *Les Posthumes* from previous genres. If in bearing a freight of philosophical ideas it resembles the *roman philosophique* while in narrating bizarre stories it resembles fantasy in the mode of *Le Diable amoureux*, *Les Posthumes* nevertheless claims from its outset to be something else, altogether sui generis.

Thus after the preface that we are assured Cazotte would have wanted, there is another section headed "Elucidations" (and even printed twice, though presumably by mistake). Here Restif stresses the unprecedented form of his work: "The little stories are unusual, of a kind absolutely new and which nobody has ever thought of."[20] The story of Duke Multipliandre is "more extraordinary, although with more romantic probability, than the Thousand-and-One Nights. . . . But there is a variety of events, always amusing, always founded on nature. His *metamorphoses*, his *love*, the persecutions which he suffers, the victories which he wins—all is new and of a kind to please the reasonable reader."[21] The "Elucidation" also informs readers that Fontlhete's correspondence terminates "with a prediction of the Revolution" made by Yfflasie and Clarendon, thanks to "the power which they have to see the future" (1:7; in the subsequent text it is Multipliandre who provides this prediction). Here too an allusion to history and perhaps also a more oblique allusion to the prophetic powers really credited by many to Cazotte is interwoven with a more perplexing but equally insistent claim for generic novelty: *Les Posthumes*, according to its "editor," offers narratives both more extraordinary *and* more probable than the *Thousand and One Nights*.

This paradox is not so much resolved as reiterated throughout the text of *Les Posthumes*. As Fontlhete begins his tale of lovers in the next life, he tells Hortense that he is preparing "stories of a kind that have never been written, because no one has had the opportunity to go back to the source as I do" (1:65). The enigmatic hint of going "to the source" may be taken as coming less from Fontlhete than from Cazotte in cryptic allusion to *his* mystic experiences; in any case, the ensuing narration about Yfflasie and Clarendon very evidently does have some claim to originality despite its equally manifest shortcomings of prolixity and unconvincing metaphysics. Lest readers overlook its novelty, which is after all its chief claim, Restif makes Hortense urge Fontlhete (whom she supposes still alive) to continue his tale of the two lovers after their death because "this is new for everybody, and very interesting for me" (1:72). The fantastic elements which give that tale its attractive air of novelty are striking even in brief outline.

After being killed by the earthquake just as they are consummating their marriage, Yfflasie and Clarendon first experience the sensuous exhilaration of flying over the whole world, from North to South Pole, going wherever they wish, carried rapidly *by* their wishes ("un desire les y transporta") with greater ease "than a Parisian can walk through his tiny garden." "Quelle volupté!" Fontlhete comments while narrating this fantasy of spiritual flight powered by mere thought (1:76–77). Here Restif keeps his readers very far indeed from any ideas of the new technology for real flight introduced by Joseph and Etienne Montgolfier nine years before Cazotte himself went to the guillotine and nineteen years before publication of *Les Posthumes*.

Yfflasie and Clarendon next learn about the cycles of reincarnation as they wander through the spiritual world encountering the souls of many famous people: Louis XIV, Richelieu, Frederick the Great, Voltaire, Rousseau, and Joan of Arc, to name only the most eminent of those who happen to be available between incarnations. The lovers just miss Racine, who was reincarnated shortly before their arrival. Yfflasie and Clarendon find Louis XIV at Versailles perched in a window where a potted bay tree grows. He is surrounded by his courtiers in miniature: "All that great crowd of admirers, numbering more than ten thousand, stood on a leaf of the little bay tree" (1:86–87).

Each soul, Yfflasie and Clarendon learn, spends one hundred years as a spirit before entering another body. During each discorporate century, spirits can remember their previous one hundred lives. Only those who have lived virtuously have a choice when it comes to the next incarnation. Richelieu, for example, who has not earned the right to choose, becomes in his next life a common murderer. There are several such narratives, some rather extensive, of the second or previous lives of famous people. The spirit world where souls live during each century between incarnations is another of Restif's utopias, but its details are of less concern here than the fact of their utterly fantastic milieu: neither a possible if unlikely island on earth as in More's prototype nor a real though future place as in Mercier's *L'An 2440*.[22] Among the anecdotes of second or previous lives lived by famous people, Restif includes high praise for Mercier (1:287) but no mention whatever of *L'An 2440*. when Beaumarchais's soul arrives, we are told about the praise of him in works (some unpublished) by "that poor *Restif Labretone*" (1:320).

Throughout the story of Yfflasie and Clarendon, complex allusions to the real world are thus interwoven with a narrative that primarily invites applause for the very audacity of its fantastic inventiveness. Hortense is surely intended by Restif to echo—or suggest—what his real readers ought to be thinking when she makes her final comment on reading the letters from Fontlhete in the first volume of *Les Posthumes:* "In truth I love these mad fancies ['imaginations folles'], because they show the gaiety of your spirit in writing them" (1:355). As the "editor" also points out, this response further heightens ironies arising from the discrepancy between Fontlhete's death and her belief that he is alive and in good spirits. But all this is mere prologue to a tale that readers are explicitly told will be yet more fantastic. Restif closes volume one

214

FANTASY AND METAFICTION

with an italicized passage promising even greater wonders: *"This Volume is not the most marvelous of the work: because it only contains the story of the disembodied souls; but it is by this that it was necessary to begin the correspondence of the couple, one of whose members wanted to preserve the other from the fear of death"* (1:356). By this explanation Restif endeavors to persuade readers that the fantasies to come, like the story of Yfflasie and Clarendon, are altogether appropriate to the frame situation of Fontlhete's attempt to prepare Hortense for news of his death. More significantly, through this explanation Restif provides a metafictional comment both remarking and endorsing the narrative quest of *Les Posthumes* for ever-greater degrees of the marvelous. This goal is next pursued in the story of Duke Multipliandre's adventures in the far future *and* in the immediate past. The futuristic fantasy in *Les Posthumes* winds up with a prophetic vision that is in fact (and form) a history of the French Revolution.

Early in volume two of *Les Posthumes*, Restif begins "The Marvelous History of Jean-Jacob, Duke Multipliandre" (2:71). After an account of his birth and adventures in the eighteenth century, the narrative goes forward in time to "The Future History of Duke Multipliandre" (4:122ff: "HISTOIRE future du Duc MULTIPLIANDRE"). A note, again from Restif in his guise of "editor," informs readers that "it is on this marvelous history that CAZOTTE founded his hopes for the success of his work. . . . The reader will doubtless agree" (2:verso of title page). Here again Restif provides a metafictional comment inviting readers to judge what follows not so much for its philosophy but for its marvelous *story* whose qualities as a fantastic tale will bear out Cazotte's hopes for the success of *Les Posthumes*. Readers are invited to measure their response to the work against the supposed author's judgment of it. The question Restif poses at the outset of Multipliandre's tale is not what will happen to him, although of course the editorial comment should heighten curiosity about this. Instead Restif focuses attention on the issue of whether readers will agree with the author that the second tale is the essential one. Multipliandre's adventures, not those of Yfflasie and Clarendon, are to be the touchstone of Cazotte's success as a writer in *Les Posthumes*. Readers are to stand back and think of the story as story in relation to its author instead of simply immersing themselves in it and accepting or rejecting the doctrines it embodies. Because the alleged author Cazotte is dead, Restif in this note also encourages readers to play the even-more-distanced role of "posterity" assessing the literary reputation of a man who flourished in the previous century—a role that Restif could not quite impose on readers under his own name in 1802.

The name "Multipliandre," we are told (2:232), derives from "multiplex-andros" and thus means "many men"—an allusion apparently to the Duke's adventures throughout the lifetimes of many ordinary men and also to his ability to project his mind into the bodies of other people to experience for awhile their situation, so that in effect he becomes many men. Multipliandre provides a vague explanation in terms of cabalistic lore of his power to live in other bodies, an ability he exercises by "efforts absolutely physical, which involve nothing of the supernatural" (2:71–72). Later there is a similar effort to explain in terms of chemistry rather than magic an invisibility powder used by Multipliandre. Restif thus tries to have it both ways: a power fantasy is introduced with gestures toward naturalistic explanation that will give it an air of plausibility denied to the supernatural. Such gestures seem futile, however, in a context where so many outright incredibilities prevail.

But again what is significant is that Restif does try. His intermittent attempts to constrain fantastic episodes within the realm of plausibility are another sign of his effort to establish a new form with elements that had previously seemed incompatible and for which there was no exact precedent. Even Mercier's procedure in *L'An 2440* hardly inspires Restif's account of future social and biological developments that are ascribed partly to the efforts of an immortal acting over many centuries. Nor does reading Mercier's uchronia provide standards by which "The Future History of Duke Multipliandre" may be judged—except of course as a failure because of those very features which are most original and have greatest affinities to many subsequent developments in futuristic fiction.

Instead of providing anything like Mercier's ideal civilization portrayed at one precisely specified moment of distant but not inconceivably distant future time in a familiar place, Restif invites readers to imagine a vast series of geological, biological, and social transformations encompassing the most remote areas of our planet, new continents, and even parts of the solar system. The story is carried through future millennia that are not dated except for one reference to the year 99,796 as a time by which earth has moved into the orbit of Venus. The narrative is otherwise so devoid of allusions to calendar time that even that figure's tenuous relationship to the present is rendered meaningless. Restif's far future appears so disconnected from present or near-future time as measured by clocks and calendars that one must wonder why he bothered to specify the temporal setting as futuristic at all. Why not resort to that once-upon-a-time which adequately serves for so much fantasy, or to that unspecified present or close past that will do well enough for tales like *Le Diable amoureux?* Indeed, why not simply go to terra incognita as in *La Découverte australe* or to another world altogether as the planetary voyagers like Cyrano had done?

Part of the answer is Restif's preoccupation with escapist dreams of wish-fulfillment taking the form of cosmological and biological fantasies whose medium of enactment must be long stretches of time—fantasies for which he claimed (however unconvincingly) a degree of possibility that could only ring even faintly true when referred to a distant future. Thousands and even millions of years ahead such things as have not happened and cannot now transpire in our world at least *might* really take place: we cannot know for sure until the time arrives (and when it does we won't be there). A very far future setting allows free rein for fantasy while it retains a tantalizing air of possibility denied to fantastic adventures in a frankly nonexistent era of "once-upon-a-time" that will *never* arrive. Another part of the answer is Restif's obsession with constructing utopias, whether sexual, social, or political. These are most powerful as calls to action or commentaries on the present when put into that realm of possibility (if not probability) uniquely afforded, as Mercier realized more clearly, by future time. Multipliandre's future adventures show how Restif attempted to solve the formal problem of connecting both fantasy and utopian speculation to history.

The initial narrative leap ahead is to an updated period vaguely specified as postrevolutionary. Multipliandre's first three wives, after living several lifetimes, have wearied and chosen to die, whereupon he retires to an enclosed country retreat, becomes a shepherd, and marries twelve women. Such marriages, Fontlhete breaks off the tale to explain to Hortense, "will be legal, thanks to a revolution which will take place in France, and which Multipliandre has predicted to me. This will be the material of several letters that I will write to you next January 1788" (4:126). Evidently, if this prediction concerns what readers in 1802 knew as the French Revolution—*their* revolution—that began in 1789, then postrevolutionary developments (including such lavish polygamy) must be referred to a remote future only distantly connected to the changes actually set in motion by the events of 1789. Restif made such temporal distancing explicit rather than implicit in his play *L'An 2000*. Because it locates its action portraying yet another variety of sexual utopia in a specified future time, this work (despite its dramatic mode) is more akin formally than *Les Posthumes* to the uchronic tradition inaugurated by Mercier's *L'An 2440*.[23] But drama was not the most congenial medium for Restif's experiments with futuristic settings. Perhaps because of residual pressures to observe dramatic unities of action and time, the stage did not so easily allow that interweaving of past, present, and future that Restif attempts in *Les Posthumes*.

FANTASY AND METAFICTION

As the account of Multipliandre's postrevolutionary life unfolds, further drastic liberalization of laws concerning divorce, multiple marriages, extramarital affairs, and related issues are described in a utopian document entitled "Plan of an absolute liberty for French Republicans" (4:128–32). The narrator—still Fontlhete supposedly writing to Hortense in the 1780s—then explains that "Multipliandre's goal was to revive within his enclosure the golden age and patriarchal customs" (4:133). Here the future explicitly becomes a potential locus for another golden age. Next there is a brief historical survey of sexual mores through the centuries in different countries, followed by a report of Multipliandre's long discourse on sexuality to "his twelve wives, who were Parisians" (4:134–37). His critique of Parisian sexual habits very obviously refers not to a distant future when everything has changed but to late eighteenth- and early nineteenth-century Paris—Cazotte's Paris, the Paris of those reading *Les Posthumes* on its publication in 1802, and of course Restif's Paris (although his identity as author remains concealed). Multipliandre's ensuing lecture on the evils of indiscriminate sexual encounters, the dangers of self-abuse, and the virtues of moderate abstention is also unmistakably directed at readers in 1802 as a lesson they should and could apply immediately without waiting for the utopian future to arrive or taking unlikely political steps toward bringing it about. Restif has slipped into his familiar didactic mode. More significantly, the narrative here has managed, albeit clumsily, to collapse distinctions between a strange future and the familiar present.

An imagined future as a metaphor of the present or as a thinly disguised satiric or didactic version of the present is so much a hallmark of later futuristic fiction that one may forget how little precedent there was to guide Restif in adopting such a strategy. *L'An 2440* did not offer a model, because Mercier makes his utopian Paris as different as possible from the France of 1771. Nor did Restif know *Memoirs of the Twentieth Century*, which might have provided some guidance. There was, to be sure, a tradition of imaginary voyages in the mode of *Gulliver's Travels* depicting strange places which are more or less defamiliarized versions of the reader's world. But it was no easy leap to future settings that might connect such places to actual history, as Restif's very clumsiness shows. One sign of the difficulty is his awkward intrusion of eighteenth-century mores into a future where they and the lecture they occasion seem conspicuously anachronistic rather than of a piece with other aspects of this future; they thereby serve as ingenious ways of *obliquely* recalling the present to consideration from a new perspective. The context does provide such a perspective. But it is not altogether sustained. The narrative too conspicuously slides into a description of the Paris known to readers around 1802. There is a kind of fluctuation of temporal reference here that seems out of control.

Early in the account of Multipliandre's future history, moreover, the verb tenses often waver irresolutely between future and preterite. This grammatical uncertainty in temporal perspective is a far more telling sign of Restif's difficulties with the formal problem of narrating an imaginary future in a way that connects it to the reader's present. He seems at first reluctant to narrate from a future rather than a present temporal viewpoint. Thus, of the enclosure where Multipliandre lives with his twelve wives, we are told: "Happiness had made (will make) its refuge out of this small corner of the universe."[24] The narrator remarks, after describing Multipliandre's program for rearing his many children to get adequate exercise, sleep, nourishment, and fresh air: "It would be impossible to report all the pains which he took (that is to say, will take) for them, in order to form men and women. He joined (or will join) to all this an ignorance of vice."[25] After further oscillations of this kind between preterite and future tenses, Restif for the most part settles down to a future-tense narration of Multipliandre's ensuing activities in an ever-more-distant future. His actions and also their strange new environment are mostly described with the future tense appropriate to prediction—the linguistic viewpoint of someone in the present looking forward.[26]

Of a fantastic new species of fruit resembling a melon but growing on trees that evolve as one result of climactic changes induced by arrival of a second moon, by close passage of a comet, and by another deluge, for example, we are told: "This fruit will have a delicious pulp resembling puree of apricot mixed with raspberries. People will taste it, not without great precautions! And it will turn out that it will nourish like rice and that it will cure fevers . . . cancers, scrofula . . . venereal diseases, etc." (4:156). When the narration has proceeded many thousands of years further ahead, Restif drops the future tense altogether in favor of preterites while calling attention to the change in a parenthetical remark apparently designed to reassure readers (or himself) that he is in control: here the future is discontinued ("on supprime ici le *futur*" [4:177]). Where a more polished (or more pretentious) writer might have gone back to revise for grammatical consistency, thus eliminating signs of authorial indecision, Restif is content to let readers follow his progress from the most conventional way of indicating a future setting (future-tense narration most appropriate for prophecy) to what became the indispensable norm for futuristic fiction: narration of future events in past tense as though from a perspective yet further ahead in time.

Apart from the ambiguous case of *Epigone*'s putative future setting that is more like alternate history, this proleptic narrative structure treating the future as if it had already happened was first used in a sustained way by Madden in *Memoirs of the Twentieth Century*. Mercier adopted essentially the same procedure without any sign of malaise, as did other early writers of futuristic fiction including eventually Restif in the final part of Multipliandre's tale. Strictly speaking, to be sure, Mercier's entire narrative does deal with a past event: the narrator's dream. The dream is about Paris in 2440, but the dream itself is over when the narrator relates it. In works adopting this dream-vision framework, the question of whether to adopt preterite or future-tense narration is less pressing, although it may arise. Restif's hesitant, groping progress toward what now seems the inevitable grammatical choice for viable futuristic fiction should not be dismissed as merely another sign of his naïvete. It is better seen as evidence of a conscious, though certainly not very deft, attempt to solve a basic problem of futuristic fiction: whether it is proper to establish the future setting grammatically or best to do so by other means while using the predominant preterite forms of conventional narrative to recount future events as though they have already occurred.

From Madden onward there was de facto consensus that, whatever *else* might be done to augment or diminish verisimilitude in a particular tale, only with the latter method of past-tense narration could a kind of fundamental verisimilitude be sustained by creating for readers the viewpoint usual in previous fiction of looking backwards to events that *have already taken place*. Narrating events, including future events, in the past tense creates a sense that what is alluded to has indeed occurred. This impression may be either enhanced or undermined by other aspects of storytelling, but in itself it always works toward sustaining plausibility. Future-tense narration, among other liabilities, invites sustained *awareness* of the dubious ontological status of what at the time of narration does not yet exist and accordingly may never exist. All fiction, to be sure, refers to what by definition does not exist and has not existed. But preterite forms do so in ways that mimic historical narratives of fact and thereby make the fictionality of their referents less obtrusive.

Restif, who habitually avoided lengthy prefaces in favor of scattering explanations throughout his works (as he does on this and other matters in *Les Posthumes*), demonstrates that the choice between past-tense and future-tense narration was neither trivial nor self-evident. There really is a choice. Future-tense narrative proved untenable. Though other early writers solved this grammatical

FANTASY AND METAFICTION

problem silently, it was (and remains) an issue fundamental to the aesthetics of futuristic fiction. Félix Bodin realized its importance in 1834 when, even more concerned with arriving at an appropriate poetics, he found it necessary to comment explicitly on the advisability of preterite-tense narration for *Le Roman de l'avenir*.

Although a sustained future-tense narration proved unworkable, it does initially serve in *Les Posthumes*—along with various non-calendric allusions to the passage of time—to convey a sense that Multipliandre's adventures carry him very far forward. His temporal progression is less toward a future that seems connected to the reader's present, however, than to a kind of increasingly surrealistic landscape where physical distortions of familiar geography are accompanied by ever-greater elongations, and some accelerations, of the time spans usually associated with human activities. Thirty-six years after marrying the twelve Parisians with whom he retires to his enclosure, Multipliandre "had 232 children and in addition 2,320 grandchildren." He leads an expedition of three ships to colonize the New Hebrides, where his venture flourishes so that "in a few years, say twenty to twenty-five years, he will have to take over another island" (4:143–44). Restif only suggests an approximate interval here, in a casual way that deflects consideration from clocks and calendars as relevant measures of this increasingly fantastic future. Concern with exact specification of time yields to preoccupation with marvels.

Along with an account of how Multipliandre's new South Pacific empire grows, Restif tells of changes wrought by arrival of earth's second moon ("La Revolution secondolunaire," 4:176), by close passage of a comet, and by the flood associated with these events. A new continent emerges, old mountains vanish, and new ones rise. Amid these geological changes evolve new minerals with astonishing properties such as the mercury-like quick-gold ("Vifor"). There are new plants with wonderful powers like the melon described above that can be taken to cure just about anything from fever to cancer. There are amazing new creatures: flying serpents, talking dogs, and a race of winged humans nicknamed "angels." Multipliandre saves old-model humans from extinction by skillfully managing an interbreeding program between them and the "angels." This produces a new winged species that is biologically stable after nine hundred years. Twenty-five hundred years later all humans have wings, along with augmented mental powers (4:174). In yet another twenty-five hundred years, the earth has moved a million miles closer to the sun (4:175). Duplication of these intervals deprives them of much particularity or relevance except as figures large enough to symbolize a long interval: it could as well have been three thousand or five thousand years without making any difference to Restif's effect.

So too for the information that six hundred fifty years is the life span of the new race of winged humans, although this figure is given some connection to the reader's time frames by a comparison with the life span of Adam (4:184). But Restif might have chosen eight hundred or a thousand years, or any such large figure, without appreciably altering the impression of creatures with a longevity that is enviably greater than ours. The time intervals specified throughout this remote future merely serve to take it further and further from meaningful relationship to the reader's era. In *Les Posthumes* Restif provides a fantasy future of almost infinite possibilities unbounded by any exact sense of how time as we experience it, or even as geologists and biologists extrapolate it backwards and forwards, might really constrain or facilitate what is imagined. If Restif was influenced by the new scientific ideas of geological time that were emerging from the work of Buffon and others, it was only to be liberated from any temporal constraint whatever in imagining a future.[27]

Like Adam, Multipliandre is eventually misunderstood and often reviled by his descendants among the new winged people. Unhappy for the first time in more than thirty thousand years, he flees with Zizi, a loyal female "angel," to a secluded polar island where he spends the next three hundred years (4:188). Their descendants, called Polarists, eventually effect a rapprochement with those from whom Multipliandre had fled, the Australians, and they in turn again revere their benefactor. Multipliandre then returns to his old enclosure where "he marries twelve new pretty peasants, and begins again to live as he had done seventy thousand years before" (4:194). After another one hundred thousand years the second moon grows cold again, and the poles of the earth are no longer habitable. This winding-down to geological old age presaging planetary death provides a suitable narrative occasion for recounting Multipliandre's afterlife replete with amazing interplanetary adventures. In due course he is metamorphosed into a star without, however, losing his individuality. This final twist, which carries the story into a future beyond any concern with time as we know it, illustrates Restif's Illuminist cosmology (presented in *Les Posthumes* as Cazotte's) and might very well have ended the narrative.

Instead, by a turn that may appear even more unaccountable than Restif's peculiar cosmology, Multipliandre's story then proceeds to loop back through time to recount his adventures during the outbreak of the French Revolution. It is largely Restif's own partially eyewitness account that we are given here, interwoven with fiction as in so many disguised autobiographical intrusions elsewhere in his oeuvre.[28] Nothing in *Les Posthumes* explicitly reveals such a genesis of the revolutionary episodes, although readers accepting the book's false attribution would probably take this part of Multipliandre's story as in some measure a veiled report of Cazotte's experiences. Even for readers aware of Restif's authorship and of the biographical imperative that so often guided his pen, however, there remains the more interesting question of why an excursion to history comes at this unlikely place. The prior narrative has proceeded chronologically, following Multipliandre from the eighteenth century to his far-future destiny; each narrated episode has been placed further and further in the future. Up to this point, the order of narration has followed the sequence of events in the story being narrated. An account of Multipliandre's adventures during the Revolution would have seemed more in keeping with this scheme if placed at the outset of Multipliandre's story. Put at the end, the placement calls attention to itself. What is gained by returning to the French Revolution only *after* the narrative in *Les Posthumes* has proceeded about as far into the future as any story could possibly go?

There are no explicit answers to the question in Restif's text. At this crucial juncture, the author only provides a note from the "editor" reminding readers of the frame-story by stating that a narration of Multipliandre's afterlife, like the tale of Yfflasie and Clarendon, is an appropriate part of Fontlhete's strategy for gradually preparing Hortense to learn about his own death (4:204). Given the persistence of such metafictional commentary on its methods at key points in *Les Posthumes,* and given too as part of such commentary the explicit announcement of a switch away from future-tense narration, one wonders at the lack of "editorial" remark from Restif to account for the more puzzling turn from far future to recent past, from fantasy to history. It is difficult to suppose him unaware of anything problematic in this unusual step. But there was no available aesthetics that provided an acceptable rationale for such an unprecedented juxtaposition of real past and fictional far future. In *L'An 2440* Mercier had merely resorted to footnotes contrasting his imaginary twenty-fifth century with the reader's eighteenth-century realities. There is no mingling of the two eras within the story after its account of the discussion with an Englishman whose criticism of France inspires the narrator's dream of a better Paris. In *Le Monde tel qu'il sera*, Souvestre occasionally suspends his account of Martha and Maurice in the year 3000 to provide character sketches of people from earlier eras (for example, an honest old veteran of the Napoleonic wars), who by contrast illustrate values that have been eliminated from the future world where machines and greed prevail. But even this strategy, which explicitly invites attention to relationships between present and future, does not entail narration

FANTASY AND METAFICTION

of actual history. The problem of connecting the real past with an imaginary future was not easily resolved.

Restif dealt with the issue by making Fontlhete revert in the tale he is telling to a previously unrecounted episode from the year 1787 when, as he explains to Hortense, Multipliandre had decided to reveal his vision of an impending French Revolution. Lest readers be confused, as they well might be, Restif (through Fontlhete) stresses this return to a prerevolutionary moment at the chronological beginning of the story whose far-future ending has just been narrated: "We are in 1787: Multipliandre, who must experience so many things; who in three or four millions or milliards of years will be the *Central-star*, is still happy with his JULIE, and his two acolytes" (4:205). Here too the span of future years is uncertain ("millions or milliards"), but it does not seem to matter so long as readers perceive that span as very long and juxtapose its end with its beginning. There follows a narration of what is described as Multipliandre's "vision" (4:207).

Aside from its role as a part of Multipliandre's story in which some of his adventures figure among actual episodes of the French Revolution, that "vision" is indistinguishable from an ordinary historical narrative. After a sampling of quotations from such inflammatory pamphlets of the prerevolutionary era as Letellier's *La Vérité* and some description of other preliminary events, we are told how matters developed on July 12 and 13. All preliminary discussion serves to introduce "the decisive day" (4:228). Fontlhete's letter dated January 7 (presumably of 1788, according to previous statements) then begins: "The 14th of July, 1789, will never depart from the memory of French people" (4:228). Capture of the Bastille is described, as the previous two days have been, in a conventional past-tense narration that here reads like a vivid eyewitness account of such events as the storming of the fortress and de Launay's decapitation. Multipliandre himself, we learn, was almost condemned by the crowd but used his invisibility powder to escape. The narrator widens the scope of his account by describing risings elsewhere in France. He shows the dangers of mob violence, which he deplores, by focusing on such horrors as the blinding of the Mayor of Troies by an infuriated woman. "The infamous Populace want anarchy, under the name of liberty!" (4:259). To illustrate further the temper of the times, he includes portions of another pamphlet by Letellier called *The Triumph of the Parisians* (4:261ff.). The national assembly of 1789 is described with comments on some of its participants, including Robespierre. All these events, we are told, are only child's play by comparison with the August 10 attack on the Tuileries (4:273). He goes on to explain political parties such as the Girondins. Multipliandre's narrative, as reported by Fontlhete, finally picks up tempo to describe the outbreak of war, the execution of Louis XVI on January 21, 1793, and the military victories achieved during the Parisians' terrible winter of hunger and hardship.

Fontlhete ends by affirming what he has narrated: "There is everything which Multipliandre told me of the things which must occur. They are . . . of a strange nature ['d'une nature étrange']. Perhaps Fontlhete will be happy not to see them" (4:287–88). In reply, Hortense writes that she can hardly believe these predictions but they unsettle her because she has faith in Fontlhete's "previsions." Before *Les Posthumes* turns to the denouement of its frame-story, Hortense comments: "But that is not possible! . . . I know this *Danton;* he is a mediocre Lawyer; this *Camille* is a stammerer who can only write" (4:288–89). Restif thus invites readers to consider how *improbable* some real history would seem if revealed beforehand, or if properly considered afterwards. The point is well taken but does not itself justify placing an account of the Revolution after instead of before the futuristic fantasy. In *Memoirs of the Twentieth Century,* Madden had remarked at greater length the improbability of much past history by way of mock justification for writing an implausible history of the future. Restif makes no such defense of his story. He does not explicitly suggest that what has

FANTASY AND METAFICTION

been told of Multipliandre's future adventures should acquire greater verisimilitude when viewed alongside actual incredibilities from the French Revolution. Nor does that idea seem implicit here. There is simply too great a disparity between the utterly fantastic impossibilities of Multipliandre's story and the unlikely but indisputably possible actions of people like Danton.

If Restif does not present real history in such a way as to lend credibility to the fantasy, placement of Multipliandre's vision nevertheless invites consideration of the French Revolution in the light of that fantasy. Readers not only have the history placed after the fantasy but are also supposed to imagine the outbreak of the Revolution narrated before it occurred, told as a prophecy by the protagonist of that fantasy. He appears, moreover, amid the real actors in the historical drama, playing a fantastic role by using his invisibility powder to escape an angry mob. Restif thus invites readers to regard the French Revolution from several new perspectives: from the viewpoint of Illuminist doctrines exemplified in Multipliandre's life over the centuries; by comparison of reality with fantasy; from a retrospective point of view, as all events are usually considered in historical narratives; and from a prospective viewpoint, *as if* seen through a prophetic "vision" that *as an account of future events* is analogous in form to the preceding "future history of Duke Multipliandre." These perspectives are not mutually exclusive. What distinguishes Restif's experiment in placing the French Revolution as an episode within the futuristic fiction of *Les Posthumes* is the multiplicity of perspectives, both temporal and generic, from which readers are invited to regard the same material simultaneously: prospectively *and* retrospectively; as history—the most realistic of all literary kinds, because it records facts—*and* as part of a fantasy.

The mixture of these perspectives does not work altogether coherently in *Les Posthumes*. Restif fails to show how the Illuminist ideas illustrated by Multipliandre's future adventures should enhance our understanding of the French Revolution. The horrors of mob violence could have been shown (and deplored) about as effectively by the same narration apart from its connection to Multipliandre's story. What that link does achieve, however, is a kind of shock effect created by the sudden plunge from escapist fantasy presented *as* mere fiction to the blood-drenched realities of the Revolution. The contrast is effective, partly because it is more of an abrupt switch from fantasy to realism than simply a mixture of fantastic and historical modes, despite the intrusion of Multipliandre with his invisibility powder. Placement toward the end adds to the power of this turn from fantasy to history, because for several volumes readers have been immersed in the state of mind appropriate to reading a fantasy that has become more and more bizarre. Despite proleptic hints early in *Les Posthumes* that a prophecy of the Revolution will be included, arrival of such a detailed account as Restif provides is neither anticipated nor prepared for emotionally by the tone of what precedes it. Wish-fulfillment fantasies of immortality, flight, and sexual utopias do not help one cope mentally with the likes of Danton, Robespierre, and the Terror, except in one respect: by following Multipliandre into his surrealistic future, readers may become connoisseurs of the strange. They are then perhaps in a better position to appreciate the narrator's statement that events during the Revolution were indeed "d'une nature étrange."

Real history becomes one more fantastic episode. This at least was Restif's apparent intention: by placing an account of the French Revolution after a series of fantastic episodes and including in that account a character from those episodes, *Les Posthumes* is well designed to achieve the effects now described as cognitive estrangement. By making readers see the revolution from perspectives that distance and defamiliarize it, Restif makes estrangement possible. That fresh look at history is at least potentially *cognitive* estrangement by virtue of the Illuminist doctrines embodied in the futuristic fantasy as its philosophical outlook. These doctrines invite readers to adopt a new way of both perceiving and assessing

FANTASY AND METAFICTION

realities such as those narrated in Multipliandre's vision of the Revolution. But if this *structure* is admirably designed to bring about cognitive estrangement, the Illuminist ideas themselves are so irrational and so unclearly expounded amid the excitements of Multipliandre's adventures and those of Yfflasie and Clarendon in the afterlife that Restif's execution of *Les Posthumes* falls short of achieving the effects for which its structure is so well suited. Such estrangement as it elicits in its account of the Revolution is only embryonically cognitive. This failure, however, should not blind us to the originality of Restif's attempt. The significance of *Les Posthumes* as an important step towards effective forms of futuristic fiction resides precisely in Restif's hesitant but unmistakable creation of a structure that invites readers to view a specific historical event of their recent past from the estranging perspective of an imaginary future—a future that is explicitly presented for readers to evaluate less as prediction or utopia than as outright fantasy.

There is a more oblique concern with history but an equally conspicuous invitation to appreciate the pleasures of fiction and fantasy as such in Jane Webb's *The Mummy! A Tale of the Twenty-Second Century*. For all its faults this lively anticipation, published anonymously in 1827 when the author was only twenty years old, was a remarkably promising beginning to what might have been a memorable literary career. Among admirers of *The Mummy*, unfortunately, was the impecunious landscape-gardening expert John Claudius Loudon, a man whose only positive contribution to futuristic fiction was a gardening encyclopedia that inspired the author of *Mrs. Maberly* to imagine the glass-domed city of Vitria. Loudon discovered, fell in love with, and finally in 1830 married *The Mummy*'s author—a disastrous event for the history of futuristic fiction, because the alliance deflected Jane Webb from writing any more tales of the future or, for that matter, much fiction at all. She published instead a series of botanical books with such dreary titles as *The Ladies' Companion to the Flower Garden*, *The Ladies' Flower*

Garden of Ornamental Annuals, and *The Ladies' Flower Garden of Bulbous Plants*. Feminists and futurists can only regard Jane Webb's transformation to Mrs. Loudon with dismay, whatever happiness she herself may have found in sharing her husband's struggle against poverty by grinding out horticultural potboilers.

In the year of her marriage she published, again anonymously, one other work that reflects her interest in time: *Conversations upon Comparative Chronology and General History from the Creation of the World to the Birth of Christ* (London, 1830). Written in the form of edifying dialogues between "Mrs. Seymour and her two daughters, Isabella and Lota," this book is a conservative treatise following the eighteenth-century chronological tradition without any hint of an impending revolution in ideas about the extent of past geological time. Webb's readers are simply informed that "the creation took place in the 710th year of the Julian period, 4004 B.C."[29] Although *Conversations upon Comparative Chronology* testifies to Webb's interest in time, its perfectly conventional attitudes about the duration of the universe and its concern with the past offer no clues to her motives or inspiration in writing one of the best and most original of the early novels set in a far future. Decipherment of the Rosetta Stone in 1821 may have turned her thoughts to Egypt and its mummies, but her impetus to experiment with the new form of futuristic fiction is less evidently connected to scientific questions about the past or future than to matters of literary form.

In *The Mummy* Webb makes no attempt to establish a plausible framework for the leap to future time, as Mercier had done by his device of recounting a present dream of things to come. Nor does she start with any claim to serious consideration as a prophet or utopian thinker. Instead she challenges readers to applaud her artistry as a teller of tales. Webb establishes a metafictional framework for *The Mummy* by prefacing it with a forthright authorial confession: "I have long wished to write a novel, but I could not determine what it was to be about. I could not bear anything common-place, and I did not know what to do for a hero." These are the first words readers encounter as they begin the book's introduction. The narrator then describes walking down "a shady lane, one fine evening in June" while mulling over the problem: "I could think of nothing that had not been thought of before. . . . '[s]urely,' thought I . . . 'there must be some new ideas left, if I could but find them.'" Coming to a hill with a "superb prospect" that is more like a painting than a real landscape—"It was quite a Claude-Lorraine scene"—the narrator sleeps. We are then reminded of how sleep on a picturesque hillside is conventionally used by writers:

> It would be of no use to go to sleep without dreaming; and, accordingly, I had scarcely closed my eyes when, me-thought, a spirit stood before me. His head was crowned with flowers; his azure wings fluttered in the breeze. . . . In his hand he held a scroll. . . . '[T]ake this,' said he, smiling . . . 'it is the Chronicle of a future age. Weave it into a story. It will so far gratify your wishes, as to give you a hero totally different from any hero that ever appeared before. . . . I will endeavour, if possible, to assist you. Look around.' I did so; and saw, as in a magic glass, the scenes and characters, which I shall now endeavour to pass before the eyes of the reader.[30]

Such an introduction encourages readers to think less about the real future than about the literary past.

Webb thus arouses curiosity about her book itself. Its classification in the subtitle as a "tale" smacks more of unabashed make-believe than of an attempt at realistically portraying some plausible future. Her introduction deflects attention from the nature of the twenty-second century—which cannot be known—to the different and entirely answerable metafictional question of whether her story will achieve literary novelty. Suspense is initially directed not at the manner of portraying the future or its difference from the present but at the author's way of finding a new kind of hero for this book. Its putative twenty-second-century events are to be compared not with life in the reader's nineteenth-century present but with the action of previous novels. Webb does not invite readers to pause at the outset for a mental survey of their own century and the possible consequences of its trends before plunging into her imagined future. Readers are to think instead of protagonists encountered in other books, because only thus can a new kind of hero be appreciated. Of course this approach does not preclude comparisons between the reader's present and Webb's imaginary future. Throughout *The Mummy* such comparisons are often elicited to satirize nineteenth-century developments in education and technology. Nor does the self-reflexive announcement of its own fictionality—its status as a work of make-believe entered in the contest of wit for the prizes awarded to originality—necessarily prevent Webb's readers from surrendering to the charm of a coherently imagined future.

The world she invents as a backdrop for her story is more consistently portrayed in its everyday details and more thoroughly subordinated to novelistic action than that of any previous futuristic fiction.[31] Webb gives her readers a concrete sense of actual life in a future distinctly different from their present. Egypt, where important episodes take place, is industrialized by English and American colonists who also install an efficient system of turnpikes "over which post-chaises, with anti-attritioned wheels, bowled at the rate of fifteen miles an hour." Canals provide flood control for the Nile, which flows through an altered landscape: "Steam boats glided down the canals, and furnaces raised their smoky heads amidst groves of palm trees; whilst iron railways intersected orange groves, and plantations of dates and pomegranates might be seen bordering excavations intended for coal pits. . . . [I]ndustry and science changed desolation into plenty, and had converted barren plains into fertile kingdoms" (p. 82). Dirigible travel is available on regular schedules. A tunnel links England and Ireland. In what might be seen as a plausible political extrapolation from post-Napoleonic developments in the Europe of Webb's time, conservative regimes—some very tyrannical—are being established throughout the world after a period of widespread democracy that had generally lapsed into mob rule. Less plausibly, but all the better for a tale with gothic elements, England has again adopted Roman Catholicism as its state religion. The country is ruled despotically but harmlessly by a lethargic queen named Claudia, while sinister, scheming priests plot to alter the royal succession. Such large and small aspects of Webb's twenty-second century are certainly intended to elicit thought about possible futures and the role of present choices in creating or forestalling them.

Webb's book is nevertheless as much a self-conscious variation on gothic and romance conventions as a response to ideas about political progress and regress, or a forecast of dirigible travel, industrialization, and other impending technology. The tone of her satire is sufficiently lighthearted to deflect attention from questions about the probable accuracy of her future as *prediction*. She attacks unmistakable nineteenth-century targets in a way that anticipates Souvestre's establishment of a futuristic dystopia by applying to present trends the method of reductio ad absurdum. Thus Webb laughs at schemes for universal education by including garrulous servants who talk in the learned jargon of college professors and cook elaborate gourmet meals while their masters speak simply and eat boiled potatoes. Doctors are mockingly replaced in Webb's future by an "Automaton Steam surgeon" (p. 313). Lax punishment of crime is satirized by twenty-second-century prisons that have become "temples of luxury" (p. 314), and the inhumanity of legal procedures is mocked in a trial presided over by "an automaton judge" who must be wound up for his summation to the jury (p. 338). At the same trial a robot lawyer runs down just as he is getting to the peroration of his speech, while another robot arguing for the defense is incorrectly programmed to speak only in French and cannot be stopped. Webb satirizes misplaced confidence in science by creating a comical mad scientist named Entwurfen—presumably from *Entwurf* (a plan or project)—who introduces himself as "the fortunate inventor of the immortalizing snuff, one single pinch of which cures all diseases by the smell; the discoverer of the capability of caoutchouc being applied to aerial purposes [India-rubber balloons that can be folded up into small packages when deflated]; and the maker of the most compendious and powerful galvanic battery ever yet beheld by mortal!" (p. 218) This figure is an exaggerated version of a familiar kind of charlatan from Webb's day, not a character only conceivable in some remote future era.

Called upon in Spain to cure an ailing general, Entwurfen demonstrates his electrical expertise with disastrous results: "an unlucky wire . . . which he did not quite understand, pointed upwards, and he tried in vain to arrange it . . . but was instantly felled to the ground by a tremendous shock, whilst a loud crash of thunder burst with violence over his head, and a vivid flash of lightening proclaimed that the ill-managed machine had drawn down the electric fluid from a heavy cloud, that happened unfortunately to be just above them, upon the head of the unfortunate general, whom it scorched to a cinder, levelling some of his officers to the earth, and scattering the rest in all directions" (p. 208). In many such episodes where Entwurfen plays the role of slapstick comedian, Webb also blends heroic romance with farcical satire. Sentenced to be burned at the stake because of his blunder in treating the general, Entwurfen and his companion Edric are rescued at the place of execution by King Roderick the Second of Ireland ("surnamed the Great") who is in Spain leading its freedom-fighters against a tyrannical government. For greater dramatic effect, King Roderick somehow disguises himself as the executioner and calls in his troops to disperse the Spaniards just when Entwurfen has given up hope. This pleasant absurdity might have been inspired—though of course it was not—by that similar moment from "the future century" in Guttin's *Epigone* when Arescie is improbably but excitingly rescued.

The adventures of King Roderick occupy a large portion of *The Mummy,* involving its plot with battles, hairbreadth escapes, feats of heroic courage, and even a beautiful princess named Zoe who disguises herself (undetected) as a page boy called Alexis in a tragically hopeless pursuit of the king, whom she loves. Zoe finally stabs herself when Roderick decides to marry her rival Elvira. Webb has an English lady named Clara disguise herself to better effect in a moment of crisis by pretending to be a Greek peasant boy, "numbers of whom at this period were rambling over England singing wild romances to their harps or lutes, and telling fortunes in a kind of doggrel rhyme" (p. 364). This part of Webb's future is neither prediction nor satire but revival of a romantic past that never was.

Such episodes, including other tangled love affairs among the aristocracy and the wicked schemes of a "wiley priest" (p. 59) named Father Morris who aims to control England, deflect attention from the future except as an exotic background—even when Webb is extrapolating to possibilities which nineteenth-century technology rendered quite plausible. There is, for example, hardly any invitation to think seriously about the real likelihood and dangers of a channel tunnel—which had actually been debated during the Napoleonic era—when Roderick leads his army from Ireland to England "through . . . the tunnel, under the sea which separates the two kingdoms" (p. 386). Webb's Irish tunnel is no prediction of things to come but merely another interesting arena for Roderick's daring adventures.

In keeping with the conventions of romance, time is marked during these episodes in the loves and wars of King Roderick not by specification of dates but by allusion to passage of the seasons, especially the arrival of winter and spring to mirror the emotional climate of events. Within Webb's futuristic fiction, there are thus protracted digressions from the twenty-second century to intervals of romance time without clear connection to the clocks and calendars that define historical relationships between fiction and fact. The future setting becomes what it had been for *Epigone* in 1659 and was to be in such works as *Eureka*: a warrant for marvelous heroic and romantic adventures that could not so easily be located in the reader's present or known past.

ORIGINS OF FUTURISTIC FICTION

The mummy itself largely serves familiar purposes that are given new warrant by resort to a future setting. Entwurfen and Edric, eager to investigate the role of electricity in sustaining life, seek a perfectly preserved corpse upon which to experiment. They travel to the pyramid of Cheops, whose mysteriously decorated, dimly illuminated burial chamber becomes the scene of a fearsome resurrection that is ambiguously associated with Edric's application of the galvanic apparatus:

> He applied the wires of the battery and put the apparatus in motion, whilst a demoniac laugh of derision appeared to ring in his ears, and the surrounding mummies seemed starting from their places and dancing in unearthly merriment. Thunder now roared in tremendous peals through the Pyramids, shaking their enormous masses to the foundation, and vivid flashes of light darted round in quick succession. Edric . . . amidst this fearful convulsion of nature . . . stood immoveable, and gazing intently on the mummy, whose eyes had opened with the shock, and were now fixed on those of Edric, shining with supernatural lustre. . . . Another fearful peal of thunder now rolled in lengthened vibrations above his head, and the mummy rose slowly, his eyes still fixed upon those of Edric, from his marble tomb. The thunder pealed louder and louder. Yells and groans seemed mingled with its roar;—the sepulchral lamp, flared with redoubled fierceness, flashing its rays around in quick succession, and with vivid brightness; whilst by its horrid and uncertain glare, Edric saw the mummy stretch out its withered hand, as though to seize him. (p. 95)

Here certainly the mode is gothic horror, melodramatic enough to verge on self-parody like so much else in Webb's tale. This quality adds to its metafictional charm without precluding enjoyment on the level at which we now take pleasure in the likes of Boris Karloff. Edric may or may not be only imagining the yells, groans, and demoniac laughter that *appeared* to ring in his ears and *seems* mixed with the thunder described in this nicely equivocal passage. But he and Entwurfen have somehow set in motion an unantici-

FANTASY AND METAFICTION

pated "convulsion of nature" that quickly gets out of control. They blame their galvanic apparatus. By describing the peals of thunder, possibly demoniac laughter, and the *supernatural* luster of Cheops's eyes, Webb allows readers to suspect a more fantastic explanation.

For Entwurfen matters then get worse (whereas from the reader's viewpoint they get better) when Cheops escapes to London by dirigible and terrorizes its populace in scenes that invite comparison between Webb's book and the works of Ann Radcliffe and other Gothic novelists. Cheops resurrected as protagonist of a futuristic fiction is indeed an original hero. In this figure Webb's novel surely satisfies expectations of literary novelty aroused by its introduction. More ambitiously, Webb also attempts to describe Cheops's revival as *he* experiences it—stressing his guilt at some past crime (later explained) and his bewilderment at trying to understand a scene that does not correspond to his notions of this world or the afterlife:

> As yet, a mist hung over his faculties, and ideas thronged in painful confusion through his mind, which he was incapable of either arranging or analyzing. . . . "Have I entered Hades, or am I still on earth?—yes, yes, it is still the earth, for there the mighty Pyramid I caused to be erected towers behind me. Yet where is Memphis? where my forts and palaces? What a dark, smoky mass of buildings now surrounds me! . . . But is this the Nile? . . . sure I must be deceived. It is the fatal river of the dead. No papyrine boats glide smoothly on its surface; but strange, infernal vessels, vomiting forth volumes of fire and smoke. Holy Osiris, defend me! Where am I? where have I been? A misty veil seems thrown upon the face of nature. Awake, awake!" cried he, with a scream of agony; "set me free; I did not mean to slay him!" Then throwing himself violently upon the ground, he lay for some moments, apparently insensible. Then slowly rising he looked at himself, and a deep, unnatural shuddering convulsed his whole frame. His sensations of identity became confused, and he recoiled with horror from himself: "these are the trappings of a mummy!" murmured he in a hollow whisper. "Am I then dead?" (pp. 108–9)

Here Webb attempts with some success the unprecedented feat of showing how an imaginary future—which in its technological aspects is largely a metaphor of her readers' present—might be seen from the doubly estranging viewpoint of someone actually from the remote past, not someone merely representing it in the manner of Duc de Levis's future Chinese traveler. But she does not sustain this portrait of Cheops as time-traveler whose ideas clash with experience of a totally different future culture in ways that further highlight the reader's differences from both past *and* future. Briefly, however, Webb forces upon readers a heightened appreciation of their present as a specific historical moment differentiated alike from past and future.

Thereafter Cheops operates at the level of magical fantasy rather than as an apparent exemplification of the scientifically plausible but nevertheless marvelous phenomenon of travel through time by means of galvanic resurrection from death. We no longer learn what Cheops is thinking. We see him only from the outside. Despite initial menacing appearances, moreover, he always acts to thwart the tale's villains while aiding its virtuous young lovers. His principle of action is out of the arbitrary world of fairy tale or supernatural gothic story. He helps all those who sincerely appeal to him for assistance in a good cause; however, those who try to enlist his aid for a vicious scheme, as the book's villains do, find that he seems to help but in fact prevents all evil plans from succeeding. Readers discover at the end that it was not galvanism but God's mysterious will that actually brought Cheops back to life. Here is another nice variation on the kind of gothic romance in which apparently supernatural events turn out to have a natural explanation. In *The Mummy* what seems like a scientific achievement—revival of a corpse by means of galvanism—is discovered to have been a genuine miracle. Realism yields to fantasy. The moral is clear: do not attempt to meddle with nature.

By treating that theme in a gothic mode without recourse to the supernatural, Mary Shelley's *Frankenstein* became a prototype for science fiction as well as an enduring myth of the way in which science may destroy those who misuse it. Webb's novel, despite the originality of a future setting which deserves very high praise, remains a comic fable without either tragic force, mythic power, or the sustained cognitive and emotional interest that may be achieved by scientifically plausible marvels of the kind Félix Bodin was soon to associate with futuristic fiction. Webb's achievement nevertheless commands respect and deserves far more recognition than it has received precisely because *The Mummy* does come remarkably close to meeting Bodin's standards. It best illustrates the incomplete evolution of futuristic fiction up to the 1830s. It also best illustrates how far an effort to sustain metafictional self-consciousness in a tale shaped by the dictates of fantasy rather than realism could serve as encouragement for creating a futuristic fiction. Writing neither as a prophet nor utopian but in an explicit effort to invent a new kind of hero in a new kind of fiction, Jane Webb almost achieved the ideal novel of the future as Bodin was to define it only seven years later.

PART THREE
The End of the Beginning, 1834

CHAPTER SEVEN

A Poetics for Futuristic Fiction: *Le Roman de l'avenir*

I started this book by glancing ahead to Félix Bodin's eloquent plea for a realistic literature of rational wonders that might be morally useful without giving up the appeal of fantasy:

> If ever anyone succeeds in creating the novel, the epic of the future, he will have tapped a vast source of the marvelous, and of a marvelous entirely in accord with verisimilitude . . . which will dignify reason instead of shocking or deprecating it as all the marvelous epic machinery conventionally employed up to now has done. . . . There [in the future] can be found the revelations of those under hypnotic trance, races in the air, voyages to the bottom of the sea—just as one sees in the poetry of the past sibyls, hippogriffs, and nymphs' grottoes; but the marvelous of the future is entirely believable, entirely natural, entirely possible, and on that account it can strike the imagination more vividly and seize it by way of realism. Thus one will have discovered a new world in an environment utterly fantastic yet not improbable.[1]

I want to conclude by looking more closely at *Le Roman de l'avenir*. Consideration of the works discussed in previous chapters underscores Bodin's originality in articulating an aesthetic ideal for futuristic fiction well before anyone had fully exemplified the genre's potential as imaginative literature. If my discussion to this point suggests that some such formulation as Bodin's was inevitable, given the experiments of his predecessors and contemporaries, I should add a reminder that it can only appear inevitable in retrospect.

Those early efforts whose tendency Bodin so clearly signals were largely independent of one another, widely scattered in time and space, and mostly unknown even to him. No writer of futuristic fiction before Bodin actually created a novel whose elements all worked coherently to elicit a sense of the marvelous within a plausible framework of realistic future setting and action. Nor did Bodin succeed. Despite his prescient understanding of the possibilities of futuristic fiction, Bodin never finished his own novel. Jules Verne later showed that wonders might indeed seem rational. But even Verne did not set his most famous tales chronologically in the future. He chose instead the more cautious technique of importing small doses of futuristic technology into the nineteenth-century readers' present or immediate past. It remained for H. G. Wells and his followers to prove that Bodin truly understood the potential of futuristic fiction. Whether his insight was inevitable as early as 1834, and I think not, what is most noteworthy now is its accuracy. In *Le Roman de l'avenir* Bodin provided a poetics of futuristic fiction.

For that he deserves the highest praise. Although Bodin hazards some speculation about the future, *Le Roman de l'avenir* should not be taken as merely novelistic prediction or a reflection of ideological trends. I. F. Clarke hardly does sufficient justice to Bodin by remarking that "the main value of his book lies in the evidence it provides for believing that the intellectual revolution implied in the idea of progress had been completed by the 1830s."[2] Bodin certainly does supply evidence that ideas of progress were widespread in 1834. Although his fragmentary novel cannot claim a high rank as fiction, it has great value as literary criticism. Bodin intended

A POETICS FOR FUTURISTIC FICTION

above all to make a metafictional statement about the possibilities of futuristic fiction. *Le Roman de l'avenir* is best understood as a remarkably astute attempt to define the aesthetics of a major transformation in the relationship between literature and time: displacement of novelistic action from past and present to future settings.

Le Roman de l'avenir also affords unequivocal evidence of many influences that shaped the early development of futuristic fiction. The new forms that emerged are of more concern to literary history than speculation about their relationships to intellectual or social contexts.[3] Available clues to the tangled matter of causation nevertheless deserve some mention, if only to show the multifarious impulses that led to viable futuristic fiction. What Loren Eiseley has candidly remarked about the emergence of Darwinian thought applies also to the literary consequences of radically changing ideas about time: "The early decades of the nineteenth century are difficult to organize. Seemingly unrelated events, diverse scientific discoveries, industrial trends, and religious outlook can all, in historical perspective, be observed to revolve in a moment of seeming heterogeneity before they crystallize into a new pattern with Darwinism at the center. It is like looking into a chemical retort which is about to produce some rare and many-sided crystal. One moment everything is in solution; there is a potentiality, no more—and yet in the next instant a shape has appeared out of nowhere."[4] As early forms of futuristic fiction, versions of apocalypse and uchronia along with futuristic satire, fantasy, and heroic romance appear in apparent isolation from one another and from any common connection to their environment of drastic social, intellectual, and technological change. Though such change stimulated writers to experiment with future settings, it did not dictate any particular method of doing so.

From some of the elements available in previous literature Bodin tried, as others had in different ways, to mold an enduring form. He is the first writer of futuristic fiction to explain why he turned to this genre and how his thinking about it took shape. He is also the first who tried to give this enterprise its own history and its own aesthetics. If his testimony is incomplete, at least it has the advantage of being firsthand. After Verne, Wells, Huxley, Orwell, and their peers, we know more about the outcome of earlier attempts, and we may fancy we know more about the dynamics of cultural change than anyone could in Bodin's day. But Bodin took part in the beginning. His perspective deserves priority. Let us examine his daring experiment and his own account of its genesis.

In the preface to *Le Roman de l'avenir*, Bodin takes up what he calls "the purely literary considerations" of writing about the future. He modestly states that there remains little for him to say, although it is always strongly tempting to provide the poetics of the genre at the outset of a work ("de faire la poétique du genre en tête de l'oeuvre," p. 28). His ensuing explicit remarks about futuristic fiction, whose key points I have cited above and in chapter 1, are indeed as notable for their conciseness as for their insight. In disclaiming any intention of describing at length the poetics of his new genre, Bodin was of course indulging in one of the hallowed stances of ironic mock modesty that authors are allowed in their prefaces. By merely mentioning how tempted he is to explain a kind of fiction that had received no critical analysis, Bodin alerts his readers at once to the need for such analysis and to the possibility that his book as a whole, not just a few pages in its preface, may serve to suggest "a poetics of the genre."

In a differently organized work, or even a more conventional one whose form was familiar, Bodin's statement might be taken at face value as a renunciation of the need for any elaborate poetics. But his disclaimer cannot so easily be overlooked in a book divided into parts that insistently invite attention to the question of what the work as a whole is doing and why. Readers of *Le Roman de l'avenir* encounter much more than just a narrative. They are confronted first with an epigram in the form of a dialogue between an Englishman and a Frenchman on the nature of hoaxes; an extensive

A POETICS FOR FUTURISTIC FICTION

dedication "to the past"; and a teasing statement that the preface is extremely tedious, unnecessary for understanding the narration, and therefore best skipped. The preface follows, then an introduction, the incomplete novel itself, a postscript, notes on the preface, a discussion of mesmerism, a survey of imaginative literature about the future, part of an earlier essay written by Bodin in 1822 predicting the situation of Athens in 1840, and finally a brief section entitled "Saint Malachy and the end of the world" on "The Prophecy of the Popes" attributed (falsely) to Ireland's Saint Malachy. Surely only the most uncurious readers could refrain from asking themselves, however fleetingly, what *kind* of work could (or should) contain all that and why it should.

Bodin's initial epigram is a reminder that some things may serve apparently contradictory purposes. To an Englishman's question "do you know what a *hoax* is?" a Frenchman replies that he does not; he is told that a hoax is something serious in a burlesque way and burlesque in a serious way ("burlesquement sérieuse et sérieusement burlesque"). For this paradoxical definition the Frenchman expresses elaborate thanks ("Monsieur, j'ai l'honneur de vous remercier") that may well be taken as an ironic expression of mystification. The Englishman replies in kind with a polite phrase ("Cela n'en vant pas la peine") and on that note Bodin ends his little "Dialogue between an Englishman and a Frenchman." This puzzling exchange alerts readers to the possibility that the book itself may be a hoax, though serious nonetheless. They themselves may or may not be the chief objects of the hoax. If so, they may still profit from the experience.

Insofar as "burlesque" implies an element of parody, Bodin's definition of hoax invites his readers not only to expect a serious joke, perhaps played on them, but also to ask exactly what is being parodied. Given the book's title, two possibilities immediately come to mind: attitudes toward the future—perhaps ideas of progress—and books about the future. Future books are another possibility, because the phrase "le roman de l'avenir" has a double meaning as a novel about the future and the novel *of* the future (that is, the kind of novel that will commonly be written in the future). Like seriousness and parody, these meanings are not mutually exclusive when coexisting in a hoax. Bodin's epigram and title, however, do more to arouse than to satisfy curiosity. If hoaxing is an activity accepted or at least understood by the English, its French literary counterpart remains unclear. Bodin makes no attempt to say beyond implying that one example is the work in hand.

Nor for that matter does Bodin name any English precedents. As a literary form the hoax is a rather shadowy and sparsely exemplified genre, falling somewhere between joke, satire, and parody. The joke may be at the expense of those who mistake it *for* what it only mocks by imitating, as in the famous case of Defoe's *Shortest Way with the Dissenters* in 1702. There Defoe parodied the bigotry of extremist High Church preachers like Sacheverell by an exaggerated imitation that exposed the intolerance of those readers sufficiently taken in by the hoax to agree with its blatantly immoral argument calling for severe persecution of English Protestants who refused to become Anglicans.[5] Works like *A Modest Proposal* and *Gulliver's Travels*, by contrast, could hardly be mistaken for the earnest projects or authentic travel books whose form they imitate. Defoe's *Shortest Way* or Poe's later balloon-hoax of 1844 actually fooled many readers. Swift's masterpieces, on the other hand, are easily seen to parody familiar forms for satiric purposes, just as Pope's *Rape of the Lock* burlesques epic conventions in ways that preclude confusing it with an actual epic. Whether Bodin would include such works by Swift and Pope in his definition of hoax because of their parodic element is not clear. His statement does not rule out this possibility and indeed seems to admit it. In any case Bodin's enigmatic "Dialogue between an Englishman and a Frenchman" at least unequivocally invites readers of *Le Roman de l'avenir* to expect from its beginning that this work will be more like some new kind of hoax than like any novel they have read before—a hoax, moreover, demanding earnest consideration of its pleasantries. From the outset Bodin establishes a tone that makes comedy a mode of serious statement. He establishes too the metafictional perspective of a work that explicitly and implicitly invites attention to its dialogic relationships, whether of parodic imitation or conspicuous difference, with previous fiction.

The first such relationship, most appropriately, is with *L'An 2440*. A six-page dedication "To the Past," which Bodin's readers encounter immediately after his epigram, unmistakably parodies the form of Mercier's "Dedicatory Epistle to the year 2440" while differing notably in substance and tone. Mercier starts by addressing to the twenty-fifth century a grim denunciation of eighteenth-century tyranny in a France whose ominous calm, he says, resembles that of tombs surrounded by walking cadavers. Bodin, by contrast, lightheartedly acknowledges the past as a source of inspiration for his novel of the future: "It is you, respectable past, who have given all the elements of this book: because when you had the advantage of being the present, you were pregnant with the future, as Leibnitz very happily said" (p. 7). Bodin thus reminds readers that time designations are partly relative; the present of his readers, especially their literary present as exemplified in the book, may also be regarded from another perspective as a future time because they are living in the past's future. By simply continuing *Le Roman de l'avenir* (especially with *L'An 2440* in mind), they may see how elements of Bodin's book were provided by the past.

Echoing the phrase from Leibnitz ("Le temps present est gros de l'avenir") that stood as epigram on the title page of *L'An 2440* serves as another signal of Bodin's initial burlesque gambit in parodying Mercier, lest readers miss the point. Allusion to Leibnitz's maxim also calls attention to the difference between Mercier's epigram for *L'An 2440* and the very different one that Bodin invented for *Le Roman de l'avenir* in concocting his dialogue between an Englishman and a Frenchman. That dialogue may also be taken as a variation of the initiatory discussion that Mercier's narrator reports having had with an Englishman whose criticisms of Paris sparked the dream of a utopian future that becomes the substance of *L'An 2440*. Mercier's epigram invites general consideration of relationships between present and future. Bodin's epigram urges attention to self-reflexive questions about ways in which the present book is related to past literary forms.

No less than *L'An 2440* as a whole, Mercier's epigram and dedication invite readers to ponder how their era may lead to—or fail to lead to—a better future. Bodin's epigram and dedication suggest comparison of *Le Roman de l'avenir* with the most famous previous work of futuristic fiction, perhaps to judge which is better. The very first, though hardly the only, question Bodin poses for his readers is how their literary past relates to a different literary present. No one alive can verify predictions about the twenty-fifth century, but every reader of *Le Roman de l'avenir* can at least see whether the form of Mercier's book itself served as a forecast of such future fiction as Bodin now provides. They have merely to continue reading to satisfy their curiosity about the literary future (Mercier's future, which is their present). A few more hours of reading time will suffice to unveil the novel of the future. It will then be clear how far *L'An 2440* served as a model. Bodin's dedication, however, is not confined to arousing some degree of suspense over these matters of literary form that are brought up implicitly but unmistakably.

Bodin continues to address the past in a bantering tone, calling it a "poor victim sacrificed to the law of progress," while he takes up the more contentious question of how it *should* be regarded. Bodin says that he is not one of those inconsiderate people who gaze incessantly "toward the Eden or the *Dorado* of future centuries" and heap blame and insult on the past for its shortcomings in serving each generation only as a steppingstone to further improvement. Conceding that in former times people were wrong to praise the past as "the apogee of perfection," Bodin notes that today, when even old men avoid nonsensical praise of the past, it is easy to fall into the opposite excess by failing to render justice to its merits. Accordingly he will guard against despising the past just

A POETICS FOR FUTURISTIC FICTION

because its people traveled modestly afoot, on horseback, or in sailboats. "Today, when we devour space, today when knowledge and riches are distributed more equally and to a larger number of individuals, there are nevertheless still many powerful thinkers who doubt that we are truly better and more happy" (p. 10). For his part, Bodin affirms, he will at least gladly acknowledge that the past had "grandeurs of which the seed is lost or will no longer germinate, glories of which the halo has vanished, sources of poetic emotion and religious enthusiasm which seem dried up, tableaux of patriarchal simplicity and royal splendors which will recur no more!" (p. 10). Here Bodin prepares for the explicit poetics that he articulates a few pages later in his preface.

He does so by suggesting in his dedication that what the present most notably lacks amid all its material advances are *scenes*, whether of grandeur or striking simplicity, that may capture the imagination. Also absent are important "sources of poetic emotion." Implicit here but shortly made explicit in his preface is the notion that any viable novel of the future must find equivalents for these affecting aspects of the past. In the preface Bodin tries to sum up this crucial point in another way by insisting that the entire poetics of the *Novel in the future* ("toute la poétique du *Roman dans l'avenir*") is contained in a phrase taken from his *Glance at the History of Civilization:* "Civilization tends to separate us from everything that is poetic in the past: but civilization also has its poetry and its marvelous" (p. 29). Thus, for Bodin, futuristic fiction should not primarily be concerned with prediction or utopian speculation. Above all its task is to recapture, in appropriate images acceptable to the modern world, imaginative equivalents of older sources of poetic emotion that can no longer serve as material for the novelist's art. Aesthetic effects must have primacy over speculative content. Readers must be moved, not simply instructed. But how this is to be achieved is by no means self-evident. Nor does Bodin's dedication do more than start preparing the ground for the poetics that he will espouse.

Bodin winds up his dedication by raising difficult questions about time and literary form that he playfully declines to answer at this stage, leaving them for readers to ponder: "Is it necessary to call in a Jeremiah to weep on the banks of that great river which carries with it into the abyss everything on earth that ends? Or a Saint John the Evangelist to break the seals, overturn the cups, sound the trumpets which announce the end of everything that has begun? Or rather is it necessary to raise toward the future, not a proud gaze of confidence in human power, but a look of pious hope in divine providence?" (p. 11). The last of these rhetorical questions implies that neither the Book of Lamentations nor the Book of Revelation provides suitable models for modern analogues of prophecy. Neither a nostalgic literature turning attention backwards from the future to seek ideals in the vanished past nor forms of apocalypse leaping over coming years to focus on the end of our world will do. Equally unsatisfactory are forms—perhaps Bodin means to imply utopian forms like those adapted by Mercier in *L'An 2440*—that serve merely as prideful delineations of future progress to be achieved by purely human means. Bodin's third question hints at the possibility of writing about human relationships to time, especially the future, in some form that will avoid all these extremes while remaining at least compatible with religious faith.

If this hint arouses curiosity, as it surely will, Bodin at this point lets readers speculate as best they can on their own: "for the moment it is not suitable for me to examine that great and serious question. I return to my dedication" (p. 11). Part of the joke here is that, having raised such very serious questions, he gives no particular reason why it is "not suitable" to consider them further. Mercier had used *his* dedication in *L'An 2440* to pursue a bit more fully those equally important issues that he proposed as themes for his book. Bodin's return to a comic mode at the conclusion of his dedication is not so much another variation upon Mercier, however, as an ironic reminder that "suitability" is a rather vague and flexible rule. Most forms, especially dedications, can include whatever the

A POETICS FOR FUTURISTIC FICTION

author chooses. In small and large ways, here with a nice comic touch, Bodin invites attention to the possibility of such choices as additional preparation for thinking about a poetics for the novel of the future that he is about to exemplify in his own narrative.

Bodin ends his dedication by parodying the conventional flourish of writers who profess no expectation of gain from their dedications to some great personage but hope that posterity will eventually do them justice: "I admit, noble past, that I pay you useless homage; but I can also boast, as people do in other dedications, that I give a high proof of independence in placing my work under the auspices of a fallen power like you. I hope nevertheless the future will be grateful to me for that politeness which is in every respect your due, if it is the case (which I strongly doubt) that the future ever has knowledge of the book and its author" (pp. 11–12). Here, as throughout, Bodin's dedication burlesques the conventions of its own form and at the same time challenges readers to consider how all books (together with those who write and read them) *should* be related to the past and future. Bodin's definition of a hoax is well exemplified by his dedication. It is burlesque because it parodies identifiable books and forms. It is serious because it raises urgent questions amid the comedy. His readers are thus prepared to expect—and perhaps accept—throughout *Le Roman de l'avenir* a similar doubleness of tone.

The preface itself is largely serious, as Bodin suggests in his ironic preliminary warning. Because it is "extremely tedious" and useless for understanding the narrative, he recommends that it be skipped "without fear of the least harm" by those who open his book only to read a novel. For all but such unreflective readers as Bodin here mocks for wanting *only* stories, this warning becomes an irresistible invitation to consider the preface carefully. To skip it in compliance with Bodin's playful invitation to do so would amount to relegating oneself to the lowest class of novel readers, those seeking nothing but entertainment. It would also be to miss explanations that do help one understand the action of Bodin's novel. In the preface Bodin's call for a literature of rational wonders, for which he there invents the term *littérature futuriste*, is put into a context of intellectual history designed to justify that call and also account for some constraints upon the content as well as the forms of futuristic fiction, including his own.[6]

Bodin first remarks that, in periods dominated by the notion of humanity's degeneration, people imagine the future fearfully and dream about "ends of the world and the last man"; conversely, in periods when the idea of progress has been accepted "like a faith," it is impossible for this idea "not to hatch religions and utopias" (pp. 15–16). To such an extent, then, Bodin identifies prevailing attitudes of optimism or pessimism towards the future as determinants of literary form—attitudes resulting in only two broad categories by 1834: utopias and apocalypses. He goes on to note that both forms have been equally deficient in novelistic action and verisimilitude. The utopias are little more than expositions of theories. Apocalyptic prophecies, though stemming from "an inspiration exalted and as a consequence poetic," are notable chiefly for "the mysterious and gigantic tableaux" of the Book of Revelation and "many other conceptions of the same kind." All such "conceptions" are stubbornly based on ideas of the Last Judgment that implicitly reject the possibility of significant improvement in this world and thereby also eliminate the possibility of novelistic action that can engage readers more closely than the baffling imagery of Apocalypse (pp. 17–18).

Underlying complicated disputes between advocates of progress who encourage utopias and those gloomier apocalyptic writers obsessed with the end of time is a basic "diversity of human constitutions," Bodin asserts, that will never admit any resolution of such arguments about future human destiny: "There will always be poetic heads and rational heads."[7] They see things differently. They will seldom agree. Thus, for Bodin, temperamental differences inherent in human nature rule out all hope of settling to everyone's

A POETICS FOR FUTURISTIC FICTION

satisfaction the nineteenth century's great debates about what the future really holds. A literature of mere prediction or utopian advocacy will accordingly always be unsatisfactory to all but small circles of believers. For the same reason, however, Bodin believes there will always be room for—and need for—a *littérature futuriste* of the kind he paradoxically defines as appealing rationally to the poetic side of human nature by imagining probable marvels.

No one can guarantee the eternity of today's dogmas and political systems given the number of similar ones that have entirely vanished from the earth, Bodin notes later in the preface (p. 25), whereas poetic temperaments will always appear: "So long as there exist good and evil, sympathies and hatreds; so long as nature displays its horrors and its riches, inflicting its scourges on men or heaping on them its benefits; so long as women, love, the religious exaltation of tender hearts, sublime souls, and the superstitious terrors of feeble brains exist; in a word (pardon this physiological blasphemy), so long as the nervous system exists, there will be poetry on the earth" (p. 24). This may seem merely another romantic manifesto, although Bodin insists towards the end of the preface that his novel is neither romantic ("if romanticism is the expression of the Middle Ages") nor classic ("because it expresses neither the social state of the ancients nor the order of ideas which served as archetypes of our literature during the two previous centuries"). Bodin does not know what literary label will serve but whimsically suggests that, if we must have a term, his novel will not be "of the tedious genre" but "of the future genre." In that way it will at least have a chance of escaping boredom by virtue of strangeness ("de sauver l'ennui par la bizarrerie," pp. 30–31).

Far more important to Bodin than available critical categories, whose paucity he thus derides, is an inevitably widening division between the spheres of "poetic" and rational activities:

> The progress it is necessary to expect is that the different systems will adapt more and more to the order of things which is proper to

each. The rational systems will prevail little by little in the material organization of society: the poetic systems will be in possession of the domain of religion and the arts. The separation of these systems will perhaps finally end the long arguments which have so far delayed everything. There will not be so much reasoning anymore on matters of sentiment or inspiration; less authority will be left to enthusiasm in matters decided according to reason and experiment. (pp. 24–25)

This prediction (which holds up rather well as a forecast) is the key idea about history underlying Bodin's poetics of futuristic fiction and his attempts in his novel.

While this forecast may at first glance seem like an early warning of what C. P. Snow called the problem of two cultures, in fact Bodin welcomes the prospect of clear separation between the realms controlled by reason and the domain of what he calls poetry. He affirms that "both will continue because they are in the nature of man, whether they exist in peace together mingled in the same country, which sometimes seems to me the true ideal of perfection, or each tries to isolate itself in some corner of the globe to cultivate itself with more liberty and apply itself entirely to forming a complete social order" (p. 25). Bodin's novel dramatizes a future in which the rational and irrational manifestations of human nature do not peacefully coexist as they would in his own utopian dream of a perfect society. Action in his story centers around a clash between underground members of the "Poetic or Anti-Prosaic Association" and the increasingly drab institutions established in a world federation ruled by the somewhat ironically termed "Civilizing Association."

Instead of explicitly noting connections between his own vision of the future and the story he tells in *Le Roman de l'avenir*, however, Bodin finishes his preface by stressing the need for a *littérature futuriste* that will appeal to the poetic side of human nature that he believed would be one of the few enduring features of *any* future. He also believed that such psychological constants (rooted in the

A POETICS FOR FUTURISTIC FICTION

facts of human physiology) are among the very few aspects of the future that *can* be predicted with any confidence. Like Samuel Madden and Restif de la Bretonne, Bodin expresses a strong sense of how improbable much actual history would have seemed if foretold before the event and how unlikely it therefore is that any novelist can be an accurate prophet. Bodin later chides Mercier (somewhat unfairly) for trying to show the twenty-fifth century while failing to foresee even the imminent changes in nineteenth-century costumes.[8] This argument that future constancies of temperament are easier to foretell than future forms of society is the immediate intellectual context within Bodin's own thought for his definition of a literature of rational wonders that will sustain its ability to move as well as instruct. Because he did not see the future as given over either to increasing rationality that might actually realize utopian dreams or to such total unreason as would warrant apocalyptic detachment from the affairs of this world, Bodin stresses the need for an aesthetic as well as speculative component in the novel of the future. The poetic side of human nature must be authentically portrayed as well as appealed to by fiction that hopes to remain meaningful.

The passages I cited at the outset of the book and at the beginning of this chapter are Bodin's most precise formulation of his poetics for a futuristic fiction—one that will carry on what he specifies as the tradition of Rabelais, Cyrano, Swift, and Voltaire in a way to produce something new and nevertheless analogous to their works ("quelque chose de nouveau et toutefois d'analogue," p. 32). Bodin also provides a loftier and even more general lineage for the "epic of the future" that has not yet been written: "Meanwhile, the epic of the future remains to be done: I hope that someone else will undertake it. In this vast literary empire, there is ample space for a Moses, a Homer, a Dante, an Ariosto, a Shakespeare, and also a Rabelais. Great and happy will be he who becomes its Moses or Homer: he will be at once the prophet, the poet, the moralist, the legislator, and the artist of future generations. At the present point of spiritual development, one would say that we lack a second Bible, one that will recount the future" (p. 31). In its way this is also utopian dreaming, as Bodin was well aware. While futuristic fiction awaits its Homer, its Moses, and its second Bible, there remains "for the moment" the lesser but more immediately achievable task of providing worthy futuristic analogues to the earthier masterpieces of Rabelais, Swift, and Voltaire. Even in this task Bodin does not claim success, as he could hardly do in publishing only an incomplete novel surrounded by explanations of what it ought ideally to accomplish. Bodin's preface closes on a somber note. After thus defining the ideal kind of futuristic fiction at its loftiest, he expresses a hope "that some one else will try it: I heartily wish that he will succeed better than I" (p. 32).

Comedy then prevails throughout the ensuing "Introduction," which completes fifty-eight pages of preliminaries placed before the commencement of Bodin's actual novel. The excessive length of this material burlesques ordinary novelistic conventions as part of Bodin's metafictional strategy of inviting readers to laugh at accepted procedures while also seriously considering other possibilities. "What then! an introduction after a preface! Isn't that duplication?" To this question at the outset of his introduction, stated in anticipation of inevitable objections from readers increasingly anxious to find a story, Bodin provides a comic answer with a ring of truth. Prefaces, he says, are grave, tedious, stiff things which authors "sometimes feel obliged to address to a very demanding segment of the public for its edification or for the sake of soothing their [the authors'] consciences or comforting their modesty." Bodin then sketches what one ordinarily covers in a preface: here is my subject; I show it to you from the highest vantage point, taking up all its aspects; you will see that I understand it better than anyone and that no one has previously seen anything like this on the topic. Or sometimes, Bodin adds, there are expressions of modesty "and many other things equally impertinent" which make it understandable that huge numbers of people never read prefaces.

Introductions, however, at least for novels, are quite another matter: "the introduction is almost an integral part of the novel, as the caretaker's lodge is part of the castle." Authors there display themselves at their most obliging, "like the agreeable cicerone who takes you through the building and explains its marvels." Accordingly it is in the introduction, Bodin ironically affirms, that he will tell us how it was possible humanly ("humainement")—without any supernatural gift of prophecy—to write *Le Roman de l'avenir*. In doing so he will also acquit himself of his duty to the largest group of novel readers, those who want to find there "the appearance of reality." By this gesture of ironic deference towards those who insist on tokens of verisimilitude they can easily understand—a slippery issue for any novel about the future—Bodin alerts readers that at this point in his introduction, along with continuing metafictional statements about the poetics of futuristic fiction, the novel *has* begun.

Its contents, we are told in an obvious flight of tongue-in-cheek fictionalizing, derive from "three hundred thirty-three thick folio notebooks" of prophetic writing left to Bodin by one Fabio Mummio, an Italian refugee in London who died on May 26, 1828. He was a mesmerist, "a poetic head, and, less politely, a madman." This *"would-be prophet* (as the English say) had mesmerized . . . beauties from three kingdoms with large blue and moist eyes, long swan-like necks, a bearing naïve and gracious on account of their timidity, and for the most part suffering from consumption" (p. 47). It is the mesmerically induced visions of these trance-maidens, giving "the future of each country of the world," which Bodin says he has quarried for his story, although not without difficulties: the reports are arranged in the greatest disorder, lacking any exact dates (p. 53). After struggling to piece together various clues in the documents, Bodin guesses that the story he is about to narrate takes place during the twentieth century—but whether in its midst or towards its close he cannot say. This uncertainty, however, will be an imaginative advantage: "On account of it, the imagination of readers does not lack space to maneuver, and many of them may hope that their grandchildren will know when to locate the action. After all, if this book is going to last until then, and from a novel become a history, I will believe it infinitely happier than it deserves to be" (p. 57). Whether his fiction becomes history by actually taking place later in the real world, an unlikely possibility in Bodin's eyes to say the least, its imprecise dating allows for one major aesthetic achievement denied to ordinary fiction: there will be greater imaginative involvement of readers who are invited by its lack of exact dates to play the game of speculating about *when* its action might possibly take place.

Bodin's conspicuous avoidance of dates within his story is another dialogic variation on Mercier's precise location of his uchronia in the year 2440. So too is the episode when a character in *Le Roman de l'avenir* arrives by dirigible to spend a day shopping for wedding presents in Paris, whose twenty-fifth century future Mercier had so thoroughly described. As a reminder to readers that self-conscious variations on Mercier's themes form one part of his technique, Bodin merely promises to show readers around the city another time (p. 217). He does not describe twentieth-century Paris and thus invites speculation about the appearance of *his* future Paris. Readers are given the pleasure of exercising *their* imaginations about some parts of Bodin's fictive future.

Bodin reports that no mesmeric procedure allowed the Italian investigator "to establish a sort of future chronology" (p. 53). Nor could the greatest prophetic efforts by Mummio and his somnambulists see beyond the twenty-first century—not surprisingly, Bodin here remarks, in view of history's unpredictable nature, as witnessed so notably by Mercier's blindness to many nineteenth-century developments. Bodin's "old friend Fabio Mummio," more apocalyptically inclined, attributed the temporal limitation to some

A POETICS FOR FUTURISTIC FICTION

impending astronomical catastrophe like a comet-strike that would end life on this world. Discounting that gloomy possibility (which is included mainly by way of satirizing prophets of doom), Bodin adds that in the notebooks there are nevertheless so many extraordinary things apparently pertaining to the late twenty-first century that he has refrained from mentioning them "for fear of putting readers' belief to an excessively hard test" (p. 56). He is only publishing "for the present a very small part" of what he could take from "that abundant literary mine." This restraint (ostensibly for the sake of maintaining verisimilitude) leaves Bodin subject to the less worrisome alternative predicament of not appearing to be a sufficiently bold inventor of marvels: "because the worst that could happen to me would be that I would not be found to be a great enough magician ['assez grand sorcier']," p. 56).

Bodin closes the introduction by satirizing another traditional stance of authors pleading for indulgence at the outset of their work. Instead of acknowledging help while nevertheless accepting in advance all blame for shortcomings, Bodin brashly denies any responsibility for whatever is bad and blames all faults on Mummio's manuscripts.[9] The introduction's penultimate paragraph, however, takes up explicitly the more serious matter of temporal point of view in futuristic fiction, an issue considered previously—and then in a more oblique, hesitant way—only by Restif de la Bretonne, whose *Les Posthumes* was apparently unknown to Bodin: "As to the form of the narration, it was necessary, in order for it to be clear and flowing, to recount all these future events in the present or past tenses, as though the novel itself was written and published two hundred years from now, as if it were addressed to the public which will exist in that time."[10] Bodin thus invites readers to play yet another imaginative game—to suppose that his novel of the future is addressed to readers of the future.

At a more technical level concerning narrative and readerly viewpoints, this too is an important part of Bodin's explicitly articulated poetics for futuristic fiction. Its readers must perforce read with the outlook of their own present day and its attitudes. They must also adopt the perspective of people living in or even *after* the future setting which is the locus of novelistic action. Although Bodin does not explore further the aesthetic implications of such imaginative leaps, he clearly defines a kind of temporal doubling of narrative viewpoint which is in fact unique to futuristic fiction and crucial to many of its effects. Novels set in their readers' present or close past do not necessarily call for any particular awareness by readers of their own location in time. Nor do even historical novels normally require that readers imagine them written and published during the era described, although such works *may* take the form of first-person narratives putatively composed in the depicted past. Only futuristic fiction, as Bodin was the first to suggest, must routinely enforce a double temporal perspective as part of its formal narrative structure. Thus amid the Shandean burlesque of his dedication, preface, and introduction, Bodin provides readers with a poetics that allows them both to understand and properly to judge his attempt at a novel of the future.

Bodin's story breaks off after 324 pages with his promise to finish it if any readers are sufficiently curious about the outcome to ask for a second volume and sufficiently indulgent to inspire him with the courage to write more. He adds that "in effect, this volume is truly no more than an exposition, and I drop the curtain at the moment when the action is going to begin" (p. 382). Apparently no one encouraged him to continue. By design or chance, therefore, his tale remains open-ended after the manner of romantic fragments. The difference is that Bodin's self-reflexive narrative invites as much consideration of how such a work should be completed in order to exemplify correctly the best potentialities of its new genre as of how its particular action might be resolved. His own intentions so far as they concern form are clear. Utopian, predictive, and philosophical elements were to remain subordinated to the requirements of plot, characterization, and, equally important, the picturesque appeal of a future designed to capture the reader's fancy as well as stimulate speculation about what may be or should be.

Again Bodin provides a clue to his poetics by inventing an epigraph, this time for his third chapter. From "the album of a schoolboy" there is a charming statement of a young writer's ambition: "When I grow up, I will write a novel of the future, and in it I will make trips through the air by machines shaped like birds; without that there is no poetry in the future." After the Mongolfiers' triumph in 1783, dirigible flight became a staple of futuristic fiction. Bodin's innovation lay in stressing the aesthetic advantage of such fantasies instead of resorting to them primarily for predictive or utopian purposes or for enhanced realism. He understood the deepest source of their appeal: not in adding verisimilitude (although such episodes *could*, because flight seemed likely to be a major aspect of the future) but rather in making futuristic fiction resonant of strange beauty in a way analogous to the older literature of supernatural marvels. If, as invention of an imaginary schoolboy's notebook implies, there is something about such beauty that may be especially attractive to the young in years or in spirit, so much the better. Bodin finds little artistic merit in visions of a future lacking such poetry and nothing to be said for readers unwilling to respond to it.

Accordingly his own novel shows a plausible world where air travel is usual for the wealthier classes and aerial battles are a major form of warfare. Even more conspicuously, it shows a world filled with wonders. Dirigibles do indeed take the beautiful form of giant birds. Bodin stresses their exotic shapes without going into technical questions. He does not speculate or invite his readers to ask themselves about how such machines might actually work. He is concerned with the phenomenology of possible futures, not technological forecast.

Steamships, for example, are not described as more advanced than nineteenth-century models but are alluded to as vomiting black columns of smoke "like the dragons of fable" (p. 241). Episodes of mesmerism are included and, unlike the business about Fabio Mummio in Bodin's introduction, are treated seriously rather than satirically. Bodin depicts trances and cataleptic states more for the sake of their marvelous atmosphere of intriguing strangeness bordering on fantasy than for didactic purposes in portraying a possible future where mesmerism has been accepted as a legitimate form of medicine. Some conversations among Bodin's characters, including discussions of philosophical topics interesting on their own account, gain drama by taking place aloft in the elegantly decorated beak-cabin of the protagonist Philirène's "Swallow." An exciting chapter entitled "An Aerial Combat" shows a fight between that craft and a more predatorily named and shaped "kite" flown by pirates. In another episode a mysterious group of female warriors, futuristic amazons, descend in a war-balloon to kidnap Philirène's fiancée Mirzala. His antagonist Philomaque, leader of the "poetic, or anti-prosaic association" in its struggle against the world federation's "civilizing association," proclaims himself "Emperor of the Air."

The poetic association is a mixed lot of idealists, artists, poets, unemployed soldiers, disaffected aristocrats from countries like England where hereditary titles have been abolished, and outright bandits who chafe under the moral constraints of civilization. These people are all blind to what the narrator calls genuine progress achieved by the civilizing association, which has succeeded to an impressive extent in abolishing slavery, polygamy, national armies and navies, and ruinous taxes. What members of the poetic association see and rebel against is the apparent price of such progress: increasing standardization of life; destruction of fine old buildings and beautiful landscapes; and disappearance of local customs along with languages like Gaelic and Basque which sustained valuable traditions. To their dismay Sherwood Forest, once the fabled home of Robin Hood, has for two centuries been cleared of trees and planted with barley and turnips (p. 302). They receive a report that Stonehenge is also threatened. They take some comfort in a study suggesting that all available coal will eventually be mined and used up, thus ending "that odious nourishment of mechanical industry . . . that powerful agent of a civilization that is sad, uniform, monotonous, destructive of all poetic life" (p. 303). But this depletion will take at least another century during which time horses, "one of our national glories," are likely to vanish altogether if specimens are not soon acquired for museums.

Members of the poetic association hold their secret meetings at evocative spots with romantic connotations of bygone days: "abbeys, cathedrals, palaces, ruined castles, or large caves. . . . This time a general meeting of the *central committee*, composed of delegates from all parts of Europe, summons them to the famous cave in *Darbyshire* named *Elden Hole* or *Poole's Hole* on account of a brigand named Poole who hid there" (p. 308). It is the ambiance of such places that concerns Bodin as much as the philosophy inspiring these clandestine meetings. His poetic association is less a forecast than an effort to symbolize part of his nineteenth-century present and some of its potential consequences in a way that maximizes dramatic interest by enhancing the reader's sense of the depicted future as an exotic setting for picturesque action. Bodin's concern is not primarily with such estrangement as a vehicle for promoting social commentary or satire—what Darko Suvin calls cognitive estrangement.[11] Instead, Bodin focuses on the novelistic task of making fictive setting and action compelling on their own accounts.

Even the most unappealing aspects of this future are often described by Bodin's characters in a fashion calculated to create a vivid sense of strangeness in setting against which personal relationships can be played out to more dramatic effect. Thus a member of the poetic association denounces modern dehumanization of combat: "that war bizarrely mechanical, of which our great industrial nations have recently given the example, that war in which long armies of machines deploy against one another without visible sign of the men who direct them, overturning and killing each other methodically, piece by piece, until no part of them remains. . . . ridiculous parodies of war, where one would believe oneself watching a masquerade of grotesque demons mocking the human species" (p. 324). Against this eerie vision of mechanized warfare in a more thoroughly industrialized future, Bodin poses the perhaps equally distasteful but undeniably more human spectacle of men rallying to "that which was poetic and great in war: a leader idolized by his soldiers and endowed with everything which speaks to the imagination, with a character of steel, a fiery spirit, a hero whose entire person could pass for a type of the beautiful and the great" (p. 323). It is this older Napoleonic ideal, already anachronistic for readers of Le Roman de l'avenir, against which Bodin's protagonist Philirène has to contend in the person of his opponent Philomaque.

By way of contrast, Philirène is described in the title of chapter 8 as "an intellectual hero." He is more reflective, less charismatic, and not at all, the narrator remarks, like the literary stereotypes of a hero. Although Philirène, like Philomaque, talks at length about the values for which he fights and espouses more appealingly liberal ideas than his antagonist, Bodin subordinates such philosophizing to the novelistic requirements of sketching two very different people as a way of explaining the grounds of their conflict. They are not intended *merely* as spokesmen for opposite trends in modern civilization. The novel's action is grounded in a portrait of temperamental differences no less than in ideological issues.

One of Philomaque's schemes, we learn in the closing pages of Bodin's story, is to enlist the still-powerful followers of Islam in his cause by winning over the abducted Mirzala, the only living direct descendant of Mohammed, and proclaiming her his "Empress of the Air." He also "thinks of employing later the largest part of his air force ['forces atmospheriques'] to capture the summits of Horeb and Sinai to celebrate there his own coronation. But these places,

A POETICS FOR FUTURISTIC FICTION

so important on account of the religious memories which consecrate them and because of their military-aerial position, had been so fortified by the Israelite government that such an enterprise will offer the greatest difficulties" (pp. 373–74). Earlier in the novel its narrator has explained that, at an unspecified date after the formation of a new Babylonian empire, there had also been a "reestablishment of the kingdom of the Jews by a company of Jewish bankers, under the protection of the Sultans of the Euphrates and the modern Pharaohs" (p. 100). Thus, when Bodin's novel breaks off, the stage has been set for a clash between forces that are emblematic of several nineteenth-century reactionary and progressive trends extrapolated to imaginary future consequences—outcomes that in 1834 were neither totally implausible nor altogether contemptible as prediction. But the idea of a reborn Israel defending Horeb and Sinai against an Islamic air force may now seem closer to the mark than it could have when *Le Roman de l'avenir* was published, and for reasons unforeseen by its author. For anyone in Bodin's France of 1834, the impending conflict sketched in his novel was even more prominently a clash whose location and antagonists were intended to evoke associations with the marvels of a vanished and more colorful past.

Such associations, in turn, are designed to augment what Bodin calls the poetry of the future: its beautiful birdlike dirigibles, their awesome battles amid the clouds, latter-day amazons, and the like. Even the drably utilitarian "civilizing association" accompanies its annual world parliament at Centropolis in the South American "Republic of Benthamia" with spectacular ceremonies: at a huge rural ampitheater (complete with a colossal statue of Bentham) one finds a chorus of one hundred thousand voices, artillery firing salutes, and fifteen hundred balloons aloft with spectators. In keeping with the poetics that he initially outlines, rather than for predictive purposes, Bodin includes such features in his novel of the future. For the same reason, but less successfully, he also models his own would-be "epic of the future" (as he terms the ideal *littérature futuriste* at one point in his introductory manifesto) on the structure and themes of epic poetry.

The initial episode plunges readers in epic fashion into the midst of things. The narrator carefully points out later that the action of chapter 8 takes place earlier in story time than the events narrated in chapter 1, "by which we have entered *mediis rebus*, as the old critics say" (p. 195). Without such explanation this particular echo of epic structure might be overlooked, because none of the action is dated by allusion to years or months. Bodin thus chooses to signal discrepancies between plot chronology and narrative sequence by allusion to epic practice, lest the parallel be missed, rather than in ordinary novelistic fashion by simply specifying the calendric time of each incident. Other invitations to read the work as a futuristic epic are equally prominent. The first chapter evokes Virgilian echoes by opening in a restored Carthage presided over by a capable woman named Politée who has founded on the old site a new empire, has been abandoned by her lover Philomaque in favor of his political ambitions, and is called the new Dido. The geographical spread of events in Bodin's story achieves epic scope. There is epic grandeur in the issue that will be decided by the impending final conflict between the poetic association and its utilitarian opponents in the world federation: nothing less than the nature of future civilization. There is even a kind of epic overtone to the discovery that Bodin's mighty opposites Philirène and Philomaque are half-brothers, although Racine's tragedy *La Thébaïde ou les frères ennemis* is more immediately evoked in Philirène's reaction to this news: "So we are brothers! Another Thebiad . . . enemy brothers!" (p. 354).

All these epic and quasi-epic features are designed to surround Bodin's future with an aura of earlier literature dealing in marvels and thereby to enhance through literary connotations the "poetic" appeal of his story. Unlike Grainville, however, Bodin did not feel constrained to imitate very closely either the marvelous super-

A POETICS FOR FUTURISTIC FICTION

natural machinery of epics or their narrative structures, apart from the gesture of starting *in medias res*. As an opening gambit, the latter is almost equally characteristic of prose fiction and equally suitable to its purposes. Thus Bodin could go further than Grainville in the direction of effective novelistic techniques. He was not so hampered by his classical model. Bodin's epic affinities do not confine him within a form that, as he suggests in his preface, was no longer viable except as a starting point in the quest for *analogous* effects; for the time being these effects had to be achieved largely by new methods in futuristic fiction that could not yet aspire to the status of a true epic of the future. Perhaps Bodin nevertheless found it harder to complete his story while following so conspicuously epic precedents that were valuable to him chiefly for their poetic connotations. Once embarked on a tale of such grand scope, he evidently had difficulty sketching concisely a totally new future world by way of exposition or resolving the complicated plot briefly.

It may be, however, that Bodin realized the value, especially high in futuristic fiction, of an *unresolved* plot that would encourage readers to think through for themselves the possible consequences of a future victory for one or another of the nineteenth-century trends that he symbolizes in warfare between "civilizing" forces of Benthamite utilitarianism and the more emotionally compelling irrationalism of "poetic" forces led by an emperor of the air.

Whatever Bodin's reasons for breaking off his story, he takes the fact of its incompletion as a point of departure for interrogating both himself and his readers about their appropriate next steps. Each has a choice of roles. To clarify these options, his "Post-scriptum" starts with questions that again introduce issues germane to a poetics for futuristic fiction; now, however, they describe possible varieties of reader response: "Is it a *post-script*, or is it not rather an *ante-script?* The name matters little. I mean to say: why stop at this volume? Why leave the reader halfway? Be willing to listen to me for a moment" (p. 383). As Bodin's plea for a little more indulgence suggests, his tone is mainly serious throughout the material at the end of his book that comprises its real conclusion: the postscript; notes on his preface; a statement of his position on controversies about mesmerism; a survey of previous futuristic fiction; a reprinting of his 1822 essay on what Athens will be like in 1840, included by way of illustrating an earlier and very different mode of writing about the future; and remarks on a famous prophecy. All this material, as the opening query of Bodin's postscript suggests, may best be considered not just as critical commentary on Bodin's own narration but also as a kind of prolegomenon to future works by Bodin or others writing in the same vein as *Le Roman de l'avenir*.

His book is only ended, Bodin continues, for those who have found it tedious or who "without *sufficiently* focusing their attention on the characters to have the least curiosity about the fate which is reserved for them, having wanted to know what form one has given to a literary conception at least bizarre, confine themselves to tasting, turning over, weighing that conception, to assign it its value" (pp. 383–84; italics added). Such readers, who will neither long for nor imagine a continuation and conclusion of his story, are the critics, Bodin adds; these are difficult people to please, especially because they differ among themselves in their fixed opinions and in their very manner of perceiving. Thus, even while taking great pains to play the critic himself by articulating a poetics for his new genre, Bodin also cautions against reading futuristic fiction *only* with a critic's eye for discovering and assessing new literary species.

The common novel reader's concern with the fate of characters about whom he cares is in Bodin's view a healthier interest, particularly for a genre that so easily deflects attention from story to ideas. His ideal audience would be "those amiable and indulgent readers who demand nothing better than to interest themselves in the characters, in the action, instead of the scene" (p. 386). By this point in *Le Roman de l'avenir*, to be sure, Bodin takes for granted that some attention to a future setting is indispensable, and accordingly that even such ideal readers as he posits will not ignore it. He only cautions against allowing such interest in a future environment to displace adequate concern with action and characterization. Though he does not allude to Aristotle, this point is a very traditional Aristotelian insistence on the priority of plot and character over spectacle. The issue warrants careful attention because, as Bodin evidently realized though he does not dwell on the paradox, futuristic fiction depends for its most distinctive effects precisely on creation of a new setting different from every reader's present environment in ways that must be conspicuous if the work is to be effective. Bodin saw the danger in making such differences so prominent that plot and character become subordinated to concern with futuristic settings.

Bodin amplifies his warning about incorrect ways to read futuristic fiction by describing the most wrongheaded critical approaches, starting with readers who take novels of the future only as prediction. The majority of dissatisfied critics will be those who do not find the depicted future close enough to the one they have imagined: "they will have judged it either too or not sufficiently similar to the present" (p. 384). Among these will be people with very particular complaints: "they will accuse me of being still too much the monarchist, too aristocratic, and of letting Christianity stand, along with ownership of property and marriage. . . . [T]o respond sufficiently to these reproaches a volume would not be adequate; I hope therefore that I may be excused for the present" (p. 386). Again Bodin strenuously tries to prevent futuristic fiction from making its primary concern, and that of its readers, the requirements of utopian planning or universally acceptable prediction. He stresses here the dangers of such misreading by refusing to engage his potential critics on their own grounds of arguing over the desirability or the likelihood of specific features of his future setting. Such debate, in Bodin's view, should play no part in the aesthetics of futuristic fiction. He argues the futility of mistaking novels of the future like his own for works in the genre of utopia or prophecy, because to do so is almost inevitably to guarantee dissatisfaction for reasons that will be irrelevant to properly novelistic works (ideals that readers do not entirely share or predictions that seem unlikely).

Bodin says that other dissatisfied critics will long for more clarity, "fewer things left without explanation" (p. 384). This too is a crucial issue. As one of the most advanced aspects of his attempt to avoid the tedium of actionless utopias wherein every last detail is recounted (usually in dialogue of excruciating length that contributes nothing to character or plot development), Bodin deliberately includes passing allusions to intriguing technological and social developments that are not fully explained. In this key matter of how much scope to leave for involving the reader's imagination, it is very hard to strike a balance that will please all critics. Still others reading his story, Bodin continues, "will regret not sufficiently finding there the dim light of metaphysical poetry, the cloudy twilight of synthesis applied to the future history of humanity; or the darkness furrowed with lightning, with the brief and figurative shapes of the verse in *Apocalypse*" (p. 384). For avoiding apocalyptic style and subjects, Bodin excuses himself on two grounds.

First, Apocalypse is located so very far ahead. In choosing too distant a future perspective ("en plaçant le point de vue d'avenir sur un plan trop éloigné"), he would be prematurely risking an attempt at what he has "called *the epic of the future*, that which ought to be the work of another time, or certainly of another man" (p. 384). Second and more immediately relevant, he writes: "Conceptions too bold, which would nevertheless pale in comparison with those of M. Ch. Fourier, that utopian armed with analogy as with a sharp instrument with whose aid he has become the most marvelous as well as the most intrepid of those who imagine the future; such conceptions, I say, would have had the inconvenience of damaging probability and interest too much ['de trop nuire à la vraisemblance et à l'intérêt'] and hindering the vast majority of

A POETICS FOR FUTURISTIC FICTION

readers from seeing what pleases them most, characters with whom they find something in common, with whom they sympathize, and above all whom they understand" (pp. 384–85). Bodin does not oppose all speculation or utopian planning in the manner of Fourier, whom he generously praises here as the most awe-inspiring as well as the boldest of philosophical futurists. Nor does Bodin altogether omit such philosophizing from his own narrative, which is laced with stimulating discussions about the advantages and limitations of various possible future societies and those philosophies upon which they might be based. It is a question instead of achieving in futuristic fiction a necessary combination of the marvelous and the probable, a combination which for Bodin distinguishes the new genre. His praise of Fourier implicitly concedes that daring utopian speculation may in effect achieve a new variety of the marvelous quite distinct from that of the supernatural machinery in older literature but nevertheless equally unsuitable to novels of the future because equally unbelievable.

With that comment on Fourier, Bodin also begins to suggest the influences he felt most strongly at work in shaping, for better or worse, the newly emerging varieties of *littérature futuriste* (including that novelistic form for which his entire book is an argument). Utopian speculations about the future in the style of Fourier, along with uchronias on the model of Mercier's *L'An 2440*, play an ambiguous role. They stimulate all kinds of writing about the future and, to that degree, encourage experiments like Bodin's own novel. But they also deflect both readers and writers from what Bodin identifies as proper concern with plot and character. In his view they are not adequate models. Nor has the Book of Revelation served as a valid model: apocalyptic fiction does not allow for sufficient verisimilitude in setting or characterization. Related modes of enigmatic forecast purporting to be divinely inspired prophecy are equally deficient, as Bodin makes clear in his two wry paragraphs on Saint Malachy's "Prophecy of the Popes."

Of that famous document purportedly from the twelfth century (but actually a forgery), Bodin mainly remarks that it seems to foretell an imminent end for the world. Because some part of the action in his novel takes place towards the end of the twentieth century, he ironically suggests, readers familiar with that singular ("curieuse") prophecy should be grateful to him for "having given some respite to this poor world which, according to the aforesaid prophecy, will not last until then" (p. 402). By this comic stroke of taking credit for prolonging the world's future, Bodin relegates all post-biblical prophecies to the status of mere fictions competing with emerging novelistic versions of the future that may be less gloomy as well as more interesting. Readers can choose the most appealing futures from a wider variety now offered to them. Futuristic novels thus displace prophecies, but without imitating their form. Bodin insistently provides such reminders that no previous forms of writing about the future could supply more than hints of what should be done by novelists.

Bodin's short survey of "literary experiments on the future," the first such account, is most notable as evidence of how few of the available works offering such hints Bodin actually knew.[12] There is no mention of *Les Posthumes* or *The Mummy*; Bodin says he does not know of any German literature set in the future. He takes the full title of *Memoirs of the Twentieth Century* from the "Biographie universelle," along with a somewhat inaccurate statement that Madden's book is very rare because it was confiscated. In any case Bodin had not read it. Nor, more surprisingly, had he "ever seen" Grainville's *Le dernier homme*, although Charles Nodier had spoken enthusiastically of it to Bodin about ten years before *Le Roman de l'avenir*. On the basis of that hearsay account of "a French poem . . . known to a small number of the curious," Bodin alludes to it along with other poetic "apocalypses and ends of the world" (including "more than one poem entitled *The Last Man*," of which "the most well-known is that of the celebrated Thomas Campbell") [p. 398]. It is unclear, however, whether Bodin had read Campbell's effort or any of the other Last Judgment poems in its dreary tradition. If so, they too played mainly a negative role in suggesting Bodin's ideas about an appropriate form for the novel of the future: it must supply the human interest they lacked.

Apart from *L'An 2440*, which Bodin clearly knew well, the only other title mentioned in his survey is *Les Voyages de Kang-Hi* "by M. de Levis, of which an analysis that I read around 1810 in the *Journal de l'Empire* made on me, at that time a schoolboy, an impression that I still remember" (p. 398). Here too Bodin is ambiguous. But whether he had read *Les Voyages de Kang-Hi* itself or only a memorable review of it, Bodin firmly relegates it to the category of "utopias without action" that do not exemplify the full potentialities of futuristic fiction. Where then did Bodin find inspiration for his impulse to improve on what he knew about existing forms of prophecy, uchronia, and Fourierist speculation?

His autobiographical "Notes on the Preface" and its companion section "On Magnetism" suggest two sources: the historical novel and mesmerism. Whether either alone would have sufficed is a moot point. Bodin was involved with both in ways that apparently reinforced synergistically his quest for a new way of writing about the future. To see why, one must first appreciate Bodin's testimony that underlying his search for the ideal novel of the future, and spurring it on, was a perfectly conventional longing to be recognized as a writer who had done something—anything—original in an age conspicuous for its creativity in all spheres of intellectual endeavor: "I had thought for a long time that, in this century so fertile in literary inventions, in historical systemizations and in religious or social creations, there should be established a sort of registry of mortgages for the preservation of ideas. I was very interested in this, I who wanted to assume the date and mortgage of several ideas, or half-ideas, or quarter-ideas. . . . But while waiting for that useful establishment, the reviews and journals supply its place to a certain extent" (p. 388). Accordingly, Bodin explains, he had published a part of his preface in the *Gazette littéraire* of

February 17, 1831, "without having written a line of the book, for fear of being anticipated." But he only published enough, he says, to establish precedence without giving away his exact plan for a novel of the future.

That idea had obsessed him for a decade, he also reports. It had left him in a state that seemed "a true nightmare: I did not read the least phrase touching on my idea, even approaching it no matter how slightly, without fearing that someone had seized that poor idea and would profit from it before me. The very word *future* made me shudder. That state was intolerable; if it had continued I would have died because of my concealed book" (pp. 388–90). In a manner reminiscent of Jane Webb's prefatory confession that what she wanted above all was an original idea for a new kind of hero, and thus credit for literary novelty of whatever kind, there is a disarming touch of self-deprecating hyperbole here in keeping with the comic tone that Bodin favors. But there is also a ring of truth sustained by his ensuing statement of doubt that "anyone could more candidly make his literary confession" (p. 390). In fact he might have said more, and I am sorry he did not. Nevertheless no early writer of futuristic fiction had said nearly so much about the motives prompting an experiment in this new kind of writing.

While *Le Roman de l'avenir* thus includes some autobiography to account for its existence and form, the anxiety that Bodin describes reveals as much about his literary context as about his engaging personality. Bodin's fear of being anticipated is a measure of the fact that developments very like the one to which he aspired were indeed in the air. Despite his incomplete acquaintance with prior fictions about the future, Bodin correctly intuited their tendency in conjunction with developments such as mesmerism and historical novels that were far more conspicuous by the 1830s.

Motivated by the same eagerness to establish a claim to priority in some new genre, Bodin also confesses that he had tried in 1822 to imitate Walter Scott in French but had desisted "after publishing scraps here and there . . . without pretending to the certificate of invention, but only to the certificate of importation" (p. 388). Then "towards 1828" Bodin had "a new half-idea in trying to apply the procedures of Walter-Scottism ['les procédés du Walter-Scottisme'] to antiquity: I wanted to show the Greeks and Romans not buskined but speaking and acting as one might suppose they spoke and acted when they were alive" (p. 389). He published fragments of a Roman drama in literary reviews and magazines "towards the end of 1830," just in time to claim some priority over similar efforts from other hands. Thus Bodin on his own admission was not only an author casting about for a new form but also a writer looking in particular for some fresh application of Walter Scott's newly elaborated methods of historical fiction. If application of those methods to narrating realistic tales of the future seems inevitable from our vantage point, and futuristic fiction accordingly appears in some measure a corollary of the historical novel and of that historicism which it in turn reflects, the connection was far from self-evident when it occurred to Bodin.

Nor without a further impetus from mesmerism might the techniques of Scott's kind of realistic historical novel have been so clearly linked in Bodin's theorizing with the idea of finding plausible equivalents of those marvelous effects formerly achieved by means of the supernatural. The marvelous and its equivalents played no necessary role in Scott's kind of historical fiction, which is quite distinct from the gothic (a mode to which Bodin does not allude). It was "in the same period, towards 1829" that he witnessed mesmeric experiments, and even undertook some himself "to get rid of my doubts, which bordered on incredulity" (p. 389). What he saw turned him from skepticism to belief in the reality of mesmeric phenomena. Apparently too he read Mesmer's most important successors, the Marquis Chastenet de Puységur and J. P. F. Deleuze, both of whom are mentioned favorably in the section "On Magnetism" (pp. 390–97) wherein Bodin reprints two essays he had published in 1829 and 1832 defending mesmerism.

After being convinced that not all mesmerists were charlatans, he then had another idea: "to introduce mesmerism in the arts and literature, as a poetic and dramatic element" (p. 389). In this effort, as he says, he had already been anticipated in Germany by Johann Zschokke. Nonetheless, the climate of opinion in France, where hostility to mesmerism still prevailed, was not yet receptive enough to risk publication of more than "a little novelistic and mesmeric scene" in several collections (p. 389). Now that proofs of mesmerism have had more impact, Bodin remarks, he sees with great pleasure "that literature seizes upon that marvelous source of emotions and interest" (p. 389). What is striking in Bodin's account of his involvement with mesmerism is the timing of that interest, its focus on Puységur and Deleuze, and the fact that Bodin did not see futuristic fiction—or fiction of any kind—as a forum for arguing the medical or philosophical virtues of mesmerism but rather saw mesmerism as affording to literature a credible new source of the marvelous.

The revival of mesmerism that was to reach its peak in France around 1850 had by the 1830s generated journalistic controversy and satires such as *La Magnétisomanie*, a drama produced in 1816, the year after Mesmer himself had died.[13] There was also a serious investigation by the medical section of the French Royal Academy of Sciences. Its 1831 *Report on the Experiments on Animal Magnetism* finally conferred some academic legitimacy on the efforts of mesmerists to explore for medical purposes aspects of the unconscious mind manifested in what were then described as states of induced magnetism, somnambulism, and catalepsy.[14] But this scientific respectability was short-lived; another report from the Royal Academy in 1837 was less favorable. Although a significant line of scientific influence can now be traced from Mesmer through the work of Braid, Liebeault, Charcot, Bernheim, and Janet on hypnosis to Freudian and related theories of neurosis as well as to the experimental psychology of motivation, it was the spiritualist wing of mesmerism that was most prominent during the first half of the nineteenth century.[15] The occult connections, too, proved most stimulating to Romantic and Victorian literature by providing a powerful impetus to quite a wide range of fiction.[16]

Bodin, however, was finally moved to begin writing during that short interval of scientific approval for mesmerism between the report of 1831 and the more damaging attitude adopted officially three years after publication in 1834 of *Le Roman de l'avenir*. The period of favorable academic attitudes was apparently helpful, whatever role may have been played by other causes not alluded to in Bodin's autobiographical remarks. In any case, he reports that finally his book "was written in about twenty days. Time had nothing to do with the affair" (p. 390). Something had broken the ice; on Bodin's testimony, that something was a swing of public opinion in favor of mesmerism as a valid new science that might be appropriated to the purposes of literature. Equally important, it was the scientific rather than the spiritualist side of mesmerism that attracted Bodin. The distinction is crucial to understanding which of the many nineteenth-century ideas about the future served as immediate catalysts for his poetics of futuristic fiction.

As Robert Darnton has well documented, mesmerism in general represents an anti-Enlightenment current of thought most conducive to those varieties of romantic literature that reflect "the nineteenth century's fascination with the supernatural and the irrational."[17] But it is precisely this fascination that Bodin rejects in calling for a futuristic literature of credible wonders "which will dignify reason instead of shocking or deprecating it as all the marvelous epic machinery conventionally employed up to now has done" (p. 20). In the burlesque figure of Fabio Mummio surrounded by his trance-maidens, Bodin satirizes the extravagant claims of those who believed (or pretended to believe) that mesmerically induced somnambulism could put people in touch with the spiritual world in order to achieve prophetic visions of the future. This kind of occult mesmerism figures in *Le Roman de l'avenir* only as a comic device enhancing its self-reflexive manner at the outset. Bodin presents episodes of catalepsy and mesmeric trance within the novel itself more seriously as illustrative instances of a marvelous but credible split between states of consciousness experienced in and out of trances—between what we might call conscious and unconscious aspects of the mind. These episodes maintain plausibility by avoiding the excesses of mesmeric spiritualism; they would gain further credibility in the eyes of readers who came to them, as Bodin apparently himself came to write them, after reading Puységur and "the good M. Deleuze" (p. 393).

Both Puységur and Deleuze take pains to dissociate scientific investigation of mesmeric phenomenon from spiritualism.[18] Neither rules out the possible existence of supernatural beings, but each stresses that such possibilities have nothing whatever to do with the case histories they present. Mesmeric "clairvoyance" of the kind they document, moreover, is sharply limited to medical prognosis: occasionally prognosis of another's disease by a physician or lay somnambulist; much more commonly by a sick person in an induced state of trance who is able to foretell with remarkable precision future crises and remissions in his own state and is also able to prescribe appropriate treatment. Many of the case histories related by Puységur and Deleuze are in themselves quite compelling narratives very well told for dramatic effect in a way that would, not incidentally, serve to stimulate any aspiring novelist's literary imagination.

There is also about such case histories an air of mystery, enhanced in the writings of Puységur and Deleuze by their frequently reiterated and often eloquent insistence that astonishing, authenticated examples of prognostic clairvoyance have causes *not* fully understood but nevertheless natural rather than supernatural. Deleuze, for example, after summing up his extensive argument "that magnetism is absolutely foreign to mystical doctrines," adds that his survey equally shows how scientific investigation of mesmerism "tends to restore to the natural order the marvelous facts ['les faits merveilleux'] which have served as the basis of superstition."[19]

A POETICS FOR FUTURISTIC FICTION

Here then is one area of thought well known to Bodin in which marvelous events were explicitly transformed from the arena of incredibilities to that of the scientifically credible though as yet inexplicable. In extraordinary case history after case history claiming truth but narrated in a novelistic manner, marvelous phenomena of a kind that would have been ascribed to supernatural agency in another era were endowed with an appearance of scientific verisimilitude.

Another distinctive feature of mesmerism as presented by Puységur and Deleuze is its invitation to reconsider the nature of human relationships to the future. Because prognostic clairvoyance was a phenomenon central to their studies but curiously restricted in the scope of its forecasts, both men wind up casting doubt on the whole enterprise of prophecy. What could actually be foretold in authenticated instances of mesmerically induced clairvoyance was a far cry indeed from visions of national destiny, the end of the world, or even the shape of things to come after a few more decades of technological change. Patients like Puységur's "Mademoiselle L" were more likely to predict with intriguing accuracy such trivia as the exact time of their next round of fever, headaches, and stomachaches. Puységur speculates that such predictions, unrecognized as merely a natural if puzzling consequence of induced trances, were probably the basis for exaggerated tales of magic: "No doubt all the magical arts were derived from this source of truth. But from the moment when it was indiscreetly divulged that some people announced with certitude, while sleeping, the crises, the perturbations, and the end of their diseases, the common people, ignorant and friends of the marvelous, believed they could readily obtain from such sleepers knowledge of all the events to come. From that error, engendered by pride and nourished by greed, there soon originated all the superstitious belief in sibyls, in prophets, and in the existence of privileged men, gifted by the gods with a supernatural power."[20] With influence from the spiritual world thus ruled out of court as an explanation for such limited mesmeric clairvoyance as Puységur, Deleuze, and others of their non-occult school had investigated, there remained the question of how any future can be known. So long as oracles could be accepted, that question could be begged. One had only to take on faith the marvel of divine inspiration of some kind or other, an inspiration which by definition was and could remain a mystery. But for natural phenomena such as mesmeric clairvoyance, there had to be a natural explanation.

Rather more insistently than Puységur, Deleuze takes up this problem at the level of philosophical speculation. His basic premise, deceptively simple, is that the future does not exist. It can be known in only two ways: either by a present vision of some future event, or by an extremely rapid grasp of all the causes which might bring about that event. Visions make sense only on the basis of several difficult hypotheses that Deleuze surveys, starting with Kant's notion that neither time nor space exists apart from our manner of perceiving the world, in which case superior intelligences (including God) might in some way have direct access to what we think of as the future. But there would then be problems in communicating such visions to humans. This hypothesis, Deleuze suggests, might account for the enigmatic nature of authentic prophecies, which can seldom be deciphered until after the events they apparently foretell.[21]

More relevant to understanding the facts of mesmeric clairvoyance, Deleuze argues, is the second method: forecasting the future by registering its present causes. One of his examples is an invitation to consider someone who stands on a river bank looking past a bridge with several arches at an approaching ship and states which arch the vessel will pass under. Its speed and direction as well as that of currents in the water must be taken into account. An experienced observer can easily make an accurate forecast, though not an infallible one: there may be a misjudgment, or the captain may decide to change course. For Deleuze the fact of free will means that the future is never fixed where humans are concerned.

A POETICS FOR FUTURISTIC FICTION

We can only guess what others will do. Our limited ability to grasp all the natural causes at work in situations more complex than that of the approaching ship introduces further uncertainty. Reviewing these home truths leads Deleuze toward a plausible hypothesis to account for mesmeric clairvoyance: those taken into a state of induced trance have thereby—somehow—been put in a position like the experienced observer looking at an approaching ship: with heightened awareness compared to their ability outside trances, they can sense causes at work in their own bodies or mental states and accordingly predict the course of their diseases. On this premise they are not experiencing any vision of the future but merely extrapolating accurately its most probable course on the basis of present observations.

Puységur follows a similar line of speculation, although with more reluctance to engage in what he calls "high questions of metaphysics."[22] But he does introduce a number of thought-provoking philosophical conundrums about the future in the very course of dismissing them for having little immediate concern with the facts of clairvoyance reported in his case histories. The main thing to understand, he insists, is that the somnambulists described "are no more prophets than their magnetizers are magicians or sorcerers."[23] Puységur also suggests that distinctions between present and future may not be so clear-cut as we suppose. Unlike Deleuze, who in effect explains mesmeric clairvoyance as an induced ability to make unusually accurate extrapolations, Puységur rejects the idea that somnambulists are only *predicting* their own future states.

He argues instead that they are experiencing a kind of expanded present: their prognostic statements are "not only the result of obscure prevision of a probable event, but really the result of a very clear vision, or rather of a present sensation of the event which is going to come about, which, already begun for them, is apparently also present to them, also distinct at the moment when they announce it, as are to us, in our natural state, the things which strike us, or the events which affect us, at the same moment when we feel their impact." This idea leads Puységur to speculate further that future events, or what we judge as such, may only be "appearances or gradual manifestations of a continuous and eternal present."[24] Again Puységur shies away from pursuing all the philosophical implications of this thought. But he certainly leaves his readers aware that, in at least some striking circumstances, we may not find the usual clear boundaries between present and future. In one significant but usually hidden area of human experience, according to Puységur's school of non-occult mesmerism, the future (albeit a very small part of it) is present as a valid topic for description by those who can sense it.

Anyone as concerned as Bodin with discovering ways of writing about the future must have found Puységur and Deleuze especially stimulating. Neither their case histories nor their explanations could provide a direct model for modes of futuristic fiction. Nor do they directly encourage speculation about future social, political, and technological changes. But they do provoke fresh philosophical consideration of how present and future are related as modes of experience within the human mind, and they reopen questions about the psychology of apprehending the future. They suggest that in significant ways the future is already a part of present experience—naturally, not supernaturally. Without attacking all varieties of religion, they discredit spiritualism and related modes of prophecy as valid forms for dealing rationally with the future. Thus in effect, though of course not by design, they further undermine confidence in apocalyptic modes of writing as acceptable instruments for consideration of what is to come. They nevertheless insist on the marvelous nature of those phenomena they describe, while insisting equally that such marvels are to be taken as credible parts of the natural world. In their evaluations of narratives detailing case histories they recur frequently to the question of how to judge probability and credibility in such accounts, arguing for a scientific basis in rendering the incredible credible. In literary terms this amounts to a preoccupation with the issue of verisimilitude.

A POETICS FOR FUTURISTIC FICTION

Puységur is especially eloquent on the need to restore a sense of wonder about the order of nature. He ends one chapter by citing Augustine's affirmation in *The City of God* that "the manner in which spirits are united with bodies is entirely marvelous: it cannot be understood by man, and it is nevertheless man himself."[25] In dissociating himself from those who take animal magnetism as a spiritual phenomenon, Puységur claims for it the *same* air of the marvelous that attends—or should attend—*all* natural phenomena not yet understood: "As for marvels, as everything in nature is marvelous, it is entirely clear that from the development of a faculty newly recognized and observed in man there have resulted new marvels. But when one has viewed them several times, one will not find them more astonishing than the marvels of the germination of a grain of wheat, of the fertilization of an egg, and all the other marvels of this kind, to which our senses and our reason are accustomed."[26] This is also a reminder that much of what we take for granted as a part of the natural world is in fact not understood. We have only grown so used to our ignorance that all sense of wonder is deadened. Discussions of mesmerism have the effect, clearly intended in Puységur's work, of inviting an estranged perspective on ourselves and our world in order to see new wonders and to wonder anew about what we have too often seen without considering. It is this invitation to reexamine the order of nature and find its marvelous dimensions that I believe must also have appealed strongly to Bodin, for whom the fictitious future had to be not only different and plausible but also "poetic."

Exactly how far such currents in the mesmeric school of Puységur and "the good M. Deleuze" may have tipped the balance of Bodin's thought toward the aesthetics of futuristic fiction that he articulated in *Le Roman de l'avenir* must remain a matter for speculation. Related attempts in romantic literature to naturalize the supernatural and rekindle a sense of wonder about the known world might also have pushed Bodin in the same direction.[27] So very certainly did the whirlwind of economic, social, and technological change sweeping over early nineteenth-century Europe. Aeronautics was an especially powerful stimulus to thinking about future possibilities. New utopian philosophies couched as programs for future action played their part, as Bodin's generous tribute to Fourier shows. Bodin's own explicit account of how he came to write the first poetics of futuristic fiction, which is our best evidence, nevertheless points most clearly to a confluence of three developments in literature and one in psychology.

First and most generally was a valorization of sheer literary originality. As in Madden's day a century earlier in England, this attitude provided strong encouragement to the quest for new genres and also created a climate of constant generic flux favoring self-reflexive modes that Bodin and others chose for futuristic fiction. Second was the transition from utopia to uchronia accomplished most notably by Mercier—a development whose enlargement of the literary imagination evidently appealed to Bodin, even while its deficiencies in novelistic action and human interest challenged him to find a remedy without sacrificing the advantages of future settings. Third was the historical novel as developed by Walter Scott. If the past as we imagine it could be dramatized realistically, why not imaginary futures? Outside of literature, but equally removed from the industrial revolutions that now seem so much more prominent as inducements to futuristic fiction, was that insistent probing of the unconscious mind practiced by Puységur, Deleuze, and the non-occult wing of mesmerism. For Bodin it was apparently their work more than any other aspect of nineteenth-century science which pointed to the prospect of finding credible marvels, whereas for Restif de la Bretonne it had been spiritualism that prompted incredible futuristic fantasies. Bodin's approach in turn allowed for futures that were at once plausible and marvelous—in his word, poetic.

I believe Bodin was right to say that, for literature, there is no point in futures that lack the appeal of poetry. He was right to make

A POETICS FOR FUTURISTIC FICTION

his dirigibles less conspicuously believable than beautiful as he describes them arcing through the air in their strange birdlike shapes. He was right to make his schoolboy say that without such things there is no poetry in the future—and, by implication, no literary interest. If we want only verisimilitude without marvels when thinking about the future, we may as well turn to our philosophers, our statisticians, and our dismal professional futurists. Even dystopian futures in the manner of *Brave New World* and *Nineteen Eighty-Four* depend in large part for their power upon a kind of converse poetry of the hideous. To be effective as literature the nightmare too must have its own compelling shape, a shape that has more to do with the strange and estranging aesthetics of the terrifying than with the logic of accurate extrapolation.

For Verne and his successors, ideas of wondrous futures—such futures as are the stuff of appealing dreams or useful nightmares—were most often stimulated by contemplation of a proliferating technology which suggested ever-more-efficient machines: machines that might one day serve us or destroy us by traveling under the sea, in the air, to other planets, and perhaps through time itself. But this was the second wave of futuristic fiction, well after the beginning whose end Bodin marks by articulating a poetics for the genre. That poetics was shaped less by the sciences of matter and their successes in changing the outward shape of civilization than by developments in imaginative literature and a new, if still uncertain and faltering, branch of mental science. Bodin's turn for inspiration to the more subjective realms of literary imagination and psychology seems altogether fitting, for it is within the mind and its dreams that all writers must seek the future.

Notes

ONE
Temporal versus Spatial Imagination

Unless otherwise noted, all translations are the author's.

1. For a bibliography of works published in the United Kingdom between 1644 and 1976, see I. F. Clarke, *Tale of the Future from the Beginning to the Present Day*, 3d ed. (London: Library Association, 1978). For continental material, see the article "Anticipation" in Pierre Versins, *Encyclopédie de l'utopie, des voyages extraordinaires et de la science fiction* (Lausanne: Editions L'Age d'Homme, 1972).

2. Aristotle, "Rhetoric," in *Aristotle: Rhetoric and Poetics*, trans. W. Rhys Roberts and Ingram Bywater (New York, Modern Library, 1954), 210 (1417B, 10–20).

3. John Donne, "Sermon Number 2: Preached at Lincolns Inne," in *The Sermons of John Donne*, ed. George R. Potter and Evelyn Simpson (Berkeley: University of California Press, 1953–61), 2:77.

4. See I. F. Clarke, *Voices Prophesying War, 1763–1984* (London: Oxford University Press, 1966).

NOTES TO CHAPTER ONE

5. See, for example, Frank E. Manuel and Fritzie P. Manuel, *Utopian Thought in the Western World* (Cambridge: Belknap Press of Harvard University Press, 1979); Darko Suvin, *Metamorphoses of Science Fiction: On the Poetics and History of a Literary Genre* (New Haven: Yale University Press, 1979); I. F. Clarke, *The Pattern of Expectation, 1644–2001* (New York: Basic Books, 1979); Chris Morgan, *The Shapes of Futures Past: the Story of Prediction* (Exeter, England: Webb and Bower, 1980); and W. Warren Wagar, *Terminal Visions: The Literature of Last Things* (Bloomington: Indiana University Press, 1982).

6. Robert Scholes, *Structural Fabulation: An Essay on Fiction of the Future* (Notre Dame: University of Notre Dame Press, 1975), 17–18.

7. Félix Bodin, *Le Roman de l'avenir* (Paris, 1834), 16: "On rêvait les fins du monde et le dernier homme."

8. Ibid., 397: "En effet, je n'ai connaissance d'aucune action romanesque transportée au milieu d'un état social ou politique futur."

9. Ibid., 17: "l'auteur n'a songé qu'à trouver un cadre pour exposer un système politique, moral ou religieux, sans rien rattacher à une action, sans donner ni relief ni mouvement aux choses ou aux personnes, sans aborder enfin la création vivante d'un monde à venir quelconque."

10. Ibid., 20: "Si jamais quelqu'un réussit à faire le roman, l'épopée de l'avenir, il aura puisé à une vaste source de merveilleux et d'un merveilleux tout vraisemblable, s'il se peut dire, qui énorgueillira la raison au lieu de la choquer ou de la ravaler comme l'ont fait toutes les machines à merveilleux épique, qu'il a été convenu de mettre en jeu jusqu'à présent. En offrant la perfectibilité sous la forme pittoresque, narrative et dramatique, il aura trouvé un moyen de saisir, de remuer les imaginations, et de hâter les progrès de l'humanité, bien autrement puissant que les meilleurs exposés de systèmes, fussent-ils présentés avec la plus haute éloquence."

11. Ibid., 26: "Chacun s'arrange un avenir à sa fantaisie; chaque système, chaque secte a le sien."

12. Ibid., 28–29: "La civilisation tend à nous éloigner de tout ce qui est poétique dans le passé: mais elle a bien aussi sa poésie et son merveilleux."

13. Ibid., 29–30: "Là peuvent se trouver des révélations de somnambules, des courses dans les airs, des voyages au fond de l'Océan, comme on voit dans la poésie du passé des sibylles, des hippogriffes et des grottes

NOTES TO CHAPTER ONE

de nymphes; mais le merveilleux de l'avenir, comme je l'ai dit précédemment, ne ressemble point à l'autre, en ce qu'il est tout croyable, tout naturel, tout possible, et dès-lors il peut frapper l'imagination plus vivement, et la saisir en s'y peignant comme la réalité. On aura trouvé ainsi un monde nouveau un milieu tout fantastique, et pourtant pas invraisemblable."

14. Ibid., 31–32: "Pour le moment, la question est de savoir si, après les grotesques et audacieuses fantaisies de Rabelais, les amusantes et satiriques inventions de Cyrano et de Swift, et les pétillans romans philosophiques de Voltaire, il était possible de trouver quelque chose de nouveau et toutefois d'analogue; quelque chose qui ne fût ni d'une fantaisie trop dévergondée, ni d'une intention purement critique, ni de cet esprit philosophique qui nuit à l'intérêt et à l'illusion en substituant toujours des idées aux personnages, et en subordonnant l'action et les caractères a la thèse qu'il soutient; et pourtant une chose à la fois fantastique, romanesque, philosophique et un peu critique; un livre où une imagination brillante, riche et vagabonde, pût se déployer à son aise; enfin, un livre amusant sans être futile. Je crois que ce livre était possible; mais je suis encore parfaitement convaincu qu'il n'est pas fait."

15. See especially Suvin, *Metamorphoses of Science Fiction*, p. 116, for speculation on why the shift to futuristic fiction "that cuts decisively across all other national, political, and formal traditions in culture, has so far not been adequately explained." For consideration of his explanation, see chapter 3.

16. Raymond Trousson, *Voyages aux pays de nulle part: Histoire littéraire de la pensée utopique*, 2d ed. (Bruxelles: Editions de l'université de Bruxelles, 1979), xxv.

17. On the uses of future settings in science fiction, see Thomas A. Hanzo, "The Past of Science Fiction," in *Bridges to Science Fiction*, ed. George E. Slusser, George R. Guffey, and Mark Rose (Carbondale: Southern Illinois University Press, 1980), 131–46; John Huntington, "Olaf Stapledon and the Novel About the Future," *Contemporary Literature* 22, no. 3 (1981): 349–65; John Huntington, "Remembrance of Things to Come: Narrative Technique in *Last and First Men*," *Science Fiction Studies* 9 (1982): 257–64; and Boris Eizykmann, "Temporality in Science-Fiction Narrative," *Science Fiction Studies* 12 (1985): 66–87. On Verne's characteristic use of present and past settings, see Marie-Hélène Huet, "Antic-

ipating the Past: The Time Riddle in Science Fiction" in *Storm Warnings: Science Fiction Confronts the Future*, ed. George E. Slusser, Colin Greenland, and Eric S. Rabkin (Carbondale: Southern Illinois University Press, 1987), 34–42.

18. Trousson, *Voyages aux pays de nulle part*, xxvii.

19. Mikhail Mikhailovich Bakhtin, "Forms of Time and of the Chronotope in the Novel," in *The Dialogic Imagination: Four Essays by M. M. Bakhtin*, ed. Michael Holquist, trans. Caryl Emerson and Michael Holquist (Austin: University of Texas Press, 1981), 84–85.

20. Ibid., 250–51.

21. Ibid., 147–48.

22. Ibid., 147.

23. See Ian Watt, *The Rise of the Novel: Studies in Defoe, Richardson and Fielding* (Berkeley: University of California Press, 1957); English Showalter, Jr., *The Evolution of the French Novel: 1641–1782* (Princeton: Princeton University Press, 1972).

24. See Katerina Clark and Michael Holquist, *Mikhail Bakhtin* (Cambridge: Belknap Press of Harvard University Press, 1984).

25. Alexandre Cioranescu, "*Epigone*, le premier roman de l'avenir," *Revue des sciences humaines* 39 (Juillet–Septembre 1974), 441–48.

26. [Jacques Guttin], *Epigone, histoire du siècle futur* (Paris: Pierre Lamy, 1659).

27. See Bernard Crick, *George Orwell: A Life* (1980; reprint, Harmondsworth: Penguin Books, 1982), 582–85.

28. See [Nicolas Lenglet Du Fresnoy], *De l'usage des Romans*, 2 vols. (Amsterdam, 1734), 2:140: "Epigone ou l'Histoire du siècle futur, par Jacques Guttin, in 8. Paris 1659. Cette petite Histoire a eu jadis quelque réputation; mais elle est aujourd'hui peu recherchée."

29. On developing techniques of realism in French fiction, which did not preclude uncertainty about chronology even during the eighteenth century, see Showalter, *The Evolution of the French Novel*, 67–261.

30. Bakhtin, "Forms of Time," 154.

31. See the article "Guttin (Jacques)" in Versins's *Encyclopédie de l'utopie*. Cioranescu ("*Epigone*, le premier roman de l'avenir," p. 447) refers to "Clodovée le Conquérant ou Louis XIV" but does not discuss the grounds or difficulties of this equation.

32. Showalter, *The Evolution of the French Novel*, 26. See too Erica

NOTES TO CHAPTER TWO

Harth, *Ideology and Culture in Seventeenth-Century France* (Ithaca: Cornell University Press, 1983), 129–79. Her discussion of intricately changing relationships between history and fable may help explain why it became harder to write futuristic fiction just about the time Guttin published *Epigone* and hence why that work had no immediate posterity, although Harth does not consider this particular issue. Nor, I think, do the trends she describes shed much light on the question of why Guttin or anyone might have been especially impelled to experiment with future settings during the heyday of heroic romances: "In the reign of the Sun King, literary truth changed in value. The *vraisemblance* that had cross-fertilized *romans* and *histoires*, contributing to the generic confusion between the two, came to be disdained in favor of the *vrai*. This change was closely linked to an important generic evolution. The multivolume heroic novel all but disappeared, and the word *roman* no longer figured prominently in titles of fictional works. History (particularly the *histoire de France* genre) went into eclipse. The replacement of the old *roman* by newer forms of fictional narrative and the virtual departure of history after Mézeray were accompanied by the progressive disengagement of truth from the constraints of verisimilitude" (p. 143).

TWO
Towards an Aesthetics of Extrapolation

1. See Marjorie Hope Nicolson, *Voyages to the Moon* (1948; reprint, New York: Macmillan, 1960).

2. Fredric Jameson, "Progress Versus Utopia; or, Can We Imagine the Future?" *Science Fiction Studies* 9 (July 1982): 148–49. Jameson also argues here that science fiction does not offer images of a real future but instead works "to defamiliarize and restructure our experience of our own *present* and to do so in ways distinct from all other forms of defamiliarization" (p. 151). The generic distinction, for Jameson, consists in a strategy of enforcing awareness of the present as history by inviting readers to view their own time from the viewpoint of its possible connections to an imaginary future. This argument has the advantage of granting to futuristic fiction a unique power which cleary distinguishes it from other genres. More debatable perhaps is Jameson's contention that we cannot ever effectively imagine real futures.

3. David Russen, *Iter Lunare: Or, A Voyage To the Moon. Containing*

NOTES TO CHAPTER TWO

Some Considerations on the Nature of that Planet. The Possibility of getting thither. With other Pleasant Conceits about the Inhabitants, their Manners and Customs (London, 1703), 44–45.

4. Nathan Bailey, *Dictionarium Britannicum*, 2d ed. (London, 1736).

5. Bailey, *Dictionarium Britannicum*.

6. *A Brief Description of the future History of Europe, from Anno 1650, to An. 1710.* ([London], 1650), 21. For the intellectual and political context of this and related works, see Keith Thomas, *Religion and the Decline of Magic: Studies in Popular Beliefs in Sixteenth and Seventeenth Century England* (London: Weidenfeld and Nicolson, 1971), especially chapter 13, "Ancient Prophecies," 389–432. Thomas argues persuasively that during the seventeenth century there was a "stabilising function" for such documents: "Political prophecies tended to be invoked at a time of crisis, usually to demonstrate that some drastic change, either desired or already accomplished, had been foreseen by the sages of the past" (p. 415). There were thus political motives prompting the writers or interpreters of these prophecies to direct attention backward more than to the future. Thomas notes too that documents purporting to be ancient prophecies foretelling present events "were a universal feature of an essentially pre-political world, that is to say, of one where innovation has to be disguised as a return to the past, and where the fact of change is essentially unrecognised" (p. 427). Underlying the eighteenth-century subversion of such attitudes, Thomas remarks, was a growing awareness of differences between past and present, differences that imply too a potentially different future instead of perpetual cycles of similar events. Thomas rightly insists, however, that "the reason for the replacement of this cyclical view of history by a linear one is one of the great mysteries of intellectual history" (p. 430).

Thomas finds that technological change was not so much the instigator as another consequence of transformations in convictions about the shaping of the future: "It was the abandonment of magic which made possible the upsurge of technology, not the other way round. . . . It was a favourable mental environment which made possible the triumph of technology. . . . The change which occurred in the seventeenth century was thus not so much technological as mental. In many different spheres of life the period saw the emergence of a new faith in the potentialities of human initiative. . . . It is . . . possible to connect the decline of the old

NOTES TO CHAPTER TWO

magical beliefs with the growth of urban living, the rise of science, and the spread of an ideology of self-help. But the connection is only approximate and a more precise sociological genealogy cannot at present be constructed" (pp. 657, 661, 666). When speculating about possible connections of technology and futuristic fiction during the eighteenth and early nineteenth centuries, it is well to bear in mind Thomas's admirably documented study of the previous era. We should not assume that technology always transformed attitudes, including attitudes about the future, instead of vice versa.

7. For an excellent survey of other relationships between typology and literature, see Paul J. Korshin, *Typologies in England, 1650–1820* (Princeton: Princeton University Press, 1982). Although futuristic fiction was apparently not prompted by typology, typological thinking did encourage novelistic use of what Korshin identifies as predictive structures arising from the depiction of known character types whose identification by any reader early in a story "enables him or her to predict how they are likely to behave" (p. 227). But such predictions are mostly confined to action within the unfolding plots of novels and do not determine the choice of their temporal settings. See also Earl Miner, ed., *Literary Uses of Typology from the Late Middle Ages to the Present* (Princeton: Princeton University Press, 1977).

8. Mikhail Bakhtin, "Forms of Time and of the Chronotope in the Novel," in *The Dialogic Imagination: Four Essays by M. M. Bakhtin*, ed. Michael Holquist, trans. Caryl Emerson and Michael Holquist (Austin: University of Texas Press, 1981), 147–48.

9. Isaac Newton, *Observations Upon the Prophecies of Daniel, and the Apocalypse of St. John* (London, 1733), 251. For the context of Newton's ideas about prophecy, see Frank E. Manuel, *A Portrait of Isaac Newton* (Cambridge: Harvard University Press, 1968), especially chapter 17, "Prophecy and History," 361–80. Manuel stresses (p. 367) that "Newton always remained firm by the principle that the truth of prophecy could be demonstrated only *after* it had been fulfilled, never before. . . . Thus while the books of prophecy were history, the history of things to come, their language could not be truly understood by ordinary men until after the events prophesied had actually happened." See also Paul J. Korshin, "Queuing and Waiting: the Apocalypse in England, 1660–1750," in C. A. Patrides and Joseph Wittreich, eds., *The Apocalypse in English Re-*

NOTES TO CHAPTER TWO

naissance Thought and Literature: Patterns, Antecedents and Repercussions (Ithaca: Cornell University Press, 1984), 240–65.

10. For another prominent English example of these attitudes, see Thomas Newton, *Dissertations on the Prophecies, Which Have Remarkably Been Fulfilled, and at This Time Are Fulfilling in the World*, 3d ed., 3 vols. (London, 1766), especially 2:215–16, 3:7–8, and 3:411–12. For an analysis of related material, see James West Davidson, *The Logic of Millennial Thought: Eighteenth-Century New England* (New Haven: Yale University Press, 1977). Davidson's survey of New England discussions shows that attempts to work out the chronology of history as foretold in the Book of Revelation neither led to consistent interpretations nor focused attention on the actual future. Instead such attempts apparently reinforced a general sense of imminence, a feeling that something crucial was about to happen: perhaps the millennium, the Second Coming, or the final judgment. This feeling in turn mainly heightened awareness of how the perplexing events of the present—such as mid-eighteenth-century earthquakes, the French and Indian wars, the American Revolution, and the French Revolution—could be assimilated as part of a coherent pattern of history that linked past with present and both much more tenuously with a future shown very darkly indeed by scriptural prophecies. Davidson makes clear the extent to which interpretation of biblical prophecy most often became an exercise in retrospection that entailed looking backward from present events to see if they are perhaps foretold by obscure biblical prophecies. He notes the small proportion of pages given to actual speculation about the nature of the millennium, even in works devoted to interpreting the Book of Revelation. See also below, chapter 4, note 6.

11. The first edition, containing only the first two parts, is Thomas Burnet, *Telluris Theoria Sacra* (London, 1681). This appeared in English as *The Sacred Theory of the Earth: Containing an Account of the Original of the Earth and of All the General Changes Which It Hath Already Undergone or Is to Undergo, till the Consumation of All Things* (London, 1684). The final two parts were added to the Latin edition of 1689 and included in the English translation of 1690 as well as in subsequent English editions.

12. For an account of Burnet's influence on English aesthetics, especially attitudes toward mountains and poetic descriptions of them, see Marjorie Hope Nicolson, *Mountain Gloom and Mountain Glory: The De-*

NOTES TO CHAPTER TWO

velopment of the Aesthetics of the Infinite (Ithaca: Cornell University Press, 1959). For the political context of Burnet's ideas, see M. C. Jacob and W. A. Lockwood, "Political Millenarianism and Burnet's *Sacred Theory*," *Science Studies* 2 (1972): 265–79; and Margaret C. Jacob, *The Newtonians and the English Revolution 1689–1720* (Hassocks, England: Harvester Press; Cornell University Press, 1976).

13. Frank E. Manuel, *The Religion of Isaac Newton* (Oxford: Clarendon Press, 1974), 39.

14. Stephen Toulmin and June Goodfield, *The Discovery of Time* (1965; reprint, Chicago: University of Chicago Press, 1982), 93.

15. [Georges Louis Leclerc, Comte de Buffon], *Théorie de la terre*, in *Œuvres complètes de M. le Cte de Buffon*, 24 vols. (Paris, 1774), 1:266: "c'est un roman bien écrit, & un livre qu'on peut lire pour s'amuser, mais qu'on ne doit pas consulter pour s'instruire."

16. Isaac Newton, *Correspondence of Isaac Newton*, ed. H. W. Turnbull (Cambridge, England: Published for the Royal Society at the University Press, 1960), 2:331, 333.

17. Newton, *Correspondence*, 333.

18. Burnet, *The Sacred Theory of the Earth*, 6th ed., 2 vols. (London, 1726), 1:xx.

19. Joseph Keill, *An Examination of Dr. Burnet's Theory of the Earth*, 2d ed. (London, 1734), 22, 139. The first edition of Keill's *Examination* appeared in 1698.

20. Arlen J. Hansen, "The Meeting of Parallel Lines: Science, Fiction, and Science Fiction," in *Bridges to Fantasy*, ed. George E. Slusser, Eric S. Rabkin, and Robert Scholes (Carbondale: Southern Illinois University Press, 1982), 51–58.

21. Burnet stresses too the utility of those hypotheses which in the normal course of science must be displaced by more accurate conjectures: "He that in an obscure Argument proposeth an *Hypothesis* that reacheth from End to End, tho' it be not exact in every Particular; 'tis not without a good Effect; for it gives Aim to others to take their Measures better, and opens their invention in a matter which otherwise, it may be, would have been impenetrable to them" (1:130). Cf. Newton's more evasive assertion added to the "General Scholium" of the second edition of the *Principia* in 1713: "Hypotheses non fingo" (I frame no hypotheses). For comments on the relationship of this notoriously perplexing assertion to Newton's actual

methods, see N. R. Hanson, "Hypotheses Fingo," in *The Methodological Heritage of Newton,* ed. Robert E. Butts and John W. Davis (Oxford: Basil Blackwell, 1970), 14–33.

22. Burnet did not include astrology among the available methods of scientific prediction: "I do not see how we are any more concern'd in the Postures of the Planets, than in the Postures of the Clouds; and you may as well build an Art of Prediction and Divination, upon the one, as the other" (2:40). For a survey of shifting attitudes toward astrology, as well as an account of its persistence, see Thomas, *Religion and the Decline of Magic;* and Bernard Capp, *English Almanacs 1500–1800: Astrology and the Popular Press* (Ithaca: Cornell University Press, 1979).

23. See R. F. Jones, "Science and English Prose Style in the Third Quarter of the Seventeenth Century" and "Science and Language in England of the Mid-Seventeenth Century," in *Seventeenth-Century Prose: Modern Essays in Criticism,* ed. Stanley E. Fish (New York: Oxford University Press, 1971), 53–111. Jones's classic essays are also conveniently available along with related material in Richard Foster Jones, *The Seventeenth Century: Studies in the History of English Thought and Literature* (Stanford: Stanford University Press, 1951).

24. Buffon, *Œuvres complètes,* 1:263, in his section "Du Système de M. Burnet": "Son livre est élégamment écrit, il sait peindre & présenter avec force de grandes images, & mettre sous les yeux des scènes magnifiques."

25. See, in addition to Toulmin and Goodfield's *The Discovery of Time,* Roy Porter, *The Making of Geology: Earth Science in Britain, 1660–1815* (Cambridge: Cambridge University Press, 1977).

26. H. G. Wells, *The Time Machine* (1895; reprint, New York: Bantam Books, 1982), 104, 186. For excellent discussions of *The Time Machine,* see Frank McConnell, *The Science Fiction of H. G. Wells* (Oxford: Oxford University Press, 1981); and John Huntington, *The Logic of Fantasy: H. G. Wells and Science Fiction* (New York: Columbia University Press, 1982).

THREE
Formal Variations

1. For the 1958 Gauss lectures, see Kingsley Amis, *New Maps of Hell: A Survey of Science Fiction* (New York: Harcourt, Brace and Co., 1960).

NOTES TO CHAPTER THREE

2. Darko Suvin, *Metamorphoses of Science Fiction: On the Poetics and History of a Literary Genre* (New Haven: Yale University Press, 1979), 3–15; Brian W. Aldiss, *Billion Year Spree: The True History of Science Fiction* (1973; reprint, New York: Schocken Books, 1975), 53. For science fiction defined as a new mode of apocalyptic literature, see David Ketterer, *New Worlds for Old: The Apocalyptic Imagination, Science Fiction, and American Literature* (Bloomington: Indiana University Press, 1974). For the generic affiliation of science fiction with varieties of mythology, see Robert M. Philmus, *Into the Unknown: The Evolution of Science Fiction from Francis Godwin to H. G. Wells* (Berkeley and Los Angeles: University of California Press, 1970); and Casey Fredericks, *The Future of Eternity: Mythologies of Science Fiction and Fantasy* (Bloomington: Indiana University Press, 1982). For the history of science fiction since Mary Shelley's *Frankenstein* in relation to the rise of modern science, see Robert Scholes and Eric S. Rabkin, *Science Fiction: History, Science, Vision* (New York: Oxford University Press, 1977). For a consideration of the liberating possibility that the whole generic system which created science fiction as a distinct form may be breaking up into more fluid relationships that call for casting our historical nets even more widely, see Mark Rose, *Alien Encounters: Anatomy of Science Fiction* (Cambridge: Harvard University Press, 1981).

3. Suvin, *Metamorphoses of Science Fiction*, 8 (italics deleted).

4. Ibid., 113: "Swift created the great model for all subsequent SF. . . . All the later protagonists of SF, gradually piecing together their strange locales, are sons of Gulliver, and all their more or less cognitive adventures the continuation of his *Travels*."

5. Aldiss, *Billion Year Spree*, 53.

6. Thomas A. Hanzo, "The Past of Science Fiction," in *Bridges to Science Fiction*, ed. George E. Slusser, George R. Guffey, and Mark Rose (Carbondale: Southern Illinois University Press, 1980), 132. See also Fredric Jameson, "Progress Versus Utopia; or, Can We Imagine the Future?" *Science-Fiction Studies* 9 (July 1982): 147–58; Boris Eizykman, "Temporality in Science-Fiction Narrative," *Science-Fiction Studies* 12 (1985): 66–87; John Huntington, "Olaf Stapledon and the Novel About the Future," *Contemporary Literature* 22, no. 3 (1981): 349–65; and John Huntington, "Remembrance of Things to Come: Narrative Technique in *Last and First Men*," *Science-Fiction Studies* 9 (1982): 257–64.

NOTES TO CHAPTER THREE

7. Suvin, *Metamorphoses of Science Fiction*, 89.

8. Ibid., 116, 72, 73.

9. See "Merchant's Time and Church's Time in the Middle Ages" and "Labor Time in the 'Crisis' of the Fourteenth Century: From Medieval Time to Modern Time," in Jacques Le Goff, *Time, Work, and Culture in the Middle Ages*, trans. Arthur Goldhammer (Chicago: University of Chicago Press, 1980), 29–52 (originally published as *Pour un autre Moyen Age: Temps, travail et culture en Occident, 18 essais* (Paris: Editions Gallimard, 1977).

10. Madden's motive in suppressing his book is not known; see the article "Samuel Madden" in *Dictionary of National Biography*, ed. Sidney Lee (London, 1909), 12: 740–41.

11. According to the National Union Catalogue, there are copies of the 1733 edition at Harvard, the Library of Congress, and the Huntington Library. Northwestern University now has a copy, on which an anonymous early annotator has recounted the tale of Madden's strange suppression of "this mysterious Work" on the day of its publication, with the result that "it is now one of the *very rarest Books in the English Language*." A 1972 Garland Press reprint edition is announced as the facsimile of a copy in Yale's Beinecke Library; it includes a four-page introduction by Malcom J. Bosse, who is not much concerned with the history of futuristic fiction. I. F. Clarke, *The Pattern of Expectation, 1644–2001* (New York: Basic Books, 1979), 16, gives six sentences to Madden, dismissing *Memoirs of the Twentieth Century* as a work of forecast whose predictions are at best of "slight interest" because the world of Madden's fiction is so unlike the real twentieth century. Anyone who looks up Madden in the *Cambridge Bibliography of English Literature* or the *New Cambridge Bibliography* will find *Memoirs of the Twentieth Century* correctly attributed but confused with an anonymous work, *The Reign of George VI* (London, 1763), which is wrongly listed as the second edition of Madden's book. Citations in the text are taken from the Huntington Library copy of [Samuel Madden], *Memoirs of the Twentieth Century* (London: Osborn, Longman, et al., 1733).

12. For the background of millennial and apocalyptic writing which Madden would have taken for granted as known at least in its general outlines to his readers, see Margaret C. Jacob, *The Newtonians and the English Revolution, 1689–1720* (Hassocks, England: Harvester Press,

NOTES TO CHAPTER THREE

1976), especially chapter 3, "The Millennium," 100–42; and Michael McKeon, *Politics and Poetry in Restoration England: The Case of Dryden's Annus Mirabilis* (Cambridge: Harvard University Press, 1975), especially part 2, "Eschatological Prophecy."

13. See Rodney M. Baine, *Daniel Defoe and the Supernatural* (Athens: University of Georgia Press, 1968), especially chapter 1, "Defoe and the Angels," 12–36.

14. See Philip Babcock Gove, *The Imaginary Voyage in Prose Fiction: A History of its Criticism and a Guide for Its Study, with an Annotated Check List of 215 Imaginary Voyages from 1700 to 1800* (New York, 1941); Marjorie Hope Nicolson, *Voyages to the Moon* (1948; reprint, New York: Macmillan, 1960).

15. See in Louis-Sébastien Mercier, *L'An deux mille quatre cent quarante: Rêve s'il en fût jamais*, 3 vols. (Paris, An VII [1798]: Brosson and Carteret; Dugour and Durand), the "Nouveau Discours Préliminaire": "Sans forcer le sens, et d'une manière claire et précise, j'ai mis au jour et sans équivoque, une prédiction qui embrassoit tous les changemens possibles, depuis la destruction des parlemens, de la noblesse et du clergé, jusqu'à l'adoption du chapeau rond. . . . Je suis donc le véritable prophète de la révolution. . . . Au milieu de cette révolution . . . il y a eu d'autres révolutions terribles et sanglantes qu'il m'étoit bien impossible de prévoir; car, comment imaginer qu'une poignée de scélérats ineptes et féroces, étrangers à la première et courageuse explosion, domineroient tout-à-coup une nation éclairée."

16. For evidence detailing the popularity of *L'An 2440*, see Everett C. Wilkie, Jr., "Mercier's *L'An 2440:* Its Publishing History During the Author's Lifetime, Part I," *Harvard Library Bulletin* 32 (Winter 1984): 5–35.

17. Aristotle, "Poetics," in *Aristotle: Rhetoric and Poetics*, trans. W. Rhys Roberts and Ingram Bywater (New York: Random House Modern Library, 1954), 263.

18. For more on relationships between history and fiction in eighteenth-century England, see Leo Braudy, *Narrative Form in History and Fiction* (Princeton: Princeton University Press, 1970).

19. Arthur C. Clarke, *Childhood's End* (1953; reprint, New York: Ballantine, 1964), 170.

20. I. F. Clarke, *The Pattern of Expectation*, 16.

21. See Paul K. Alkon, *Defoe and Fictional Time* (Athens: University

NOTES TO CHAPTER THREE

of Georgia Press, 1979), especially chapter 2, "Setting and Chronology," 23–80.

22. Although written two years before the appearance and suppression of *Memoirs of the Twentieth Century* in 1733, Swift's poem was not published until 1739. For an account of its textual history, see Arthur H. Scouten and Robert D. Hume, "Pope and Swift: Text and Interpretation of Swift's Verses on His Death," *Philological Quarterly* 52 (1973): 205–31. I cannot say whether Madden knew of "Verses on the Death of Dr. Swift" or whether Swift read Madden's book. Even if there was no influence of one work upon the other, the climate of literary experimentation is noteworthy for the resort of both authors in the same decade to a parallel strategy built upon a similar device of double temporal perspective involving the future. Swift's resort to a future setting for considering his own death may also be of more than incidental interest for the history of science fiction. See in this connection David Ketterer, "Death and the Denial of History: The Textual Shadow of the SF Author," *Science-Fiction Studies* 9 (1982): 228–30; and Gregory Benford, "Death and the Textual Shadow of the SF Author, Again," *Science-Fiction Studies* 9 (1982): 341. Ketterer and Benford plausibly suggest that futuristic fiction may sometimes be occasioned by the author's need to deal acceptably with powerful fantasies about his or her own death.

23. I. F. Clarke (*The Pattern of Expectation*, 16–22) suggests that *The Reign of George VI* is written in the manner of David Hume's *History of England* and that the portrait of George VI applies ideals taken from Viscount Bolingbroke's *Idea of a Patriot King*.

24. *The Reign of George VI, 1900–1925* (London, 1763), vi–viii. Invitations to interpret the story as alluding to eighteenth-century politics are on pages xi, xiii, and xv; comparisons with Swift's political allegory are on pages vi, vii, and viii. We are told, for example, that in *The Reign of George VI*, "Our historian, in the gloomy portrait which he draws of the nation, at the beginning of his work, alludes very strongly to a late dangerous crisis. . . . The character of the future Duke of Bedford, will easily lead us to think of a nobleman of the present times, who has headed an opposition to the government of his King; and the parliamentary proceedings in the reign of George the sixth, may be considered as a well turned compliment to the legislature of George the third" (p. xiii).

NOTES TO CHAPTER FOUR

FOUR
From Utopia to Uchronia

1. Charles Renouvier, "Uchronie, tableau historique apocryphe des révolutions de l'empire Romain et de la formation d'une fédération européenne," *Revue Philosophique et Religieuse* 8 (1857): 187 ff. This is the first part of a work that Renouvier published as a book in 1876. In defining *uchronie* as "utopie des temps passés," Renouvier says too that the term is designed for "une pensée neuve et un genre insolite" (a new kind of thinking and an unusual genre).

2. For an excellent survey and critique of recent thinking about the historical novel, see Harry E. Shaw, *The Forms of Historical Fiction: Sir Walter Scott and His Successors* (Ithaca: Cornell University Press, 1983). Alternate history is seldom considered a valid form of historical fiction, although it should be.

3. Raymond Trousson, *Voyages aux pays de nulle part: Histoire littéraire de la pensée utopique*, 2d ed. (Bruxelles: Editions de l'université de Bruxelles, 1979), 121.

4. Everett C. Wilkie, Jr., "Mercier's *L'An 2440*: Its Publishing History During the Author's Lifetime, Part I," *Harvard Library Bulletin* 32 (Winter 1984): 16, 22; Everett C. Wilkie, Jr., "Mercier's *L'An 2440*: Its Publishing History During the Author's Lifetime, Part II: Bibliography," *Harvard Library Bulletin* 32 (Fall 1984): 348–400. For the German translation of 1772 and relevant information on Mercier's reception in Germany, see Louis-Sébastien Mercier, *Das Jahr 2440: Ein Traum aller Träume*, trans. Christian Felix Weisse, ed. Herbert Jaumann (Frankfurt am Main: Suhrkamp Verlag, 1982). See also Trousson's valuable introduction to Louis-Sébastien Mercier, *L'An deux mille quatre cent quarante: Rêve s'il en fut jamais*, ed. Raymond Trousson (Bordeaux: Editions Ducros, 1971), 1–73, especially 61–73. Subsequent references to *L'An 2440* in the text are to this edition, which reprints the earliest version of Mercier's work.

5. Frank E. Manuel and Fritzie P. Manuel, *Utopian Thought in the Western World* (Cambridge: Belknap Press of Harvard University Press, 1979), 4, 431–32, 20. For their discussion of Mercier, see pages 458–60. Their preference for "rationalist, systematic utopias" is often expressed,

NOTES TO CHAPTER FOUR

starting on page 3, where they say of utopian fiction: "The novels portraying encapsulated and protected pictorial utopias, while they have continued to be sold in millions of copies into our own time, were often in content residual and derivative, dependent upon revolutionary utopian theory that others had propounded." Though true, this statement begs the question of how literary form, especially new forms, contributed to such remarkable diffusion of utopian ideas.

6. For a fascinating account of the background, however, see Clarke Garrett, *Respectable Folly: Millenarians and the French Revolution in France and England* (Baltimore: Johns Hopkins University Press, 1975). See too James West Davidson, *The Logic of Millennial Thought: Eighteenth-Century New England* (New Haven: Yale University Press, 1977); and Ernest L. Tuveson, *Millennium and Utopia: A Study in the Background of the Idea of Progress* (Berkeley: University of California Press, 1949). Tuveson's classic study shows an affiliation of millennial thought and utopian speculation, but the author does not note the transition to futuristic uchronia. Utopias had to exist before they could be put into future time, to be sure; but their mere existence, however indebted to millennialism, did not necessarily lead to future settings. Davidson, as I have mentioned above in chapter 2, note 10, provides ample evidence for the extent to which interpretation of biblical prophecy rather paradoxically focused attention more on the past and present than on the future. Garrett stresses that "millenarianism was one more current in the religious revival of the later eighteenth century" (p. 229). Properly regarded as but one feature among a cluster of irrationalist phenomena that included mesmerism, Swedenborgian mysticism, and cabalism, millenarianism may be allowed at best a role so minor in the development of early futuristic fiction that, with the interesting exception of Grainville, whom I discuss in chapter 5, there are no specific textual connections of any significance in accounting for emergence of the new form. In a very general way I suppose it is true that what Garrett and others note as the Protestant rejection of Augustinian metaphoric interpretations of Revelation (starting most notably in 1627 with Joseph Mede's *Clavis Apocalyptica*) opens more possibilities for speculation about events on this earth before as well as during the millennium. But this hardly accounts for the forms invented by Mercier and Geoffroy. See Garrett's chapter 6, "The Millenarian Tradition in English Dissent," p. 121 ff.

NOTES TO CHAPTER FOUR

7. For the most complete bibliography of books with future dates for their titles, see André-Clément Decouflé and Alain-Michel Villemur, *Les Millésimes du futur: Contribution à une bibliographie des anticipations datées* (Paris: Laboratoire de Prospective Appliquée & Temps Futurs, 1978). Copies may be read at the Bibliothèque Nationale in Paris and the Maison d'Ailleurs at Rue du Four 5, 1400 Yverdon, Switzerland.

8. For Orwell's 1943 outline under the title *The Last Man in Europe*, see Bernard Crick, *George Orwell: A Life* (1980; reprint, Harmondsworth: Penguin Books, 1982), 582–85. Crick also prints (p. 546) a letter which Orwell wrote in 1948 stating "I haven't definitely fixed on the title but I am hesitating between NINETEEN EIGHTY-FOUR and THE LAST MAN IN EUROPE." He made the right choice. In addition to serving as an extraordinarily effective emblem for Orwell's message, the title also provides our only unequivocal dating for the story's events because inhabitants of Big Brother's Oceania are denied accurate information about time. We are told early in the narrative that, although Winston Smith begins a diary bravely enough with the heading "April 4, 1984," in fact he "did not know with any certainty that this *was* 1984. . . . It was never possible nowadays to pin down any date within a year or two" (George Orwell, *Nineteen Eighty-Four* [New York: Harcourt, Brace, 1949], 8.).

9. Brian Stableford, "Near Future," in *The Science Fiction Encyclopedia*, ed. Peter Nicholls (Garden City, N.Y.: Doubleday, 1979), 419–21.

10. "Délivré des prestiges d'un sommeil favorable, je crains, hélas! je crains plutôt que ton soleil ne vienne un jour à luire tristement sur un informe amas de cendres et de ruines!" (p. 78).

11. Bronislaw Baczko, *Lumières de l'utopie* (Paris: Payot, 1978), 165 n. 22.

12. Michael Holquist, "How to Play Utopia: Some Brief Notes on the Distinctiveness of Utopian Fiction," *Yale French Studies* 41 (1968): 106–23; reprint in *Science Fiction: A Collection of Critical Essays*, ed. Mark Rose (Englewood Cliffs, N.J.: Prentice-Hall, 1976), 132–46.

13. Trousson, *Voyages aux pays de nulle part*, 178.

14. I refer to the first edition. Some of Mercier's subsequent additions to his text, which were extensive, have more predictive intent—for example, his chapter on balloons ("L'aérostat").

15. Alexandre Cioranescu, *L'Avenir du passé: Utopie et littérature* (Paris: Editions Gallimard, 1972), 196.

NOTES TO CHAPTER FOUR

16. The familiar ideals, as Trousson (*Voyages aux pays de nulle part*, 177) remarks, of Montesquieu, Rousseau, Beccaria, Voltaire, the *Encyclopédie*, and all those around 1770 who had faith in the future.

17. The paragraph to which this note is appended summarizes and translates observations in Baczko, pp. 155–67.

18. Holquist, "How to Play Utopia," 138.

19. Renouvier, "Uchronie," 207.

20. See I. F. Clarke, *The Pattern of Expectation, 1644–2001* (New York: Basic Books, 1979), 1–89.

21. Louis Geoffroy, *Napoléon et la conquête du monde—1812–1832—Histoire de la monarchie universelle (Napoléon apocryphe)* (1836; reprint, Paris: Editions Tallandier, 1983), 339. Subsequent references are to the Tallandier edition, which reproduces in facsimile the 1896 edition (with preface by Jules Richard). This in turn was based on Geoffroy's 1841 edition with his final revisions, retitled *Napoléon apocryphe*.

22. Geoffroy, *Napoléon et la conquête*, 350: "La pensée, devenue plus rapide, avait besoin d'instruments qui eussent de sa célérité; la sténographie devint l'écriture commune, et des machines à touches, des *pianos d'écriture*, peignaient, avec la plus grande rapidité, la pensée a peine jaillie de l'âme."

23. Ibid., 221–22: "La tradition mahométane annonçait depuis longues années l'arrivée d'un autre messie qui la frapperait à mort. . . . Les événements qui venaient de les écraser leur apprirent que le temps était arrivé, et pour eux la grande victoire de Jérusalem était la destruction de leur croyance et l'accomplissement des prophéties." I must leave to those concerned with European orientalism the question of how accurately or inaccurately Geoffroy represents Islamic theology. Decisive victory over the Turks was a recurrent idea in millenarian fantasies. As Garrett observes (*Respectable Folly*, 116), "the assumption that the last great battle before the millennium would be fought against the Turks was six centuries old by 1790." While Geoffroy certainly exploits this familiar dream, in no way that I can see does it account for the uchronic form that he invented.

24. See Marc Angenot, "The Emergence of the Anti-Utopian Genre in France: Souvestre, Giraudeau, Robida, *et al*.," *Science Fiction Studies* 12 (July 1985): 129–35.

25. Geoffroy (*Napoléon et la conquête*, 336) adds a carefully reasoned defense of this reform, hinting somewhat ambiguously that even God finally had to accept it as a fait accompli: "Il n'y eut rien alors de sacrilège

dans ce décret. Si l'essence du catholicisme est l'unité et l'universalité; si, au milieu de cette confusion de langues et de ces Etats *hachés*, comme dit M. de Maistre, la nécessité d'une langue religieuse universelle avait été reconnue, afin que, dans le même instant, les mêmes paroles élevassent sur tous les points du globe les mêmes prières et exprimassent les mêmes respirations des âmes, ainsi que les appelle un philosophe; aujourd'hui que l'empire et le langage français étaient universels, cette langue devait être acceptée comme un fait accompli, comme l'expression du culte des hommes pour Dieu."

26. Ibid., 332: "Il y avait bien une politique, permise seule à l'empereur, c'était la *police*, immense réseau enveloppant l'univers, que tout le monde sentait, et que personne n'osait apercevoir."

27. See Philip K. Dick, *The Man in the High Castle* (New York: Putnam's, 1962); Winston S. Churchill, "If Lee Had Not Won the Battle of Gettysburg," in *If It Had Happened Otherwise: Lapses into Imaginary History*, ed. John Collings Squire (London: Longmans, Green, 1931); American edition titled *If; or, History Rewritten* (New York: Viking, 1931). See also the articles "Delisle de Sales" and "Uchronie" in Pierre Versins, *Encyclopédie de l'utopie, des voyages extraordinaires et de la science fiction* (Lausanne: Editions L'Age d'Homme, 1972). For Delisle de Sales's uchronic chapter, see the edition of *Ma République* entitled *Eponine, ou de la République* (1793), 2: 181–202: "Ch. XXI. D'une nouvelle Séance Royale." On another variety of embryonic uchronia, see Claire Le Brun, "Les chansons de geste: La tentation de l'uchronie au moyen âge," *Imagine: revue de science-fiction québécoise* 4 (Autumn 1982): 44–49. See also Barton C. Hacker and Gordon B. Chamberlain, "Pasts That Might Have Been: An Annotated Bibliography of Alternate History," *Extrapolation* 22 (Winter 1981): 334–78. This bibliography is also available in *Alternative Histories: Eleven Stories of the World as it Might Have Been*, ed. Charles G. Waugh and Martin H. Greenberg (New York: Garland, 1986).

28. Orwell, *Nineteen Eighty-Four*, 271.

29. Ibid., 270.

FIVE
The Secularization of Apocalypse

1. Félix Bodin, *Le Roman de l'avenir* (Paris, 1834), 397.
2. Mark Rose, *Alien Encounters: Anatomy of Science Fiction* (Cam-

NOTES TO CHAPTER FIVE

bridge: Harvard University Press, 1981), 99. Rose also suggests (p. 195) that "because it represents the logical limit of the dialectic between the human and the non-human, science fiction inevitably moves toward apocalypse. Meaningless in itself, the idea of apocalypse is nevertheless the necessary condition for the creation of meaning through the genre."

3. Robert Galbreath, "Ambiguous Apocalypse: Transcendental Versions of the End," in *The End of the World*, ed. Eric S. Rabkin, Martin H. Greenberg, and Joseph D. Olander (Carbondale: Southern Illinois University Press, 1983), 56, 68.

4. M. H. Abrams, *Natural Supernaturalism: Tradition and Revolution in Romantic Literature* (1971; reprint, New York: W. W. Norton, 1973), 13.

5. Galbreath, "Ambiguous Apocalypse," 54.

6. David Ketterer, *New Worlds for Old: The Apocalyptic Imagination, Science Fiction, and American Literature* (Bloomington: Indiana University Press, 1974), 13; italics deleted. See also pages 4–14 for a useful survey of critical use of the terms *apocalypse* and *apocalyptic*.

7. For information on relevant contexts and Grainville's early thinking about his work, see Henry F. Majewski, "Grainville's *Le dernier homme*," *Symposium* 17 (Summer 1963): 114–22. See also A. J. Sambrook, "A Romantic Theme: The Last Man," *Forum For Modern Language Studies* 2 (January 1966): 25–33; and Jean de Palacio, "Mary Shelley and the 'Last Man': A Minor Romantic Theme," *Revue de Littérature Comparée* 42 (January–March 1968): 37–49.

8. [Herbert Croft], *Horace éclairci par la ponctuation* (Paris, 1810), 78–80: "Si jamais le monde voit une Epopée plus faite pour vivre jusqu'au dernier homme que celles d'Homère et de Milton, j'ose dire que son auteur la calquera sur le plan de ce petit ouvrage; qui n'est après-tout, peut-être, que la sublime ébauche d'une grande conception" (p. 79).

9. Charles Nodier, "Observations préliminaires du nouvel éditeur" in *Le dernier homme, ouvrage posthume; par M. de Grainville, homme de lettres, Seconde édition, publiée par Charles Nodier*, 2 vols. (Paris, 1811; facsimile reprint, Slatkine Reprints: Geneva, 1976), 1: v–xii.

10. She explains that *Proso-Poésie* means "prose and poetry," an allusion to cantos that have individual verse prologues but are otherwise a combination of dialogue and narrative (Elise Gagne, *Omégar ou le dernier*

NOTES TO CHAPTER FIVE

homme: Proso-poésie dramatique de la fin des temps en douze chants [Paris, 1859], ii.)

11. J[ules] Michelet, *Histoire du XIXe siècle*, 3 vols. (Paris, 1875), 3: 91–109, quotations on 101, 104, 103; in an appendix to volume 3 (pp. 459–68), Michelet outlines the plot of *Le dernier homme*, which he sees as a great conception quite apart from the wording of Grainville's text.

12. Unless otherwise noted, quotations in English from *Le dernier homme* are taken from the anonymous translation entitled *The Last Man, or Omegarus and Syderia, A Romance in Futurity*, 2 vols. (London: R. Dutton, 1806). Citations in French are taken from the second edition, published in 1811 by Nodier.

13. Michelet, *Histoire du XIXe siècle*, 3: 96–97.

14. For comments on the Terrestrial Genius as an anticipation of later fiction dealing with the ambiguous role of scientists, see the article on Grainville in Pierre Versins, *Encyclopédie de l'utopie, des voyages extraordinaires et de la science fiction* (Lausanne: Editions L'Age d'Homme, 1972). Versins also remarks eloquently and rightly that *Le dernier homme* is "un des ouvrages les plus méconnus et pourtant les plus importants que nous ait valu ce curieux état d'esprit dont la vision ne cesse pas aux bornes de la réalité accessible" (p. 376).

15. Majewski ("Grainville's *Le dernier homme*," 117–20) remarks that while Grainville's "conception of a novelistic treatment of the end of the world" is original, aspects of the love story ring changes on attitudes and images "peculiar to pre-romantic literature since Prevost's *Cleveland*" while also anticipating themes of "physical frustration and a desire for the purity of spiritual love" articulated by Stendhal in the very different context of *Armance*. More relevant to Grainville's formal innovations than such affinities is the analogy to eighteenth-century geological speculation which Majewski also suggests: "It is but a step from Buffon's world in disorder at its formation (*Epoques de la Nature*, 1778) with his description of our earliest ancestors' horror before geological catastrophe to Grainville's disintegration." The shortness of that step is far more apparent in retrospect, however, than it ever was to Buffon's contemporaries. If it was one small step for Grainville, it was a giant leap for his readers. So too for the other analogues correctly suggested by Majewski: "images of a perishable universe in Le Tourneur's translation of Ossian (1777), Hubert

Robert's painting of the Louvre in ruins (1784)" and Mercier's various "complacent descriptions of catastrophe" outside the pages of *L'An 2440*. Such fleeting images of future disaster are an important part of Grainville's intellectual environment, but they are not close enough in form to provide models for his innovations or, more important, to have provided his readers with precedents allowing assimilation of *Le dernier homme* to familiar paradigms of interpretation.

16. W. Warren Wagar, *Terminal Visions: The Literature of Last Things* (Bloomington: Indiana University Press, 1982), 16.

17. The adjectives "aethereal" and "golden" supplied by the 1806 translator slightly augment for English readers the conventional cast of Grainville's imagery without distorting his meaning. Cf. the 1811 ed., 2: 80: "Des anges placés aux pieds du trône de Dieu, sonnent les trompettes du dernier jour, dont les éclats sont entendus jusqu'aux limites de l'univers."

18. 1811 ed., 2:84: "Il commence à croire que cette secousse n'est peut-être qu'un prélude éloigné de la résurrection des morts."

19. Again the 1806 English translator rushes matters somewhat, thus making Grainville's text slightly more conventional than it actually is, by referring to the "resurrection" of bones as though they had already and instantaneously been brought back to life. Grainville, dividing events into stages, refers only to the initial *eruption* of human remains from their resting places beneath the earth so that they will be conveniently available *later* for resurrection: "Trois heures suffisent pour l'éruption des dépouilles humaines, tant elle est violente et rapide!" (1811 ed., 2:82).

20. Here the 1806 translator has added the phrase, "that symbol of time," making Grainville's meaning more explicit without doing violence to his intention except by making the statement a bit less subtle: "Alors la pendule séculaire, en sonnant la dernière heure du jour, tire Omégare de sa rêverie. Ces coups lugubres qui, frappés douze fois par l'horloge du temps retentissent dans le silence des ténèbres, l'affectent douloureusement. Il dit d'une voix triste: *le dernier jour de la terre commence*" (1811 ed., 2:101–2).

21. C. M. LeRoy de Bonneville, *Etude biographique et littéraire sur Cousin de Grainville* (Havre, 1863), 31: "Il est fâcheux, selon nous, qu'il ait entièrement perdu de vue la régénération religieuse de l'homme par le rédempteur; il est à regretter qu'il ait donné un certain reflet de Déisme à

NOTES TO CHAPTER FIVE

son ouvrage, en y généralisant trop l'idée de Dieu." Bonneville also objects to the Terrestrial Genius and other allegorical figures in the work as resembling too much the machinery of pagan epics with their inferior gods and goddesses. For Bonneville, Grainville's most innovative departures from both Christian doctrine and conventional mythology are a major flaw: "On est choqué de voir, comme dans les épopées païennes, en face du Dieu suprême, figures, comme des dieux inférieurs, le Génie de l'avenir, le Génie de la terre, la Nature, la Nuit, les Ténèbres, la Mort, les Esprits du feu, tous ces êtres bâtards qui n'appartiennent pas complètement à la mythologie antique et qui sont absolument étrangers à la cosmogonie chrétienne" (p. 31). Another flaw for Bonneville is the love story which Michelet chose to read as the work's central theme. Bonneville stresses its incompatibility with affirmation of an apocalyptic ending for life on this world: "Toute l'action du poëme tend d'une part à faire réussir le mariage d'Omégare, et d'autre part à en empêcher les effets. L'ambassade d'Adam n'a que ce but, et elle aboutit, en dernier résultat, à pousse Omégare à abandonner Sydérie, sa femme, la mère de son enfant, au moment du plus affreux des cataclysmes, comme si Dieu pouvait lui ordonner, lui imposer ce crime, j'allais dire cette lâcheté" (pp. 31–32).

22. Michelet, *Histoire du XIXe siècle*, 3:103: "Elle ne doit rien aux machines toutes faites du merveilleux convenu. Grainville n'emprunte rien au paganisme classique, rien au merveilleux chrétien. Le premier homme, le jugement, n'appartiennent pas au christianisme; ce sont des idées communes à une foule de religions."

23. Gagne, *Omégar ou le dernier homme*, viii.

24. For an introduction to various earlier traditions, see C. A. Patrides and Joseph Wittreich, eds., *The Apocalypse in English Renaissance Thought and Literature: Patterns, Antecedents and Repercussions* (Ithaca: Cornell University Press, 1984).

25. Joseph Anthony Wittreich, Jr., *Visionary Poetics: Milton's Tradition and His Legacy* (San Marino: Huntington Library and Art Gallery, 1979), 44.

26. See Jeffrey R. Smitten and Ann Daghistany, eds., *Spatial Form in Narrative* (Ithaca: Cornell University Press, 1981).

27. A. Creuzé de Lesser, *Le dernier homme, Poëme imité de Grainville* (Paris, 1831), xiv.

28. Camille Flammarion, *La fin du monde* (Paris, 1894). This was

translated into English as *Omega: The Last Days of the World* (New York: Cosmopolitan, 1894).

29. Gagne, *Omégar ou le dernier homme*, i–iv. She explains (pp. ii–iii) that a work may conform to Church doctrine but set a date for the last day and introduce fictional characters because doing so contradicts nothing in the Bible: "La fin du monde, prédite par l'Ancien et le Nouveau Testament, est un article de foi que nul chrétien n'oserait mettre en doute. Ce principe posé, il doit être permis à l'écrivain de la rapprocher ou de l'éloigner à son gré, puisqu'elle n'a point de date précise, et de placer dans le drame terrible qui s'y jouera tous les acteurs enfantés par son imagination. Donc, convaincue que nous ne portions aucune atteinte aux dogmes de l'Eglise, objets de notre profonde vénération, nous avons supposé la terre arrivée aux dernières limites de sa durée, et ses nombreux habitants endormis du sommeil de la mort, à l'exception d'Omégar et de sa famille."

30. Creuzé de Lesser, *Le dernier homme*, xviii–xxii.

31. Ibid., xxiv: "J'ai sur-tout tâché d'imprimer au merveilleux une marche plus ferme, et à-la-fois plus hardie et plus régulière."

32. A priest, Grainville had married during the revolution to escape the guillotine, only to find himself ostracized and unemployed later because of that defection from his clerical vows; on a winter day in 1805, publication year of *Le dernier homme*, he drowned himself in the Somme. The story is best read as told by Michelet in his chapter on Grainville.

33. [Cousin de Grainville], *Discours qui a remporté le prix d'éloquence, de l'académie de Besançon, en l'année 1772. Sur ce sujet: Quelle a été l'influence de la philosophie sur ce siècle? Par M. l'Abbé de Grainville* (Paris, 1772), 1, 11: "Les hommes restèrent à peindre. Mais quels hommes! froids & raisonneurs comme la Philosophie qui les a formés, offrent-ils un grand trait à saisir? Ils se suivent avec le même scrupule que des troupeaux qui paissent sur une montagne, & le nombre des caracteres & des actions vraisemblables diminua avec les progrès de l'imitation."

34. Grainville, *Discours*, 13. The phrase that I have translated as "actions with verisimilitude" could also be rendered as "probable actions," which I believe amounts to the same idea in Grainville's statement: "Le besoin d'actions vraisemblables, multiplia les Poemes didactiques, l'uniformité des caracteres produisit les Drames métaphysiques; la Mythologie

NOTES TO CHAPTER FIVE

détruite, fit place aux descriptions physiques & savantes; c'est-à-dire, que la Philosophie tint le sceptre de la Littérature."

35. Creuzé de Lesser, *Le dernier homme*, xxiv–xxv.

36. Mary Shelley, *The Last Man*, ed. Hugh J. Luke, Jr. (Lincoln: University of Nebraska Press, 1965), 4.

37. The celestial spirit, to whom Grainville gives the last word in *Le dernier homme*, is explicit about the moral of his revelation and equally clear about the importance of communicating it to a wide audience as a task of greater priority for the narrator than pursuit of his personal ambitions. With pardonable prophetic license, however, the spirit remains enigmatic about how readers are to apply the lesson: "J'ai voulu seulement te rendre le témoin du triomphe d'Omégare, et t'apprendre comment, par son obéissance aux ordres du ciel, il doit un jour abréger le règne du temps, et hâter celui de l'éternité. Mes desseins sont remplis: révèle aux hommes cette histoire du dernier siècle de la terre; sacrifie à ce devoir glorieux que je t'impose, la fortune et les desirs de l'ambition. Je rendrai les heures de ton travail si douces, qu'elles seront les plus heureuses de ta vie" (2:175).

38. Wagar, *Terminal Visions*, 15–16.

39. See Shelley, *The Last Man*, 187 and 326, for the allusions to Defoe.

40. See Wagar's excellent survey in *Terminal Visions* and see also the essays in *The End of the World*, ed. Eric S. Rabkin, Martin H. Greenberg, and Joseph D. Olander (Carbondale: Southern Illinois University Press, 1983).

41. More immediately, as Jean de Palacio notes in "Mary Shelley and the 'Last Man'" (pp. 41, 48–49), Shelley's book simply took its place among a temporary vogue for last men living in various periods, mainly past and present. Thus in 1826 appeared Cooper's *The Last of the Mohicans*. Later there were the efforts of Bulwer-Lytton, which Palacio regards as a more successful use than Shelley's or Grainville's of the last man theme: *The Last Days of Pompeii* (1834); *Rienzi, or the Last of the Tribunes* (1835); *The Last of the Barons* (1843); and *Harold, the Last of the Saxon Kings* (1848). Although doubtless more widely read than Grainville in England, these resort to the past for settings. A subsequent anonymous work not mentioned by Palacio again turns to the future: *The Last Peer* (London, 1851). For more on this book, see chapter 6, pp. 195–96.

NOTES TO CHAPTER SIX

SIX
Fantasy and Metafiction

1. Thus, in commenting on "the sudden outpouring of futuristic stories that began in 1871," I. F. Clarke remarks in *The Pattern of Expectation, 1644–2001* (New York: Basic Books, 1979), 140–41: "a full explanation would show how this remarkable advance in the power and popularity of the tale of the future was the primary result of dominant ideas about mankind, industrialism and the future of society that had come together for the first time in the 1860s. The oldest and most potent of these was the idea of progress which had animated utopian fiction from the start in Sébastien Mercier's *L'An 2440*. When this was fused—or sometimes confused—with the Darwinian ideas that became general knowledge after the publication of *The Origin of Species* in 1859, the revised doctrine of progress provided new matter for tales of the future at the same time as it seemed to add the sanction of evolutionary theory to the description of life in the centuries ahead." For an excellent account of related developments in more recent futuristic fiction, see Brian Stableford, *Scientific Romance in Britain, 1890–1950* (London: Fourth Estate, 1985).

2. Robert Scholes, *Structural Fabulation: An Essay on Fiction of the Future* (Notre Dame: University of Notre Dame Press, 1975), 18.

3. Eric S. Rabkin, *The Fantastic in Literature* (Princeton: Princeton University Press, 1976), 181–82. See also chapter 4, "The Fantastic and Genre Criticism" (pp. 117–50) for a persuasive argument, which I accept too as another basis for my discussion, that the fantastic is not an exclusive mode but rather a variety of devices allowing various degrees of departure from realism within particular works and genres that may thus be ranged along a spectrum from minimal to maximum resort to fantasy. A more restrictive definition of fantasy is offered in Tzvetan Todorov, *Introduction à la littérature fantastique* (Paris: Editions du Seuil, 1970). For additional investigation of this topic and useful bibliographical references, see Rosemary Jackson, *Fantasy: The Literature of Subversion* (London: Methuen, 1981); Kathryn Hume, *Fantasy and Mimesis* (London: Methuen, 1984). To identify fantastic elements in the early futuristic fiction that concerns me, I have found no need for those elaborate definitions of fantasy that some later developments in other genres have occasioned, or for Todorov's restriction of fantasy to cases wherein the text is ambigu-

ous about the natural or supernatural cause of narrated events that are so far outside the range of ordinary experience as to appear marvelous.

4. On Souvestre's place in the dystopian tradition, see Marc Angenot, "The Emergence of the Anti-Utopian Genre in France: Souvestre, Giraudeau, Robida, *et al.*," *Science-Fiction Studies* 12 (July 1985): 129–35.

5. Emile Souvestre, *Le Monde tel qu'il sera* (Paris: W. Coquebert, [1846]), 7.

6. *The Last Peer*, 3 vols. (London, 1851), 3:367.

7. Pierre-Marc Gaston, Duc de Levis, *Les Voyages de Kang-Hi, ou nouvelles lettres chinoises*, 2 vols. (Paris, 1810), v.

8. *L'An 2440* is not mentioned by name, but the reference to Mercier is unmistakable: "Quant au second genre de fiction, l'on a vu, il y a environ trente ans, publier à Paris un ouvrage où l'auteur anticipant de plusieurs siecles sur les évènements, et se livrant à toute la chaleur de son imagination, présentoit, à l'exemple de Platon, de Morus, et de quelques autres, de nouveaux plans d'institutions politiques, civiles et religieuses. Les hommes en adoptant ses idées ne pouvoient manquer, disoit-il, de devenir tout-à-coup heureux et sages" (Levis, *Les Voyages de Kang-Hi*, vii).

9. [R. F. Williams], *Eureka: A Prophecy of the Future*, 3 vols. (London, 1837), ix. Subsequent citations in the text are given parenthetically.

10. *Eureka*, xi. For an account of the intellectual currents prompting this partly serious, partly parodic endorsement of the imagination, see James Engell, *The Creative Imagination: Enlightenment to Romanticism* (Cambridge: Harvard University Press, 1981).

11. To the narrator's objection that portrayal of future changes in "governments, religions, and philosophy" may be "too serious for the novel reader," Wilhelm responds: "It matters not whether the time sought to be illustrated be of the past, of the present, or of the future: each may be made equally laughable, equally pathetic, and equally philosophical" (*Eureka*, pp. x–xi). Here for the first time in Western literary criticism is an explicit statement that past, present, and future are *equally* valid subjects of imaginative writing. Wilhelm's status in the introduction as an object of satire—the sickly student coughing and scribbling fiction as he dies at the University of Göttingen—shows that the author of *Eureka* was hesitant to argue in his own name against the weight of more traditional views that had prevailed for so many centuries. But there is no mistaking Williams's implication: if futuristic fiction has no less trouble than other

novels in seriously dealing with government, religion, and philosophy, neither is there any *more* difficulty simply by virtue of future settings. Questions of plausibility are for Williams easily handled by reference to cyclical theories of history. To the question "how is it possible to convey any thing like a natural picture of the state of existing nations at so remote a time?" Wilhelm responds: "By a reference to what is already known of the growth, maturity and decay of nations. . . . Every thing has its age. The tree cannot flourish beyond a certain time—nor can a country. . . . [N]ow we have the glories of London and Paris, and Berlin and Vienna, and these will exist their period, and then gradually fall into decay" (*Eureka*, pp. xiv–xvi). Williams also refutes the idea that limitless technological progress will prop up existing governments and thus rule out political change as a topic for speculative fiction. Against Wilhelm's cyclical view, the narrator objects that "the superior civilization we enjoy, must prevent our retrograding. . . . Think of our steam-engines, our railroads, our wonderful discoveries in science and mechanics, and our extraordinary advancement in intelligence; we are rising, and we shall continue to rise." But Wilhelm is given the last word: "We cannot rise above the top . . . and after that we must go down" (*Eureka*, p. xvii).

12. [John Banim], *Revelations of the Dead-Alive* (London, 1824), 9–10. The protagonist continues his explanation of the ontological distinction between dream and trance in a way that seems emphatically to prepare for a story that will maximize verisimilitude: "Dreams cannot give the certainty of features and words that I accompanied with my mind; nor the certainty of sun and air, and of crowded and joyous existence; nor the truth, in fact. All my own dreams, at least, which I enjoyed independently of this riper knowledge, ever were, and continued to be, snatches and disarrangements, and transformations of time, place, and persons; mist and doubt, as if they had happened in twilight; and then waking mistrust and vexation. In trance, on the contrary, I conversed with individuals as seemingly real as this life could present, and observed events as consistent as fate itself could make them; and this the sequel will show" (pp. 9–10). At the story's end there is some invitation to consider paradoxes involved in actually traveling to the future through a trance. The protagonist wonders how his pregnant, future-world wife can be said to exist: "I suddenly start, and wonder where is she at all with the precious burden committed to her charge? The whole affair then seems to me like a stolen

NOTES TO CHAPTER SIX

marriage between myself and the creature of another world, who shortly after the ceremony, flitted back into her eternal space, or burst, as a bubble on the air; and I conclude by assuming that the 'Loves of the Angels' were nothing to it" (p. 337). A love affair with a time-traveler is thus presented as neither unlike the more familiar fantasies of relationship between human and more-than-human, nor exactly the same.

13. *Mrs. Maberly; or, The World as It Will Be*, 3 vols. (London, 1836), 1–2.

14. Charles A. Porter, *Restif's Novels, or An Autobiography in Search of an Author* (New Haven: Yale University Press, 1967), 340.

15. [Nicolas-Edme Restif de la Bretonne], *Les Posthumes; Lettres reçues après la mort du mari, par sa femme, qui le croit à Florence. Par feù Cazotte*, 4 vols. (Paris, 1802). The "faux titre" is *Lettres du tombeau*.

16. See Edward Pease Shaw, *Jacques Cazotte (1719–1792)*, Harvard Studies in Romance Languages, vol. 19 (Cambridge: Harvard University Press, 1942), especially pp. 25–35 and 57–68. Cazotte's story, as well as a prophecy about the French Revolution attributed (dubiously) to him, are now conveniently available with an excellent preface and helpful annotation in Jacques Cazotte, *Le Diable amoureux suivi de la "Prophétie de Cazotte" rapportée par La Harpe, de ses "Révélations," d'extraits de sa correspondance ainsi que d' "Ollivier" et de l' "Histoire de Maugraby"*, ed. Georges Décote (Paris: Gallimard, 1981). See also Georges Décote, *L'Itinéraire de Jacques Cazotte (1719–1792): De la fiction littéraire au mysticisme politique* (Geneva: Droz, 1984).

17. The psychology of writing futuristic fiction as a means of dealing acceptably with fantasies about one's own death is considered in David Ketterer, "Death and the Denial of History: The Textual Shadow of the SF Author," *Science-Fiction Studies* 9 (1982): 228–30; and Gregory Benford, "Death and the Textual Shadow of the SF Author, Again," *Science-Fiction Studies* 9 (1982): 341.

18. But it works the other way too with equal insistence: in various subtle as well as not-so-subtle ways, Restif tempers evocation of reality with the pleasures of dreaming. In addition to Porter, see Pierre Testud, *Rétif de la Bretonne et la création littéraire* (Geneva: Droz, 1977), especially chapter 2, "Le réel et l'imaginaire," 81–186. Testud warns persuasively against mistaking Restif's famous realism for a simple transcription of experience intended mainly as a record of how it really was. More

often, Testud suggests, even in those apparently realistic narratives that prompted Paul Bourget to call Restif "le pithecanthrope de Balzac," Restif mingles fact with fiction in a way that moves history toward the imaginary while in turn lending the imaginary an air of verisimilitude. Thus of Restif's frequent habit of locating fictional action in known streets, Testud remarks: "Il est du reste difficile de décider si, par ces précisions, Rétif cherche à lester de réalité ses histoires, ou s'il désire compromettre la réalité dans l'imaginaire, rendre par là romanesques et fabuleux les lieux familiers de son existence" (p. 116). Testud thus sums up Restif's way of investing reality with the qualities of dreaming and fantasy: "L'imagination rétivienne n'aboutit pas à une vision plus approfondie et plus vraie du réel, à la différence de l'imagination des grands romanciers du XIXe siècle. Elle substitue au monde réel le monde féerique des coïncidences, des quiproquos, des amours incessantes et des paternités innombrables, des tragédies et des histoires exemplaires, des communautés utopiques rassemblées dans un enclos bourguignon ou austral. Il existe bien un monde rétivien, mais il ne cherche pas à faire concurrence à l'état-civil et à la vie. Il cherche à concurrencer tous les rêves et, par le livre qui en porte témoignage, à leur donner une réalité qui les confond avec l'expérience vécue" (p. 183). Restif's attraction to fantasy was by no means expressed only in such overtly fantastic works as *La Decouverte australe* and *Les Posthumes;* only in the latter, however, does it elicit a corresponding move toward futuristic fiction.

19. See Auguste Viatte, *Les Sources occultes du romantisme: Illuminisme-théosophie 1770–1820*, 2d ed., 2 vols. (Paris: Champion, 1969).

20. "Les Historiettes sont singulières, d'un genre absolument neuf, & auquel Personne n'avait jamais pensé" (1:6).

21. "Plûs extraordinaire, quoique plûs dans la vraisemblance romantique, que les Mille-e-une NUITS. . . . Mais c'est une variété de faits, toujours amusante, toujours fondée sur la Nature. Ses *métamorphoses*, son *amour*, les persécutions qu'il éprouve, les victoires qu'il remporte, tout est neuf, & d'un genre à plaire au Lecteur raisonable" (1:6–7).

22. For the intellectual context of utopian elements in *Les Posthumes*, see Mark Poster, *The Utopian Thought of Restif de la Bretonne* (New York: New York University Press, 1971).

23. Testud remarks that *"L'An 2000* se référait, par son titre sinon par son sujet, à *L'An 2440* de Mercier" (*Rétif de la Bretonne*, p. 336, n. 172).

NOTES TO CHAPTER SIX

Testud also notes (p. 341) that Restif deliberately sought the static scenic effects of a tableau in *L'An 2000*, which essentially deals with a single public ceremony (a marriage).

24. "Le bonheur avait (aura) fait son asile, de ce petit coin de l'Universe" (4:133).

25. "Il serait impossible de rapporter tous les soins qu'il en prit (c'est-à-dire prendra), afin d'en faire des Hommes et des Femmes. Il joignit (ou joindra) à tout-cela l'ignorance du vice" (4:141).

26. For some account of the grammatical choices available in referring to the future, and the epistemological consequences of opting for one or another possibility, see Suzanne Fleischman, *The Future in Thought and Language: Diachronic Evidence from Romance* (Cambridge: Cambridge University Press, 1982), 1–31.

27. For an account of shifting ideas about geological time, see Stephen Toulmin and June Goodfield, *The Discovery of Time* (1965; reprint, Chicago: University of Chicago Press, 1982). See also Roy Porter, *The Making of Geology: Earth Science in Britain, 1660–1815* (Cambridge: Cambridge University Press, 1977); and Anthony Hallam, *Great Geological Controversies* (Oxford: Oxford University Press, 1983).

28. Bear in mind, however, the caution in note 18 above. Testud also warns against assuming that reports presented as eyewitness accounts in Restif's publications, especially accounts of events during the Revolution, are necessarily based on his own firsthand experiences: "Rétif est un témoin douteux de l'Histoire de son temps. Des événements révolutionnaires, il n'a rien vu, sinon quelques cortèges qui ont passé sous ses fenêtres, rue de la Bûcherie. La comparaison entre ses notes du *Journal* et les tomes XV et XVI des *Nuits de Paris* montre quel crédit peut être accordé aux texts 'historiques' de Rétif. Tout son information est une information de seconde main: il utilise les propos entendus au Café Manouri, ou dans la librairie de la veuve Duchesne . . . pour imaginer des scènes de rue où il joue un rôle de premier plan. Son égocentrisme ne lui permet pas de se représenter en simple spectateur; le monde extérieur ne l'intéresse que s'il peut, d'une façon ou d'une autre, l'annexer à sa propre existence. Du reste, au Café Manouri comme chez la veuve Duchesne, l'Histoire contemporaine lui parvient sous forme d'histoires; le processus narratif est déjà amorcé, et il n'a plus qu'à le poursuivre dans sa création littéraire" (p. 109). Even outside his most overtly fantastic narratives,

NOTES TO CHAPTER SIX

Restif thus seldom provides a glimpse of history unmediated by fiction. Nevertheless the intrusion of historical events within a fantasy such as *Les Posthumes* creates a very different effect.

29. [Jane Webb], *Conversations Upon Comparative Chronology and General History from the Creation of the World to the Birth of Christ* (London, 1830), 1, 5. For an account of the developments that were casting doubt on traditional biblical chronology, see Toulmin and Goodfield, *The Discovery of Time;* on eighteenth-century chronological writing, see Paul K. Alkon, "Johnson and Chronology," in *Greene Centennial Studies: Essays Presented to Donald Greene in the Centennial Year of the University of Southern California*, ed. Paul J. Korshin and Robert R. Allen (Charlottesville: University Press of Virginia, 1984), 143–71; on Webb's role in opening careers in professional gardening to women, see Bea How, *Lady with Green Fingers: The Life of Jane Loudon* (London: Country Life, 1961).

30. Mrs. Loudon [Jane Webb], *The Mummy! A Tale of the Twenty-Second Century* (London: Frederick Warne & Co; New York: Scribner, Welford & Armstrong, [1872]), v–viii. References are taken from the Eaton Collection's copy of the second edition. The "Publisher's Preface," dated August 1872, suggests that by the latter part of the nineteenth century earlier futuristic fiction of all kinds was being assimilated in readers' eyes to the mode of predictive extrapolation: "This Novel was written by the late Mrs. Loudon, many years since. It lays the scene in the twenty-second century, and attempts to predict the state of progress to which this country might possibly arrive. It has always been considered a successful book, and it is hoped that this first cheap edition will make the Novel more widely known and appreciated." As I hope my discussion will sufficiently show, in 1827 Webb hardly intended *The Mummy* as a book designed primarily "to predict the state of progress" to which England might aspire.

31. Its closest rival in presenting a consistently imagined future world is doubtless Julius von Voss, *Ini: Ein Roman aus dem ein und zwanzigsten Jahrhundert* (Berlin, 1810).

SEVEN
A Poetics for Futuristic Fiction

1. Félix Bodin, *Le Roman de l'avenir* (Paris, 1834), 20–30.
2. I. F. Clarke, *The Pattern of Expectation, 1644–2001* (New York: Basic Books, 1979), 72.

NOTES TO CHAPTER SEVEN

3. See R. S. Crane, "Critical and Historical Principles of Literary History," in *The Idea of the Humanities and Other Essays Critical and Historical* (Chicago: University of Chicago Press, 1967), 2:45–156.

4. Loren Eiseley, *Darwin's Century: Evolution and the Men Who Discovered It* (1958; reprint, Garden City, N.Y.: Doubleday Anchor Books, 1961), 57.

5. See Maximillian E. Novak, "Defoe's *Shortest Way with the Dissenters:* Hoax, Parody, Paradox, Fiction, Irony, and Satire," *Modern Language Quarterly* 27 (1966): 402–17; and Paul K. Alkon, "Defoe's Argument in *The Shortest Way with the Dissenters,*" *Modern Philology* 73 (May 1976): Suppl. 12–23; and the discussion of *Moll Flanders* as hoax in Laura A. Curtis, *The Elusive Daniel Defoe* (Totowa, N.J.: Barnes and Noble, 1984), 138–60.

6. Bodin, *Le Roman de l'avenir,* 26. In mock apology for inventing the term *littérature futuriste,* Bodin adds parenthetically: "J'ai la manie aussi, moi, tout comme les autres, de faire des mots nouveaux."

7. Ibid., 23: "La querelle interminable des spiritualistes et des physiologistes, des dogmatiques et des empiristes, des ascétiques et des utilistes, etc., etc., est apparemment fondée sur la diversité des organisations humaines. Il y aura toujours aussi des têtes poétiques et des têtes positives."

8. Ibid., 54–55: "Quelle tête politique chez les anciens eût pu imaginer la possibilité d'un état social sans esclaves? . . . Quel génie, au dix-septième-siècle, eût pu concevoir l'idée de ce qui se passe depuis cinquante ans dans les deux hémisphères? L'honnête et quelquefois amusant déclamateur Mercier, qui crut, il y a une cinquantaine d'années, rêver l'an 2440, ne poussait pas même jusqu'au gouvernement représentatif, aux pantalons et aux cheveux à la Titus. Il ne va-pas plus loin que les idées de quelques philosophes et économistes français en vogue de son temps; et sa monarchie philantropique, qui n'est qu'une modification du pouvoir absolu, ne paraît guère plus avancée que les têtes de ses citoyens futurs sur lesquelles il croit innover audacieusement en se bornant à les blanchir d'un *soupçon de poudre,* et en revelant les cheveux en chignon."

9. Ibid., 58: "Tout ce qu'on y trouvera de mauvais, j'en décline hardiment la responsabilité, qui doit peser tout entière sur les manuscrits que j'ai consultés."

10. Ibid., 57–58: Quant à la forme de la narration, il a fallu, pour qu'elle fût claire et coulante, raconter toutes ces choses futures au présent

ou au passé, comme si le roman lui-même était écrit et publié dans deux cents ans d'ici, comme s'il s'adressait au public qui existera dans ce temps-là."

11. Darko Suvin, *Metamorphoses of Science Fiction: On the Poetics and History of a Literary Genre* (New Haven: Yale University Press, 1979).

12. Bodin, *Le Roman de l'avenir*, 397–99; "Des essais littéraires sur l'avenir."

13. See Robert Darnton, *Mesmerism and the End of the Enlightenment in France* (Cambridge: Harvard University Press, 1968).

14. See J. C. Colquhoun, trans., *Report of the Experiments on Animal Magnetism, made by a Committee of the Medical Section of the French Royal Academy of Sciences: Read at the Meetings of the 21st and 28th of June, 1831* (Edinburgh, 1833; reprint, New York: Arno Press, 1975).

15. For the contribution of mesmerism to scientific psychology, see Edwin G. Boring, *A History of Experimental Psychology*, 2d. ed. (New York: Appleton-Century Crofts, 1957), 116–33, 694–701.

16. See Maria M. Tatar, *Spellbound: Studies on Mesmerism and Literature* (Princeton: Princeton University Press, 1978); and Fred Kaplan, *Dickens and Mesmerism: The Hidden Springs of Fiction* (Princeton: Princeton University Press, 1975).

17. Darnton, *Mesmerism and the End of the Enlightenment in France*, 127.

18. See Marquis Chastenet de Puységur, *Mémoires pour servir à l'histoire et à l'établissement du magnétisme animal*, 3d. ed. (Paris, 1820); A. M. J. Chastenet de Puységur, *Recherches, expériences et observations physiologiques sur l'homme dans l'état de somnambulisme naturel, et dans le somnambulisme provoqué par l'acte magnétique* (Paris, 1811); J. P. F. Deleuze, *Histoire critique du magnétisme animal*, 2 vols. (Paris, 1813).

19. Deleuze, *Histoire critique du magnétisme animal*, 1:294–95.

20. Puységur, *Recherches*, 109–10.

21. Deleuze, *Histoire critique du magnétisme animal*, 1:278ff.

22. Puységur, *Recherches*, 57.

23. Ibid., 55.

24. Ibid., 55–56.

25. Ibid., 39: ". . . vous direz sans doute avec Saint-Augustin: *modus quo corporibus adherent spiritus, omnino mirus est, nec comprehendi ab homine potest; et hoc ipse homo est*. 'La manière dont les esprits sont unis

aux corps est tout à fait merveilleuse: elle ne peut être comprise par l'homme, et c'est cependant là l'homme lui-même.' (De la *Cité de Dieu*.)"

26. Puységur, *Recherches*, p. 101.

27. See M.H. Abrams, *Natural Supernaturalism: Tradition and Revolution in Romantic Literature* (New York: W. W. Norton, 1971).

Index

Abrams, Meyer Howard, 159, 160
Absalom and Achitophel (Dryden), 109
Aeronautics. *See* Flight
Aldiss, Brian W., 89, 90, 111
Allegory: time in, 31, 32, 35, 109; and prophecy, 60; and futuristic fiction, 60–61
Alternate history: in *Epigone*, 39–41, 43, 44; invention of, 115; used to examine causation, 116; and future, 129–30, 132–33; realism and fantasy in, 146; and forms of utopia, 146–48; real and fictive pasts in, 152; boundary of possible and probable in, 152; time in, 153; and uchronia, 153; precursors of, 154; *Nineteen Eighty-Four* as, 156. *See also* Geoffroy, Renouvier
Amis, Kingsley, 89
L'An 2000, 218
L'An 2440 (Mercier): and *Epigone*, 43–44; and *Memoirs of the Twentieth Century*, 98–99; and French Revolution, 99, 124, 126; publishing history of, 117; dream frame-story of, 118, 123–24, 232; verisimilitude in, 122, 125; Mercier's birthdate and setting of, 122–23; connection to history, 122–29; and prediction, 123, 126; 1772 English version titled *Memoirs of the Year Two Thousand Five Hundred*, 123; as commentary on eighteenth-century France, 124–25; footnotes in, 125, 226; fantastic in, 127–28; new paradigm for utopia, 127–28; and Geoffroy, 133; formal affinities of, to uchronia of alternate history, 153; and Apocalypse, 162; and *Les Voyages de Kang-Hi*, 198–99; and *Les Posthumes*, 216–18; and *L'An 2000*, 218; past-tense narration in, 221; epigram from Leibnitz in, 251; and

327

INDEX

L'An 2440 (cont'd)
   Le Roman de l'avenir, 251, 254, 259, 262, 288
Ancients and Moderns controversy, 50
Angenot, Marc, 317 (n. 4)
Apocalypse: and science fiction, 158–59; and credibility in fiction, 160; phenomenology of, 167–74; and verisimilitude, 168; traditional representations of, 179; imagery of, in Shelley's *The Last Man*, 189–90; and utopia, 196; Bodin avoids, 274. *See also* Grainville, Shelley
Ariosto, Ludovico, 259
Aristotle, 3, 103–4, 106, 109, 273
Augustine, Saint, 287
Aulicus his dream of the kings sudden comming to London (Cheynell), 3
Avidius Cassius, 116

Bacon, Francis, 119
Baczko, Bronislaw, 125, 126–28, 153
Bakhtin, Mikhail, 12–16, 17, 33, 42, 62, 128
Balloons, 47, 265. *See also* Flight
Banim, John, 203
Barjavel, René, 17
Bastille, 118, 124, 227
The Battle of Dorking (Chesney), 11
Beauharnais, Fanny de, 211, 212
Beaumarchais, Pierre-Augustin Caron de, 214
The Beggar's Opera (Gay), 103, 112
Bellamy, Edward, 20
Benford, Gregory, 304 (n. 22), 319 (n. 17)
Bentham, Jeremy, 269, 271

The Bickerstaff Papers (Swift), 101, 103
Bodin, Félix, 16, 160, 161, 186, 211, 241. *See Le Roman de l'avenir*
Bonneville, C. M. Le Roy de, 176, 183
Rosse, Malcom J., 302 (n. 11)
Braudy, Leo, 303 (n. 18)
Brave New World (Huxley), 289
Brecht, Bertolt, 89
A Brief Description of the future History of Europe (anon.), 59–61
Buffon, Georges-Louis Leclerc, Comte de, 64, 67, 83, 84, 85, 224
Bulkeley, John, 168
Burgess, Anthony, 17
Burnet, Thomas. *See The Sacred Theory of the Earth*
Byron, George Gordon, sixth baron, 205

Caesar, Julius, 40
Calendar. *See* Time
Capitalism, 47, 91–92, 112
Capp, Bernard, 300 (n. 22)
Causation: in literary history, 247
Cayley, Sir George, 6
Cazotte, Jacques: Illuminist beliefs of, 207, 210; death of, 207, 213; *Les Posthumes* falsely ascribed to, 207–12, 215; reputation as a prophet, 209, 212; allusions to, in *Les Posthumes*, 225; *Le Diable amoureux*, 207–8, 212, 215, 217
Chamberlain, Gordon B., 309 (n. 27)
Change, 109, 110–11, 143
Channel tunnel, 237
Chaucer, Geoffrey, 205
Cheops, 183, 238–40

328

INDEX

Chesney, Sir George Tomkyns, 11
Cheynell, Francis, 3
Childhood's End (Clarke), 104–5
China, 198–202
Christianity, 129, 211
Chronology: in prose fiction, 24–25; Jane Webb on, 232. *See also* Time
Chronotope. *See* Bakhtin
Churchill, Winston S., 154
Cioranescu, Alexandre, 17, 126
The City of God (Augustine), 287
Clairvoyance: mesmeric, 282–86
Clarke, I. F., 11, 105, 246, 316 (n. 1)
Clovis, 38
Cognitive estrangement: defined, 89; and science fiction, 90–91; fantasy as means of, in *Les Posthumes*, 229–31; in *The Mummy*, 240–41; in *Le Roman de l'avenir*, 267; mesmerism and, 287
Commodus, 116
Condorcet, Marie Jean Antoine Nicolas de Caritat, Marquis de, 119
Conte philosophique, 11
Conversations upon Comparative Chronology (Webb), 232
Cook, James, 194
Cosmology, 183–84
Crick, Bernard, 294 (n. 27), 307 (n. 8)
Croft, Herbert, 161
Curtis, Laura A., 323 (n. 5)
Cyrano de Bergerac (Savinien), 10, 23, 48, 217, 259

Daghistany, Ann, 313 (n. 26)
Dante Alighieri, 259

Danton, George-Jacques, 228, 229, 230
Darnton, Robert, 281
Darwin, Charles R., 247
Dates: effects of specifying in futuristic fiction, 24–25; as titles for books, 121–23; in *Les Posthumes*, 217; in *Le Roman de l'avenir*, 262, 270. *See also* Time
Davidson, James West, 298 (n. 10), 306 (n. 6)
Decoufle, André-Clément, 307 (n. 7)
La Découverte australe (Restif de la Bretonne), 206, 217
Defamiliarization. *See* Cognitive estrangement
Defoe, Daniel, 91, 109, 143, 190, 197, 250
Deleuze, J. P. F., 279, 282–85, 288
Delisle de Sales, 154
Le dernier homme (Grainville): as secularization of Apocalypse, 161–91 passim; Croft praises, 161; Nodier introduces second edition, 161; English translation, 161; as epic, 161, 165, 196–97; adaptations of, 162, 182–85, 187–88; Michelet's romantic reading of, 162, 166, 176; and forms of Apocalypse, 163–64, 176–80, 196–97; plot, 164–67; Christianity in, 165–66; allegorical figure of scientist in, 166, 181–82, 187–88; phenomenology of Apocalypse represented in, 167–74, 180; tempo of action in, 168–72; and history, 171; mythic future in, 172; combination of realism, fantasy, and allegory in, 174; doctrines of Apocalypse questioned by, 174,

INDEX

Le dernier homme (cont'd)
181–83; plot time in, 177; scenes and novelistic progression in, 177–80; dream-visions in, 177–80; spatial form and, 180; point of view in, 180; utopia rejected in, 181, 196; mixture of genres in, 183; and Shelley's *The Last Man*, 188–90; as transitional form of futuristic fiction, 190–91; and Bodin, 270–71, 276.

Le dernier homme, poëme imité de Grainville. See Lesser

Description de la Chine et de la Tartarie chinoise (Du Halde), 199

Le Diable amoureux (Cazotte), 207–8, 212, 215, 217

Dick, Philip K., 154

Discours qui a remporté le prix d'éloquence, de l'académie de Besançon (Grainville), 186–87, 314 (nn. 33, 34)

Donne, John, 3

Don Quixote (Cervantes), 53

Drama, 218

Dreams: temporal relationships in, 34, 35; as narrative framework in *L'An 2440*, 118, 123–24; in *Le dernier homme*, 177–80; choice of verb-tense in narrations of, 222

Dryden, John, 109, 205

Du Halde, Jean Baptiste, 199

The Dunciad (Pope), 100, 103, 105

Dystopia. See Utopia

Eiseley, Loren, 247

Eizykmann, Boris, 293 (n. 17), 301 (n. 6)

Entretiens sur la pluralité des mondes (Fontenelle), 55, 56

Epic: and futuristic fiction, 8, 11, 245, 259–60; conventions of, in *Le dernier homme*, 196–97; conventions of, in *Le Roman de l'avenir*, 270–71

Epigone (Guttin): inaugurates futuristic fiction, 17–44 passim; intentions of, 17; distancing in, 18–19; verisimilitude and future setting of, 18; and romance conventions, 18, 32, 35, 42; and frame-stories in later futuristic fiction, 19–21; dedication to the Marquise de Gouvernet, 22; dates omitted from, 24–26; predictions in, 25, 38–39, 40, 43; narrative sequence in, 26–27; names in, 28–29; allegory in, 28–29, 31; space-time relationships in, 31–33; tempo of action in, 31–35; and dreams, 34; satire in, 36, 37; and calendar time, 36–39, 42, 43–44; French history in, 38–41; as alternate history, 39–42, 120, 221; spatialization of time in, 42–43, 128; ontological status of future in, 44; not model for *Memoirs of the Twentieth Century*, 93

Epistemology, 159–60, 191

Esquisse d'un tableau historique des progrès de l'esprit humain (Condorcet), 119

An Essay on the Principle of Population (Malthus), 162

Eschatology: and concern with future, 14, 62; and science fiction, 158–59; and *Le dernier homme*, 174; and *The Last Man*, 190

Estrangement. See Cognitive estrangement

INDEX

Eureka (Williams), 202–3, 237, 317–18 (n. 11)
Evolution, 84–85
Extrapolation: defined, 46; Burnet's aesthetics of, 63–85

The Faerie Queene (Spenser), 109
Fantasy: and realism in futuristic fiction, 7, 192–93; in *Epigone*, 18–19; and alternate history, 146; and epistemology, 159; and the marvelous, 186–88; in *Le dernier homme*, 191, 196; and metafiction, 192–241 passim; as catalyst of generic change, 193; in *Le Monde tel qu'il sera*, 194–95; avoided in *The Last Man*, 197; in *Mrs. Maberly*, 205–6; in *Les Posthumes*, 206, 212, 216, 224, 229–31; in *The Mummy*, 240; in *Le Roman de l'avenir*, 266
Far future, 121–22, 183, 184, 217–18
Fesch, Joseph, 137
Fiction: futuristic defined, 3; and science, 67–68
Fielding, Henry, 104
La Fin du monde (Flammarion), 162, 183–84
Flammarion, Camille, 162, 183–84, 191
Fleischman, Suzanne, 321 (n. 26)
Flight, 47, 213, 224, 265–66, 288
Fontenelle, Bernard le Bovier, 55, 56
Fourier, Charles, 274, 275, 277, 288
Frank, Joseph, 180
Frankenstein (Shelley), 12, 90, 166, 190
Fredericks, Casey, 301 (n. 2)
French Revolution, 129, 143, 186; in

Les Posthumes, 209, 212, 215, 218, 225–31
La Fronde, 40
Future: eschatology deflects attention from, 14; ontological status of, 42; past-tense narration used for description in futuristic fiction, 90, 221–23; investigation of versus prediction of, 125–26, 133; and alternate history, 129–30; possible influence of futuristic fiction on, 195–96; as metaphor of present in futuristic fiction, 219; and past in futuristic fiction, 219–20, 226–27; aesthetic appeal of, in *Le Roman de l'avenir*, 265, 267–68, 269; mesmerism and ideas about, 283–86. See also Far future

Gagne, Elise, 183, 191; on role of female writers, 176; *Omégar ou le dernier homme*, 161, 184–85
Galbreath, Robert, 158, 159, 160
Garrett, Clarke, 306 (n. 6)
Gay, John, 103, 112
Gazette littéraire, 277
Genre: futuristic fiction as, 5; concepts of and futuristic fiction, 11–15; parodic and futuristic fiction, 103; experimentation with and futuristic fiction, 112–13; fantasy as catalyst of changes in, 193
Geoffroy, Louis. See *Napoléon et la conquête du monde*
Geology: and futuristic fiction, 63–85 passim; imaginary in *Les Posthumes*, 217; and Jane Webb, 232
Godwin, Francis, 23

INDEX

Goethe, Johann Wolfgang von, 134
Golden age: myths of, 14; *Les Posthumes* portrays future, 219
Goodfield, June, 64
Gothic fiction, 279; and science fiction, 89, 90; and *The Last Man*, 190; and *The Mummy*, 235, 238–40
Gouvernet, Marquise de, 22
Grainville, Jean-Baptiste Cousin de, 4, 59, 78, 84; *Discours qui a remporté le prix d'éloquence, de l'académie de Besançon*, 186–87, 314 (nn. 33, 34). See *Le dernier homme*
Guardian angels, 94–95
Gulliver's Travels. See Swift
Guttin, Jacques, 3, 45, 153, 154, 236. See *Epigone*

Hacker, Barton C., 309 (n. 27)
Hansen, Arlen J., 68
Hanzo, Thomas, 90, 109
Harrington, James, 12
Harth, Erica, 294 (n. 32)
Histoire comique (Cyrano de Bergerac), 23; Russen's commentary on, 48–58
Historical novel: and uchronia, 146; temporal viewpoint in, 264; and futuristic fiction, 277–79, 288
History: and future history, 103; and uchronia, 120–29; and utopian speculation, 218; juxtaposed with imaginary future in *Les Posthumes*, 218–19, 225–31. See also Alternate history, Geoffroy, Mercier
Hoax: as literary form, 249–50, 255
Holquist, Michael, 125, 128

Homer, 161, 259, 260
Huet, Marie-Hélène, 293 (n. 17)
Hume, Kathryn, 316 (n. 3)
Hume, Robert D., 304 (n. 22)
Huntington, John, 293 (n. 17), 300 (n. 26), 301 (n. 6)
Huxley, Aldous, 4, 155, 248, 289

Illuminism, 210–12, 225, 229–31. See also Cazotte
Imaginary voyages, 46–47
Imagination, 202–3, 317–18 (n. 11)
India, 200–201
Industrial revolutions, 288
Ini (von Voss), 322 (n. 31)
Inquisition, 117
Islam, 135–36, 268–69
Iter Lunare (Russen): publishing history, 48; as commentary on Cyrano de Bergerac's *Histoire comique*, 48–58; cyclical concept of history in, 49–51; view of science in, 51; rejects idea of progress, 51; atemporal extrapolation in, 52; on genre of Cyrano's *Histoire comique*, 53–54; on plurality of worlds, 54–55; and science fiction, 54–55; and Newtonian physics, 56; theology of and speculation about the future, 57–58; and technology, 58
Itinerarium Extaticum (Kircher), 23, 95

Jackson, Rosemary, 316 (n. 3)
Jacob, Margaret C., 299 (n. 12), 302 (n. 12)
Jameson, Fredric, 47, 295 (n. 2)
Jefferson, Thomas, 117

INDEX

Jeremiah, 254
John the Evangelist, Saint, 254
Johnson, Samuel, 96
A Journal of the Plague Year (Defoe), 109, 190, 197
Judaism, 137–38, 269

Kant, Immanuel, 284
Kaplan, Fred, 324 (n. 16)
Keill, Joseph, 67, 68, 70
Ketterer, David, 159–60
Kircher, Athanasius, 23, 95
Korshin, Paul J., 297 (nn. 7, 9)

The Ladies' Companion to the Flower Garden (Webb), 231
The Ladies' Flower Garden of Bulbous Plants (Webb), 232
The Ladies' Flower Garden of Ornamental Annuals (Webb), 231–32
Book of Lamentations, 254
The Last Day (Bulkeley), 168
Last Judgment: paintings of, 167–68; poems about, 168; traditional imagery of, 168–69; vision of, in *Le dernier homme*, 178–79
The Last Man. See Shelley
The Last Man, or Omegarus and Syderia, A Romance in Futurity: anonymous English translation of Grainville's *Le dernier homme*, 161
The Last Peer (anon.), 195–96
Launay, Bernard-Reñe-Jordan, Marquis de, 227
Le Brun, Claire, 309 (n. 27)
Le Goff, Jacques, 302 (n. 9)
Le Guin, Ursula K., 17

Leibnitz, Gottfried Wilhelm, 251
Lem, Stanislaw, 17
Lesser, Auguste-François Creuzé, Baron de, 183, 191; *Le dernier homme, poëme imité de Grainville*, 161, 181, 184–85, 187–88
Lessing, Gotthold Ephraim, 13
Lettres persanes (Montesquieu), 198, 199
Levis, Pierre-Marc Gaston, Duc de. See *Les Voyages de Kang-Hi*
Lilienthal, Otto, 6
Lisbon earthquake, 208
Littérature futuriste: Bodin invents term, 4, 11, 255
Lockwood, W. A., 299 (n. 12)
Looking Backward (Bellamy), 20
Loudon, John Claudius, 205, 231
Loudon, Mrs. John Claudius. See Webb
Louis XIII, 38
Louis XIV, 38, 40
Louis XVI, 154, 228

McConnell, Frank, 300 (n. 26)
McKeon, Michael, 303 (n. 12)
Madden, Samuel, 4, 19, 45, 85, 120, 121, 143, 192, 211, 228. See *Memoirs of the Twentieth Century*
Magic mirrors, 20, 163, 164, 188, 233
La Magnétisomanie, 280
Majewski, Henry F., 310 (n. 7), 311 (n. 15)
Malachy, Saint, 249, 275–76
Malthus, Thomas Robert, 162, 166
The Man in the Moone (Godwin), 23
Manuel, Frank Edward, 64, 118–20

INDEX

Manuel, Fritzie, 118–20
Marcus Aurelius, 116
Ma République (Delisle de Sales), 154
Marmor Norfolciense (Johnson), 96
Marvelous, the: in futuristic fiction, 8, 9, 186–88, 275; in *Epigone*, 44; in *Napoléon apocryphe*, 134–40; in adaptations of *Le dernier homme*, 184, 185; in *The Mummy*, 237; mesmerism as a source of, in fiction, 280–83, 286–87
The Masks of Time (Silverberg), 96
Mathematics, 92
Mede, Joseph, 306 (n. 6)
Memoirs of the Twentieth Century (Madden): time-travel in, 19, 85; and *Epigone*, 45; publication and suppression of, 92; satire in, 93, 94–98, 102; and *Itinerarium Extaticum*, 95; utopian elements in, 97–98; epistolary framework of, 98–99; self-reflexive quality of, 100; and eighteenth-century literary innovation, 103, 112–13; verisimilitude, 104–8, 110–11; remarks improbability of history, 107–8, 120, 228, 259; double temporal perspective in, 108–9; past-tense narration in, 109, 221, 222; and scientific discovery, 111; new aesthetics in, suggested by science, 114; distancing in, 128; compared with *Napoléon apocryphe*, 143; comic inversion of apocalypse in, 162–63; and early futuristic fiction, 192, 219, 276
Memoirs of the Year Two Thousand Five Hundred (English translation of Mercier's *L'An 2440*), 123

Mercier, Louis-Sébastien, 4, 5, 11, 19, 25, 43, 103, 116, 153, 171, 193, 214, 226, 254, 275. See *L'An 2440*
Mesmer, Friedrich Anton, 280
Mesmerism: in *Le Monde tel qu'il sera*, 194, 198; in *Le Roman de l'avenir*, 261–63, 266, 281; influence of, on Bodin, 279–88; and futuristic fiction, 279–88 passim; and romantic literature, 281; scientific and spiritualist schools of, 281–82; and clairvoyance, 282–86; and ideas about the future, 283–86; and the marvelous, 286–87; and verisimilitude, 286–87
Metafiction: and fantasy, 192–241 passim; defined, 193; and realism, 193; in *Les Voyages de Kang-Hi*, 198, 202; in *Eureka*, 202; in *Mrs. Maberly*, 203–5; in *Les Posthumes*, 207, 215–16; in *The Mummy*, 233–34, 238, 241; in *Le Roman de l'avenir*, 247
Michelet, Jules, 162, 166, 176, 182, 183
Millenarianism, 119, 306 (n. 6)
Milton, John, 161, 182, 205
Mimesis, 7, 54
Miner, Earl, 297 (n. 7)
Mrs. Maberly (anon.), 203–6, 231
A Modest Proposal (Swift), 250
Mohammedanism. See Islam
Molière, Jean-Baptiste Poquelin, 21
Le Monde tel qu'il sera. See Souvestre
Montesquieu, Charles de Secondat, Baron de, 198, 199
Montgolfier, Jacques Etienne, 213, 265

334

INDEX

Montgolfier, Joseph Michel, 213, 265
More, St. Thomas, 11, 119, 214
Morgan, Chris, 292 (n. 5)
Moses, 259, 260
The Mummy (Webb): metafictional framework of, 232–33; preface of, 232–35; novelty sought in, 232–35; satire in, 234, 235–36; dystopian elements of, 235; gothic elements of, 235, 238–40; romance conventions in, 236–37; self-parody in, 238; point of view in, 240; fantasy in, 240–41; cognitive estrangement in, 240–41; compared with *Frankenstein*, 240–41; place of, in development of futuristic fiction, 241; unknown to Bodin, 276; not predictive, 322 (n. 30)

Napoléon apocryphe. See *Napoléon et la conquête du monde*
Napoleon Bonaparte, 162, 171, 211, 212; alternate history of, in *Napoléon apocryphe*, 130–54
Napoléon et la conquête du monde—1812 à 1832—Histoire de la monarchie universelle (Geoffroy; second edition titled *Napoléon apocryphe*): publication, 115, 116; as uchronia of alternate history, 129–54 passim; technological progress described in, 130–32; the uncanny in, 134; the marvelous in, 134–40; Islam in, 135–36; Protestantism and Catholicism in, 137; Judaism in, 137–38; title of second edition self-reflexive, 140; and real history, 140–45; improbability of history remarked in, 141–44; verisimilitude in, 141–44; Napoleon criticized in, 144–46; as utopia, 146–48; *Nineteen Eighty-Four* and, 148, 151; dystopian elements of, 148–52

Natural supernaturalism, 159, 170, 176, 287
New Theory of the Earth (Whiston), 84
Newton, Isaac, 56, 62, 64–66, 75, 84, 149, 297 (n. 9)
Newton, Thomas, 298 (n. 10)
Nineteen Eighty-Four. See Orwell
Nodier, Charles, 161, 183, 276
Novak, Maximillian E., 323 (n. 5)

Observations Upon the Prophecies of Daniel, and the Apocalypse of St. John (Newton), 62
Oceana (Harrington), 12
Omégar ou le dernier homme. See Gagne
Orwell, George, 4, 5, 6, 12, 17, 148, 151, 248, 289; *Nineteen Eighty-Four*: title of, 25, 121, 307 (n. 8); as uchronia, 116, 154–57; near future setting of, 121; dystopian features of, 154–56

Partridge, John, 101
Past: concern with and futuristic fiction, 14–16
Patrides, C. A., 297 (n. 9), 313 (n. 24)
Pénaud, Alphonse, 6
Peri Bathous (Pope), 103, 105
Phaeton myth, 73–74

335

INDEX

Philmus, Robert M., 301 (n. 2)
Philosophiae Naturalis Principia Mathematica (Newton), 56, 64
Planetary voyages. *See* Space travel, Imaginary voyages
Plato, 11
Plot: role of, in futuristic fiction, according to Bodin, 272–73
Poe, Edgar Allan, 250
A Poem on the Last Day (Young), 168
Poetics (Aristotle), 103–4
Point of view: 222, 229–31, 240, 263–64. *See also* Cognitive estrangement, Time
Polo, Marco, 199
Pope, Alexander, 112, 205; *The Dunciad*, 100, 103, 105; *Peri Bathous*, 103, 105; *The Rape of the Lock*, 103, 250
Porter, Charles A., 206
Porter, Roy, 300 (n. 25)
Poster, Mark, 320 (n. 22)
Les Posthumes (Restif de la Bretonne): fantasy and realism in, 206, 207, 212, 214, 216, 230; weaknesses of, 206–7; significance of, 206–7, 231; time in, 207, 217, 219, 220, 223, 224; ascription of, to Cazotte, 207–12, 213, 215, 216; and *Le Diable amoureux*, 207–8, 215; frame-story of, 208–9, 213–15, 226; composition and publication, 209; and Restif's impending death, 209; genre of, 210, 212, 216–17, 219, 229; Illuminist doctrines in, 210–12, 225, 229–31; verisimilitude, 211, 212, 216; utopian speculation, 214, 218–20; reincarnation imagined in, 214; future history of Duke Multipliandre in, 215–31; wish-fulfillment fantasies and far-future setting of, 217–18; French Revolution in, 218, 225–31; sexual mores considered in, 219; preterite and future verb-tense alternation in, 220–21; geological changes imagined in, 223, 225; biological evolution imagined in, 223–24; narrative sequence of, 225–26, 229–31; and cognitive estrangement, 230–31
Les Précieuses ridicules (Molière), 21
Prediction: and futuristic fiction, 125–26
Prévost, Antoine-François, l'Abbé, 167
Private Letters from an American in England to his Friends in America (anon.), 120–21, 196
Probability: in futuristic fiction, 103–11; concepts of, altered by science, 114; of real and alternate history in *Napoléon apocryphe*, 141–45; in *Le Monde tel qu'il sera*, 195
Progress, 7, 9, 51, 127, 181, 192–93, 194, 198, 246, 256
Prophecy: and futuristic fiction, 58–63, 75–76; style of, 78; and dreams, 123; and *Le dernier homme*, 163–64, 176–80; generic attributes of, 180; mesmerism and, 283–85; and politics, 296 (n. 6); directs attention to past, 298 (n. 10)
Prophecy of the Popes (falsely attributed to St. Malachy), 275–76

INDEX

Puységur, Marquis Chastenet de, 279, 282–83, 285–86, 288

Rabelais, François, 10, 259
Rabkin, Eric S., 193
Racine, Jean, 270
Radcliffe, Ann, 89, 239
The Rape of the Lock (Pope), 103, 250
Reader response, 271–74
Realism: and fantasy in futuristic fiction, 7, 192–93; and future settings, 112; in *The Last Man*, 190; in *Revelations of the Dead-Alive*, 203, 318 (n. 12); in *Mrs. Maberly*, 205–6; and fantasy in *Les Posthumes*, 206, 212. *See also* Verisimilitude, Fantasy
The Reign of George VI, 1900–1925 (anon.), 4, 112–13, 120
Religion: and science fiction, 57–58; and futuristic fiction, 59–63; decline of, 186; and futuristic fiction, according to Bodin, 254. *See also* Apocalypse, Burnet, Grainville, Prophecy, Russen
Renouvier, Charles, 147; invents term *uchronia*, 115; writes *Uchronie*, an alternate history of the Roman Empire, 115–16, 129–30
Republic (Plato), 11
Restif de la Bretonne, Nicolas-Edme, 4, 193, 259, 263, 276; compulsion to record own experiences in fictional form, 209, 225; obsession with utopias, 218; and spiritualism, 288; *La Découverte australe par un homme volant*, 206, 217; *L'An 2000*, 218. See *Les Posthumes*
Revelation, Book of, 8, 60, 63, 73, 122, 163–64, 168, 177–80, 196, 254, 256, 275. *See also* Apocalypse, Grainville, Shelley
Robin Hood, 266
Robinsonade, 11
Robinson Crusoe (Defoe), 108, 190
Romance: conventions of, and *Epigone*, 18, 35, 42; end of vogue for in seventeenth-century France, 42; futuristic, 43–44; seventeenth- and eighteenth-century definitions of, 54; conventions of, in *The Mummy*, 235, 236
Le Roman de l'avenir (Bodin): term *littérature futuriste* invented in, 4, 256; comments on previous futuristic fiction in, 4, 8, 276–77; ideals for futuristic fiction proposed in, 7–11; past-tense narration recommended for futuristic fiction in, 223, 263; calls for literature of rational wonders, 245; originality of aesthetics in, 245–46; not predictive, 246, 253, 265–66, 273; as metafiction, 247, 251, 260; poetics for futuristic fiction outlined in, 248; divisions of, 248–49; epigram of, 249, 251–52; hoax, burlesque, and parody in, 249–50, 255, 260, 263; dialogic relationship with previous fiction, 251; dedication of, to the past, 251, 254–55; allusions to *L'An 2440* in, 251, 254–55, 259, 262; tone of, 251, 255; self-reflexive opening of, 252; past discussed in,

INDEX

Le Roman de l'avenir (cont'd)
252–53, 255; on emotional power of futuristic fiction, 253, 257, 259, 269; time and literary form considered in, 254; rejects Lamentations and Revelation as models for futuristic fiction, 254; preface of, 255–60; deficiencies of futuristic utopias and apocalypses remarked in, 256; ideas of progress and regress discussed in as determinants of literary form, 256; rational and poetic temperaments distinguished in, 256–58; neither classic nor romantic, 257; plot and characters in, 258, 266–67, 268, 270, 271, 272–73; literary tradition of, 259; improbability of history remarked in, 259; epic of the future called for in, 259–60; introduction of, 260–64; mesmerism and, 261–63, 266, 279–88; dates in, 262, 270; reader responses to, 262, 264, 271–74; flight in, 265; picturesque appeal of future in, 265, 267–68; ideas subordinated to action in, 267–68; warfare in, 268; Islam in, 268–69; past evoked by future settings in, 269; epic conventions in, 270–71; novelistic techniques in, 271; Fourier praised in, 274; reasons given in for avoiding apocalyptic style and subjects, 274; influences on futuristic fiction considered in, 275–76; "Prophecy of the Popes" discussed in, 275–76; Bodin's autobiographical account of its origins in, 277–81; romantic literature and, 287; major influences on, 288

Roman Empire: alternate history of, in *Uchronie,* 115–16

Rose, Mark, 158

Rosetta Stone, 232

Rousseau, Jean-Jacques, 187

Royal Academy of Sciences (France), 280

Royal Society (England), 51, 78–79

Russen, David, 66. See *Iter Lunare*

Russian Formalists, 89

Sacheverell, Henry, 250

The Sacred Theory of the Earth (Burnet): influence of, on English poetry, 63; and science fiction, 64; Flood explained in, 66; final conflagration explained in, 66, 73–74, 76; aesthetic affinities of science and fiction remarked in, 68–74, 81–82; on Scripture as guide to the future, 74; on credibility of speculation about the future, 74; biblical exegesis in, 75–76; on difficulty of reading and writing about the future, 76–77; on style appropriate for writing about the future, 77–80; constraints of verisimilitude in, 79–82; and futuristic fiction, 83–85; *Le dernier homme* compared with, 167–68

St. Serf, Thomas, 48

Sartre, Jean-Paul, 6, 7

Scholes, Robert, 6–7, 192–93

Science: and fiction, 53, 67–68, 106–7, 109–11; and theology in

INDEX

seventeenth-century England, 65, 66; and ideas of probability in life and in literature, 111, 113–14, 186–87; and decline of religion, 186. *See also* Burnet, Russen

Science fiction: and futuristic fiction, 5, 12, 90–91, 158; in *Iter Lunare*, 54–55, 57; and religion, 57–58; and aesthetics of scientific hypothesis, 68; defined, 89–90; and cognitive estrangement, 89–90; and Gothic fiction, 89–90; as proleptic narrative, 90, 109; and technological change, 90; *Gulliver's Travels* as archetype of, 90; and the sublime, 90; verisimilitude of, and scientific laws, 94–95; new wave, 158; and apocalypse, 158–59; and epistemology, 159–60

Scott, Sir Walter, 134, 278–79

Scouten, Arthur H., 304 (n. 22)

Self-consciousness: in futuristic fiction, 11, 192

Shakespeare, William, 205, 259

Shelley, Mary: *Frankenstein*, 12, 90, 166, 190; *The Last Man*, 188–90, 197

The Shortest Way with the Dissenters (Defoe), 250

Showalter, English, Jr., 294 (nn. 23, 32)

Silverberg, Robert, 96

Smitten, Jeffrey R., 313 (n. 26)

Snow, Charles Percy, 258

Souvestre, Emile: *Le Monde tel qu'il sera*, 148, 194–95, 198, 226, 235

Space: and time in literature, 12–16, 18, 44, 128

Space travel: in early fiction, 23, 46–47; and ideas about the future, 52; and theology, 57; and *Les Voyages de Kang-Hi*, 199

Spatial form: in prophecy, 180

Spiritualism: in *La Fin du monde*, 183; and mesmerism, 281–88 passim; and Restif de la Bretonne, 288

Stableford, Brian, 121

Stendhal (pseudonym of Marie-Henri Beyle), 134

Sterne, Laurence, 205

Sublime: theories of, and science fiction, 90; and futuristic fiction, 112

Suvin, Darko, 11, 89, 90, 91, 92, 111, 267

Swift, Jonathan, 10, 54, 110, 259, 260; *Gulliver's Travels*, 90, 91, 92, 103, 112–13, 119, 154, 199, 220, 250; *Windsor Prophecy*, 96; *A Tale of a Tub*, 100, 103, 105; *The Bickerstaff Papers*, 101, 103; *Verses on the Death of Dr. Swift*, 112, 154; *A Modest Proposal*, 250

A Tale of a Tub (Swift), 100, 103, 105

Tatar, Maria M., 324 (n. 16)

Technology, 5, 58, 113, 289

Tertullian, 105

Testud, Pierre, 319–20 (n. 18), 321 (n. 28)

La Thébaïde ou les frères ennemis (Racine), 270

Théorie de la terre (Buffon), 84

Thomas, Keith, 296–97 (n. 6)

The Thousand and One Nights, 212

INDEX

Time: and genre, 13–15, 237, 247; calendric in fiction, 24–25, 36–39, 42, 43–44, 121–23, 171, 177–80, 217, 223, 262, 270, 307 (n. 8); emblematic, 29; in fairy tales, 33; in realistic fiction, 34; in dreams, 34, 35; and space in futuristic romance, 44; in utopias and uchronias, 120–29; as distancing device, 128; varieties of, in fiction, 153; mythic, 156, 189; apocalyptic, 168; representational tempo of, in *Le dernier homme*, 168–72; in Last Judgment scenes, 178; unity of, 218; distortions of, in *Les Posthumes*, 219, 223–24; geological, 224, 232; and point of view in *Les Posthumes*, 229–31; in *The Mummy*, 237; in Jules Verne, 246; relationships of, with literature and future settings, 247; reader's location in, 264

The Time Machine. *See* Wells

Time-travel, 19–20, 85, 95–96. *See also* Wells

Todorov, Tzvetan, 316 (n. 3)

Tom Jones (Fielding), 104

Toulmin, Stephen, 64

Trousson, Raymond, 11, 12, 117, 125

Turgot, Anne Robert Jacques, Baron de l'Aulne, 119

Typology, 60, 109, 297 (n. 7)

Uchronia: defined, 115–16; forms of, 115–57 passim; and alternate history, 116, 153; purposes of, 119; and millenarian thought, 119; realism and fantasy in, 146; time representation in, 153; impact on Bodin, 288. *See also* Alternate history, Renouvier, Utopia

Uchronie (Renouvier), 115–16, 130

Unconscious mind, 280, 282

Unities, 218

Utopia (More), 11, 53

Utopia: monogenesis of, 11; futuristic and alternate past forms of, called uchronia, 115–16; and uchronic forms of, 116–57 passim; relationships to historical time in, 122–29; and alternate history, 146–52; and dystopias, 148–52, 155; Orwell and, 154–57; limitations of, in futuristic fiction, 160; Grainville rejects, 196; and *Les Voyages de Kang-Hi*, 199; and history, 218; and Restif de la Bretonne, 218. *See also* Geoffroy, Mercier, Time, Uchronia

Verisimilitude: Bodin on role of, in futuristic fiction, 8; in *Epigone*, 18; and future settings, 19, 60, 91; and chronology in fiction, 25; and scientific extrapolation, 54; Burnet on role of, in speculation about the future, 79–82; in science fiction, 94–95, 111; Madden on, 103–8, 110–11, 113–14; in *L'An 2440*, 122, 125; in *Napoléon apocryphe*, 134–45; in alternate history, 148; and apocalyptic themes, 159–60, 168; Grainville on science and, 186–87; and predictive fiction, 193; in *Le Monde tel qu'il sera*, 195; in *The Last Man*, 197; in *Les Voyages de Kang-Hi*, 200–201; and past-tense narration in futuristic

INDEX

fiction, 222; and mesmerism, 286–87; concepts of, in seventeenth-century France, 294–95 (n. 32)

Verne, Jules, 9, 10, 47, 246, 248, 289

Verses on the Death of Dr. Swift (Swift), 112, 154

Versins, Pierre, 11, 38

Villemur, Alain-Michel, 307 (n. 7)

Voltaire, François-Marie Arouet, 10, 208, 259–60

Voss, Julius von, 322 (n. 31)

Les Voyages de Kang-Hi (Levis): dialogic relationship of, with *L'An 2440*, 198; *Lettres persanes* and *L'An 2440* as models for, 198; utopian speculation and, 198, 201; present customs projected to future in, 199; distancing in, 199; metafiction in, 200, 202; fantasy avoided in, 200; verisimilitude in, 200–201; India in, 200–201; novelistic elements of, 201; compared with *The Mummy*, 240; known to Bodin, 277

Wagar, W. Warren, 167, 189–90

Walpole, Horace, 89

Washington, George, 117

Watt, James, 162

Webb, Jane, 193, 206; marriage, 231–32; *The Ladies' Companion to the Flower Garden*, 231; *The Ladies' Flower Garden of Ornamental Annuals*, 231–32; *The Ladies' Flower Garden of Bulbous Plants*, 232; *Conversations upon Comparative Chronology*, 232; sources of her interest in futuristic fiction, 232. See *The Mummy*

Wells, Herbert George, 5, 10, 17, 19, 47, 85, 94, 197, 246, 248; *The Time Machine*, 5, 85, 98–99, 121, 183

Whiston, William, 84

Wilkie, Everett, Jr., 117

Williams, Robert Folkestone: *Eureka: a Prophecy of the Future*, 202–3, 237, 317–18 (n. 11)

Windsor Prophecy (Swift), 96

Wittreich, Joseph Anthony, Jr., 180

Wright Brothers (Orville and Wilbur), 6

Young, Edward, 168

Zamyatin, Yevgeny, 4, 155

Zschokke, Johann, 280

THE END

www.ingramcontent.com/pod-product-compliance
Lightning Source LLC
Chambersburg PA
CBHW030127240426
43672CB00005B/48